JULIAN BOND'S
TIME TO TEACH

JULIAN BOND'S
TIME TO TEACH

A HISTORY OF THE SOUTHERN CIVIL RIGHTS MOVEMENT

JULIAN BOND

Edited by Pamela Horowitz and Jeanne Theoharis
Foreword by Pamela Horowitz
Introduction by Jeanne Theoharis
Photographs by Danny Lyon
Afterword by Vann R. Newkirk II

BEACON PRESS
BOSTON

BEACON PRESS
Boston, Massachusetts
www.beacon.org

Beacon Press books
are published under the auspices of
the Unitarian Universalist Association of Congregations.

24 23 22 21   8 7 6 5 4 3 2 1

This book is printed on acid-free paper that meets the uncoated paper
ANSI/NISO specifications for permanence as revised in 1992.

Text design and composition by Kim Arney

Library of Congress Cataloging-in-Publication Data

Names: Bond, Julian, 1940–2015, author. | Horowitz, Pamela, editor. |
Theoharis, Jeanne, editor. | Lyon, Danny, illustrator.
Title: Julian Bond's time to teach : a history of the southern civil
rights movement / Julian Bond ; edited by Pamela Horowitz and Jeanne
Theoharis ; photographs by Danny Lyon ; afterword by Vann R. Newkirk II.
Other titles: Time to teach
Description: Boston : Beacon Press, [2020] | Includes
bibliographical references and index.
Identifiers: LCCN 2020029089 (print) | LCCN 2020029090 (ebook) |
ISBN 9780807033203 (hardcover) | ISBN 9780807033388 (ebook)
Subjects: LCSH: Student Nonviolent Coordinating Committee (U.S.)—History. |
Civil rights movements—Southern States—History—20th century. |
African Americans—Civil rights—History—20th century.
Classification: LCC E185.61 .B685 2020 (print) | LCC E185.61 (ebook) |
DDC 323.0975/0904—dc23
LC record available at https://lccn.loc.gov/2020029089
LC ebook record available at https://lccn.loc.gov/2020029090

To Professor Bond's students,
past and future

CONTENTS

FOREWORD

by Pam Horowitz

FOLLOWING THE "UNITE THE RIGHT" white supremacist rally in Charlottesville, Virginia, in August 2017, Julian's cousin Cynthia Bond, writing in the *Village Voice*, wondered if the rally's organizers, Richard Spencer and Jason Kessler, both University of Virginia graduates, Spencer in 2001 and Kessler in 2009, had taken Julian's course on the history of the civil rights movement, which he taught at their alma mater from 1992 to 2012.[1]

We don't know, but it's highly unlikely. We do know that many of the more than five thousand students who did take the course found it transformative. "The class and its teacher changed my life" is not an atypical comment.[2] It was in Julian's class that students learned to appreciate, many for the first time, the centrality of race in American history and, as importantly, what that meant for them personally. As one of his teaching assistants put it, "He helped his students understand that history changed because of people like them."[3] In other words, they could change the world. "I left class each week feeling empowered not only by the actions of those who came before me, but also in my own ability . . . to make meaningful contributions to civil rights," said one.[4]

Just as Julian's students loved learning it, Julian loved teaching them that they could be agents of social change. For him, that was teaching's greatest reward. He liked to tell the story of a student from Danville, Virginia, who knew nothing of the bloody civil rights history of her hometown until Julian's lecture. After class, she thanked him profusely and vowed to go home and confront her local school board so future students would not share her ignorance.

When Julian himself was a student—at Morehouse College in 1960—the Southern civil rights movement changed his life. His participation in the Atlanta sit-in movement led to his attendance at a meeting of hundreds of students from across the South in Raleigh, North Carolina, over Easter weekend. It was there that the Student Nonviolent Coordinating Committee was founded. Julian would serve as SNCC's communications director for the next five years.

In this role, Julian "was at the nerve center of information essential to insiders and critical for outsiders. Handling this huge responsibility with sensitivity and awareness of the booby traps all around him was fundamental to the success of SNCC."[5] Throughout a lifetime of achievement and awards, Julian regarded his SNCC years as the highlight of his career and his SNCC colleagues as his soul mates.

Not unlike Black Lives Matter today, which Julian greatly admired, SNCC was bold and disruptive, challenging not just racial strictures but the very structures of society. Julian reveled in the discovery that President John F. Kennedy had called SNCC "sons of bitches."[6] And that President Jimmy Carter said, "If you wanted to scare white people in Southwest Georgia, Martin Luther King and the Southern Christian Leadership Conference wouldn't do it. You only had to say one word: SNCC."[7]

Just when Julian launched his political career, with a successful campaign for the Georgia House in 1965, SNCC issued a statement against the war in Vietnam. Julian did not write the statement, but he supported it. Using this as its reason, the legislature refused to seat him. It would require two more electoral victories and a unanimous opinion of the US Supreme Court for Julian to take his rightful place in the legislature.[8] The national publicity surrounding his fight for his seat made him a household name and led to his nomination for vice president of the United States in 1968. The first African American so nominated, at age twenty-eight, Julian was too young to serve.

After a twenty-year political career, half in the Georgia House and half in the Georgia Senate, Julian began a second career as an academic. It was his "time to teach," just as his only book, published in 1972, was titled *A Time to Speak, a Time to Act*. And he would teach about a time: the era of the modern Southern civil rights movement. He often joked that they wouldn't let him teach physics. He gravitated to academia naturally, his father, the noted educator Horace Mann Bond, having been the first Black president of Lincoln University, known then as "the Black Princeton." After teaching first at the University of Pennsylvania, Drexel, Harvard, and Williams, Julian then taught at the University of Virginia for twenty years and concurrently at American University for twenty-five.

Whether as a politician or an academic, Julian was in the vanguard of nearly every social movement of his time. Having been a leader of both the civil rights and antiwar movements, he joined a sit-in in San Francisco in 1977 on behalf of disability rights, long before the passage of the Americans with Disabilities Act of 1990. His first arrest came during the civil rights movement, but his post-movement activities also sometimes led to arrest—once at the South African Embassy in Washington, DC, in the 1970s in protest of apartheid and later at the White House, protesting against the Keystone Pipeline in 2013. Virtually alone among Black leaders, Julian was an early and passionate supporter of gay rights, insisting that LGBTQ rights were human rights. As chairman of the NAACP, the nation's oldest and largest civil rights organization, from 1998 to 2010, he was the force behind its historic vote in 2012 in support of marriage equality.

He was as cool as he was committed. He hosted *Saturday Night Live* and appeared in movies, including *Ray* (2004) and *5 to 7* (2014). He was a master narrator, most notably of the fourteen-part singular documentary of the civil rights movement, *Eyes on the Prize*. In demand as a speaker throughout his career, he spoke on college campuses across the United States and abroad.

Oddly, though I had heard Julian speak countless times and written many of the speeches, I had never gone to a class or read his class lectures. When I began reading them for this book, I could hear his voice. It was magical.

Adding to the magic are Danny Lyon's photographs. Danny, then a newly minted graduate of the University of Chicago, took pictures for SNCC from 1962 to 1964. Julian described him as "inquisitive, New York-y, rumpled," and said, "SNCC's idea of photography was functional [e.g., for press releases and fundraising]. Danny Lyon took this function and made it art."[9]

Julian said of SNCC: "In a scale of militants and aggressive behavior . . . in a nonviolent context . . . we were first."[10] Julian never lost his militancy. His cousin Cynthia called him "a firebrand, elegant and wise." Spencer and Kessler probably fancy themselves as "firebrands," but no one would mistake them for being "elegant and wise." They could have learned something from one who was.

WHAT JULIAN BOND TAUGHT ME

by Jeanne Theoharis

A MID PROTESTS in the summer of 2016 around the police killings of Alton Sterling and Philando Castile, Kasim Reed, then mayor of Atlanta, invoked Martin Luther King Jr.'s roots there to affirm the city's longstanding commitment to freedom of speech. But then, explaining the large police presence at downtown protests, he scolded the young demonstrators: "Dr. King would never take a highway."[1]

Earlier that year, Reverend Barbara Reynolds took to the pages of the *Washington Post* to criticize this new generation of protesters: "Many in my crowd admire the cause and courage of these young activists but fundamentally disagree with their approach. Trained in the tradition of Martin Luther King Jr., we were nonviolent activists who won hearts by conveying respectability and changed laws by delivering a message of love and unity. BLM [Black Lives Matter] seems intent on rejecting our proven methods."[2]

Across the political spectrum, many have held up the civil rights movement to critique and chastise Black Lives Matter. These framings misrepresent the movements BLM activists are building across the country. And they greatly distort the history of the civil rights movement—as I first learned it from Professor Bond and as he lays out in this book.

Of course, King took many a highway, most famously in the Selma-to-Montgomery march, upset business as usual, and, perhaps most significantly, believed in the necessity of disruption to highlight and transform unjust policies and realities. The movement wasn't unified, and there was much disagreement and debate about the right tactics and approaches. It was deeply disruptive and made people uncomfortable then, like it does today. And even in the moments when activists purposefully donned "respectable" attire and rooted their protest in God and country, they were regularly treated as "un-American" and unreasonable.

Calling out these myths, as Professor Bond would insist, is more than setting the historical record straight. The troubling ways the civil rights movement is being invoked in the age of Black Lives Matter are dangerous because they grossly distort how the civil rights movement actually proceeded. And they are comfortable because they allow many Americans to keep today's movements at arm's length. Professor Bond highlighted the dangerous and seductive power of the "master narrative" and the urgency of seeing a fuller history of the civil rights movement for understanding our past and where we must go from here.

I had the great good fortune to take a class with Julian Bond when I was an undergraduate at Harvard University and then two years later to serve as one of his teaching assistants. Julian Bond was a lifelong freedom fighter and a titan of social justice leadership. But alongside that persevering voice for justice, one of his greatest gifts was that of a teacher and movement intellectual.

To teach about the Southern civil rights movement was a way to carry it forward to a new generation, and he thrilled to this. It was a way to disrupt the stultifying, politically convenient myths—the master narrative—that had grown around the movement. That narrative, he quipped, reduced the movement to "Rosa sat down, Martin stood up, then the white folks saw the light and saved the day."[3] Or, in a less sassy fashion, he critiqued its problematic assumptions:

Traditionally, relationships between the races in the South were oppressive. In 1954, the Supreme Court decided this was wrong. Inspired by the court, courageous Americans, Black and white, took protest to the street, in the form of sit-ins, bus boycotts, and freedom rides. The protest movement, led by the brilliant and eloquent Dr. Martin Luther King Jr., aided by a sympathetic federal government, most notably the Kennedy brothers and a born-again Lyndon Johnson, was able to make America understand racial discrimination as a moral issue. Once Americans understood that discrimination was wrong, they quickly moved to remove racial prejudice and discrimination from American life, as evidenced by the Civil Rights Acts of 1964 and 1965. Inexplicably, just as the civil rights victories were piling up, many African Americans, under the banner of Black Power, turned their backs on American society.[4]

IN THIS MASTER NARRATIVE, as Professor Bond made clear, injustice is obvious, decent people took action, and the good guys triumphed—and then Black Power came along and ruined everything. Challenging this romanticized and dangerous fable, Professor Bond's classes sought to give us a much fuller, more accurate, and much deeper sense of the movement's origins and effects, its many players, and its many opponents. He also aimed to help us think about the uses behind this mythmaking—to see the ground-shaking challenge to American society and politics the civil rights movement had wrought, its unpopularity at the time, and the tremendous amount of work still to be done. To see the movement in its full complexity, to understand what it took—the strategy and the organizing, the many, many people who pushed it forward, and the many, many people who stood in its way—was necessary to understanding our own way forward.

The point, then, was not to tell us young people what to do—that the activists of old had the right way that needed to be drummed into us. Rather, he sought to challenge the fables that had grown up around the movement and the popular memory of it to ensure that we grasped the difficulty and necessity—the complications, joys, and work—of building movements and the power of youth leadership.

This book aims to make Professor Bond's teachings available to a wider audience—to present in narrative form his history of the Southern civil rights movement. Part of what has made this possible was that he was a meticulous teacher. He wrote his class lectures out in full sentences. Over the years, he rewrote them, improved them, added new material when he learned things or read new books, and polished them again. He was always reading, and the lectures reflect that, not just his own knowledge but all that he gleaned from the growing scholarship on the modern Black freedom struggle. Most of the lectures were revised for fifteen to twenty years—and most of the ones we use here were last revised in 2006, 2007, or 2008.

The heart of the book are the lectures focused on events of the Southern civil rights movement, on events he witnessed and shaped, knew players in, understood the background for, and had a broader context to bring to bear. Pam Horowitz and I, with the help of our research assistant, Erik Wallenberg, have compiled the lectures, edited them slightly, and sewed them into a narrative history. To make this book readable and affordable, and not overly long, we could not include all of them. We have pared down his early lectures focused before World War II; trimmed the more detailed political history, including lectures that described presidential and congressional machinations; and abridged the last lectures, in which he quickly skimmed many of the events of the late 1960s. We have edited them a bit for readability and clarity. Julian would teach with Power-Point—often including long quotes from various movement actors, scores of photos, leaflets, presidential Oval Office recordings, FBI records, and material from congressional leaders. We have shortened the quotes considerably and are not including flyers, statements, or other movement ephemera that he used in his PowerPoints. But we have attempted to maintain the ways he delved into the motivations of political elites alongside those of civil rights activists—firmly believing you needed to understand how the rulers thought and moved, backstabbed and schemed, alongside the movement. He had a whole lecture devoted to music, but without the music, we could not replicate it here. We could not find a full lecture on the Vietnam War or one on SNCC and women and the Waveland conference (though I remember it from when I TA-ed the class).

We have tried to include citations wherever possible—and Erik has done yeoman's work in tracking many down. In some places, Professor Bond had included citations or partial citations; in other places, we had to try to track them down. His lectures reflected decades of reading, and we were able to acknowledge only some of what he read. There is a lot we couldn't necessarily piece together. He read widely and built these lectures over many years, adding to them all the time, according to Pam. Quite simply, he loved the burgeoning literature on the movement, read it assiduously, and, unlike some movement contemporaries who worried about outsiders writing their history, continuously revised his own interpretations from new evidence and analyses scholars produced. We have also included an annotated bibliography Julian used for the civil rights tours he gave from 2007 to 2015 through the University of Virginia, and we have provided short lists of suggested readings for each chapter. We have tried to credit sources Julian used or relied on for his syllabi, but, in the spirit of his commitment to keep up with the latest historiography on the movement, we have also included some more recent works in the suggested readings.

Knitting together his lectures provides a narrative history of the Southern civil rights movement—a master class—as Julian Bond taught it to me and hundreds of other undergraduates over two decades, so that a new generation of students, along with other interested readers, can continue to learn from him. The point of his lectures was not just to tell stories—though, of course, people could listen to those stories for days—but also to impart broader insights about how the direction of the nation changes, about the nature of injustice and the forces that protect it, and about our role in challenging it.

WHAT HE TAUGHT ME IN SEVEN LESSONS

Lesson 1: Movements are made; they don't just happen. It wasn't "Rosa Parks sat down and then people boycotted the buses." Julian Bond started back in the 1930s and 1940s. He showed not just what happened but also how it happened. His treatment of the Montgomery bus boycott—what led to it, what it took, how it worked—spanned three classes. There I sat, my twenty-year-old self, so excited to be taking a class with *the* Julian Bond but wondering why he was taking so long to get through this first campaign. Character by character, he detailed the various people who came together to turn Rosa Parks's bus stand into the Montgomery bus boycott and how they sustained that effort for 382 days. That indelibly changed how I understood—and ultimately how I would teach and write about—the civil rights movement.

In the popular narrative, the movement just happens. Rosa Parks refuses to give up her seat, people rise up and boycott, and ultimately bus segregation is defeated. It is the perfection of the American dream. What Julian Bond showed so vividly was that people made decision after hard decision after hard decision. There was nothing predestined about it. The connections they had built over years and the experiences they had informed what they did. America wasn't naturally moving toward justice, nor did a movement just happen once someone made a courageous stand. People chose, amid searing conditions, amid threats to their person and to their livelihood, to make it happen.

So, starting decades before, he traced all the people who would come together: from E. D. Nixon to Jo Ann Robinson to Claudette Colvin to Parks herself, from the Brotherhood of Sleeping Car Porters to the bus boycott in Baton Rouge. And then, painstakingly, once Parks made her courageous stand, he took us hour by hour, day by day, to show us who talked to whom, what decisions were made, how a movement flowered from Parks's courageous refusal. Rosa Parks called Fred Gray, who called Jo Ann Robinson; E. D. Nixon called the ministers and reporter Jo Azbell; Jo Ann Robinson snuck into her office at Alabama State College and ran off fifty thousand leaflets; and on and on. By showing how the civil rights movement happened, it also became possible to imagine how we could do it again.

Lesson 2: The changes the civil rights movement accomplished were not the province of presidents or charismatic speakers but accomplished by the efforts and freedom visions (and sacrifices) of everyday local people possessing great courage and vision. And many, many of those people were young people. He insisted that those local people have to be known, their particular contributions detailed and lifted up—and so he did: Annie Devine, E. W. Steptoe, Johnnie Carr, Fred Gray, Unita Blackwell, Reverend T. J. Jemison, Fannie Lou Hamer, and many, many others.

He showed us the key leadership roles that young people played— Barbara Johns, Claudette Colvin and Mary Louise Smith, the Little Rock Nine (who had inspired him)—and his many friends and comrades in SNCC—Dave Dennis, Ruby Doris Smith, Charles McDew, Bob Moses, Diane Nash, Bernard and Colia Lafayette, and many, many more. They held up a mirror to the nation's professions and its practices, forcing it to confront its original sin of systemic racism. Young people lead, he would teach, and the nation will ultimately be forced to follow. He also highlighted the elders who supported and nourished their work and how cherished that support was.

He made clear that this kind of youth leadership scared many people then, just as it scares many people now. Many white and Black people did not like or support what SNCC did. (March on Washington organizers made SNCC chair John Lewis edit his speech because they thought it too angry and confrontational, Professor Bond schooled us.) So he cautioned that we shouldn't be surprised when adults, even adults sympathetic to our cause, would be some of the first to criticize us or say we weren't going about it the right way, because that was what had happened throughout the civil rights movement.

Lesson 3: Social change and social oppression are about choice. There was nothing destined about the civil rights movement. Fate didn't determine Dr. King's leadership. He had to choose to step forward, again and again.

Professor Bond spent a lot of time detailing the sit-ins and Freedom Rides—how people imagined what was possible beyond what others thought feasible or reasonable. How they stepped forward, how they insisted on not stopping, and that by acting they went beyond what they thought they could do—thereby changing the freedom they could imagine.

He told a funny story of his own initiation into the struggle.

"What do you think about the Greensboro sit-in?" fellow Morehouse student Lonnie King asked twenty-year-old Bond.

> "I think it's great!"
> "Don't you think it ought to happen here?" he asked.
> "Oh, I'm sure it will happen here," I responded. "Surely someone here will do it."
> Then [came] to me, as it came to others in those early days in 1960, a query, an invitation, a command: "Why don't we make it happen here?"[5]

In his graceful way, he showed how he—like us—admired courageous action but had imagined someone else would take it forward. And then he realized that it needed to be him; that assuming someone else would summon the courage was part of how oppressive systems were maintained. One of the things he stressed about the sit-ins was that they arose from a younger generation frustrated with people decrying injustice but not acting. And so they decided to take action themselves.

Four college freshmen in Greensboro. Four friends. If you had three friends, you could start, his lectures made clear. The Freedom Rides too, when they encountered massive violence in Anniston and CORE pulled back, the young people of SNCC stepped forward. They were determined that the message could not be that violence could stop the movement—and by pushing forward, they forced the nation to see and the Kennedys to act.

Professor Bond also stressed the choice of inaction, the choice of silence, the choice of preferring order to justice. Birmingham police commissioner Bull Connor, Alabama governor George Wallace, and Medgar Evers's killer, Byron de la Beckwith, were not the only villains in his lectures. So, too, were the people who sat on the sidelines and allowed white resistance against Black equality—be it physical violence, economic assassination, or social ostracism—to grow and spread. He reminded us how uncomfortable people were with the movement's disruptive tactics fifty years ago—colleges suspended SNCC students, newspapers editorialized against them, moderate leaders decried civil disobedience and disruptiveness, and allies traded their rights away. So, to just focus on the likes of Bull Connor missed what made the movement so very hard and why many of its goals remain unattained today.

Professor Bond made sure we understood that when Dr. King went to jail in Birmingham, one of the most violently racist cities in the country, King nonetheless zeroed in on the problem of the white moderate. "I have almost reached the regrettable conclusion that the Negro's great stumbling block in the stride toward freedom is not the White Citizens' Council-er or the Ku Klux Klanner, but the white moderate who is more devoted to 'order' than to justice; who prefers a negative peace which is the absence of tension to a positive peace which is the presence of justice; who constantly says 'I agree with you in the goal you seek, but I can't agree with your methods of direct action.'" Opposition to the civil rights movement went far beyond water hoses and burning crosses to those who claimed allegiance to the goals but constantly decried their tactics or their bluntness.

Lesson 4: Movements take years and decades, and they are unpopular. The civil rights movement began long before it was publicly recognized, long before the *Brown v. Board of Education* decision and the Montgomery bus boycott. And it continued long after the Voting Rights Act was signed and the TV cameras packed up and went home.

Professor Bond made sure we understood that many of these civil rights heroes and heroines spent years and decades in the wilderness, taking stand after stand but not knowing if they would see change in their lifetime. Most Americans kept the struggle at a distance. The task of social justice requires years and decades of perseverance. The idea that once King or SNCC had revealed injustice to the country most Americans got on board to change it was a convenient falsehood. It required doing it again and again, creating a sense of persistent uncomfortableness to make it impossible for people to continue to dismiss the issues.

The majority of Americans in the 1960s did not support the civil rights movement. In May 1961, in a Gallup survey, only 22 percent of Americans approved of what the Freedom Riders were doing, and 57 percent said that "the sit-ins at lunch counters, freedom buses and other demonstrations by Negroes were hurting the Negro's chances of being integrated in the South."[6] In 1966, a year after the Selma-to-Montgomery March and the passage of the Voting Rights Act, 85 percent of white people and 30 percent of Black people nationally believed that civil rights demonstrations by Black people hurt the advancement of civil rights.[7] Seventy-two percent of Americans had an unfavorable view of King.[8] Lest we see this as Southerners skewing the national sample, in 1964, a year before the passage of the Voting Rights Act, in a poll conducted by the *New York Times*, a majority of white New Yorkers said the civil rights movement had gone too far and spoke of Black people receiving "everything on a silver platter" and of "reverse discrimination" against whites.[9]

No amount of respectability protects one from the relentlessness and fury of the opposition, Professor Bond made clear. Yet he was a "hopeless optimist," as he put it, saying, "I always believe things will work out." Not because things just naturally work out. Not because injustice once revealed is automatically fixed. Not because if one acts right and tries hard and wears a nice dress or a suit, then things have a way of working out. But because of what he knew from firsthand experience: the power of ordinary people to change this country through their will, tenacity, and perseverance.

And so Professor Bond made clear that the popular embrace of the civil rights movement happened years and decades after the movement's peak. Your righteousness will not be validated in the moment, he taught us. Rather, it requires faith and steadfastness, building community, and embracing sheer orneriness—because you will repeatedly be made to feel crazy, off-base, even seditious. But we must not fall prey to nihilism, because what he knew, what he had seen, is that things do change from the most unlikely places, from "the stone that the builders rejected."

Lesson 5: There was nothing inexplicable about Black Power. The civil rights and Black Power movements, as his lectures showed, were often inextricably linked. From Rosa Parks to Robert Williams to Gloria Richardson, many key activists believed in the right of self-defense and the power of nonviolent direct action; they held a variety of goals, from economic justice and opposition to US foreign policy to independent Black political power and desegregation. Professor Bond insisted that the story of Black Power needed to start much earlier, and he took issue with the ways that Black militancy was often framed as coming out of nowhere when there was a long history of often-frustrated struggle and Black grievances that preceded it. So you couldn't look at SNCC's turn toward Black Power in Lowndes County, Alabama, he made clear, without seeing the sellout of the Mississippi Freedom Democratic Party by Democratic Party leaders and other liberal allies. The uprisings of the mid-1960s were preceded by movements against school and housing segregation and police brutality that had made few gains. The Civil Rights and Voting Rights Acts were not the ends but crucial, hard-won steps on a much longer road for full social justice. The movement's growing demands and its growing militancy were an outgrowth of the immense opposition, deep silence, and shallow commitments from supposed allies and the American public that they faced time and again.

And the movement carried on long after the cameras went home. The Black freedom struggle was part of a larger global human rights struggle. And so SNCC activists made global connections—from ardent opposition to the Vietnam War and South African apartheid to the connections with anticolonial struggles and Palestinian self-determination. They were lambasted for being outside the bounds of civil rights, just as the Movement for Black Lives making common cause with Palestinian struggles has been today. When MLK took the pulpit of Riverside Church in 1967, the *New York Times* blasted him; the *Washington Post* blasted him; the NAACP blasted him.[10] Dr. King was supposed to stay in his lane. So, too, Julian Bond, who was elected to the Georgia legislature but whose colleagues refused to seat him because of his opposition to the war. He fought all the way to the Supreme Court and finally was seated because civil rights were part of a larger global struggle for human rights.

Professor Bond decried the sentimentalization of the movement. A persistent supporter of gay rights, he refused to attend Coretta Scott King's funeral because it was held not at the King family church, Ebenezer Baptist Church, but at New Birth Missionary Baptist Church, run by the homophobic Reverend Eddie Long. This was a disservice to her and her lifetime of human rights work—and he was not going to participate in it.

He rejoiced and supported new movements of Dreamers, Dream Defenders, and Black Lives Matter activists. He loved the energy, vision, and tenacity of youth organizing around police violence, mass incarceration, and immigration policy, saying they reminded him of himself when he was young. He did not engage, like some of his movement comrades, in the "you're not doing it the right way, and why are you so angry" criticism of youth militancy. Professor Bond understood why they were angry because he was too.

Lesson 6: Learning is essential for movements and for teachers. Twelve-hour-meetings, mistakes, disagreements: the civil rights movement was made by people who were figuring and thinking and acting and learning and rethinking and adjusting. Professor Bond wasn't afraid to talk about that process, about the learning that happened in the movement. They were young people. There were serious generational and ideological divides, and they didn't always agree or get it right the first time. By learning and changing, by pressing forward, and by course-correcting, the movement carried on. Study groups, study groups, study groups, he stressed.

Key to that was not to be ashamed when you don't know the whole story. When I started working on my biography of Rosa Parks,

I interviewed him.[11] I aimed to detail her post-Montgomery activism in Detroit, not just her time in Montgomery, but he didn't have much to add, ruefully admitting, "I met her numerous times over her lifetime. . . . I just talked to her about innocuous things and never delved deeper. . . . I thought I knew everything to know about her."[12] And so he opened countless doors for me to try to help me get the bigger story. And then when I published the book, he made sure people heard about it, even the hard parts. In fact, it was during a conversation we were having about Rosa Parks's suffering—and how this little radical NAACP chapter in River Rouge, Michigan, run by Black Communists shamed the national NAACP into helping Parks with the medical bills she couldn't afford—that he decided that the whole executive board of the NAACP needed to hear this story. History is not what people like to hear, Bond believed; it's what people need to learn to better understand our past and our future.

Lesson 7: Mentorship is powerful and transformative. What an incredible gift it is to have a teacher who believes in the power of movements, a mentor who sees the potential of young people to change the course of history, and a visionary who reveals the capacity of our darkest demons to change over time.

SNCC embodied the leadership and organizing abilities of every person. People like Ella Baker and organizations like Highlander Folk School put that philosophy into practice through leadership building. One of my favorite stories Professor Bond told was about Ella Baker, one of SNCC's most invaluable mentors. SNCC meetings would last for hours and hours, and people would smoke. Ella Baker would sit there hour after hour with them, wearing a face mask (because the smoke bothered her), taking part, listening, occasionally offering a comment until people got where they needed to go.

Like Ella Baker with her face mask, Julian Bond was not a fair-weather mentor. He didn't just write a blurb or make an introduction—any of which would have been an incredible honor. He was a movement mentor, understanding what it takes to help someone find her voice. And part of the work of mentoring that Baker and Bond both embodied is to place themselves in the background, not to dispense advice from on high or insist on how things "should be done."

Julian Bond mentored in matter-of-fact, often understated ways. At a moment when people were always remarking how busy they were, how full their plate was, Professor Bond was different. He wrote letters, opened doors, and sent notes like it was no big deal, like he wasn't too busy and didn't have to remind you of all the work he was doing, of how much he knew, or how he had been there long before you.

He thrilled to the surge of youth movements, seeing himself in them and encouraging them forward. In the end, mentoring is not about being The Mentor; it's about enabling young people to fly beyond what has come before.

That was the power of the civil rights movement, as Julian Bond taught it—a launching pad for us, so we could imagine going further and demanding more of the nation. Rest in power, Julian Bond. Your lessons continue.

JULIAN BOND'S
TIME TO TEACH

INTRODUCTION TO THE COURSE

by Julian Bond

WELCOME. I INTEND to share with you a rapidly expanding historiography of the movement for civil rights. There are new books appearing almost weekly. Speaking in the largest generalities, the course of civil rights scholarship over the last decades has changed radically from an emphasis on "great men"—Martin Luther King, Presidents Kennedy or Johnson—and a top-down narrative to state and community studies where the efforts of individuals and local groups are prominent. Rather than looking at the movement through a telescope, scholars are beginning to look at it through a microscope, and what I teach is informed by these new views as well as older interpretations of what the movement was and who made it.

I also teach from my own experiences. I spent most of my early years in the South, in rural Georgia and urban Atlanta. I grew up on university campuses—at Fort Valley State College outside Macon, Georgia, and on the campus of Lincoln University in Pennsylvania. My father was an academic and my mother a schoolteacher and then librarian.

I am fortunate to have been born in 1940—too soon to be a baby boomer but old enough to have been eyewitness to and participant in much of the history we are going to study. I was in Atlanta in February 1960 when the sit-ins began there, and I helped to organize them and was arrested there at Atlanta's City Hall for the first time.

I was one of several hundred students from across the South who gathered in Raleigh, North Carolina, on Easter 1960 to found the Student

Nonviolent Coordinating Committee (SNCC), and I became the organization's communications director, a position I held for five years.

I helped to organize Atlanta's sit-in movement, which successfully integrated the city's lunch counters, parks, and tennis courts and movie theaters over the next several years.

On May 13, 1961, I met with the Freedom Riders as they passed through Atlanta, never dreaming that they would be viciously attacked and beaten—some of them near death—in Anniston and Birmingham the next day.

I was in Albany, Georgia, in 1961 when a movement, built by the Student Nonviolent Coordinating Committee and then joined and led by Dr. Martin Luther King Jr., fought and floundered.

I was in rural Southwest Mississippi in 1961 when SNCC established its first beachhead in the most resistant state, and I met a man who was later murdered because he dared to try to register to vote.

I was in Birmingham late on the afternoon of the bombing that morning of the Sixteenth Street Baptist Church that killed four schoolgirls.

I was at the 1963 March on Washington when Dr. King delivered his "I Have a Dream" speech.

I was in Selma when that movement began in 1963 and in Montgomery in 1965 when the Selma-to-Montgomery marchers arrived.

And in 1965, as the civil rights movement began to shift from confrontational protest tactics back to electoral strategies, I was elected to the Georgia House of Representatives. I was expelled from the legislature because of my opposition to the war in Vietnam and my seat declared vacant; I ran for the vacancy, won the election, and was expelled again. One of my constituents, Dr. Martin Luther King Jr., led a march on the Georgia State Capitol protesting my exclusion. I ran a third time, and, in the interval, the US Supreme Court decided that the Georgia House was wrong to deny me my seat, and I served—in the Georgia House and Senate—for the next twenty years.

In the course of these years I met many of the movement's participants—leaders and less-well-known personalities—Martin Luther King and Malcolm X and Ella Baker and Fannie Lou Hamer and James Farmer and James Forman and many, many others.

Where I can, I am going to draw on my own experiences, as a young Black Southerner, college student, and movement activist, as the movement unfolded around me. In my life, there has never been anything like it. I was surrounded by other people my age—we were running this thing. We raised the money. We did the work. These people are my closest friends today. You come so close to the people with whom you work that you are bound to them for the rest of your life.

ONE

WHITE SUPREMACY AND THE FOUNDING OF THE NAACP

I N 1968, THE YEAR HE WAS KILLED, Martin Luther King Jr. spoke about the successes and failures of the civil rights movement. He said then:

> While this period represented the frontal attack on the doctrine and practice of white supremacy, it did not defeat the monster of racism. If we are to see what is wrong we will have to face the fact that America has been and continues to be largely a racist society. And the roots of racism are very deep in this country, started a long time ago. . . . Racism is a faith, a form of idolatry; it is the dogma that one ethnic group is condemned to eternal inferiority and another ethnic group is somehow given the status of eternal superiority.[1]

King was speaking more than four hundred years after racism—white supremacy—was introduced to these shores, but he might as well have been speaking today. Here racism is the subordination of Blacks based on skin color. It is a self-perpetuating system of advantage based on race. It is prejudice plus power. White supremacy is the ideology that justifies white domination.

We think of racism in terms of individual behavior and individual actions, but it is a complex set of societal actions and attitudes. There are two kinds of racist behavior, active and passive. They are conscious and unconscious, and each provides benefits, both material and psychological, for its practitioners. Active racist behavior is like walking forward at top speed on a moving sidewalk. Passive racist behavior is like standing still on a moving sidewalk, but the sidewalk carries the rider forward nonetheless. Unless the standee turns around and runs backward faster than the sidewalk can carry him forward, he receives the same benefits as do the active racists who are racing forward at top speed.

Everyone here imagines he or she belongs to a race. But we know now that race is a social construct, not a biological absolute. But if race is insignificant biologically, it has enormous significance culturally—an idea invented as a way of assigning special status and privilege. It isn't just a pigment of our imagination.

To illustrate the complications of our racial history, consider my own family's heritage. On my father's side, my grandfather was born a slave in Kentucky in 1863. He and his mother were property, like a horse or a chair. As a young girl, she had been given away as a wedding present to a new bride, and when that bride became pregnant, her husband—that's my great-grandmother's owner and master—exercised his right to take his wife's slave as his mistress. From that union came two children, one of them my grandfather.

On my mother's side, my great-grandmother was also a slave. She recalled that her grandfather was an Irishman. She explained how the slave system worked: "You know, when a [white] man would marry, his father would give him a woman for a cook and she would have children right in the house by him. . . . A white woman would have a maid sometime who was nice looking, and she would keep her, and her son would have children by her. [My master] had twenty-five slaves up here in Tennessee, and I reckon he had thousands in Mississippi, and lots of them were his children. [His children] had to work just like we did, and they had to call him Master too, and the overseer would take them down and whip them just like the others."

With that great-grand-parentage, under the American idea of race, I am a Black man, not a dark-skinned white man. We are such a young nation so recently removed from slavery that only my father's generation stands between Julian Bond and human bondage. Like many others, I am the grandson of a slave.

My grandfather James Bond was born in 1863, in Kentucky; freedom didn't come for him until the Thirteenth Amendment was ratified in 1865. At age fifteen, barely able to read and write, he hitched his tuition—a steer—to a rope and walked across Kentucky to Berea College, and the college took him in. My grandfather belonged to a transcendent generation of Black Americans, a generation born into slavery, freed by the Civil War, determined to make their way as free men and women.

The consequences of slavery were neither incidental nor secondary aspects of American history but constitute its central theme. Rather than the exception to America's grand themes of liberty and freedom, slavery and the racism it required and engendered are a constant reminder of the shallowness of these ideas. What "race" means—and, in the American context, what "Black" and "white" mean to whites and Blacks alike—is at the root of the American dilemma today.

In the summer of 1905, William Edward Burghardt Du Bois convened a group of Blacks in Niagara Falls, New York. They formed the Niagara Movement; it eventually developed thirty branches, but its membership remained small. Later that year, Du Bois outlined a program that he believed the new organization as well as all American Blacks ought to try to pursue.

> We must complain . . . plain, blunt complain, ceaseless agitation, unfailing exposure of dishonesty and wrong. . . . Next, we propose to work. To press the matter of stopping the curtailment of our political rights; to urge Negroes to vote honestly and effectively; to push the matter of civil rights; to organize business cooperation; to build schoolhouses and increase the interest in education; to bring Negroes and labor unions into mutual understanding; to study Negro history; to attack crime among us . . . to do all in our power to increase the efficiency of our race, the enjoyment of its manhood rights, and the performance of its just duties. This is a large program. It cannot be realized in a short time. . . . This is the critical time.[2]

BLACK SOUTHERNERS WERE denied access to the political process, miseducated in pathetically inadequate public schools, dehumanized in the popular culture. But they were stirring against their oppression, and the world around them was changing, and they created a rich interior life, hidden from and almost incomprehensible to whites.

They faced a system of racial division enshrined in custom—de facto segregation—and by law—de jure segregation. Historian John W. Cell described what it meant:

> When they rode public transportation, they sat in the black section in the rear. If they wanted to drink, eat or go to the toilet, they might be lucky enough to find facilities reserved for them; otherwise they had to do without. Parks, beaches, golf courses, tennis courts and swimming pools excluded them; again comparatively rarely, they might find separate but undoubtedly inferior facilities. If they ran afoul of the law, they were sworn on separate but equal Bibles, and if convicted by usually all-white juries, were sentenced by white judges to segregated jails. When they died, they were embalmed in black funeral parlors . . . and buried in black cemeteries.[3]

New Orleans segregated prostitutes. Oklahoma segregated telephone booths.

As the twentieth century dawned, Southern extremists influenced public opinion in the North and South. They published a spate of ultra-racist books—*The Negro a Beast* and *The Negro: A Menace to American Civilization*.[4] They argued that Blacks were innately inferior, immoral, and a criminal race, and that the end of slavery had caused a reversion to barbarism. Distinguished anthropologists and anatomists regarded Blacks as a separate species next to the ape, and historians and political scientists reinterpreted Reconstruction as a Black failure.[5]

In 1900, three-quarters of the eight to ten million Southern Black people lived in rural communities. Ninety-five percent of all Black Americans lived south of the Ohio River and east of Central Texas. Improved roads and the Model-T Ford, and the pull of the city, freed both Black and white Southerners from rural life and plantation ties. There were differences between North and South and West, between big city, small town, and rural countryside, but in all parts of the country a color line existed, limiting where Blacks could live, work, and send their children to school.

Nowhere was the color line so rigid—and the penalty for violating it so harsh—as in the South. By the 1890s, a new generation of Blacks was reaching adulthood, young women and men who had never been slaves. As children, they had witnessed the violent overthrow of Reconstruction.

But most white Southerners believed the children of slaves were fixed at a lower level of mental and moral development. The Southern plantation had been a school, a Southern historian wrote, and most whites thought the end of slavery had dismissed the pupils too soon. Actual schools for Blacks ranged from the inadequate to the abysmal. In 1916, the Southern states spent an average $10.32 for every white public school student and $2.89 for each Black student.

Whites were confident that Blacks were the perfect labor force—easily coerced, unlikely to organize, readily available—because they lacked ambition and skills to do otherwise. This confidence was accompanied by fears—fears that this almost barbaric race would engage in angry rebellion. The fears were bolstered by memories—Reconstruction memories of Black men voting, Black men serving in government, Black men carrying guns, Black men taking their employers to court. And, above all, this, the greatest fear—the specter of interracial sex, made most fearful because Blacks might initiate it, not whites—was common throughout the region.

The Black press—10 newspapers in 1870, 31 in 1880, 154 in 1890—widened the circle of Black hope, illuminated the possibility of a better life, and agitated for increased militancy.

But as Blacks celebrated the fiftieth anniversary of the Emancipation Proclamation in 1913, whites were in the midst of a counter-celebration; Norfolk, Richmond, Roanoke, Greensboro, Atlanta, and Baltimore passed or proposed laws requiring residential segregation. My grandfather James Bond was arrested in Atlanta in 1917 for moving onto a street reserved for whites. North Carolina tried to segregate farmland. And the administration of Woodrow Wilson instituted Jim Crow (legalized segregation) in federal employment in Washington.

Du Bois, the Blacks who had formed the Niagara Movement, and the liberal whites who later formed the National Association for the Advancement of Colored People (NAACP) had little reason for optimism and less reason to trust the white South. Reconstruction had collapsed. Blacks were disfranchised across the South, beginning in Mississippi in 1890; by 1910, state constitutions barred Black voters in North Carolina, Alabama, Virginia, Georgia, and Oklahoma. In Louisiana, slightly more than 50 percent of the electorate was Black in 1890; by 1910, less than 0.1 percent was Black.[6]

Murder and brutality—including lynching, ritual human sacrifice, state-sponsored and private terror—accompanied the removal of Blacks from every sphere of public life. Between 1880 and 1923, a Black person was lynched every two and one-half days in the United States.

HISTORIAN C. VANN WOODWARD argued in his classic *The Strange Career of Jim Crow* that the most hostile legal and extralegal forms of racial segregation emerged during the last years of the nineteenth century when states and localities enacted laws providing for the systematic separation of Blacks and whites in every aspect of social, cultural, economic, and political life. According to Woodward, there had been an earlier pattern of fluid race relations, and that before the codification of race laws, relations were malleable, not fixed. But a latter cadre of historians—Leon Litwack, Richard Wade, Joel Williamson—argued that Woodward underestimated early white resistance to a multiracial, democratic society, and his use of the imposition of segregation laws as a marker—the appearance of de jure segregation—ignored an older pattern of de facto segregation that had existed since the Civil War.[7]

Tennessee adopted the first segregation laws in 1875; the rest of the South soon followed. By 1885, most states required segregated schools, and, in 1886, the Supreme Court upheld "separate but equal" in *Plessy v. Ferguson*. To paraphrase Frederick Douglass, former slaves were free of their individual masters but were the slaves of society. And many remained slaves of their masters too.

John Hope Franklin described the South at the end of the nineteenth century: "Clashes between the races occurred almost daily, and the atmosphere of tension in which people of both races lived was conducive to little more than a struggle for mere survival, with a feeble groping in the direction of progress. The law, the courts, the schools, and almost every institution in the South favored the white man. This was White Supremacy."[8]

In 1903, Du Bois described the condition of the average Southern Black person: "He felt his poverty; without a cent, without a home, without land, tools, or savings, he had entered into competition with rich, landed, skilled neighbors. . . . Before this there rises a sickening despair that would disarm and discourage any nation save that black host to whom 'discouragement' is an unwritten word."[9]

This story is a history of those who refused to be discouraged. It is a history of the fight for civil rights. "Civil rights," as used here, are the rights guaranteed by the US Constitution, articulated in the Thirteenth, Fourteenth, and Fifteenth Amendments. "These Amendments . . . abolished the institution of slavery, mandated national birthright citizenship, guaranteed the right of due process to all persons, and established the right of suffrage without regard to race."[10] These rights have been the central demand of the Black movement, always accompanied by calls for economic and social justice.

IN THE EARLY YEARS of the twentieth century, the United States had become an empire, with foreign trade greater than any other nation except England. For many Americans, prosperity followed; for Blacks, it did not. Southern terror and hardship increased Black migration to urban America, North and South, an outpouring that would slow and then resume in the 1940s.

In 1910, there were 5,700 Black people living in Detroit and 91,000 in New York. Fifteen years later, Detroit had 81,000 Black people; New York had almost 300,000. By 1900, there were seventy-two cities with Black populations greater than 5,000; Blacks outnumbered whites in Charleston, Savannah, Montgomery, Jacksonville, Shreveport, Vicksburg, and Baton Rouge. New Orleans, Baltimore, and Washington each had more than 75,000 Blacks. Between 1910 and 1920, Chicago's Black population more than doubled, Cleveland's quadrupled, and Detroit's multiplied by seven times. Competition for jobs and housing led to further segregation: organized labor was hostile to Blacks, and cities began segregating housing by law in 1912 and 1913.

Again, John Hope Franklin: "The century, which had opened on such a note of optimism, very early revealed overtones of despair that equaled, if they did not surpass, any which the Negro had experienced."[11]

There was a positive in this negative. Urban segregation and ghettoization, squeezing and locking Blacks of all classes in all-Black communities where they shared social institutions, made developing communications networks easier and helped class divisions subside. Race—not class or educational level—meant Blacks shared a collective predicament and therefore could envision exercising collective strength. Skin color ensured that all the talents and skills of the group were concentrated in a single community.

But the negative spiraled forward. More than 100 Blacks were lynched in the first year of the new century; 105 in 1901; 85 in 1902; 84 in 1903; 76 in 1904; and 57 in 1905. By the beginning of World War 1, more than 1,100 had been murdered by lynch mobs.[12] There were serious race riots in Statesboro, Georgia, and Springfield, Ohio, in 1904; in Greensburg, Indiana, Brownsville, Texas, and Atlanta in 1906. White mobs dragged Blacks from streetcars in Philadelphia and New York and beat them; towns in Indiana and Ohio forbade Blacks to settle within their limits.

Most frightening was the riot in Springfield, Illinois, in August 1908, the hundredth anniversary year of the birth of Springfield's most famous citizen, Abraham Lincoln. It took five thousand militiamen to put down the white mob that rampaged through Springfield's streets, destroying Black businesses and homes. Two Blacks were lynched within half a mile of the only home Lincoln had ever owned and within two miles of Lincoln's grave.

HORRIFIED BY THE SPRINGFIELD RIOT, a group of liberal whites resolved to act. In February 1909, Oswald Garrison Villard, the grandson of abolitionist William Lloyd Garrison, issued a call signed by fifty-three others to join in "the renewal of the struggle for civil and political liberty."[13] The call produced a new organization—the National Association for the Advancement of Colored People. Du Bois, named director of publications and research for the new organization, was the only Black officer.

Du Bois was more than agitator and organizer of protest; he remains the towering intellectual figure of the modern freedom struggle. Born in Great Barrington, Massachusetts, in 1868, he graduated from Fisk University in 1888. He became Harvard's first Black PhD recipient in 1895 and began teaching at Atlanta University. In 1903, he launched a public attack on Booker T. Washington, arguing that Washington "practically accepts the alleged inferiority of the Negro races."[14] Blacks could not gain their rights, Du Bois argued, by throwing them away. During his long life, he supported both Black capitalism and Marxism, interracialism and separatism. He was an elitist who fought throughout his life for the welfare of the Black masses. His attack on Washington in 1903 polarized Black America into two camps—the Washingtonians and the radicals, whose most prominent and articulate spokesman was Du Bois.[15]

THUS BEGINS THE FREEDOM STRUGGLE at the dawn of the twentieth century, which should not be taken as the beginning of the struggle for civil rights. Whether called that or "the black liberation movement" or "the freedom fight" or by any other name, that contest began for Americans of African descent in Jamestown and continues on today.

Dr. Du Bois came to Lincoln University where my father was president in 1943. He and my father in our kitchen cracked open a bottle of champagne and held a ceremony dedicating me to a life of scholarship. So my own journey also begins with W. E. B. Du Bois.

TWO

ORIGINS OF THE
CIVIL RIGHTS MOVEMENT

T HE NAACP WAS founded at a low, low point in the lives of American Blacks. Blacks entered the twentieth century stripped of the promises of democracy, left by the law to the tender mercies of their white neighbors. The Supreme Court had capitulated to the racist fury that swept the South, reneging on the promises of a color-blind Constitution made in the heat of the Civil War and Reconstruction with the passage of the Thirteenth, Fourteenth, and Fifteenth Amendments. Following the end of Reconstruction, a wave of terror had descended on the South, where nine of every ten Blacks lived, three-fourths in rural areas. The national government abandoned Blacks to state control; most were reduced to peonage, a condition of near slavery. As historian Harvard Sitkoff observed, "The Southern way had become the American way."[1]

By 1900, the eugenics movement—the pseudoscience of racial differences—was in full flower. It claimed nature—not nurture—accounted for and required the superiority of white over Black. While white misbehavior was attributed to poverty, family disorganization, and poor education, Black failings were due to inherent racial inferiority. The eugenics movement described a vertical racial hierarchy, with whites on top and Blacks at bottom, and most white Americans believed that the superior whites should rule over the baser races, including the inferior Blacks. The most progressive whites believed in gradualism, and they emphasized that

Blacks should prepare themselves for citizenship through education, religion, and economic uplift, while decrying strategies of agitation, force, or political activity.

Du Bois writes that whites received a "psychological wage" from living in a society where members of their racial group occupied the leading positions. When the group you belong to receives social esteem, prestige, and material benefits, these arrangements seem so familiar as to be virtually natural. Any changes in this relationship or challenges to it are so disquieting that the challenges must be vigorously repulsed and the challengers marginalized. Even if economic benefits will result from altering the status quo, the accompanying loss of privilege and prestige is too high a cost to pay.

Even as white supremacy was being codified, Blacks, particularly in the urban South, responded by building a culture of resistance and accommodation and an institutional infrastructure, best exemplified by the growth of a small number of Black businesses—morticians, barbers, bankers, insurance companies, and others—almost all catering to a Black clientele.

In the early twentieth century, the NAACP and other Black reformers operated in a culture that assumed Black people to be incapable of pursuing or articulating any common interests independent of whites. As the United States prepared to enter the First World War, there was not one Black policeman in the South, not one Black judge anywhere in the country, and the parade of barbarity continued. In 1911, the townspeople of Livermore, Kentucky, bought tickets to participate in a lynching at a local theater; orchestra seat holders were allowed to fire as many bullets as they chose into the hanging Black body; those in the gallery's cheaper seats could only fire one shot. A crowd of ten thousand watched the stabbing, mutilation, and burning alive of a disabled Black youth in Waco, Texas, in the public square; his remains were sold as souvenirs, the teeth for five dollars each.[2]

No political party—Progressive, Democratic, Prohibition, Republican, Socialist, or Socialist-Labor—wooed the Black vote in 1912, and not one word about civil rights appeared in any party platform. By the middle '20s, membership in the Ku Klux Klan rose to eight million—they controlled the state governments of Indiana and Colorado. In 1924, a new magazine, *Time,* put the Imperial Wizard of the Ku Klux Klan on its cover.[3]

The period between the First and Second World Wars saw an awakening of Black protest. The chief agency of this awakening was the NAACP, but other forces played a role as well. One, of course, was the First World War itself, which helped the slow stream of Black migration from South to North and West grow into a flood, pushed out because Southern life was hard and pulled out because Northern opportunity beckoned. Between 1910 and 1920, three hundred thousand left; over the next ten years, 1.3 million; in the 1930s, 1.5 million left; and in the 1940s, 2.5 million.

Almost four hundred thousand Blacks had served overseas, many as stevedores and laborers. In France, the US military asked the French not to "spoil" Black troops by treating them as equals. Black troops enjoyed freedoms in Europe not permitted on American soil but returned home in 1919 to find their reward was a summer of bloody race riots. The war they fought reflected intra-European arguments over Africa, and the war brought home to many the realization that the majority of the world was colored, not white. For some white Americans, including many in the military, this was a war fought not to make the world safe for democracy but for white supremacy.

For many Blacks, the war held great promise for added equality at home. Du Bois understood the war and the effect it would have on returning Black servicemen. He wrote in the May 1919 issue of the NAACP magazine *The Crisis*: "Make way for Democracy! We saved it in France, and by the Great Jehovah, we will save it in the United States of America, or know the reason why."

In its tenth year, the NAACP had almost one hundred thousand members. For the next two decades the NAACP's work was threefold: it attacked individual instances of racial injustice, it attacked the South-wide denial of the right to vote, and it continued prosecuting a series of court cases against legalized Jim Crow.[4]

The most prominent counter to the interracialism of the NAACP was the Universal Negro Improvement Association (UNIA), led by the nationalist Marcus Garvey, born in Jamaica in 1887, who had immigrated to the United States in 1916. By the '20s, Garvey had built the largest and broadest mass movement of Blacks America had ever seen. By the mid-'20s the UNIA had more than seven hundred branches in thirty-eight states, in every corner of the country, and more than two hundred branches outside the USA. His plans, spelled out in 1925, were very different from those of the NAACP.

Garvey argued for a return of some American Blacks to Africa, the liberation of Africa from European colonialism, the creation of Black businesses, and rigid separation of the races here. Blacks deserved political and economic equality, he argued, but whites would never permit it. The center of Garvey's message was absolute rejection of white denigration of Africa and African Americans. Africa had agriculture and advanced culture—written languages, advanced medicine, and mathematics—when Europeans were still naked barbarians, he proclaimed. But modern Africa had been spoiled by Europeans, and Africans in America had been robbed of the legacy their African forebears had created for them.[5]

BY 1921, GARVEY'S UNIA may have had ten times as many members as the NAACP. At its height in 1923, the UNIA boasted six million members, the largest Black mass movement in American history. In 1923, Garvey was convicted of mail fraud, sentenced to five years in federal prison, and then pardoned by President Coolidge and deported in 1927. He had risen to great influence, attracting hundreds of thousands of followers, before the government brought him down. He had aroused the anger and enmity of other Blacks; Du Bois called him "the most dangerous enemy of the Negro race in America and in the world . . . either a lunatic or a traitor."[6] *The Messenger*, published by labor leader A. Philip Randolph, referred to Garvey as "the supreme Negro Jamaican Jackass" and an "unquestioned fool and ignoramus."[7] But thousands upon thousands loved and followed him; they did so because he tapped into the strong stream of nationalism, race preservation, cultural revitalization, group identity, and self-defense that has been ever-present in Black America since slavery.

Garveyism represented psychological liberation from mental slavery imposed by white supremacy. "The world has made being black a crime," Garvey said. "I intend to make it a virtue."[8] He linked black aspiration for cultural and economic independence from white domination with the American striving for success, and, if the effect was not much change in the physical circumstances of Garvey's followers, he radically altered their mental state and political outlook and kept alive that ever-present strain of Black Nationalism that continues in America today.

THE TEN YEARS following World War I saw improvements in the economic lives of Blacks, but a quick decline followed. When the stock market crashed in October 1929, many Blacks were already in the middle of a depression. "Even in starvation there was discrimination," a historian wrote.[9] Relief distribution was governed by racial preferences, and Blacks were totally excluded from some welfare programs.

Building Black political power, for many Blacks, offered a way out. Dissatisfaction among Blacks with the Republican Party began in 1928 when the party tried to replace its Black supporters and rebuild an all-white organization in the South, destroying the influence of prominent Black party leaders. One result was an increased Black vote in the 1928 presidential election for Alfred E. Smith, the Democratic candidate. Smith lost to Republican Herbert Hoover, in part because the Republicans were willing to exploit anti-Catholic sentiments in the South and were willing to shoulder their loyal Black supporters aside to attract white Democrats. Republicans learned that prejudice was politically profitable; Blacks learned that blind loyalty to any party was foolish.

By the time Herbert Hoover ran for reelection in 1932—against the little-known Democratic governor of New York, Franklin Roosevelt—a few Blacks were willing to abandon Abraham Lincoln's party. One-half of all urban Black Southerners were out of work. Most Blacks voted for Hoover, who lost, but, within a year, Roosevelt's personality and his politics began to win the allegiance of more Blacks, as well as many other Americans, as he began an all-out attack on the Depression. In his four terms from 1933 to 1945, he never supported a single piece of civil rights legislation and scarcely spoke a single word against discrimination. Racial discrimination persisted in federal programs. Blacks, however, did benefit from various New Deal measures, and Black federal employees increased from fifty thousand in 1933 to nearly two hundred thousand by 1946.

New Deal policies that worsened the positions of Blacks were not overtly racist but undoubtedly had racist effects. Most telling was the exclusion of farm laborers and domestic workers from coverage under the Social Security Act and the National Labor Relations Act of 1935 and the Fair Labor Standards Act of 1938. Since most Southern Blacks and relatively few Southern whites were concentrated in these lowly paid occupations,

Black exclusion meant most Blacks were left out of the new welfare state and denied the same chance to escape poverty available to many poor whites. It is undeniable that, in comparison with whites, Blacks became relatively worse off. New Deal programs helped fuel the modern wealth gap between Blacks and whites.[10] Nonetheless, the material circumstances of Blacks improved, and, on average, Blacks were better off in 1950 than they had been in 1930.

Eleanor Roosevelt played an important role in shaping both white and Black perceptions of her husband's administrations; she was on intimate terms with noted Black educator Mary McLeod Bethune. Mrs. Roosevelt visited Black schools and federal projects targeted to Blacks, and represented an egalitarianism never seen in the White House before. By 1936, a majority of Blacks were Democrats, and Roosevelt—in contrast to his twentieth-century predecessors in the White House—was viewed fondly by most Blacks.

Franklin Roosevelt's 1932 election and subsequent terms increased the power of the Presidency. The Depression also changed the nature and role of government. The Depression of the 1930s was—and is—the greatest crisis Americans confronted in the twentieth century. America was fighting for its life and future. There had never been a time when the government was so engaged in the lives of its citizens. Americans began to re-think and question the role of government in insuring economic stability and in helping individuals protect themselves from larger economic and social forces they could not confront alone. The Depression and New Deal changed forever the nature of the American workplace—unemployment insurance and Social Security created a safety net for millions of Americans.

BY 1935, AMERICA had begun to leave behind the unregulated capitalism that had created so much misery. Even the arts were changed by the Depression—writers, photographers, composers, artists, and painters hired by the Works Progress Administration and the Farm Security Administration began to celebrate the lives and struggles of ordinary women and men. Art was for everyone, they believed—not just for an elite.

The Depression, the New Deal measures taken to end it, the relative racial liberalism of many in the Roosevelt Administrations, and the

assertiveness of Black Americans helped raise Black expectations, overcome powerlessness, and diminish white hostility. Supreme Court decisions had begun to reverse the anti-Black counterrevolution of the late
1800s; cases involving Black exclusion from juries, the right to picket
against employment discrimination, disenfranchisement, racially restrictive housing covenants, unequal pay for Black teachers made Blacks "less
freedmen and more free men."[11]

In 1932, Southern politicians had been loudest in demanding government action to beat back the Depression and had supported Franklin Roosevelt enthusiastically. New Deal programs poured money into the South,
most of it intended to help the poor and most of it controlled by and ben-
efiting landowners and their business associates. Big planters in the Black
Belt, the region that was the backbone of the segregationist South, saw
their fortunes secured.

But within a few years, the New Deal began to upset some time-
honored Southern economic and political relationships and to challenge
others. Work relief programs and the legalization of labor unions threatened to upset the supply of cheap labor and destroy the culture of agricul-
tural dependency. Workers flocked to labor unions—to the United Mine
Workers and the Amalgamated Clothing Workers in 1933 and in 1934. In
1935, industrial unions organized the Congress of Industrial Organizations (CIO), and in its militancy and social and political outlook it differed
widely from the racially restrictive and politically conservative American
Federation of Labor (AFL).

The promise of federal interest—if not federal protection—spurred
racial militancy and inspired efforts to secure the right to vote. NAACP
membership swelled. Black youth joined the left-wing American Youth
Congress, the American Student Union, and the Southern Negro Congress. In Georgia and South Carolina, Blacks attempted to vote in white
primaries (the primaries were run like private clubs in which only whites
could participate).

In 1936, with the economy on the upswing and a popular program of
jobs, credit, and relief, Roosevelt easily won reelection, creating a new majority: big-city political machines, the Southern and border states (pow-
ered by labor militancy), and Black votes. Yet, at the same time, white
resistance to integration was certified by a Roper poll in 1939. Only one in
eight Americans believed Blacks should live wherever they wanted to live;

seven in ten said Blacks were less intelligent than whites, and in 1944, half believed in affirmative action for whites, agreeing that whites should have the first chance at any kind of job. Half said they wouldn't like it if they were in a hospital with a "Negro nurse"; six of ten told the Gallup poll in 1948 they would object to mixing the races in the military.

THREE

WORLD WAR II

A NOTHER WAR—WORLD WAR II—reshaped American society and reordered American thinking toward racism. For Blacks, the war against fascism was a personal struggle. When Italy invaded Ethiopia, a Black nation had been attacked, and Black America reacted with outrage. Hitler's notion of a master race was an old and frightening story to American Blacks; in him they saw the worst demagogues of the South now threatening to take over the entire world.

If the war caused many Americans to raise questions about whether and how well democracy was applied at home, the Cold War that resulted from it fostered a strident American nationalism that shut down debate and eliminated dissent in the postwar period. It created a new world physically and politically divided between Soviet and American spheres. It also marked the end of European expansion that had begun in the fifteenth century with the slave trade.

Like the First World War, the economic engine of the Second created jobs for many and another great migration—again Blacks left the South for the North and West. Between 1940 and 1945, the Black population of Los Angeles doubled; the Black population of other cities increased as well. Between 1940 and 1965, the Black population of New York grew from 6 percent of the total to 16 percent; Chicago's from 8 to 27 percent; Detroit's from 4 to 18 percent; and Washington, DC's from 28 to 63 percent.

Above all else, the war and postwar conversion rejuvenated American capitalism. Disposable family income rose. It was $1,055 in 1940; by 1956, that was the income of the average teenager. Corporate profits, the gross national product, the number of civilian jobs, Americans' personal expenditures—all expanded after the war.

The war quickened the integration of the South into the nation's economic and political life. Defense dollars stimulated Southern industrial development. The federal government spent $4 billion on Southern military facilities during World War II, building and expanding bases and shipyards—more than one-third of the total spent nationally.

An explosion of job opportunities swallowed up surplus labor that had been mired in agriculture, and job opportunities outside the region pulled Southerners away. In the 1930s, one of every seven Southerners left the region; in the 1940s, one of every five left. More than 1.5 million Blacks left the South in the 1940s. Those who stayed behind became an urban population—by 1950 in Georgia, for example, Blacks were more urbanized than whites. Cities offered Blacks higher living standards, even for the poor. Public housing was superior to sharecroppers' shacks. And cities offered the safety of numbers, and those numbers meant that institutions—like churches, schools, businesses—were more available than in the countryside.

Those Blacks who left created a civil rights constituency in Northern, Midwestern, and Western states, electing Democrats who countered their Southern colleagues' objections to any civil rights advance. Those who stayed behind were active too—Black voter registration efforts flourished, much of it prompted by returning veterans. Mississippi's Progressive Voters League grew to five thousand members in the most repressive state in the union. In Atlanta, the United Negro Veterans marched by the hundred to demand Black policemen. In Savannah, 12,000 new Black voters registered in seventeen days, and the number of new Black voters in Georgia rose from 20,000 in 1945 to 136,000 by the end of 1946.

By 1950, there were half as many Black sharecroppers as there had been in 1930. By 1960, two-thirds of those had left the farm. The demise of sharecropping meant the death of direct control of Blacks by landlords, the weakening of the most powerful rural white supremacist authority since slavery.

In the 1940s, the percentage of Blacks acquiring a high school education shot upward, a reflection of increased Black prosperity and the white

South's increased funding for Black schools to lower pressure for school integration. The number of Blacks in college increased 150 percent in the 1940s; this growth in educational access and achievement meant a corresponding growth in confidence and the courage to demand equal rights.

The war also helped to throw a spotlight on the nation's acquiescence to racial segregation. The gulf between promise and practice further fueled Black militancy. Even before the December 1941 attack on Pearl Harbor and American entry into the war, war preparation and production had begun. Black leaders were anxious to ensure their constituents would not be left behind in the promised prosperity.

IN EARLY 1941, A. Philip Randolph, president of the Brotherhood of Sleeping Car Porters, threatened a mass march on Washington to protest discrimination in defense industry hiring. Black unemployment had reached 25 percent. The contrast between employment segregation at home and America's claims to be a freedom-loving, democratic alternative to fascist Germany abroad only heightened the frustration Blacks felt on the eve of the war.

Randolph represented a radical, socialist critique of the struggle for equal rights. Born in Florida in 1889, Randolph came of political age in Harlem just before and during the First World War. His conversion to socialism informed his view that the racial struggle was a class struggle too, one that should be waged with the Black working class in the foreground. Neither the NAACP nor the National Urban League drew its leadership from the working class. Randolph became a caustic critic of civil rights organizations that did not share his view and an even more pointed critic of white supremacists.

Randolph had waged a decade-long struggle to organize railroad porters into a union, the Brotherhood of Sleeping Car Porters, and won certification in 1937. His experience and his victory gave him entree into the national councils of organized labor, where he became a constant prod to the exclusionary practices of most unions. President Woodrow Wilson called Randolph "the most dangerous Negro in America."[1]

Randolph, the NAACP's Walter White, and an Urban League spokesman visited Roosevelt in September 1940 to complain about defense plant job discrimination. Randolph left the meeting convinced that only mass action would force a presidential response. Randolph warned that one hundred thousand Blacks would march on Washington to bring their "power and pressure to bear on the agencies and representatives of the Federal Government to exact their rights in National Defense employment and the armed forces of the country."[2]

The Black response was overwhelming, even from the less militant NAACP and Urban League. With the march set for July 1, 1941, Randolph wrote as a member of the newly formed March on Washington Committee: "Dear Fellow Negro Americans: Be not dismayed in these terrible times. You possess power, great power. Our problem is to harness and hitch it up for action on the broadest, daring, and most gigantic scale!"[3]

Roosevelt tried to stop the march, enlisting the services of his wife, Eleanor, a popular figure among Blacks nationally, and the aid of New York mayor Fiorello H. LaGuardia. They failed, and the president called a White House meeting with Randolph and three others.

The four insisted on a quid quo pro for canceling the march. On June 25, Roosevelt gave it to them. He issued Executive Order 8802, which declared: "There shall be no discrimination in the employment of workers in defense industries or government because of race, creed, color or national origin."[4]

The order did not desegregate the military, as the movement had demanded, but it did establish a Fair Employment Practices Committee (FEPC), empowered to investigate and recommend but without enforcement powers. Like many of the victories won by Black Americans, the executive order was ineffective, only grudgingly given, and then granted only in response to threatened disruption and international embarrassment. Roosevelt paid little attention to the merit of the arguments that Randolph and others made; what interested him was an expedient way of canceling the march.

The FEPC, which largely died after the war, did represent a dramatic new commitment to Blacks from an American president. The March on Washington movement, kept alive by Randolph, played an important role in laying the groundwork for the civil rights movement that would follow in the 1950s. Not only did it show the effectiveness of threats of disruptive protest; it provided early training for a generation of activists—among them James Farmer and Bayard Rustin—and it built a base of activists standing ready for the nonviolent movement to begin.

As the 1940s began, Black Americans were poised for another leap forward. Franklin Roosevelt's New Deal had raised expectations and, in some instances, created new opportunity. It had especially changed American expectations of government's role in combating poverty and had erased Black loyalty to the Republican Party. Black life chances had improved between 1930 and 1940—literacy among Blacks was up, the number of Black skilled workers was up, life expectancy increased, the percentage of young Blacks attending school had risen.

Black Americans had enjoyed boosts from sports, with Joe Louis's championships from 1937 to 1949 and Jesse Owens's four gold medals won over the objections of Adolf Hitler at the 1936 Olympics; and from the arts in 1939, when Mrs. Roosevelt resigned from the Daughters of the American Revolution over their refusal to let Marian Anderson sing at Washington's Constitution Hall, when *Native Son* by Richard Wright became a 1940 best seller, and when Paul Robeson, Canada Lee, Katherine Dunham, Duke Ellington, Lena Horne, and others began to enjoy popular success.

They had also gotten a boost from the US Supreme Court in a series of lawsuits sponsored by the NAACP and others, including *Gaines v. Canada*, a 1938 decision declaring that states had to provide equal facilities for Blacks even if separate facilities existed; *Smith v. Allwright* in 1944, in which the court struck down Texas's white primary; *Morgan v. Virginia* in 1946, where the court banned segregation in interstate travel; and in 1948 in *Shelley v. Kraemer*, in which the court said racially restrictive housing covenants were unconstitutional. If the NAACP's legal victories did little to dent white supremacy, they did educate Blacks about their civil rights, mobilized local communities, and strengthened the NAACP's position as the dominant organization fighting for civil rights. Membership in the NAACP increased greatly by 1945—acknowledgment of the association's increased militancy and the growing desire by Blacks for an organized vehicle to promote racial progress.

As in World War I, the employment opportunities created by World War II and the desire by Southern Blacks to improve their lives and escape Southern terror changed the demographics of Black America. The government encouraged recruiting Southern Black workers as a wartime emergency measure. Both Southern Black women and men were motivated to move by harsh racial conditions, but women faced another fear: sexual exploitation at the hands of whites.

The wave of outmigration built a Black industrial working class in Northern cities. On a much smaller scale, a similar class grew in the South. But, North or South, they worked the most difficult, dangerous, and low-paying jobs. Despite increased opportunity, segregated jobs remained the rule. In 1940, 62 percent of Black men were farmers, farm laborers, or other laborers; only 28 percent of white men had similar jobs. Almost 30 percent of white men had professional, semiprofessional, proprietary, managerial, and clerical and sales jobs; only 5 percent of Black men were so employed. Fifteen percent of white men were skilled craft workers; only 4 percent of Black men were. Among women who worked outside the home, 56 percent of Northern Black women were domestic workers; only 12 percent of Northern white women were maids. Fifty-one percent of white women had professional, managerial, sales, or clerical jobs; only 9 percent of Black women had such work.[5]

And when white women were urged to enter the factory to replace their husbands, absent in the war, Black women were urged to enter the laundry, the cafeteria, or other service jobs white women had left behind. Only 100 of the 96,000 female production workers in Detroit's plants in late 1942 were Black.

In the military itself, race remained the determinant for employment. In the Marines, Blacks could only serve as stewards. In the Navy, 80 percent of Blacks—and 2 percent of whites—were stewards, cooks, and stewards' mates. The Army had one white officer for every five white enlisted men; every Black officer served seven Black enlisted men.

But the war mobilized thousands of Black men into a military force and inspired them and others like them to fight for freedom. For most Black Americans, the war had two goals—"a double V": victory over fascism and Hitler's master race theories abroad; victory over racism at home. The NAACP's Walter White wrote in 1945 that "Negro militancy and implacable determination to wipe out segregation grew more proportionately during the years 1940 to 1945 than during any other period of the Negro's history in America."[6]

Four thousand Black women served in the Women's Army Corps, about 10 percent of all WACs. But in the WAC and the Army Nurse Corps, Black women were assigned to segregated units and seldom sent overseas. They were barred from the Women's Reserve of the Navy until 1944. And segregation at restaurants, movie theaters, and other places of public accommodation served as daily reminders to Blacks they were not considered a part of the public.

THE UNITED STATES found it at least rhetorically difficult to fight a war against racial supremacy in Europe and the Far East while tolerating white supremacy inside the United States. The Japanese made race-based appeals to nonwhites in China, Latin America, and India. The author Pearl S. Buck wrote: "Every lynching, every race riot, gives joy to Japan. . . . 'Look at America' Japan is saying to millions of listening ears. 'Will white Americans give you equality?'" She argued: "We cannot . . . win this war without convincing our colored allies—who are most of our allies—that we are not fighting for ourselves as continuing superior over colored peoples."[7]

And in his 1944 classic *An American Dilemma*, Swedish sociologist Gunnar Myrdal noted that "the German radio often mentions America's harsh treatment of Negroes in its propaganda broadcasts to European peoples."[8] Myrdal's two-volume study offered a radical reformulation of America's racial problems. Racism contradicted whites' own "American creed" of liberty, equality, justice, and fair opportunity for everyone. But Myrdal wrongly postulated that discrimination and racial inequality were the products of irrational prejudice and not integral to the structure and functions of our politics and institutions. Thus, the Myrdal paradigm, adopted by most Americans, treated racial prejudice as a largely psychological phenomenon rather than acknowledging race was a political construct created and employed to pursue power and maintain control. *An American Dilemma* sold an unusual one hundred thousand copies. In 1954, the Supreme Court cited Myrdal's study in its *Brown v. Board of Education* ruling.

World War II did make democracy, for many Americans, more than an abstract concept; it was an ideal for which they were fighting and dying. But even that ideal had contradictions. American soldiers died in segregated trenches in a segregated army; the enemy was often characterized in racist terms—the "yellow Jap" and the "savage Hun." At home, Japanese Americans became scapegoats for the war and victims of anti-Japanese hysteria. In 1942, 112,000 Japanese Americans were rounded up and herded into camps, their property confiscated.

In March 1942, two thousand miles of the West Coast, by order of President Roosevelt, was designated an evacuation area; 120,000 Japanese people who lived on the West Coast, two-thirds of them American citizens, were forced into ten concentration camps—the only prison camps ever designed for Americans who had committed no crime. Ten thousand Germans and German Americans and ten thousand Italians and Italian Americans were placed in camps for shorter periods; the ten thousand Italian Americans were forced to relocate from California's coast.[9]

As the pogroms against Jews and the death camps in Europe became common knowledge, racial supremacy understandably lost currency; Hitler gave racism a bad name.

On Tuesday, August 14, 1945, I was sitting in the segregated balcony of a downtown movie theater in Nashville when the movie suddenly stopped, the lights came on, and a man walked in front of the screen to the center of the stage. "Ladies and gentlemen," he said in a deep Southern accent. "The war is over!"

FOUR

PRESIDENT TRUMAN
AND THE ROAD TO *BROWN*

T HE AMERICAN VICTORY in World War II created a changed international landscape; the war's aftermath changed it even further. By
1946, the Soviet Union, recent ally to the US, was now seen by the US as
a threat to world peace. Although the war had been won together, each
seized upon the peace as an opportunity to consolidate power—to control their own populations—through purges, internal exile, and prison in
Russia and with greater sophistication in the United States. Competition
between the Soviet Union and the United States became a secular religion—opposition to Communism became the national faith.

The choice, President Harry Truman told Congress in March 1947, was
stark and real. One way of life, the president said, is "distinguished by free
institutions, representative government, free elections, guarantees of individual liberty, freedom of speech and religion, and freedom from political
oppression." But Truman was describing a way of life most Black Southerners had never known. Then he described the Communist choice, a way
of life that "relies on terror and oppression, a controlled press and radio,
fixed elections, and the suppression of personal freedoms."

"It will be the policy of the United States," the president said, "to support free peoples who are resisting attempted subjugation by armed minorities or by outside pressures."[1] Except that Black people in the US were
not free. Truman had easily described the day-by-day existence of most
Blacks living south of the Mason-Dixon Line—resisting subjugation.

Truman's listeners had heard what would be called the Truman Doctrine, a commitment to stop the expansion of Communism everywhere. It would not be limited to foreign affairs; both domestic and foreign policy initiatives would now be evaluated to see whether or not they contributed to Communism's spread or undercut attempts at Communist infiltration at home.

One effect of concentrated anti-Communism and the escalation of the Cold War at home was the weakening and red-baiting of interracial organizations. Following the November 1948 election, the Southern Conference for Human Welfare and the Southern Negro Youth Congress disbanded; Highlander Folk School and the Southern Conference Education Fund remained the lonely Southern interracial battlers for integration.

TRUMAN HAD COME TO OFFICE when President Roosevelt died suddenly in April 1945. It is fair to say that while most Americans mourned his death, Black Americans were especially bereft. Truman had flirted with the Ku Klux Klan in his political youth, but 20,000 Black voters in Kansas City, Missouri, and another 110,000 across the state served as an antidote to moderate his views and were an important factor in his first election to the Senate in 1934. He accepted segregation as the norm but was a racial moderate, a supporter of antidiscrimination legislation, including a permanent Fair Employment Practices Commission, and an opponent of the poll tax.

Following the limited success of his threatened March on Washington in 1941, A. Philip Randolph had created the National Council for a Permanent Fair Employment Practices Commission. It attracted solid support, including from the Socialist and Communist Parties and even in the 1944 Republican platform. Truman, as vice president, had strongly supported a permanent FEPC. In the months after Roosevelt's death, he kept the FEPC alive through executive orders but was unable—some thought unwilling—to win congressional authorization.

Blacks remained skeptical, even more so after Truman appointed South Carolina senator James Byrnes to be secretary of state. An unapologetic racist, Byrnes was leading the resistance to implementation of the 1944 Supreme Court ruling that outlawed the exclusion of Black voters from Democratic Party primaries.

Having won that 1944 victory, the NAACP continued to press Truman and continued its legal fight as well. In 1947, in *Patton v. Mississippi*, the Supreme Court found the exclusion of Blacks from juries unconstitutional. In 1948, the NAACP won *Sipuel v. University of Oklahoma*, a decision that required a state to provide legal education for Blacks at the same time it was offered to whites. In 1950, *Sweatt v. Painter* held that an equal education meant more than equal facilities; *McLaurin v. Oklahoma State Regents* held that Black students could not be segregated within a university.

These court victories were tempered by a wave of violence that swept the South following the war. My earliest memory of racial violence is the nightstick beating and blinding of Sergeant Isaac Woodard in Aiken, South Carolina, in 1946. Woodard was returning home after three years in the army and arrested after an argument with the bus driver because he wanted to use the restroom. He was brutally beaten by police officers, including being jabbed in the eyes with nightsticks. The Aiken police chief was indicted for the beating but was acquitted as a courtroom full of whites cheered. I will remember the newspaper photographs of Sergeant Woodard, his bandaged eyes beaten into darkness, as long as I live.[2] I was six years old.

Later that summer, Macio Snipes, the only Black voter in his Georgia district, was killed in his home by whites. In July 1946, in Monroe, Georgia, Roger Malcolm was arrested for fighting with a white man. When he was released, his white employer drove Malcolm, his wife, and two friends down a back road to a waiting mob—all four were shot and killed.

Liberal groups—representatives of forty-six civil rights, religious, and labor organizations—spurred by Southern violence, established the National Emergency Committee Against Mob Violence and quickly moved to mobilize mass opinion. They met with Truman in September 1946 to call for federal action against lynchers. Walter White described the Woodard beating, and Truman rose from his chair and said, "My God! I had no idea that it was as terrible as that! We've got to do something!"

Truman took advantage of the committee's meeting to announce the establishment of a presidential commission, already under consideration, to study racial violence and to recommend federal action. Foremost in the president's mind were the upcoming midterm elections. Black Democrats were expressing dissatisfaction with the administration's civil rights efforts. Truman announced the commission in December to mixed notices.

The year 1946 had not been a good one for civil rights. Racist Georgia governor Eugene Talmadge and Mississippi senator Theodore Bilbo had been reelected; legislation ending the poll tax, outlawing lynching, and establishing the FEPC had been defeated; attacks on Black voting rights and widespread racist violence continued. Japanese Americans seeking compensation for their wartime losses made little progress.

Despite these setbacks—or perhaps because of them—more and more groups and organizations took up the cause of civil rights, and several reached across racial barriers to form coalitions. Blacks and Mexican Americans joined together in San Antonio to elect a Black to a college trustee board and a Mexican American to the school board. The Japanese American Citizens League supported a permanent FEPC, Japanese Americans condemned racism, and Black newspapers spoke out against anti-Japanese prejudice. Blacks, Jews, labor and church groups supported FEPC laws in twenty-seven states; ten enacted them.[3]

The leadership of the NAACP pushed for integrated schools, despite evidence that some Blacks were pleased to have facilities that, if separate, were truly equal. In the early 1940s, the NAACP had opposed the construction of all-Black hospitals and supported the integration of existing, segregated facilities. When the government proposed building an all-Black hospital in Mississippi, a *Negro Digest* poll showed that 34 percent of those asked supported it, 28 percent opposed it, and the rest were undecided.

Increasingly, the pro–civil rights rhetoric of white elites—as well as Blacks—was colored by international politics. Secretary of State Dean Acheson wrote in April 1946 of the "adverse effect [the existence of discrimination] has on our relations with other countries. . . . Frequently we find it next to impossible to formulate a satisfactory answer to our critics in other countries."[4]

Formed in 1946, the United Nations Human Rights Commission soon became an international forum for grievances. In October 1947, the NAACP filed a petition, "An Appeal to the World," before the commission over the opposition of the State Department and the US delegate to the commission, Eleanor Roosevelt. The appeal created a worldwide stir, demonstrating the availability of international embarrassment as a lever in the fight for equal justice.

Truman would have to face the voters as president for the first time in 1948 and secure Black votes. In October 1947, the President's Committee on Civil Rights released *To Secure These Rights.*[5] It codified the demands of the then civil rights movement and gave them presidential approval.

Henry Wallace of the anti-segregation Progressive Party formally announced as a third-party candidate on December 29, 1947. "Voting for a Democrat or Republican is like voting for different ends of the same egg," Charles Houston said. "Wallace offers the American people something different."[6] Truman countered with a special message to Congress on civil rights on February 2, 1948, the first time an American president had sent such a message to Capitol Hill. He recommended many of the same suggestions put forth in *To Secure These Rights*: abolishing the poll tax, a permanent FEPC, federal protection against lynching, and creation of a civil rights division in the Department of Justice.

There was no direct attack on segregation, except in interstate travel, where the Supreme Court had already spoken. What Truman did do, however, was to outline the nature of the struggle for civil rights over the next two decades. As enthusiasm for the Wallace campaign waned, Truman's popularity fell too. Some elements in the Democratic Party even tried to dump Truman in favor of war hero General Dwight "Ike" Eisenhower, who had not committed to either major party.

The Eightieth Congress, dominated by the Republican Party, passed almost none of Truman's civil rights program; indeed, the president hardly seemed to promote the program he had announced earlier in the year. As the election approached, Truman's record showed promises made and promises delayed.

The Democratic Convention in Chicago in July 1948 produced a civil rights plank only slightly stronger than the one in the Democrats' 1944 platform. But it featured a bruising floor fight and made a civil rights hero of young Minneapolis mayor Hubert Humphrey, who brought the hall alive.

> To those who say that we are rushing this issue of civil rights, I say to them, we are one hundred seventy-two years too late. To those who say that this civil rights program is an infringement on States' Rights, I say this, that the time has arrived in America for the Democratic Party to get out of the shadow of States' Rights and to walk forthrightly into the bright sunshine of human rights.[7]

SOME SOUTHERNERS WALKED OUT. The civil rights plank adopted by the Democratic Convention in 1948 so angered the racist white South that many bolted the convention, formed the States' Rights Party, and nominated segregationist governor Strom Thurmond of South Carolina as their presidential candidate.

On July 26, 1948, Truman delivered a long-awaited civil rights bombshell. He issued two executive orders. The first declared the policy of "fair employment throughout the federal establishment without discrimination because of race, color, religion, or national origin" and established a Fair Employment Board in the Civil Service Commission. The second called for "equality of treatment and opportunity for all persons in the armed services without regard to race, color, religion, or national origin."[8]

Earlier that year, in March, A. Philip Randolph had told a congressional committee he would counsel Black youth to refuse induction into a segregated army. He had begun to threaten that young Black men would refuse to register for the draft, set to begin August 16, unless the president outlawed military segregation. Truman's actions were as much a ploy for Black votes and a response to Randolph as they were an attempt to paint the Republican Congress as a "do-nothing" body. Its failures and an appeal to the "little man" were his central election themes. He told a Southern Illinois audience, for example, that "big business Republicans have begun to nail the American consumer to the wall with spikes of greed!"[9]

The Republican nominee, Thomas Dewey, who had a decent if largely unknown race relations record as New York governor, made little effort to attract Black voters, and Wallace continued to fade. Attacks from Southern congressmen on Truman's civil rights program helped him with Black voters. Thurmond's attacks on Truman's FEPC as similar to the "Communistic Russian all-races law promulgated by Stalin" helped convince Black voters that the Truman campaign was where they should be.[10]

In the last week of the campaign, Truman made a bold appeal for the votes of American minorities. He began in multiethnic Chicago, assailing the "crackpot forces of the extreme right wing" who were "stirring up racial and religious prejudice against some of our fellow Americans." It is these "dangerous men," he said, "who are trying to win followers for their war on democracy, are attacking Catholics, and Jews, and Negroes, and other minority races and religions."[11] In Boston, he denounced religious bigotry against Catholics, and in New York, he identified himself with Israel, reaffirming his sometimes tenuous support for a Jewish homeland.

And then, on October 29, the first anniversary of his Committee on Civil Rights report, he became the first president to speak in Harlem. He told an audience of 65,000 that he would work for equal rights "with every ounce of strength and determination that I have."[12]

Black votes made a difference in Truman's victory. He won California by over 17,000 votes, Black voters in Los Angeles giving him a 25,000-vote margin over Dewey. He carried Illinois thanks to Black Chicago voters and Ohio because of Black Cleveland. Although Truman's civil rights program was an important part of his victory, his ability to make himself the heir to the New Deal helped him to succeed with Blacks as well. Class interests joined race interests to create a Truman landslide among Blacks. From 1936 forward, the class interests of the majority of Black voters led them closer and closer to a solid identification with the Democratic Party and away from loyalty to the Republicans that had begun with Abraham Lincoln. The Democrats were the "bread and butter" party for Blacks even though the Republicans were thought by many to have a modest edge overall in civil rights.

By solidifying the shaky relationship between Black voters and the Democratic Party, Truman prompted some racist white Democrats to look elsewhere. Civil rights was still a sectional issue in 1948 and, outside the South, largely a contest between Southern and Northern wings of the Democratic Party. The States' Rights Party candidacy of white supremacist Strom Thurmond showed white Southerners there were alternatives to the Democratic Party—his Dixiecrats carried South Carolina, Mississippi, Alabama, and Louisiana.

In 1952, war hero Dwight David Eisenhower, opting to run as a Republican, was elected president, defeating Adlai Stevenson and shattering the solid Democratic South that had been so important to the Democrats in the past. The Republicans won control of the House of Representatives and tied for control of the Senate. Stevenson had courted the South too; his unwillingness to make a strong statement on civil rights created hesitancy among many Blacks to support the Democratic ticket, but he still received three out of every four Black votes, similar to Truman's totals four years earlier.

The Roosevelt and Truman years had seen an expansion of Black protest and politics, with each attempt at legislation or regulation, effective or not, stirring other attempts, energizing more people. A generation of Black and white civil rights activists battled with the federal government, others fought lonely battles in the South, but all stood poised and ready for the next leap forward. There was much hope that the momentum built up under Roosevelt and Truman would continue under Eisenhower.

If there is one distinguishing feature of the struggle of Black Americans, it has been a willingness to try many methods; that was true when the twentieth century began, and it was even more true at the century's halfway point.

FIVE

BROWN V. BOARD
OF EDUCATION

O N MAY 17, 1954, Supreme Court chief justice Earl Warren conducted about forty minutes of routine court business and then announced: "I have the judgment and opinion of the court in No. 1—*Oliver Brown et al. v. Board of Education of Topeka*. . . . In these days, it is doubtful that any child may reasonably be expected to succeed in life if he is denied the opportunity of an education. Such an opportunity, where the state has undertaken to provide it, is a right which must be available to all on equal terms." Then, he came to the crucial question: "Does segregation of children in public schools solely on the basis of their race, even though the physical facilities and other 'tangible' factors may be equal, deprive the children of the minority group of equal educational opportunities? We believe that it does."

"The doctrine of 'separate but equal,'" Warren said, "has no place!"[1]

I was fourteen years old when this happened. I remember this feeling my parents had of great joy and optimism about it. I don't think they thought things would change overnight. But they thought this was a sign of change. Things were looking up.[2]

The *Brown* decision came from a long history of Black efforts to obtain an equal education. The formation of the NAACP formalized the drive for access to education. The strategy was designed by Charles Houston and carried forward by Thurgood Marshall after Houston's death in 1938. Beginning in 1936 with *Pearson v. Murray*, integrating the University of Maryland's law school, the NAACP won a series of lawsuits that aimed at forcing separate to be truly equal, thus making segregation so expensive it would have to be abandoned. The NAACP then shifted from trying to make separate facilities equal, and winning equal pay for segregated Black teachers, to a direct attack on the beast itself.

In 1951, Marshall began to coordinate lawsuits attacking segregated education as unconstitutional on its face, even if the separate facilities were equal. The suits hailed from Clarendon County, South Carolina; Prince Edward County, Virginia; New Castle County, Delaware; the District of Columbia; and Topeka, Kansas. On December 9, 1952, the Supreme Court heard oral argument on all five cases, combined them under the name of the petitioner listed first—Oliver Brown of Topeka, Kansas, suing on behalf of his daughter Linda. Linda Brown lived three blocks from a segregated school; instead of attending that school, she rode a bus each day to an all-Black school two miles away.

When the case first came before the court, both its presenters and the justices who heard it understood its historic potential. In an unusual but not unheard-of procedure, the case was argued in the 1952 term and reargued the next.

Among other issues, the court struggled with the meaning of the Fourteenth Amendment, that portion of the Constitution adopted after the Civil War, guaranteeing equal protection of the laws as well as due process. In its earliest cases defining the Fourteenth Amendment, for instance, in *Strauder v. West Virginia* in 1880, the court had said: "It ordains that no state shall deprive any person of life, liberty or property without due process of law, to deny to any person within its jurisdiction the equal protection of the laws."

"What is this," the court asked, "but declaring that the law in the States shall be the same for the black as well as the white; that all persons, whether colored or white, shall stand equal before the laws of the States, and, in regard to the colored race, for whose protection the amendment was primarily designed, that no discrimination shall be made against them by law because of their color?"[3]

From that noble beginning there emerged, only a few years later, the disgraceful doctrine of "separate but equal" in *Plessy v. Ferguson*.[4]

In 1952, a half century after *Plessy*, for the first time the court confronted "separate but equal" head-on. The court asked the lawyers to prepare written responses to five questions, two of them dealing with the history of the

Fourteenth Amendment. The NAACP turned to scholars, including my father, and constitutional experts for assistance. While C. Vann Woodward and John Hope Franklin were studying post-Reconstruction policies regarding Southern race relations, my father researched the intentions of the ratifying states with respect to school integration.

My father believed so strongly in school integration that in 1947 my sister and I were plaintiffs in a lawsuit to integrate the schools of tiny Lincoln Village in Pennsylvania. Before that case could come to trial, the district closed the all-Black school, and my sister and I and the other Black children integrated the formerly all-white school.

In the end, the court regarded the historical evidence as "inconclusive" and "a draw," which meant victory for the NAACP.[5] *Plessy* had said Congress condoned segregation; now free to look for guidance elsewhere, the court was able to speak for what one historian called "the American conscience."[6]

The day *Brown* was announced, the NAACP held a news conference to announce an ambitious new agenda. To Thurgood Marshall, *Brown* was the Magna Carta of Black America, a declaration of our rights. School segregation would be eliminated, he thought, within five years. He was right about the former; he was obviously wrong about the latter.

Southern whites, with some exceptions, were adamantly opposed to *Brown*. The governors of South Carolina, Georgia, and Mississippi threatened to close public schools rather than permit integration. A Richmond newspaper wrote that the justices were "an inept fraternity of politicians and professors" and the decision "repudiated the Constitution, spit upon the Tenth Amendment, and rewrote the fundamental law of this land to suit their own gauzy concepts of sociology."[7] Yale-educated Mississippi judge Tom Brady wrote a book called *Black Monday*, distributed widely by the White Citizens' Council. He expressed the attitude and fears of many when he wrote:

> When a law transgresses the moral and ethical sanctions and standards of the mores, invariably strife, bloodshed and revolution follow in the wake of its attempted enforcement. The loveliest and purest of God's creatures, the nearest thing to an angelic being that tread this celestial ball is a well-bred, cultured Southern white woman or her blue-eyed, golden-haired little girl. . . . We have, through our forefathers, died before for our sacred principles. We can, if necessary, die again.[8]

THOSE WHO PREDICTED the promised land would be slow in coming were proved right on May 31, 1955, a year and two weeks after the initial decision. The first decision, in 1954, announced that school segregation was illegal and must end; the second decision, in 1955, said yes, but not today, not now, in fact not at any time soon. Rather, the court ordered the affected states to make haste slowly, in a masterpiece of ambiguity, to "admit to public schools on a racially nondiscriminatory basis *with all deliberate speed* the parties in these cases."[9]

The court did not set a date, as the plaintiffs had hoped. It did not ask for plans of action within three months, as the federal government's brief had requested. *Brown II* represented the costs of unanimity. Chief Justice Warren had believed a divided court would have been "catastrophic." For the first time, the Supreme Court had stated a right and delayed its exercise.

Delay and the promise of more delay gave the opposition time to organize, defend, and attack. It allowed the collapse and abdication of responsible white leadership and their replacement by extremists and opportunists. The vacillation of the Eisenhower administration gave no encouragement to white liberals or moderates. Instead, Eisenhower's hopes of building on and enlarging the Southern white votes he had received in 1952, and his administration's ignorance of the white South's potential for angry explosions, laid the foundation for the crisis yet to come in Little Rock in 1957, one of more than five hundred instances of violence and reprisals against Southern Blacks between 1955 and 1958.[10]

Southern members of Congress organized themselves to fight against the school decisions. Defiance of the court became proof of Southern loyalty and support of the white race. In 1956, 101 members of Congress, including every member from Alabama, Arkansas, Georgia, Mississippi, Louisiana, South Carolina, and Virginia, signed a "Southern Manifesto," asking their states not to obey the Supreme Court and warning against "meddlers" who might provoke Southerners to "unlawful acts," thereby disclaiming, predicting, and sanctioning violence all at the same time.

The Southern states passed more than 450 laws to block school integration and attack those who promoted it. The all-out attack on the NAACP—injunctions in Texas and Alabama, removal of tax-exemption in Georgia, South Carolina's forbidding public employment to NAACP members—reduced the NAACP's Southern membership, but it also unintentionally opened the door for more dynamic leadership, including some members of the Black clergy, previously better known for caution than courage.

Brown destroyed segregation's legality and gave a nonviolent army license and power to attack and destroy segregation's morality as well. The Southern protest movement was emboldened by *Brown*. The decision's anniversary quickly became a celebratory signpost for the growing movement for civil rights. Martin Luther King's first national address was at the 1957 Prayer Pilgrimage at the Lincoln Memorial on *Brown*'s third anniversary. I marched with several thousand others when the Atlanta student sit-in movement held its largest protest—a march on the Georgia State Capitol—to commemorate *Brown*'s sixth anniversary in 1960. The Freedom Rides were expected to end their tour through the South in New Orleans on the seventh anniversary of *Brown* in 1961.

When schools opened in the fall of 1956, some modest desegregation occurred, most often in school districts in the Upper and Border South, but resistance quickened. For the first ten years after 1954, the emphasis was more on "deliberate" than speed. The focus was on dismantling the dual school systems in the South, the products of de jure segregation, and, in Southern accents, "all deliberate speed" meant any conceivable delay. Integration was more a legal fiction than actual fact. President Eisenhower had lobbied Chief Justice Warren to rule for the South; he never endorsed *Brown*, and the resistant white South, encouraged by his silence, reacted with evasion and delay. Its tactics included violence, establishment of private segregation academies, plans to abolish all public education, repealing compulsory school attendance laws, state support to escaping white students, and the long-discarded theories of interposition and nullification, put forth in the 1830s by South Carolinian John C. Calhoun, who argued that states could "nullify" federal law. Prince Edward County, Virginia, closed its public schools for five years, believing children were better off uneducated than integrated. Ten years after *Brown*, more than 97 percent of all Southern Black children still attended segregated schools.

A second phase occupied the five years from the Civil Rights Act of 1964 until 1969. The Civil Rights Act prohibited discrimination wherever federal funds were spent, and for the first time, under a Southern president, Lyndon Johnson, the federal government took an active role. The percentage of Black children in school with white ones rose from 3 percent to 13 percent.

But there were great costs too. In North Carolina, from 1963 to 1970, the number of Black elementary school principals dropped from 620 to 170. Black secondary school principals went from 209 to 10. By 1973, only 3 were left. By 1972, 3,051 Black North Carolina schoolteachers—one-fifth of the state's Black teachers—had lost their jobs as Black and white schools merged. Across the South, an estimated 31,000 Black schoolteachers lost their jobs. Lost as well was history—revered school names, mottoes, mascots, traditions. Black students found themselves in formerly all-white schools that retained the identity they had acquired in the segregated past. Wherever Black school buildings were retained, their names were changed. Plaques, trophy cases—all the artifacts that honored Black achievement—disappeared.[11]

In the ten years after the 1964 act, the Department of Justice brought actions against more than five hundred school districts, and the Department of Health, Education, and Welfare filed more than six hundred complaints. But it was a full thirteen years after *Brown* that the court—in the 1968 *Green* decision—declared "separate but equal" extinct—and required school districts to dismantle segregation "root and branch" and produce integration plans "*now!*"[12]

Then Richard Nixon, in his victorious 1968 campaign for president, courted white votes with promises to roll back integration enforcement. Evasion and delay were given new life in the Supreme Court's 1974 decision in *Milliken v. Bradley.* By 1991 and 1992, a Supreme Court shaped by President Ronald Reagan gave school systems permission to disassemble desegregation plans despite remaining vestiges of segregation.[13]

Despite the dismal picture seen when viewed backward, in its immediate aftermath, in the middle 1950s for Black Southerners, *Brown* was a great emblem of success and held out great promise. In his history of the *Brown* decision, Richard Kluger writes: "Not until the Supreme Court acted did the nation acknowledge it had been blaming the black man for what it had done to him. His sentence to second class citizenship had been commuted; now the quest for meaningful equality—equality in fact as well as in the law—had begun."[14]

Brown became more than an occasion for annual celebration; it served as sanction and certification that the effort for equality was just and right.

If the Depression in 1929 had convinced America it was obliged to protect its citizens' well-being, the court's decision in *Brown* began to convince reluctant white Americans they would have to share their bounty, their knowledge, and their world. Critics who scoff at *Brown* as if the advantages to Black children were to be gained simply by sitting next to white ones in a classroom miss the point of integrated schools. A public educational system that is truly integrated and treats minorities and whites equally is the antithesis of the larger society, which is profoundly segregated and unequal.

IN THE WAKE of the *Brown* decisions, the attorneys general of Louisiana, Alabama, and Texas won court orders against the NAACP. Virginia passed seven laws to restrict the organization. South Carolina made it illegal for schoolteachers to be members. By 1957, the NAACP was facing debilitating litigation and legislation in seven states; it was completely banned in Alabama.

The South's crackdown on the NAACP resulted in an immediate drop in membership; the number of Southern branches dropped from 60 percent of the total in 1955 to 52 percent in 1958. In 1955, 45 percent of the dues-paying, card-carrying membership was Southern; by 1957, only 28 percent of the NAACP's members came from the South. As the NAACP grew weaker, activists looked for other organizations, and many created new ones.

Brown gave white racists a rallying cry throughout the South. The KKK was invigorated, and the White Citizens' Councils organized. They created a firm organizational base for terror and intimidation in each of the Southern states. One result was a series of attacks on voting rights activists that reverberated throughout Black America in 1955: Reverend George Lee was gunned to death in Belzoni, Mississippi, May 7, 1955. His friend and fellow activist Gus Courts was shot six months later but survived the attack, and Lamar Smith was assassinated on August 13 on the courthouse steps in Brookhaven, Mississippi.[15]

THEN, IN AUGUST 1955, fourteen-year-old Emmett Louis Till was lynched. He had come from his home in Chicago to Money, Mississippi, to live for the summer with his uncle, Mose Wright. Before he left his mother told him, "If you have to get down on your knees and bow when a white person goes past, do it." Leaving a country store, Till allegedly said "Bye, baby" to the white wife of the store's owner. That night, the store owner, Roy Bryant, and his half-brother, J. W. Milam, came to Mose Wright's home and took young Till away. They beat him, shot him in the head, and tied his body to a seventy-five-pound cotton gin fan and dumped it in the Tallahatchie River. "What else could I do?" one of the killers asked later. "He thought he was as good as any white man." Bryant and Milam were acquitted by an all-white, all-male jury in sixty-seven minutes.[16]

Till's mother insisted on an open casket at his funeral: "I want the world to see what they did to my boy." The Till case became a cause célèbre across the United States; his death sent terrifying signals to young Blacks everywhere. I was a year older than Emmett Till and can remember thinking, "If they'll do that to him, what will they do to me?"

Well-publicized in Black America, spoken of in barbershops and poolrooms, in churches, nightclubs, and social gatherings, the murders were done to instill fear and teach a lesson: that those who dared to challenge the color line could be stopped by brutal death. They did instill fear, but they also increased determination.

JUST AS THESE terror attacks were beginning, Roy Wilkins became the third executive secretary of the NAACP. At that point, the NAACP was the only national organization of Black people fighting for civil rights. As we have seen, it had won impressive court victories against racially restrictive housing covenants, segregated transportation, and segregated public facilities, culminating in the 1954 and 1955 school decisions, and Black Americans had some cause for cautious optimism. But it would take more than court victories to destroy segregation.[17]

Wilkins was born in 1901 and educated at the University of Minnesota, where he edited the school's paper, *The Daily.* He had become managing editor of the *Kansas City Call* before joining the NAACP staff in 1931, succeeding Du Bois as editor of the NAACP's magazine, *The Crisis.* When NAACP executive secretary Walter White died, Wilkins succeeded him, taking over the nation's oldest and largest civil rights organization just as events in Montgomery, Alabama, the former capital of the Confederacy, would change the nature of the racial struggle and give it new techniques, personalities, and organizations.

SIX

THE MONTGOMERY
BUS BOYCOTT

TO HISTORIANS OF the civil rights movement, the Montgomery bus boycott is like the Civil War for nineteenth-century American historians; it is the most studied event of the movement. It provides a case study of how a social movement starts, develops, and grows. Such movements begin with a concrete, precipitating event but are usually the result of known or shared incidents on the part of the participants. If the movement is to grow and succeed, it must use certain mechanisms. It must continue agitation, foster fellowship, sustain morale, and develop tactics. The Black citizens of Montgomery did all these things.

As we look at Montgomery—and at Albany, Birmingham, Selma, and other movements that seem confined to a single city or state—remember that, taken together, they constitute a series of events that are called the civil rights movement, a drive to eliminate racial segregation and win equal rights. When these are considered individually, each reflects the efforts of the Black people of a town or state to achieve local aims. Looking at the collected whole—the national movement—we see the important roles played by larger-than-life figures like Martin Luther King and presidents. The local movements show us how important unknown figures, men and women, were to making the movements that preceded and produced the larger, nationally known persons and events. These lesser-known leadership figures built the movements that built the reputations of Kings and presidents. We do not diminish Martin Luther King when we study these others; we see, instead, how countless people helped to make the larger movement a success.

The people and events we will study are only examples; there are many, many other personalities, places, and times that could profitably occupy our attention. There are numerous heroes and heroines, brave and cowardly men and women, Black and white scoundrels and devils we have chosen to pass by. What follows is the struggle to achieve democracy in the middle of twentieth-century America and some of the people who helped and hindered along the way.

"By the 1950s," sociologist Aldon Morris writes, "Southern whites had established a comprehensive system of domination over blacks. This system of domination protected the privileges of white society and generated tremendous human suffering for blacks." The system controlled Blacks economically, politically, and personally. Morris calls it a "tripartite system of domination."[1] Economic oppression kept Blacks in the lowest-paid, dirtiest jobs. Political oppression excluded Blacks almost absolutely from any participation in public affairs, including the most important, voting. Personal oppression reinforced the other two. It included laws separating Blacks from whites, relegating Blacks to the worst housing, schools, and other public facilities, denying Blacks protection by police. It included customs that proscribed human behavior; thus, Emmett Till's mother advised him to kneel before whites if he must. It was supported by terror, both state-sponsored and private, random and planned, including ritual human sacrifice, carried out by the forces of the state and by private citizens.

This system of oppression created, as a reaction, an environment of protest and collective strength, especially in the urban South. Black churches, colleges, and businesses thrived in the segregated city; Black social and civic organizations and institutions grew as well. These kept alive a tradition of protest that can be traced forward from slave rebellions to the Underground Railroad to the Garvey movement to the March on Washington movement.

Central to the protest community were what Morris calls "movement halfway houses."[2] These are organizations that, despite a lack of prominence, played important roles in the civil rights movement. He describes them as a "group of organizations . . . only partially integrated into the larger society because its participants are actively engaged in efforts to bring about . . . change." They are distinctive, he writes, in "their relative isolation from the larger society and the absence of a mass base."[3] They lack broad support and a visible platform. But halfway houses are valuable to emergent organizations and movements—like the Montgomery bus boycott, the sit-ins, and the Student Nonviolent Coordinating Committee. They can provide resources, skilled and experienced activists, tactical training, protest songs, educational programs, and publicity.

There are many such halfway houses; Morris concentrates on three and the roles they play in the movement. These three also play important roles—usually behind the scenes—in the Montgomery bus boycott and beyond:

> *The Highlander Folk School* was founded in Monteagle, Tennessee, in 1932. Highlander's philosophy was that oppressed people best know the answers to their problems and that solutions would only arise from the experiences and imagination of the group. It brought potential leaders together to identify and analyze common problems and to return to their communities to replicate this process. In the 1930s, its focus was on union organizing; in the 1940s, it widened its focus to encourage Black and white Southerners to struggle against racial discrimination. Over the years it attracted people who would become important leadership figures in the civil rights movement.
>
> *The Fellowship of Reconciliation*, organized in England in 1914 and the US in 1915, though small, became the major pacifist organization in the US and a training ground for the architects of nonviolent protest in America, including A. J. Muste, Bayard Rustin, James Farmer, James Lawson, and Glenn Smiley. The FOR gave birth to the Congress of Racial Equality in 1942 and provided training for the Montgomery bus boycott.
>
> *The Southern Conference Education Fund*, which grew from the Southern Conference for Human Welfare, founded in 1938 by liberal Southerners, was dedicated to labor reform and ending discrimination. Internal and external problems, chiefly red-baiting, caused SCHW to collapse in 1948—only SCEF, its tax-exempt arm, survived. SCEF was a non-membership organization dedicated to assisting Blacks in overthrowing all forms of racial discrimination in the South.

These halfway houses and others will appear as our story goes on.

Every Southern town or city had Black leadership; a few of the leaders were energetic and bold; most were powerless, and many were self-selected or chosen by whites to speak for Blacks. A crisis in a community—like Rosa Parks being arrested—could put the passions of the Black community into the hands of the dynamic leadership, making them spokespersons, pushing them forward into the light.

In the middle 1950s, recent events had shaken white Montgomery. The Supreme Court's May 1954 ruling against segregated schools and the hiring of the city's first Black policemen caused great consternation among the city's white, predominately segregationist population.

In April 1954, twenty-five-year-old Martin Luther King Jr. preached his first sermon as the official pastor of Montgomery's Dexter Avenue Baptist Church. He could not have known that in nine years he would be the most famous Black American, speaking at the March on Washington to the largest gathering of civil rights supporters in the nation's history. And he could not have imagined that in fourteen years he would be dead.

Ten days after that first sermon, the French colonial empire in Indochina collapsed; a faraway garrison called Dien Bien Phu was overrun. No one thought then that 58,000 Americans would lose their lives in Vietnam or that the war fought there would define the limits of American power for a generation.

MARTIN LUTHER KING JR.

Martin Luther King Jr. was born in Atlanta, Georgia, on January 15, 1929, and named after his father, Martin Luther King Sr., pastor of Ebenezer Baptist Church, active with the Atlanta NAACP and a member of the boards of Morehouse College and the local Black bank.

Young Martin King attended segregated public schools and spent his seventh- and eighth-grade years at the private Laboratory High School of Atlanta University. When it closed, he transferred to Booker T. Washington High School. There he skipped the ninth and twelfth grades and entered Atlanta's Morehouse College in 1944 at age fifteen. He spent the summers of 1945 and 1947 working in the Connecticut tobacco fields, his first taste of life beyond the Cotton Curtain. He quit a 1946 summer job because the foreman insisted on calling him "nigger." He first considered becoming a doctor or lawyer. By 1947, he had decided on the ministry; he was ordained and made assistant pastor of his father's church.

He graduated from Morehouse in 1948 and entered Crozer Theological Seminary in Chester, Pennsylvania, graduating in 1951. He then entered Boston University's doctoral program in theology. While in Boston, he met a politically minded student at the New England Conservatory of Music, Coretta Scott of Marion, Alabama; in 1953, they were married.

King's early years were spent in the comfortable shelter of middle-class Black Atlanta, protected from the rigors of the segregated city. His father was a powerful figure in Black Atlanta who demanded the respect of whites—young King recalled his father insisting on being called "Reverend," not "boy," in downtown stores and refusing to accept second-class treatment. His teachers at Morehouse College altered his skeptical, cynical view of his father's profession and made it more attractive—"the shackles of fundamentalism were removed" there, and his Morehouse experience also began to shape his views on race.[4] He was active in the campus NAACP and in intercampus interracial organizations with white students from other Atlanta schools.

He blossomed academically at Crozer, read Marx for the first time, heard lectures on pacifism and Gandhi's success with nonviolence in India, and took courses on the "social gospel," which insisted the institutionalized church must be involved with real human problems, not just with the hereafter. He served as a student pastor in a church in Elmhurst, New York, in the fall of 1950; the pastor gave him low marks for exhibiting a "snobbishness which prevents his coming to close grips with the rank and file of ordinary people."[5]

At Boston University, his intellectual development continued. His teachers tried to interest him in an academic career, but he felt his future lay with the church. The senior King promoted an invitation to join the Morehouse faculty, but King Jr. demurred.

He preached a trial sermon at Chattanooga's First Baptist Church and then heard that a church in Montgomery, Dexter Avenue Baptist, had dismissed its pastor, the controversial and outspoken Vernon Johns. King agreed to preach a trial sermon at Dexter Avenue, and in March 1954 the church voted to offer him the pulpit.

Dexter Avenue was small compared to Ebenezer, its congregation largely middle class, many of them teachers and administrators at Alabama

State and in Montgomery's segregated schools. King spent his early months at Dexter Avenue seizing control of the church and reorganizing its internal structure, including a new social and political action committee. He joined the Montgomery NAACP and attended meetings of the only interracial organization in Montgomery, the Alabama Council on Human Relations. In August 1955, he received a letter from the secretary of the NAACP, Rosa Parks, telling him he had been named to the NAACP's executive committee. In November, he considered running for the presidency of the local NAACP branch but rejected it in favor of family and church duties.

According to the 1950 census, the small city the new King family settled into reflected the economic realities of the mid-century segregated South. Seventy percent of all working Black males were unskilled, and 70 percent of all working Black females were private household maids or service workers. Only 3 percent of Black men were classified as "professional" or "managers"; most of these were teachers, school administrators, or clergymen.

CORETTA SCOTT KING

King's new wife was reluctant to go to Montgomery, although it was less than one hundred miles from her home. She was born on a farm ten miles from Marion, Alabama, and wanted to escape from the segregated South. Her father, through hard work, had accumulated several hundred acres of farmland. As a girl, she had chopped and picked cotton and scrubbed clothes in a washtub. She and her siblings left the farm to attend private Lincoln High School in town, which was established by Congregational Church missionaries after the Civil War. The school, with an integrated faculty, provided a superior education, which enabled her to follow her older sister to Antioch College in Yellow Springs, Ohio. At Antioch, she was active in the campus NAACP and a race relations committee and supported Henry Wallace's third-party bid for president, attending the 1948 Progressive Party convention as a student delegate. She graduated in 1951 and entered the New England Conservatory of Music that fall.

Unlike her husband-to-be, Coretta Scott had to work to support herself in school, despite a one-time scholarship she received from the State of Alabama, intended to keep Alabama's graduate schools all white. On their first date, Martin Luther King Jr. told Coretta Scott, "You have everything I have ever wanted in a wife. . . . The four things that I look for in a wife are character, intelligence, personality and beauty. And you have them all. I want to see you again. When can I?"[6]

They were married on June 18, 1953. She had decided years earlier that she would not follow the marriage ceremony's promise to "obey" her husband; Reverend King Sr., who presided, reluctantly agreed. The couple spent their wedding night at the home of a family friend who was an undertaker in Marion; no decent hotel that would admit Black people was closer than Montgomery.

The newlyweds spent the rest of that summer living in his parents' home in Atlanta. He served as assistant pastor of his father's church; she worked as a clerk in Atlanta's Black bank.

They returned to Boston in the fall; he, to finish residency requirements and to begin his thesis, "A Comparison of the Conceptions of God in the Thinking of Paul Tillich and Henry Nelson Wieman," and she, to finish her degree in music education. King commuted to Montgomery from Boston through the summer of 1954. In June 1955, he received his PhD from Boston University.

RALPH DAVID ABERNATHY

While at Morehouse, King had befriended a Montgomery minister who was studying at Atlanta University, Ralph David Abernathy. Abernathy, born in 1926, was raised on his father's five-hundred-acre farm in Linden, Alabama. Drafted into the US Army in 1944, he rose to sergeant but fell ill and was discharged before seeing combat. Returning to Alabama, he entered Alabama State College in Montgomery and in his first year led a successful campus-wide boycott of the school cafeteria and a protest against poor housing at the school for veterans.

In 1948, he decided to become a minister. After graduating from Alabama State in 1950, Abernathy spent a summer working as an insurance salesman and entered Atlanta University seeking a master's degree in sociology. After gaining his master's in 1951, he returned to Montgomery to become dean of men at Alabama State and the pastor of a small church in Demopolis, Alabama. At twenty-six he became the pastor of First Baptist Church in Montgomery—until the great migration of 1917, the largest Black church in the United States. In August 1952, he married Juanita Odessa Jones, a schoolteacher and, like Coretta Scott, a native of Perry

County, Alabama, who also insisted the preacher drop the word "obey" from their ceremony.

While a graduate student in Atlanta, Abernathy had briefly met Martin Luther King; in Montgomery in 1954, their friendship grew, and soon the two became inseparable.

BUS SEGREGATION

In Montgomery, as in every Southern town and city, buses were segregated by law, as was every other aspect of daily life. It was even illegal for Blacks and whites to play checkers together.[7] Under a 1900 law, all city transportation had to "provide equal but separate accommodations for white people and Negroes . . . by requiring the employee in charge thereof to assign passenger seats . . . in such a manner as to separate the white people from the Negroes where there are both whites and Negroes on the same car." An exception allowed Black nurses caring for white children or "sick or infirm white persons" to sit with their wards in the white sections. Bus drivers had "the power of a police officer." In 1955, there were fourteen different bus routes, several nearly all-Black or all-white. On some Black lines, the company ran "special" buses for Blacks only.[8]

In 1955, sixty-two buses traversed fourteen routes carrying thirty thousand to forty thousand Black passengers and as many whites. Each bus had thirty-six seats. The first ten—two bench seats facing each other at the front and the first row of parallel seats—were reserved for whites, even if there were no whites on the bus. In theory, the ten seats at the very rear—the bench seat across the rear and two bench seats facing each other—were similarly reserved for Blacks, but this reservation was much less rigorously enforced.

On the thirty-six total bus seats, Blacks were seated from the rear forward and restricted to the ten rear seats; whites had the first ten seats in the front, with a "no man's land" separated by a "dead line" in between, which adopted the racial character of those who sat in it. When more whites boarded the bus than there were "white" seats, the driver would "equalize," the seats and the line separating the races moved backward. If there were more Black riders than there were Black seats, Blacks could not sit in empty seats in the white section. The seats in the rear were located over the engine and in summer were especially uncomfortable.

Additionally, Black passengers were required to buy their tickets at the front and then disembark and board the bus through the rear door. Frequently drivers would speed away, leaving the Black passenger who had paid standing on the street; other drivers would accelerate suddenly as a Black passenger was making her way toward the rear. Discourtesy was normal treatment—calls of "nigger bitch," "whore," "cow," and "heifer" were common.[9]

Segregated public transportation was a special form of torment for Black Southerners, who knew whites did not mind physical closeness when Blacks were maids, cooks, nurses, farmhands, or other servants, or when illicit sex was demanded. Whites objected to proximity only when it suggested equal status, as in side-by-side seating on a bus or train. As Blacks became an urban population, their dependence on public transportation grew; in most Southern cities, Blacks were the majority of streetcar or bus riders. But no Southern city employed Black drivers.

Black people had long objected to segregated transportation. In his 1850 autobiography Frederick Douglass mentions the "mean, dirty and uncomfortable car set apart for colored travelers called the 'Jim Crow' car" and his efforts to physically resist being forced to sit in it. Blacks in Philadelphia carried on a successful battle of several years, beginning in 1864, to be permitted to ride the streetcars of that city.[10]

In 1865, Mississippi passed laws forbidding "any freedman, negro or mulatto to ride in any first-class passenger cars, set apart, or used by and for white persons." According to C. Vann Woodward, in 1865, "Florida prevented whites from using cars set apart for Negroes and Negroes from using cars for whites." In 1866, Texas required all railroad companies to "attach to passenger trains one car for the special accommodation of freedmen."[11]

By the end of the nineteenth century, Blacks had boycotted streetcar lines in more than twenty-seven cities. Blacks protested segregation on railroads and steamships too. W. E. B. Du Bois—then at Atlanta University—and other Black Atlantans protested an 1899 law that segregated railroad sleeping cars. In 1904, Du Bois and Booker T. Washington planned a lawsuit against the Pullman Company, but it never materialized. That same year, the editor of Richmond, Virginia's Black newspaper, *The Planet*, led an unsuccessful yearlong boycott of the city's segregated streetcars.

In 1890, Louisiana passed the Separate Car Law to ensure passenger "comfort" by ordering railroads to provide "equal but separate" cars for

Blacks and whites. No member of one race could occupy seats in a car reserved for the other. In 1891, a group of Louisiana Blacks formed a committee to test the law, hired a lawyer, and then had Homer G. Plessy sit in the white-only railroad coach. He refused to move when ordered to do so and was arrested. The state argued that separating the races was legal, as long as the facilities were equal. In 1896, in *Plessy v. Ferguson*, the US Supreme Court agreed, giving federal approval to separate but equal that would stand until 1954.

Blacks in Montgomery conducted a two-year boycott of the city's streetcars that lasted from 1900 to 1902. They won the right to keep their seats, if an open seat wasn't available—but that city ordinance was not enforced.

The first National Negro Conference, meeting in 1909, protested against Jim Crow railroad laws, and the NAACP made removal of segregated trains and streetcars part of its early agenda. On August 23, 1917, the men of the all-Black Third Battalion of the Twenty-Fourth Infantry Regiment defended themselves against a white mob angered by a dispute over bus seating in Houston, Texas. When the air cleared, seventeen whites were dead and nineteen Black soldiers were hanged for mutiny and forty-one jailed for life.

Twentieth-century Southern streetcar and bus company files and police records are full of reports of Black passengers throwing the signs that separated the white and Black sections out of the bus window; arguments, often violent, between Black passengers and white drivers and passengers over refusals to move to accommodate whites; Blacks refusing to pay or objecting to being insulted by drivers or white passengers.

During World War II, there were also instances of white drivers shooting and killing Black passengers. In July 1942, a Black army private in Beaumont, Texas, who refused to vacate a bus seat reserved for whites, was arrested and shot while in police custody. In 1944, army lieutenant Jackie Robinson, future Hall of Fame baseball player, refused an order to move to the back of a segregated army bus. He was arrested and court-martialed but acquitted.

In 1943, fourteen-year-old Martin Luther King Jr. and his high school teacher were returning to Atlanta from an oratorical contest in South Georgia when the bus driver ordered them to surrender their seats to white passengers. Young King refused but finally complied. Twenty years later he said, "It was the angriest I have ever been in my life!"[12]

The bus, after all, was one place where Southern Blacks and whites could see each other being segregated under the same roof. Whites saw Blacks standing over empty seats and did and said nothing. Blacks saw the empty seats as they stood, and their anger grew.

THE BATON ROUGE BUS BOYCOTT

In March 1953 in Baton Rouge, Louisiana, Black leaders requested first-come, first-served seating *within* the segregated system. The city council agreed and passed an ordinance to that effect. But the all-white bus drivers' union refused to permit any alteration of the segregated system and ordered Blacks not to sit in the front. When the city insisted on its new rule, the drivers conducted a four-day strike, and Louisiana's attorney general declared the city ordinance illegal, in conflict with state segregation laws.[13]

Like Blacks in Montgomery and every other Southern city, Baton Rouge's Blacks had a long history of maltreatment on the city's buses. In June they began a boycott in protest. Revered T. J. Jemison became the boycott's leader. Pastor of Mount Zion Baptist Church, he was a graduate of Alabama State and Virginia Union University and had studied at New York University. He had moved to Baton Rouge in 1949. He had served one term as president of the Baton Rouge NAACP and was active in the Baton Rouge Community Group, a local civic organization.

Baton Rouge's Black leadership constructed an umbrella organization to direct the boycott, the United Defense League (UDL). The UDL organized a carpool, Operation Free Lift, raised money to finance it, held nightly mass meetings of 2,500 to 3,000 people, and reduced Black patronage of the bus company by 90 percent. On the sixth day, the city suggested a compromise: the two side seats of each bus would be reserved for whites, the long back seat reserved for Blacks; all other riders would sit on a first-come, first-served segregated basis. A mass meeting attended by eight thousand Blacks approved the compromise, although a sizeable minority wanted the boycott to continue, apparently unaffected by Jemison's promise that the question of bus segregation would be settled by a court decision.

The Baton Rouge protest proved that segregation could be challenged by mass action. The compromise victory wasn't won by middle-class Blacks seeking integration; few of them rode buses anyway. This was a triumph for the bus-riding public, the working class. Like the Montgomery bus boycott that would follow in two years, the Baton Rouge bus boycott drew on Black churches for participants, communication, and fundraising. Like Martin Luther King, Jemison was an educated, articulate leader. Like King, he was a newcomer with few obligations to existing patterns of political behavior. He was too new to have engendered any distrust within his own community. Like King, he was both novice *and* privileged insider—a leader in the community's most stable and independent organization, the Black church.

News of the Baton Rouge boycott quickly spread through the organizational networks of Black America. Jemison's father had been president of the National Baptist Convention, the largest organization of Blacks in America, for twelve years, and Jemison became secretary of the Baptist Convention in 1953. Future boycott leaders—including King and Abernathy in Montgomery, Reverend K. C. Steele in Tallahassee, Reverend A. L. Davis in New Orleans—were all members of the Baptist Convention and in communication with Jemison when they organized boycotts in their own cities.

THE WOMEN'S POLITICAL COUNCIL

In Montgomery, a group of Black women was poised to boycott the city's buses. They were members of the Women's Political Council, an organization founded in 1946 by Dr. Mary Fair Burks, chair of the English Department at Alabama State. Modeled on the League of Women Voters, which was closed to Blacks, WPC members were professional women, largely schoolteachers and administrators from Alabama State and the city's public schools. By 1955, the WPC had grown to three chapters of one hundred members each, spread throughout Black Montgomery.[14]

An increasing concern of the council was the mistreatment of Blacks on city buses, especially Black women. In 1945, a woman was arrested for not having "correct change" and for talking back to the white driver. In 1949, two women and two children from New Jersey, unused to segregation, were arrested for refusing to give up their seats to white riders. In 1950, police shot and killed a Black man who had argued with a bus driver. In 1953, a woman was beaten by a driver and arrested for disorderly conduct, one of thirty complaints received by the WPC that year alone.[15]

JO ANN GIBSON ROBINSON

In 1950, the presidency of the WPC passed from Dr. Burks to Jo Ann Robinson. Born on a farm near Macon, Georgia, Robinson received a BS from Georgia State College at Fort Valley, an MA from Atlanta University, and in 1949 accepted a position in the English Department at Alabama State. On her first day at Alabama State, she met Dr. Burks and joined the WPC. She also joined Dexter Avenue Baptist Church.

Like so many Blacks in Montgomery, Jo Ann Robinson had a traumatic experience with racism on the city's buses. In December 1949, a driver ordered her to move to let a white passenger sit down. When she did not move fast enough, he ordered her from the bus. Like with King the experience was searing. Thirty-seven years later she wrote: "In all these years I have never forgotten the shame, the hurt of that experience. The memory will not go away."[16]

Under Robinson's leadership, the WPC initiated meetings with Mayor W. A. "Tacky" Gayle and the city's other two commissioners, or aldermen, and began to monitor meetings of the city commission. By 1954, the WPC had begun to discuss plans for a bus boycott. After the *Brown* decision came down, Robinson wrote to the mayor demanding action on the buses or people would organize a citywide boycott.

E. D. NIXON

Another group that had complained about the mistreatment of Blacks was the Progressive Democratic Association, headed by E. D. Nixon.

Edgar Daniel Nixon was born in Montgomery on July 12, 1899, the fifth of eight children. He received the equivalent of a third-grade education and at fourteen left school for a lifetime of hard work and service to his community. In 1924, he became a Pullman porter. He was one of "thousands of black men who punched pillows, lifted bags, shined passengers' shoes and prepared their berths."[17] Because the owner of the Pullman Company was George Pullman, they were called "George Pullman's boys"—or usually just "George." Porters were said to have the best job in the Black community and the worst job on the train. Still it was an attractive job for many. Morehouse College president Benjamin Mays, NAACP lawyer and Supreme Court justice Thurgood Marshall, NAACP executive director Roy Wilkins, and Matthew Henson, who reached the North Pole with Admiral Robert Peary in 1906, all spent time as Pullman porters.

Nixon tried to organize his fellow porters in 1925 and 1926, inspired by A. Philip Randolph. He heard Randolph speak in St. Louis in 1928. "After the meeting," Nixon wrote later, "I put a dollar in the collection plate, and . . . shook hands with him, and he said, 'Where are you from, young man?' I told him, 'Montgomery, Alabama.' He said, 'We need a good man down there.' So I joined the Brotherhood."[18]

Nixon organized the Montgomery NAACP in 1928 and served as its first president. In the 1930s he and Myles Horton of the Highlander Folk School tried to unionize cotton pickers. In 1934, Nixon organized the Montgomery Welfare League to help Blacks hurt by the Depression, forcing fairer administration of New Deal programs in Montgomery.

Randolph and the Brotherhood of Sleeping Car Porters won recognition from the Pullman Company in 1937; in 1938, Nixon founded the Montgomery Division of the Brotherhood and was its president for the next twenty-five years. In 1940, he and others organized the Montgomery Voters' League. In 1944, Nixon and the league led a march of 750 Blacks to the board of registrars, demanding they be allowed to register. In November 1955, Nixon invited New York congressman Adam Clayton Powell to Montgomery; Powell met with Nixon, King, Rosa Parks, and others and told a mass meeting at Alabama State about his leadership of consumer boycotts in Harlem, including a 1944 bus boycott. He argued that economic pressures would change patterns of segregation.

In 1955, Mr. Nixon was fifty-six years old. He was a past president of the Montgomery NAACP and served in 1955 as president of the State Conference of NAACP Branches. He had been president of the Brotherhood of Sleeping Car Porters in Alabama for seventeen years. Some middle-class Blacks in Montgomery looked down on the uneducated Nixon, put off by his grammar and his manner, but when Montgomery's Blacks were in trouble with the police, it was Nixon whom they called. His employment with the Pullman Company gave him an independence most Montgomery Blacks did not have; his paycheck came from Chicago, and his work schedule gave him time to immerse himself in civic affairs. When Martin Luther King expressed interest in becoming president of the Montgomery NAACP, Nixon politely let him know that he supported another candidate.

The WPC spoke to city officials about conditions on the city's buses, accompanying a delegation of ministers, including Montgomery newcomer

Martin Luther King. WPC members, including Robinson, also met with the manager of the bus company, who maintained he was powerless to change the pattern of segregation. Finally, members of the WPC testified against a fare increase before the city commission, arguing that the rude and cruel service tendered Blacks did not merit an increase in the fare.

Then, on March 2, 1955, an incident occurred that heightened tensions in Black and white Montgomery. A fifteen-year-old high school honor student and NAACP Youth Council member, Claudette Colvin, was arrested for refusing to give up her seat, handcuffed and dragged, kicking and screaming, from the bus. News of Colvin's arrest spread quickly, and Nixon thought he had a candidate for a suit against the city's bus lines.

But when Nixon investigated Colvin more closely to see if she was a good candidate to personify the mistreatment on Montgomery's buses, his support waned. During the scuffle that led to her arrest, she was charged with disorderly conduct and assault and battery as well as violating the bus segregation law. Colvin was convicted on the assault charge, but the segregation and disorderly conduct charges were dismissed, leaving little grounds for a segregation challenge. Seen as "feisty" and "emotional," the fifteen-year-old Colvin would not do.[19]

At subsequent meetings with city and bus company officials, Black leaders argued that neither the Montgomery city segregation law nor state statutes required anyone to give up a seat to accommodate a member of another race and urged adoption of a segregated first-come, first-served seating plan, such as Mobile already employed. The white officials angrily refused.

One of the people who had fundraised for Colvin was Mrs. Rosa Parks.

ROSA LOUISE MCCAULEY PARKS

Rosa Louise McCauley was born in Tuskegee on February 14, 1913. Her father was a carpenter; her mother had been a schoolteacher. Young Rosa was educated in a rural school. "By the time I was six, I was old enough to realize that we were not actually free." At eleven she enrolled in the private Montgomery Industrial School for Girls, run by white women from Massachusetts. When it closed, she attended segregated Booker T. Washington Junior High School and then Alabama State Teachers College High School, but her grandmother's illness and death prevented her

This was the segregated South
the movement confronted.

The movement's
opposition.

Some individuals were prepared to attack demonstrators on their own, as was this driver in Atlanta.

Protesting could mean arrest, which happened to Taylor Washington in Atlanta.

These protestors also were arrested in Atlanta.

Under arrest in Cambridge, Maryland: Gloria Richardson, in pants; to her left is Stokely Carmichael, and to Carmichael's left is Cleve Sellers.

Eddie Brown being arrested in Albany, Georgia.

Police in Clarksdale, Mississippi, show their feelings as ministers march to a local church.

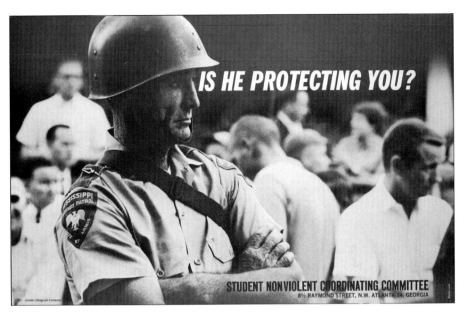

A SNCC poster asks a question we might ask today.

SNCC members Ivanhoe Donaldson, Marion Barry, and Jim Forman at a mass meeting against police brutality in Danville, Virginia, in 1963.

Prison could mean being on a work squad such as this 1963 one in Pine Bluff, Arkansas.

Ella Baker called the meeting that led to the formation of SNCC in 1960.

The young Julian Bond in his SNCC years.

Participants in the Albany, Georgia, movement, which SNCC helped organize in 1962.

Teenagers held in Leesburg, Georgia, stockade for demonstrating in Americus, near Albany.

from finishing the eleventh grade. She finished high school in 1933 at age twenty. She had childhood memories of segregated trolleys in Montgomery. "When we black people got on," she wrote, "we had to go as far back in the car as we could."

She married Raymond Parks, a barber, in 1932. Parks had less formal education than his new wife, but he was a proud, political man and active in the NAACP. He was, Mrs. Parks remembered, "the first man of our race, aside from my grandfather, with whom I actually discussed anything about the racial conditions."[20] Rosa and Raymond Parks worked together in defense of the "Scottsboro Boys," nine young Black men—fourteen to nineteen—falsely accused of raping two white women in Scottsboro, Alabama, in 1931.

Mrs. Parks was no stranger to Montgomery's buses. On one occasion she had boarded the bus in the front, paid her fare, and walked through a group of Blacks standing at the division line between Black and white seats. The driver ordered her to get off the bus and reboard through the back door. She replied that she was already on and saw no need to exit and reboard, especially since Black passengers were already squeezed into the stairwell. The driver (the same driver who would arrest her twelve years later) responded that if she couldn't go through the back door she would have to get off the bus. "I stood where I was," she remembered. "He came back and took my coat sleeve" to escort her from the bus. On the way out, she dropped her purse and sat on a front seat to retrieve it. The driver bent over her.

"Get off my bus," he said. Mrs. Parks replied, "I will get off." The driver looked as if he might strike her. She said to him, "I know one thing. You better not hit me."[21]

In 1954, she started sewing on the side for Virginia and Clifford Durr, one of Montgomery's few civil rights–supporting white families, when she helped prepare the trousseau for a Durr daughter. In 1955, Rosa Parks was secretary of the Montgomery Branch of the NAACP, secretary of the State Conference of NAACP Branches, and advisor to the NAACP Youth Council. She had become active in the NAACP a dozen years earlier after seeing a newspaper photograph of a classmate, NAACP activist Mrs. Johnnie Carr. Mrs. Parks had not known women worked with the NAACP until she saw Mrs. Carr's photo; that motivated her to visit the branch offices in

December 1943 to visit her friend. Instead, she was the only woman present at the annual election of officers, and, when her dues were paid, she was chosen secretary. Few women had been active in civil rights work in her youth, Mrs. Parks recalled. Once while working with Mr. Nixon, he told her, "Women don't need to be nowhere but in the kitchen."

"What about me?" she questioned. He replied: "But I need a secretary and you are a good one."[22]

In 1955, she was working as a tailor's assistant at Montgomery Fair Department Store. That summer, at Virginia Durr's suggestion, Mrs. Parks attended a two-week workshop at Highlander Folk School on implementing desegregation, where she met and was inspired by activist and former teacher Septima Clark. She came back further resolved to work with her NAACP Youth Council to find ways to challenge segregation.

TWO MONTHS LATER, in October 1955, a white woman asked a bus driver to make eighteen-year-old Mary Louise Smith get up from her seat. Smith refused and was arrested. Again, Montgomery's Black leadership seemed poised for action, and again their hopes were frustrated. Nixon decreed that Smith was no better suited than Claudette Colvin had been to carry Black Montgomery's fight forward. Smith's father was rumored to be an alcoholic, and the family lived in a rural shack; Smith, they believed, would not be able to stand the rigors of the publicity that would follow a suit against the segregated system.[23]

THURSDAY, DECEMBER 1

On the late afternoon of December 1, 1955, Mrs. Parks left work and boarded the Cleveland Avenue bus for her regular ride home. She sat in the aisle seat on the front row of the middle section with three other Black riders; within a few blocks, the bus was filled, with twenty-two Blacks seated from the rear and fourteen whites seated from the front.

At the third stop, a white man boarded, and driver J. P. Blake called out, "Let me have those seats." Blake, who had ejected Mrs. Parks from a bus in 1943, meant that the four Blacks sitting in the most-forward Black row, including Mrs. Parks, should get up so a lone white man could sit down. All four Blacks had to move to provide space for one white man;

the law did not permit Blacks and whites to occupy separate seats in the same row. Furthermore, the etiquette of white supremacy insisted Blacks and whites could not share any facility equally; to do so was to diminish the white person's advantaged position, both actual and psychological.

When nothing happened, Blake stood up and said in a louder voice with a threat clearly implied: "You all better make it light on yourselves and let me have those seats."

The man sitting next to the window on Mrs. Parks's side of the row got up, and Mrs. Parks let him cross in front of her into the aisle and the rear of the bus; two Black women sitting on the other side of the aisle did the same. Blake asked her again if she was going to move, and Mrs. Parks replied, "No, I'm not!"

"Well," he said, "if you don't stand up I'm going to call the police and have you arrested."

"You may do that," Mrs. Parks said.

Blake fetched two policemen. One asked Mrs. Parks if the driver had asked her to move, and she replied that he had. He said: "Why don't you stand up?"

She answered, "Why do you push us around?"

He answered, "I do not know but the law is the law and you're under arrest."[24]

Even before Mrs. Parks was arraigned, word of her arrest had begun to spread through Black Montgomery. Unlike Colvin and Smith, Mrs. Parks was well known in Black Montgomery for her civic activism. Word quickly passed from witnesses on the bus to Nixon.

From the jail, Parks called home. Her mother answered, whose first question was standard: had her daughter been beaten? "No. Put Raymond on," Mrs. Parks said.

Nixon's first call was to attorney Fred Gray, a new lawyer in Montgomery, who had represented Claudette Colvin. Gray was away. Nixon then called the city jail to ask what charge was lodged against Mrs. Parks. He was told it was none of his dammed business. Nixon then called attorney Clifford Durr. Durr, a white Alabaman, had been a New Dealer and FCC commissioner who had resigned his post to represent early victims of the Truman loyalty program. Durr had next to no law practice because of his politics, but he had conferred with Gray on the Colvin case.

The police told Durr that Parks was charged with violating the seg-regation law. Nixon drove to the Durr home, picked up Clifford and Virginia, and the three of them drove to the jail where Nixon signed a bond and Mrs. Parks was released.

Nixon believed he had found his symbol. Rosa Parks was everything Claudette Colvin and Mary Louise Smith were not; her demeanor, the respect she commanded throughout Black Montgomery, her history of civil rights activism and bravery made her the ideal candidate to carry the fight against bus segregation. Nixon and the Durrs went back to the Parkses' apartment in Cleveland Courts to talk about what would come next. Both her mother and husband were frightened. "The white folks will kill you, Rosa," Raymond pleaded. He worried that the Black community wouldn't stick with her, as had happened with Claudette Colvin.

"If you think it will mean something to Montgomery and will do some good, I'll be happy to go along with it," she said.

Later that evening, attorney Gray began returning the calls he had missed during the day. One of the calls was from Rosa Parks, whom he knew well from the NAACP. She asked him to be her lawyer. He said yes.

Another was from Jo Ann Robinson. Gray was born in Montgomery in 1930 and received a BA from Alabama State, where Jo Ann Robinson had been his teacher. Black people were not allowed to attend law school in Alabama; instead, the state paid for him to get a law degree from Case Western Reserve in Ohio. He practiced law with Charles Langford and was assistant pastor at the Holt Street Church of Christ.

After agreeing to represent Parks, Gray called Robinson. She told him the Women's Political Council was thinking of calling for a one-day boy-cott on Monday, December 5, the day of Mrs. Parks's trial. Robinson wrote out a leaflet at home. It read:

> Another Negro woman has been arrested and thrown in jail because she refused to get up out of her seat on the bus for a white person to sit down. It is the second time since the Claudette Colvin case that a Negro woman has been arrested for the same thing. This has to be stopped. Negroes have rights too, for if Negroes did not ride the buses, they could not operate. Three-fourths of the riders are Negroes, yet we are arrested, or have to stand over empty seats. If we do not do something to stop these arrests, they will continue. The next time it may be you,

or your daughter, or mother. This woman's case will come up Monday. We are, therefore, asking every Negro to stay off the buses Monday in protest of the arrest and trial. Don't ride the buses to work, to town, to school, or anywhere on Monday. You can afford to stay out of school for one day if you have no other way to go except by bus. You can also afford to stay out of town for one day. If you work, take a cab or walk. But please, children and grownups, don't ride the bus at all on Monday. Please stay off all buses Monday.[25]

Robinson called the chairman of the Business Department at Alabama State; he had access to the school's mimeograph machine. When Robinson told him her plans, he said he too had been mistreated on the city buses. Robinson and two of her students met him in the school's duplicating room. By 4:00 a.m. they had duplicated 52,500 leaflets, with three messages on each page, and spent until 7:00 a.m. mapping distribution routes. By 8:00 a.m. the bundles of leaflets were stashed in their cars, and Robinson and her two students were in her 8:00 a.m. class.[26]

FRIDAY, DECEMBER 2

After class, Robinson called the WPC membership, alerting them to the boycott plans and explaining the leaflet distribution system. She and the two students drove to prearranged street corners where WPC members waited. Other bundles were dropped off at "business places, storefronts, beauty parlors, beer halls, factories, barber shops and every other available place."[27]

Rosa Parks's arrest was reported at the bottom of page 9 of the December 2 *Montgomery Advertiser*. The headline said, "Negro Jailed Here for 'Overlooking' Bus Segregation."

When Robinson returned to the campus for her 2:00 p.m. class, the president demanded to see her. After quizzing her on the origin of the leaflet and extracting a promise that the WPC would pay for the mimeograph paper she had used and that the college would not become embroiled in the proposed boycott, he gave her his hesitant endorsement.

Nixon, whom Robinson had called in the middle of the night, had been trying since 5:00 a.m. to line up clerical support for the boycott. His first call was to Ralph Abernathy, secretary of the Baptist Ministers' Alliance; then to his own minister, Reverend H. H. Hubbard, the alliance president;

and then—at Abernathy's urging—to Martin Luther King, to seek King's support and to ask if a meeting could be held at the most convenient location, King's downtown church. King, a newcomer in Montgomery, the father of a new baby, and the busy new pastor of a church, hesitated. He supported the boycott's aims; he did not want additional responsibilities. "Brother Nixon," he said, "let me think about it a while and call me back." Nixon said he had already told several ministers—and Abernathy was telling others—to meet at Dexter Avenue Baptist Church that evening. King agreed. One drop-off spot for Robinson's leaflets had been the regular Friday morning meeting of the Montgomery Black clergy; many knew before Abernathy or Nixon called them that a boycott was in the works.

Nixon also called Joe Azbell, city editor of the *Montgomery Advertiser*, and asked that they meet at the train station before Nixon left on his weekly trip. He promised him "the hottest story you've ever written." They met—Nixon wearing his white coat and porter's cap. Nixon handed Azbell one of the leaflets and left on his weekly Montgomery–Atlanta–New York–Atlanta–Montgomery run.

That night, seventy Black leaders gathered in Dexter's basement meeting room. Abernathy and Nixon had agreed that the Reverend Roy Bennett, president of the Interdenominational Ministerial Alliance would preside. Refusing to allow either debate or discussion, Bennett droned on for over half an hour, so long that over half of those present left. One told King, "This is going to fizzle; I'm leaving." King replied, "I would like to go too, but it's my church." Finally, Abernathy seized the floor and insisted that those remaining be allowed to speak.[28] Parks spoke, laying out her tiredness with segregation, the circumstances that had led to her arrest, and the need for collective action. And then Robinson took the floor and demanded that all those present endorse a boycott for Monday and a mass meeting on Monday night. A new leaflet would be prepared, adding the announcement about the mass meeting, and those present would meet on Monday afternoon to plan the meeting's format.

Abernathy and King remained at Dexter Avenue until midnight, mimeographing a new leaflet.

SATURDAY, DECEMBER 3
Early Saturday morning, leaflet distribution continued. Montgomery's eighteen Black taxi companies agreed to carry passengers on Monday for

the ten-cent bus fare. The first news of the upcoming boycott appeared in Montgomery's smaller newspaper, the *Alabama Journal*, that afternoon.

Reverend Robert Graetz, the white pastor of the all-Black Trinity Lutheran Church, heard rumors on Saturday about an arrest and boycott, but his own congregation could not—or would not—give him the details. Finally, he called his best friend outside his own congregation, a woman who used his church as a meeting place for the NAACP Youth Council. "Mrs. Parks," he said, "I just heard that someone was arrested on one of the buses Thursday."

"That's right, Pastor Graetz," Parks replied.

"And that we're supposed to boycott the buses on Monday to protest."

"That's right, Pastor Graetz."

"Do you know anything about it?"

"Yes, Pastor Graetz."

"Well, who was it?"

There was a moment of silence.

Then in a quiet voice she replied, "It was me, Pastor Graetz."[29]

SUNDAY, DECEMBER 4

That morning the *Montgomery Advertiser* carried a front-page story by Azbell headlined: "Negro Groups Ready Boycott of Bus Lines." The main news in the Sunday paper was the story of a riot by Georgia Tech students at the Georgia State Capitol, angered over their governor's refusal to let Tech play in the Sugar Bowl against the University of Pittsburgh. The governor had forbidden Tech to play because Pitt had one Black player, a reserve back, and Sugar Bowl officials had agreed Pitt's fans could be seated on a nonsegregated basis. The boycott story announced that a "secret meeting" of Montgomery Blacks, who planned to boycott the buses on Monday, would be held Monday evening at the Holt Street Baptist Church.

The Sunday story insured that nearly everyone in Montgomery, including Blacks who had not seen a leaflet or read the Saturday story in the *Alabama Journal*, knew about the Monday boycott, trial, and mass meeting. A number of ministers trumpeted the announcement from their pulpits too—Graetz, Abernathy, King, and other pastors urged their congregations to stay off the buses and attend the meeting Monday night.

City police commissioner Clyde Sellers, a white supremacist, announced on radio and television that Black "goon squads" had been organized to keep Montgomery Blacks off the buses and that the city's policemen were ready to help Blacks ride the buses peacefully. Sellers's announcement further spread news of the boycott and helped to frighten any Blacks who may have planned to ride.

Nixon was overjoyed at the publicity the boycott had received; the news media with their front-page story and the city's promise to send police were unwittingly serving to ensure the one-day boycott's success.

MONDAY, DECEMBER 5

Nixon and the Kings were up early Monday morning. The South Jackson line was called the "Maid's Special," and as it rolled by the King home it was empty. So were the next buses. King got in his car and drove around for several hours and saw only eight Black riders.

Another *Advertiser* story by Azbell on Monday morning reinforced the boycott. "Negro goon squads reportedly have been organized here to intimidate Negroes who ride Montgomery City Line buses today," it began. Police cars followed some buses, further terrifying potential Black riders, and, as the boycott's success became evident, it offered further proof to the police that the "goon squads" were larger than they had believed. The police finally arrested Fred Daniels, a nineteen-year-old college student helping an elderly Black woman into his car; he was the only "goon" police arrested that day.

At Mrs. Parks's trial that morning, the prosecutor replaced the city charge with a state charge. The city law required that a passenger could be asked to move only if another seat was available, the argument Montgomery's Blacks had been making to city and bus company officials for several years. The state law required segregation and gave bus drivers the power to enforce it. After testimony from driver Blake and two white witnesses, and an argument from attorney Gray that the law was unconstitutional, the judge declared Parks guilty and imposed a ten-dollar fine and four dollars in court costs. The trial took little more than five minutes.

Parks and Nixon had been shocked by crowds gathered outside the courthouse to support her that morning. When Nixon left the courtroom to post an appeal bond for Mrs. Parks, he was shocked to see over five hundred Blacks waiting in the corridors, overflowing the halls, and spilling into the street, as nervous policemen carrying shotguns looked on. He promised he would produce Mrs. Parks, unharmed, as soon as her bond was signed; someone shouted that the crowd would storm the courthouse if Nixon and Parks did not soon appear.[30]

Abernathy and Reverend Edgar N. French of Hilliard Chapel AME Church were in the crowd; they met at Nixon's downtown office to plan a strategy for the afternoon leadership meeting and the mass meeting that night. The success of the one-day boycott and the crowd that had gathered at the courthouse meant that Black Montgomery was ready—was eager—for more. The men agreed to seek a continuation of the boycott until three concessions were met: (1) the adoption of the first-come, first-served seating plan Robinson had been urging for over a year; (2) courtesy from all drivers, and bus company discipline against those who did not comply, and (3) opening bus-driver jobs to Blacks.

Other leaders separately agreed that Bennett was a disaster as a presiding officer of the boycott and that Nixon, uneducated and rough, would be an equally poor choice. Independently, one suggested that his minister, King, would be the best choice; he was well educated and could appeal to Montgomery's middle class, whose support was important even though most did not ride the buses and had little experience with the kind of indignities suffered by working-class Blacks. He was a minister and could help bring other clergymen into the protest.

At the afternoon meeting which neither Parks nor Robinson was invited to, Abernathy planned to give Nixon the floor; Nixon would yield to French, who would list the three grievances and their proposals for organizing the protest. Bennett refused to recognize Abernathy, and when the president of the NAACP charged that there were "stool pigeons" in the meeting, fear struck the crowd. For security's sake, an eighteen-person executive committee was selected to meet in the pastor's study. En route, Abernathy got Bennett to agree to recognize him, and Abernathy told King that he would propose an organizational structure at the smaller meeting. At this smaller meeting, the grievances were quickly adopted, and a name—the Montgomery Improvement Association—suggested by Abernathy, was chosen.

One minister, reminding the others that reporters would be present at the mass meeting and that their names might appear in the next day's newspaper, suggested that the three grievances should be mimeographed and distributed to the mass meeting crowd; they could then vote on them without any public discussion, thereby keeping anyone from being publicly identified as a supporter of the boycott. The pastor of Holt Street Baptist said reporters had been calling him and that several would attend the meeting.

Nixon exploded: "I am just ashamed of you. You said that God has called you to lead the people and now you are afraid and gone to pieces because the man tells you that the newspaper men will be here and your pictures might come out in the newspaper. How do you think you can run a bus boycott in secret? Let me tell you gentlemen one thing. You ministers have lived off these wash-women for the last 100 years and ain't never done nothing for them."[31] He called them cowards who let women bear the brunt of poor treatment on the buses while they hid like "little boys." "We've worn aprons all our lives," he said. "It's time to take the aprons off. . . . If we're gonna be mens, now's the time to be mens." King spoke quickly: "Brother Nixon, I'm not a coward. I don't want anybody to call me a coward."[32]

A call quickly followed for the nomination of officers. Longtime Montgomery activist and Alabama State faculty Rufus Lewis quickly nominated his pastor, Martin Luther King, in part to forestall the nomination of his rival, E. D. Nixon. Someone swiftly seconded the nomination. King said, "Well, if you think I can render some service, I will." When an attempt was made to organize the evening's program, panic ensued again. King said he had a conflict and could not attend the entire meeting, but he would "give his blessings to the occasion." Bennett said he couldn't preside. One minister said he was hoarse but would read the scripture. It was agreed that if the proposals were enthusiastically received, the boycott would go forward; if not, the threat of another boycott could be used to wring concessions from whites.

King returned home with less than an hour to prepare to speak at the mass meeting that night. Elliot Finley, a friend from Morehouse, picked him up for the drive to the church, but the crowds that surrounded it made it impossible for them to park nearby. "You know something, Finley," King said as they left the car, "this could turn into something big."[33]

Clifford and Virginia Durr never got closer than three blocks away.

The newspapers—hostile to the protest from the first—estimated the crowd at five thousand. Blacks thought it was three times larger. Reverend Graetz was the only friendly white face inside.

As the meeting began, ministers who had earlier that afternoon insisted they were too busy or too ill to take part in the program now told King and Abernathy they were eager to offer their support.

The meeting opened with two hymns: "Onward, Christian Soldiers" and "Leaning on the Everlasting Arms." A minister offered a prayer, another read scripture, and then the pastor of the Holt Street Baptist Church called Martin Luther King to the pulpit.

King's speech summarized what the boycott—one day old—was all about.

There comes a time when people get tired of being trampled over by the iron feet of oppression. There comes a time, my friends, when people get tired of being plunged across the abyss of humiliation, where they experience the bleakness of nagging despair. . . . And I want to say that we are not here advocating violence. . . . The only weapon that we have in our hands this evening is the weapon of protest. . . . My friends, don't let anybody make us feel that we are to be compared in our actions with the Ku Klux Klan or with the White Citizens Council. . . .

And we are not wrong, we are not wrong in what we are doing. (Well) if we are wrong, the Supreme Court of this nation is wrong. If we are wrong, the Constitution of the United States is wrong. If we are wrong, God Almighty is wrong. If we are wrong, Jesus of Nazareth was merely a utopian dreamer that never came down to earth. If we are wrong, justice is a lie. . . . And we are determined here in Montgomery to work and fight until justice runs down like water, and righteousness like a mighty stream.

Highlighting the "Americanness" of the boycott and protest, almost as if to protect the boycott from red-baiting charges, he reminded the audience that what happened to Mrs. Parks had happened time and time again, but now, we are tired of taking it, and we're not going to take it anymore. But we are going to be peaceful—we're not going to act like the Klan or the White Citizens' Council.

We aren't wrong, he says, because if we are wrong: the Supreme Court is wrong, the Constitution is wrong, and God is wrong. God, of course, is never wrong, at least not at the Holt Street Baptist Church. He uses a phrase he will use over and over again: "until justice rolls down like water and righteousness like a mighty stream." He asks Black Montgomery to stick together and is rewarded with an outpouring of support. He reasserts that they have the right to protest for right. And in a prescient statement, he closes by saying, "Right here in Montgomery, when the history books are written in the future, somebody will have to say, 'There lived a race of people—a *black* people . . . who had the moral courage to stand up for their rights. And thereby they injected a new meaning into the veins of history and of civilization."[34]

FOLLOWING KING'S SPEECH, Rosa Parks and Fred Daniels were presented to the crowd, and Abernathy read the three demands for the meeting's overwhelming approval. King left the mass meeting to keep a previously scheduled speaking engagement at a YMCA banquet. Later that night King and Abernathy sent the bus company an unsigned copy of the three demands.

That first mass meeting began the process of creating a movement. All the ingredients were present. A concrete, precipitating incident had occurred: Mrs. Rosa Parks, a well-known, respected figure, had been arrested for refusing to stand up so a white man could take her seat. Her experience was not unique. It had happened to Jo Ann Robinson, to Martin Luther King as a schoolboy, and those Blacks in Montgomery who had not been personally subjected to such indignity on the buses but had seen it happen to others.

The mass meeting collection that night raised over two thousand dollars. At future mass meetings, two groups of women competed to see which could raise the largest amount of money for the MIA. Georgia Gilmore, a cook who had been arrested on a city bus headed one, the Club from Nowhere. Through cake and pie sales the club made weekly donations to the MIA and was soon in friendly competition with the Friendly Club, run by Inez Ricks. Now the movement was developing a fellowship.[35]

Sometime that week, Virginia Durr wrote to a friend: "Something wonderful is happening in Montgomery!"

TUESDAY, DECEMBER 6

The next morning, the *Montgomery Advertiser* reported on the first mass meeting of the brand-new Montgomery Improvement Association. King met with reporters for the first time. He emphasized that the boycott's aims were not integration of the seating system but fair treatment within the strictures of segregation: "We are not asking for an end to segregation. That's a matter for the legislature and the courts. . . . All we are seeking is justice and fair treatment in riding the buses. We don't like the idea of Negroes having to stand when there are vacant seats. We are demanding justice on that point." The boycott would continue, King said, until it gained "concrete results."[36]

WEDNESDAY, DECEMBER 7

On Wednesday, the MIA's executive board met for the first time. Its membership showed how decisively the city's Black clerical leadership had taken control of the boycott from the Women's Political Council and Nixon, who had begun it. In addition to King as president, ministers were chosen as vice president, recording secretary, corresponding secretary, and parliamentarian. Nixon was treasurer. Ministers enjoyed a degree of financial independence from white Montgomery and were used to filling leadership roles; indeed, most of them expected it. Their major purpose was to organize committees to manage the boycott most had thought would not last beyond one day.

At the board meeting that day of the Alabama Council on Human Relations, members made plans to bring the boycott leadership and the city and bus company to the negotiating table.

THURSDAY, DECEMBER 8

The next morning the two sides met. King, Abernathy, Gray, Robinson, and eight others represented the MIA. The three city commissioners and several lawyers represented the city and the bus company. King told the gathering, "We are not here to change the segregation laws." The MIA, King said, had "a plan that can work within the laws of the state"—the equally segregated system in use in Mobile and Huntsville, Alabama, that the Women's Political Council had earlier requested. King also mentioned that the MIA wanted "better treatment and more courtesy" toward Black riders, and Black drivers hired. "We are merely trying to peacefully obtain better conditions for Negroes," he said.[37]

The bus company spokesman replied by saying that the seating plan the MIA proposed was contrary to state law. If there were specific complaints against drivers, they would be reprimanded. The time was not right for Black drivers, even on all-Black lines; instead the bus company would make every other bus on predominately Black lines an all-Black "special" with no white riders; on the "special," Blacks could have all the seats. His argument reflected a common view that where there were no whites to resent a challenge to their superior status, Blacks could sit anywhere they chose. He explained the whites' position: "If we granted the Negroes these demands, they would go about boasting of a victory they had won over the white people."[38]

The whites refused to surrender; the Blacks were astounded. "We thought that this would all be over in three or four days," Abernathy remembered later. "Since our demands were moderate," King remembered later, "I had assumed they'd be granted with little question."

Discouraged, the MIA sent a letter to National City Lines of Chicago, the owner of the Montgomery company, asking them to send someone to Montgomery to negotiate.

Whites were worried too. A few buses had been fired upon, and someone fired into a Black policeman's home. The chief of police announced that armed policemen would follow some buses, and the bus company's manager, admitting that patronage was down 75 percent, announced that service on some lines might be discontinued.

That threat prompted a call from King to Reverend T. J. Jemison in Baton Rouge. Jemison told King about the organization of Baton Rouge's boycott and carpool. It was important, Jemison said, to have one set of pickup points for people going to work in the morning and another set of pickup points for people returning home in the evening. What had been done in Baton Rouge could be done in Montgomery, Jemison said, if enough cars were volunteered and if coordination between cars and pickup points were maintained.

Thursday night the MIA's second mass meeting was held at St. John AME Church. Following a pattern that would be repeated at each meeting that would follow, King told the crowd about the failed meeting with city and bus company officials, the letter sent to Chicago, and his conversation with Jemison.

FRIDAY, DECEMBER 9

On Friday, the organization of the carpool was underway. The city announced it would require cabs to charge the minimum fare—forty cents—in an attempt to break the boycott (bus fare was then ten cents), and the bus company announced it would discontinue two Black routes on Saturday, December 10. Removing bus lines forced even reluctant boycott supporters into active participation; riding a bus in defiance of the boycott was no longer an option.

MONDAY, DECEMBER 12

At the mass meeting on the first-week anniversary of the boycott, the MIA announced that a carpool would begin the next day, December 13. The transportation committee established forty-two morning stations and forty-eight evening ones; a Black owned parking lot in downtown Montgomery would serve as the central command post. More than two hundred volunteer drivers had been recruited; middle-class Montgomerians donated their cars or drove them in the carpool. Over time the organization was able to buy fifteen station wagons to supplement the volunteer cars.

The morning stations—Black churches, funeral homes, and stores—were open from 6:00 a.m. until 10:00 a.m.; hourly service was instituted from then until 1:00 p.m. when domestic workers—maids, cooks, and nurses—began to leave work. Afternoon pickup stations were downtown locations frequented by whites and Blacks; the afternoon service continued until 8:00 p.m. In time, the transportation committee employed fifteen dispatchers (Rosa Parks served as a dispatcher briefly) and twenty full-time drivers six days a week, providing ten thousand to fifteen thousand rides per day. There were seventy-four part-time unpaid volunteer drivers. Dispatchers were stationed at the downtown parking lot.[39]

TUESDAY, DECEMBER 13

On Tuesday, cracks between local (MIA) and national (NAACP) interests began to appear, caused by the MIA's requests for equal treatment within the segregated system versus the NAACP's desire for integration, and by the NAACP's legalistic approach versus the direct-action boycott technique of the MIA.

As we shall see later, this local-national conflict will reappear again and again when Martin Luther King brings his troops into a Southern town and his national goals conflicted with more limited local aims. But in Montgomery in 1955, King was the local leader. The visitor was W. C. Patton, the NAACP's director of voter registration, based in Birmingham. Patton reported to NAACP executive secretary Roy Wilkins, "King assured me" that the MIA's "ultimate goals are the same as those of the NAACP."[40]

THURSDAY, DECEMBER 15

At Thursday night's mass meeting, transportation committee chairman Rufus Lewis reported that 215 volunteer drivers were making the transportation system a success. The carpool and the weekly mass meetings helped create and cement movement strength and solidarity. The carpool eased class divisions among Montgomery's Blacks as professionals shared their cars with domestic servants. The mass meetings' ability to combine church services with political education and testimony from boycotters insured that all shared the boycott experience; each triumph was a success story participated in and shared by all.

SATURDAY, DECEMBER 17

At their next negotiating session, King reiterated the MIA's goals and relaxed one. The MIA would settle for the bus company's receiving applications from Black drivers; they would not have to be immediately hired. The mayor announced he had appointed a special "citizens committee" of eight whites and two Blacks; the Blacks were the mayor's choices, his invitees to the meeting, and were not a part of the MIA. The MIA, he said, could have three representatives on the committee. The mayor, of course, was following a long-established practice of white leadership—selecting Black leaders for the Black community. When Jo Ann Robinson objected to the handpicked candidates, the mayor named six MIA representatives— King, Abernathy, Robinson, Reverend Hubbard, and attorneys Gray and Charles Langford. The "special committee" was able to agree only on a resolution calling for courtesy on the buses toward everyone.

MONDAY, DECEMBER 19

As the committee met again, King spotted a new face among the whites, the secretary of the Montgomery Chapter of the White Citizens' Council. King objected to his presence and was told that the mayor had chosen him and added a non-voting white woman as recording secretary. King protested that the White Citizens' Council secretary was biased; the whites responded by charging that King himself was biased. For whites like the mayor, the White Citizens' Council and the NAACP—the only Black organization they knew of—were simply two different interest groups. King favored integration and the White Citizens' Councils opposed it, they were opposite equals. Abernathy came to King's rescue, saying King spoke for all the Blacks present. Again, no agreement could be reached.

The MIA was taken aback by the refusal of the city and bus company to agree to the slightest modification of segregated seating. They began to reassess their approach, and while attorney Gray told reporters that the MIA was not asking "for an abolition of segregation at this time," the editor of the *Birmingham World* reported, "plans are being made for a 12-month campaign."[41]

THURSDAY, DECEMBER 22

The MIA's executive board met and expressed disappointment with the negotiations and decided not to meet with the city again until some concessions were forthcoming. In an attempt to explain their position to all of Montgomery, they prepared a detailed statement—printed in the *Advertiser* on Christmas Day—outlining past grievances suffered on the city's buses and repeating their proposal for separate-but-equal seating.

The bus company reduced the number of routes it served, announced that all bus service would be canceled for several days over the holiday period, and warned that the lack of business might call for a fare increase early in 1956.

In his mass meeting speeches, King began to mention Gandhi and nonviolence more frequently. The MIA's newspaper ad read, "This is a movement of passive resistance, depending on moral and spiritual forces. We, the oppressed, have no hate in our hearts for the oppressors, but we are nevertheless determined to resist until the cause of justice triumphs."[42]

White Montgomery had tried to pick the representatives for Black Montgomery and had tried to pack the negotiating committee with an admitted racist; now they tried to undermine King's growing status in the community. They spread rumors that "outside agitators" were responsible for the boycott, that King was stealing from the MIA, that he occupied a leadership position that should have gone to an older, more established preacher. In response, the MIA and Black Montgomery closed ranks around him. On December 30, 1955, a Montgomery policeman told a local FBI agent he had been instructed "to uncover all the derogatory information he could" about King; two Montgomery policemen traveled to Atlanta to investigate King but concluded "he was clean as a hound's tooth." This was the beginning of a long FBI campaign to discredit King.[43]

From New York, NAACP executive secretary Roy Wilkins wrote to W. C. Patton that the organization could not help with Mrs. Parks's legal appeal; the NAACP could not associate itself with the MIA "on any other basis than the abolition of segregated seating on the city buses." NAACP lawyers were already pursuing a case to integrate city buses in Columbia, South Carolina; they could not enter another case "asking merely for more polite segregation."[44] Wilkins was being disingenuous; the NAACP could easily have supported the legal suit, which attacked the segregation law, without agreeing to a continuation of segregation.

JANUARY 1956

The Montgomery City Bus Lines, admitting that the boycott was 100 percent effective, announced it was losing twenty-two cents every mile a city bus traveled and faced bankruptcy; it asked the city for a 100 percent fare increase, from ten cents to twenty cents. The city agreed to raise the adult fare to fifteen cents.

FRIDAY, JANUARY 6

A letter to the editor of the *Montgomery Advertiser* suggested the boycott violated the state's anti-union boycott law. The evening of January 6, the city commissioner in charge of police announced to a 1,200-person rally of whites that he had joined the White Citizens' Council. *The Advertiser* noted, "In effect, the Montgomery police force is now an arm of the White Citizens' Council." He told the crowd, "I wouldn't trade my Southern birthright for a hundred Negro votes."[45]

MONDAY, JANUARY 9

Once again the two sides met; once again the MIA presented its polite segregation plan; once again the city and bus company refused. King noted the effect of the boycott: "Either the bus company will have to meet our demands or fold up." But he also tried to separate the MIA's moderate seating requests from the lawsuit appealing Mrs. Parks's conviction: "We are fighting the question of segregation in the courts."

During the week, the Reverend Robert Graetz's car was vandalized, and King announced on January 15 that mass meetings would be conducted six nights a week instead of two. The movement was taking steps to strengthen its support, to counter the city's intransigence. King announced that the MIA's "separate but equal" seating demand had cost the MIA the support of the NAACP. "Frankly," he said, "I am for complete integration. Segregation is evil, and I cannot, as a minister, condone evil." On January 17, Police Commissioner Sellers told the Junior Chamber of Commerce, "We must at all costs strive to preserve our way of life."[46]

On January 9, the *Montgomery Advertiser* published a story titled "Rev. King Is Boycott Boss." This was not just white Montgomery's first look at King; it was their first serious look at anything Black, the first time the newspaper had given any consideration to the Black community—or a Black figure. Prior to this, the paper had profiled the minister many whites thought was the brains behind the protest—the white Lutheran minister Robert Graetz.

SATURDAY, JANUARY 21

On Saturday, the mayor met with three Black ministers, none of them members of the MIA, and announced to the press that a boycott settlement had been reached. The announcement would be printed in the Sunday *Advertiser*, an obvious collaborator in this fraud. The Associated Press sent a story out on its national wire that the Sunday paper would announce that unnamed "prominent Negro ministers" had agreed to a plan that would retain the present system of ten seats reserved for each race.

A reporter for the *Minneapolis Tribune* named Carl Rowan read the story; he had been in Montgomery two weeks earlier, and now he called King to ask him what he knew of the agreement. When King said he knew nothing, Rowan called Gray, and when the MIA's lawyer was unable to confirm the statement, Rowan called the Associated Press to tell them the story was false. He then called Commissioner Sellers, who refused to name the ministers who had agreed to end the boycott, but conceded they were not members of the MIA. Rowan told King what Sellers had said, and King called the MIA leadership to his home. They decided to awaken every Black minister in Montgomery to tell them the lie the morning newspaper would tell and urge them to repudiate it from their pulpits. King and another group went into Montgomery's bars and nightclubs.

The boycott held.

THURSDAY, JANUARY 26

King was arrested for going thirty miles per hour in a twenty-five-mile-an-hour zone while transporting boycotters. Several dozen Blacks arrived at the jail upon hearing of King's arrest; he was released on a signature bond.

FRIDAY, JANUARY 27

On Friday night, sitting in his kitchen, King experienced a religious moment setting him on the path that would consume the rest of his life. A year after he arrived in Montgomery, he had been thrust into the leadership of a boycott most had believed would last a few days, but which had continued for almost two months. Whites in Montgomery were painting King as the major obstacle to settling the boycott and asking older, established Blacks why King, the new man, was in charge, why they had ceded their rightful position of power to this upstart, who probably was stealing money from the movement.

"I almost broke down under the continual battering," King said.[47] But Montgomery's Black community was beginning to appreciate his leadership, and the community's leaders recognized his diplomatic skills. He was achieving national and international recognition. Telephoned threats against him were numerous and growing; Montgomery's white power structure seemed determined not to give in, even to the moderate demands of the MIA. That night another telephone call had awakened him. The caller said: "Nigger, we are tired of you and your mess. And if you aren't out of this town in three days, we're going to blow your brains out and blow up your house." Unable to go back to sleep, he sat in his kitchen and made a cup of coffee. Eleven years later, speaking in Chicago in 1967, he remembered how he had felt in his Montgomery kitchen.

> It was around midnight. You can have some strange experiences at midnight.
>
> . . . And I got to the point that I couldn't take it any longer. I was weak. Something said to me, . . . "You've got to call on that something in that person that your Daddy used to tell you about, that power that can make a way out of no way." And I discovered then that religion had to become real to me, and I had to know God for myself. And I bowed down over that cup of coffee. . . . And it seemed at that moment that I could hear an inner voice saying to me, "Martin Luther, stand up for righteousness. Stand up for justice. Stand up for truth. And lo I will be with you, even until the end of the world." . . . I heard the voice of Jesus saying still to fight on. He promised never to leave me, never to leave me alone. No never alone. He promised never to leave me, never to leave me alone.
>
> Almost at once, my fears began to go. My uncertainty disappeared.[48]

POLICE OFTEN SAT at the pickup stations giving MIA drivers dozens of tickets. Jo Ann Robinson got seventeen tickets in just a short time. As the city's response became more and more hostile, some MIA members suggested that the organization should organize its own transportation system with a city franchise. A city license would let the MIA charge its passengers, something it could not do with the car-pool system. Costs for gas, oil, tires each week were huge and supported entirely from the mass meeting collection plate. Mrs. Parks's appeal through the state courts would be subjected to delays. Because there had been no other seat available to her, her conviction might be overturned without disturbing the segregation laws. Her attorneys agreed that a frontal attack, based on the 1954 *Brown v. Board of Education* decision, would have to be mounted. Gray, with the help of NAACP lawyer Robert Carter, began to draw up a lawsuit.

MONDAY, JANUARY 30

While the MIA Monday night meeting was in progress at Ralph Abernathy's First Baptist Church, a dynamite bomb blew the front porch off

King's house. Coretta Scott King and a friend heard a bump and footsteps running away from the house; they had just moved into a back room when the bomb exploded. By the time King got home, several hundred Blacks surrounded his house, all of them angry, many threatening the police who were frightened themselves. Commissioner Sellers, a new member of the White Citizens' Council, asked King to calm the crowd. From the bombed porch, with Sellers on one side and Mayor Gayle on the other, King spoke: "Everything is all right. It is best for all of you to go home. The police are investigating, nobody has been hurt, and everything is under control."

He then spelled out what the movement's response to violence would be—this night and in the future: "We are not advocating violence. We want to love our enemies. I want you to love our enemies. Be good to them. This is what we must live by. We must meet hate with love."

"I did not start this boycott," he continued. "I was asked by you to serve as your spokesman. I want it known the length and breadth of this land that if I am stopped, this movement will not stop. If I am stopped, our work will not stop. For what we are doing is right. What we are doing is just. And God is with us."[49]

After the mayor and police commissioner spoke to the crowd, promising to do all they could to find the bombers, King again asked the crowd to disperse. "Go home and sleep calm. Go home and don't worry. Be calm as I and my family are. We are not hurt and remember that if anything happens to me, there will be others to take my place."[50]

Thereafter King and Abernathy decided to carry guns for their own and their families' protection. The two ministers visited the one white Alabama political figure who was a potential ally, Governor James "Big Jim" Folsom, to ask for help in obtaining pistol permits, but a request to the county sheriff for permits was denied. The men of Dexter Avenue Baptist Church organized dusk-to-daylight shifts of armed guards to protect their pastor's home.

FEBRUARY 1–2

On February 1, the MIA filed a suit in federal court seeking an injunction against segregated bus seating and an end to harassment of the carpool. The plaintiffs were all women—Claudette Colvin, Mary Louise Smith, Susie McDonald, and Aurelia Browder—who had suffered harassment or worse on the city's buses. Gray had also wanted a minister to be part of the case, but none was willing.

Nixon's home was bombed on the evening of February 1; he was away, and little damage was done. Ralph Abernathy's home was bombed also.

On Tuesday, February 2, under a court order won by the NAACP, the University of Alabama admitted its first Black student, Autherine Lucy. Students rioted against her on February 7, and she was suspended. She was expelled on February 29 for making "untrue" and "outrageous" statements about university officials.[51]

HARASSMENT INTENSIFIES

Jo Ann Robinson saw a uniformed Montgomery policeman throw a rock through a plate glass window of her home; later someone threw acid on her car. Other cars were vandalized; paint was thrown on homes. Fred Gray's draft board removed his ministerial exemption and classified him 1-A; he was later indicted on a trumped-up charge of barratry.

Not all whites in Montgomery were as hostile to the movement as the city's leaders; a group of thirty-seven white businessmen, the Men of Montgomery, made an attempt to settle the boycott. By February 20, the MOM group had managed to convince the city to offer a plan reserving ten seats for each race but insuring no one would have to stand over an empty seat, the least possible modification of the present seating plan. The bus company urged agreement to keep it from bankruptcy. Reverend Ralph Abernathy presented the plan to the regular Monday mass meeting; from the several thousands gathered at St. John AME Church, only the Reverend Roy Bennett and his assistant pastor voted to accept it.

The next morning, February 21, a grand jury indicted almost 115 members of the MIA under the state anti-boycott law. Rumors of the indictments had circulated through Black Montgomery for more than a week. When they came, the MIA organized a mass surrender at the courthouse to demonstrate that this latest effort would fail to stop the boycott or intimidate its leaders. A Black Montgomery businessman who had been one of the Blacks selected by Mayor Gayle to sit on the negotiating committee provided bail money. Four thousand people attended the mass meeting that night. So did thirty-five reporters from across the country.

Only 89 of the 115 indicted were actually arrested. In mid-February, Mrs. Virginia Durr wrote to friends:

> I thought I would write you and tell you what is going on down here and how exciting and thrilling it is. . . . [Mrs. Parks] is so brave and so intelligent and so determined. So as the Negroes said when they "messed with her they messed with the WRONG ONE" and the whole Negro community united overnight, and with each stupid and vicious attack on them they get madder and madder and more determined, and instead of a handful you now have forty or fifty thousand simply determined to stick it out until Hell freezes over.
>
> To arrest all of their leaders was the very thing that was needed to make them more determined, and especially to arrest their preachers. I have picked up and carried numbers during the boycott, and they all express the same determination. . . .
>
> But there is another side to the story. . . . The White Citizens Council grew apace day by day and there is real blackmail going on. They work the blocks and the buildings and ask each one to join, and if they don't—well there is no doubt you get on a blacklist.[52]

The mass indictments insured the Montgomery bus boycott and its young leader a place in the news across the country. Both the *New York Herald Tribune* and the *New York Times* carried front-page stories; network television began to cover the boycott and King. Others were paying attention to what was happening there too. One was Bayard Rustin.

BAYARD RUSTIN

Bayard Rustin was born in 1910 into a family of caterers in West Chester, Pennsylvania. As a young boy, he adopted an English accent, which he kept throughout his life. Poverty and the Depression interrupted his college education, and he moved to New York's Harlem, worked at odd jobs, including backup singer for folksingers Leadbelly and Josh White, attended free night classes at City College, and joined the Young Communist League.

For several years he was a successful Communist Party organizer and recruiter, but when Hitler invaded the Soviet Union in June 1941, the party ordered him to close down his anti-segregation activity. They intended to use all their energies fighting foreign Nazis, not domestic ones. He resigned and found a temporary job with A. Philip Randolph's March on Washington movement. When the March on Washington was halted by Roosevelt's capitulation, Randolph got Rustin an appointment to see A. J. Muste at the Fellowship of Reconciliation, and Rustin became FOR's youth secretary. FOR, an international Christian-based nonviolent organization, was founded in England in 1914. One of Rustin's tasks was helping a new organization that FOR helped to organize, the Congress of Racial Equality.

In 1943, Rustin refused to be drafted and renounced his right to conscientious objector status and noncombatant work as a Quaker. He spent the rest of World War II in Lewisburg Penitentiary, emerging after twenty-seven months in 1946 just as World War II had ended and the Cold War begun. In 1947, he joined a CORE-sponsored bus ride through the Upper South to test a new Supreme Court decision that Black passengers on interstate buses could not be forced to sit in rear seats. He was beaten and arrested and served time on a South Carolina chain gang. Other arrests followed. Rustin was a gay man, and he was arrested on a morals charge in 1953, for which he served thirty days in jail.[53]

THREE YEARS LATER, traveling on money raised by Randolph, Rustin arrived in Montgomery on a Tuesday just as the indictments were being issued and went to Abernathy's home. He soon met Nixon, joined the indictees at the courthouse lawn on Wednesday, and had a friend wire him five thousand dollars, which he gave to Nixon to use for bail bonds. He attended a mass meeting and an MIA transportation committee meeting, met with the executive director of the Alabama Council on Human Relations, and heard King preach on Sunday. He had his first long talk with King, beginning a friendship that would last until King died. Some of the out-of-town reporters recognized Rustin; he did not help by introducing himself as a representative of *Le Figaro* and the *Manchester Guardian*. Worried about being linked with a former Communist, homosexual pacifist, MIA officials soon persuaded Rustin to leave town. He continued to advise King, over the years, spending hours discussing nonviolence. He wrote an article for King's signature, describing the Montgomery movement as a refutation of stereotypical notions of Blacks, printed in *Liberation* magazine, the first writing published under King's name. In countless conversations, Rustin enlarged King's rudimentary understanding of non-violence and mass organizing. He once said: "King couldn't organize vampires to go to a bloodbath."[54]

Gandhi's nonviolence and his struggles against British colonialism were attractive to Black Americans, especially intellectuals. He identified himself as a Black man and was fighting a powerful white nation. Among Gandhi's early Black admirers were Howard Thurman, the chapel dean at Boston University when King was a student there, and Dr. Benjamin Mays, Morehouse College president when King was a Morehouse student.

NONVIOLENCE

Nonviolence is widely misunderstood.

"Self-defense" against racist violence had always been practiced in African American communities. For King, under Rustin's tutelage, nonviolence became an alternative to wanton violence. For him, it was courageous, not cowardly. It was active resistance to evil, not passive acceptance of it. It led toward the creation of what he came to call "the beloved community." It attacked an evil system, not the evildoers themselves. It eradicated not only physical violence but "the violence of the spirit." It used love as a lever, tilting the majority toward justice and equality.

After the bus boycott, as we shall see, and beginning with the 1960 sit-ins, many came to believe nonviolence and self-defense were not mutually exclusive and could be used by the same people in different situations. Self-defense was neither the opposite of nonviolence nor the equivalent of violence. Many believed nonviolence might succeed on the picket line, but few were willing to embrace it in their private lives. King's argument that nonviolence could wear down and defeat *any* enemy ran counter to the common sense of most Blacks. For some it was debasing. It might have limited tactical utility but not personal application.[55]

King himself grew to understand and articulate distinctions in the nonviolence/violence construct—he believed there were three categories of behavior: pure nonviolence, self-defense, and "the advocacy of violence as a tool of advancement, as in warfare, deliberately and consciously."[56] Like Gandhi, King understood the militancy of direct action, not passive or acquiescent. And like Gandhi, King sanctioned self-defense for those unable to adopt and accept pure nonviolence. "When the Negro uses force in self-defense," he said, "he does not forfeit support—he may even win it, by the courage and self-respect which it reflects."[57]

ON MONDAY, FEBRUARY 27, Rustin's replacement arrived, the Reverend Glen Smiley, a white Texan. Rustin managed to introduce King to Smiley before he left. For the next four years, Smiley was in and out of Montgomery, attending the movement's strategy sessions and running workshops in nonviolence. His white face and Southern accent allowed him to move among Montgomery's whites, who were still convinced local Blacks were incapable of running the successful protest.

STRUGGLE AND VICTORY

Conducting the boycott was expensive. Birmingham attorney Arthur Shores, the senior Black lawyer in the state, had agreed to represent the indicted MIA members for one hundred dollars apiece. The carpool cost three thousand dollars a week; the MIA now had several paid employees working from the MIA office located in Rufus Lewis's Citizens Club. Roy Wilkins wrote King to say the NAACP would bear the full costs of the MIA defense, the suit against the bus segregation laws, and Rosa Parks's appeal as well.

The anti-boycott trials were set to begin on Monday, March 19. King would be tried first. The state intended to prove that the MIA had begun and maintained the boycott illegally—without "just cause or legal excuse." As expected, King was found guilty and fined. Attorney Shores announced he would appeal and posted a thousand-dollar bond.

Then, on April 23, the US Supreme Court upheld a lower court decision striking down segregated seating on buses in Columbia, South Carolina. The Montgomery City Bus Lines announced that its drivers would no longer enforce segregated seating on the city's buses. But Mayor Gayle announced that even if the bus company wouldn't, the city would, and the city would arrest any bus driver who failed to do so. King announced that the boycott would go on, and, at a mass meeting, three thousand people shouted affirmation of a resolution continuing the boycott until at least May 11, when the federal suit filed by Fred Gray would be tried in Montgomery.

At the May 11 trial, the Black female plaintiffs and Mayor Gayle and Commissioner Sellers testified. When Claudette Colvin testified, she was asked who the leader of the boycott was. She answered, "Our leaders is just we, ourselves."[58]

The three-judge panel voted 2 to 1 to strike down Montgomery's segregation law. Because the city appealed to the US Supreme Court, the boycott remained in effect.

The State of Alabama struck against the NAACP on June 1. Alabama attorney general John Patterson, arguing that the New York–based organization was "organizing, supporting, and financing an illegal boycott by Negro residents of Montgomery," obtained a court order banning most NAACP activities within the state. When the NAACP resisted an order to turn over its membership rolls and contributors' lists to the state, the judge imposed a $100,000 fine. It would take eight years and several trips to the US Supreme Court to win the right to operate in Alabama again.

In late August, Reverend Robert Graetz's home was bombed, and on September 8 the insurance policies on seventeen of the MIA's station wagons were canceled. Only the intervention of a Black Atlanta insurance executive with Lloyd's of London allowed the carpool to continue. In October, the city of Montgomery asked a state judge to issue an injunction against the carpool as a violation of the bus company's franchise. A hearing was set for November 13. King sat in the courtroom, sure that the judge would outlaw the carpool, effectively ending the transportation system that had allowed the boycott to succeed. During a recess, an Associated Press reporter gave King a story datelined Washington, DC, that the Supreme Court that morning had affirmed the lower court decision outlawing segregation.

King announced that Montgomery's Blacks would return to the buses as soon as the Supreme Court's order reached Montgomery. That night, ten thousand Blacks gathered to celebrate their victory. Despite the Supreme Court ruling, the state judge issued an order declaring the carpool illegal, ending the transportation system that made the boycott a success.

The City of Montgomery, however, petitioned the Supreme Court for a rehearing, further delaying the issuance of the final order and, with it, an end to the boycott. Without the carpool, the MIA organized a neighborhood-based "share-the-ride" system that kept the boycott intact.

While they waited for the order, the MIA put together a weeklong Institute on Nonviolence and Social Change to help Black Montgomery adjust to riding integrated buses. King was the first speaker at Holt Street Baptist Church, where the boycott had begun a year before. In his speech, King said the boycott had taught six lessons:

(1) We have discovered that we can stick together for a common cause; (2) Our leaders do not have to sell out; (3) Threats and violence do not necessarily intimidate those who are sufficiently aroused and nonviolent; (4) Our church is becoming militant, stressing a social gospel as well as a gospel of personal salvation; (5) We have gained a new sense of dignity and destiny; and (6) We have discovered a new and powerful weapon: nonviolent resistance.[59]

Finally, on December 17, the Supreme Court rejected the city's last appeal; the order arrived in Montgomery on December 20. At two mass meetings that night, King reminded the crowds to follow the suggestions for riding integrated buses they had received: to maintain "a calm and loving dignity" telling riders, "Do not deliberately sit by a white person, unless there is no other seat."[60]

On December 21, Montgomery City Bus Lines resumed service on all of its routes. That morning, King, Abernathy, Smiley, and Nixon boarded a bus and took a front seat. Mrs. Parks had decided to stay home, but *Look* magazine came to find her, insisting that she ride so they could get a picture. She posed sitting in front of UPI reporter Nicholas Chriss, and the iconic bus boycott photograph was created.[61] During the photo shoot, one of the drivers was none other than James Blake, but the reporter missed the significance. Three hundred and eighty-two days after it began, the boycott was over.

In the days that followed, forty carloads of Klansmen paraded through Montgomery; this time, Blacks left their homes and stood in the streets as the Klansmen rode by. Some followed the procession, jeering and laughing. The Klan slunk away.

BOYCOTT AFTERMATH

Despite the drama and emotion of the boycott, Montgomery remained a segregated city; even the buses remained voluntarily segregated, as few Blacks chose to take front seats. The violence also continued. Someone fired a shotgun at King's home. There were other incidents—on January

10, bombs damaged five Black churches and Reverend Graetz's home. Eight months after the boycott's end, still facing death threats and unable to find work, the Parks family was forced to leave Montgomery for Detroit, where Mrs. Parks's brother and cousins now lived.

THE BOYCOTT PROVED one standard assertion of Southern whites—that Blacks and whites could solve their disputes without outside interference—absolutely wrong. The refusal of whites to consider the smallest of alterations of segregation and their refusal to even discuss the issue with Blacks left Blacks no alternative except seeking outside assistance, and they found it in the federal courts. Whites learned a fatal lesson—great political gains, however temporary, could be won by rejecting Black requests for changes in the racial status quo. But, as white resistance stiffened, Black aggressiveness increased.

The Montgomery bus boycott's greatest effect may have been beyond Montgomery. It introduced Martin Luther King to the nation and the world, and his articulation of nonviolence struck a spark in the minds of Blacks across the South. One hundred years earlier, Frederick Douglass had said: "The struggle for freedom is a struggle to save Black men's bodies and white men's souls!"[62] Now in Montgomery, King had preached the same message, couched in the common evangelical Christianity of Southern Blacks and whites. His message in 1955 and 1956 was restoration and redemption, rejection of evil. Just as the South had rejected slavery, it could reject segregation too, King argued, and although few whites in Montgomery listened, he had struck a theme that would eventually resonate among whites and Blacks.

For the national news media, the boycott's dramatization of Southern Blacks' strength, determination, and solidarity was a new phenomenon. The story of "good Negroes" and "bad white racists" was irresistible, and it drew more journalists to the region. In 1956, news magazine coverage of civil rights issues tripled from the previous year. *Life* magazine carried one civil rights story in 1955; the next year it ran thirty-five. In 1957, its sister publication, *Time* magazine, put Martin Luther King Jr. on the cover.[63]

White hostility toward the media insured journalists' sympathies would lie with the Black victims of violence. The immediate white response was disappointment, disapproval, and anger. For some, the anger flowed from a feeling of betrayal, as if an old and trusted family retainer had absconded with the family jewels.

Much as we today hear denunciations of programs designed to strike down discrimination, perversely described as creating and widening the division they were intended to heal, in Montgomery and its aftermath, as Black demands quickened, white Southerners argued that federal court orders and Black aggressiveness drove a wedge between the races, upsetting the historical myth of benign race relations that many whites—and no Blacks—deeply cherished.

SEVEN

THE 1956 PRESIDENTIAL ELECTION AND THE 1957 CIVIL RIGHTS ACT

WHILE MONTGOMERY'S FIFTY thousand Blacks were teaching the nation a new method of fighting segregation, introducing a new leader and a new civil rights vocabulary, and demonstrating that unified mass action was an effective weapon against segregation, civil rights battles were being fought on the political front as well. These political battles would do more than change the nature of the struggle for civil rights; they would affect the lives and futures of three politicians, changing the way the country viewed them and enhancing their prospects for higher office. Their reaction to Black demands for increased freedom would shape the country's future as well.

In 1955, the Leadership Conference on Civil Rights agreed to press Congress and President Dwight D. Eisenhower to pass a series of civil rights measures, including bills that would guarantee Black Southerners the right to vote. The Supreme Court's 1954 school desegregation decision, *Brown v. Board of Education*, had heightened resistance to racial integration generally, while making the South's objections to Black voting less justifiable.

The first five years of the decade had brought some victories—and some defeats—in the fight for equal rights. Win or lose, the half-decade was five years of motion and emotion for Black Americans, signaling the growth of a new determination to push against the barriers to equality.

If there was progress it was heralded across the country, preached about from pulpits, talked about in barbershops and beauty shops. If there were steps backward, or acts of terror and brutal resistance, these too became a part of the folklore. If they were intended to frighten, they served instead to stiffen the determination of Black Americans to overcome—in any way that seemed possible.

In June 1950, the Supreme Court ruled in *Sweatt v. Painter* that equal education meant more than identical physical facilities; Herman Sweatt of Houston was ordered admitted to the University of Texas, the South's largest university. Also in June, the court ruled in *McLaurin v. Oklahoma* that once a Black student is admitted to a previously all-white school, no distinctions can be made on the basis of race; McLaurin had been segregated within the University of Oklahoma law school.

THE KOREAN WAR BEGAN, and Black soldiers fought beside whites. In September, African American diplomat Ralph Bunche was awarded the Nobel Peace Prize. In April 1951, the University of North Carolina admitted Black students, and, in May, segregation in Washington's restaurants was declared illegal. In July, Illinois governor Adlai Stevenson called out the National Guard to put down a mob of three thousand whites who rioted over the presence of a Black family in the Chicago suburb of Cicero. On Christmas Day, a racist's bomb killed NAACP leader Harry T. Moore at his home in Mims, Florida.

In January 1952, the University of Tennessee agreed to admit Black students, and Tuskegee Institute reported in December 1952 that for the first time in seventy-two years no lynching had occurred, the Southern Regional Council reported an increase in racist bombings—forty for the year. The ten-day boycott of city buses in Baton Rouge, Louisiana, in June 1953 succeeded. Atlanta University president Rufus Clement was elected to the Atlanta Board of Education, and Hulan Jack was elected first Black president of the borough of Manhattan in December 1953. President Eisenhower named J. Ernest Wilkens assistant secretary of labor, making him the highest-ranking Black person in the federal government. And in May 1954, in *Brown v. Board of Education*, the Supreme Court ruled unanimously that racial segregation in public schools was unconstitutional. *Brown* overruled the 1896 *Plessy v. Ferguson* ruling.

In the words of Richard Kluger: "No more would [the Black man] be a grinning supplicant for the benefactions and discard of the master class. No more would he be a party to his own degradation. He was both thrilled that the signal for the demise of his class status had come from on high; and angry it had taken so long and first extracted so steep a price in suffering."[1]

In the world outside the United States, change was occurring too. There had been riots in Johannesburg against apartheid in 1950; that year Great Britain recognized Communist China; and the United States recognized Saigon as the capitol of a divided Vietnam and began to send arms and men to instruct in their use. In 1951, there were anti-British riots in Egypt, and a state of emergency was declared in Kenya after the rise of a secret organization called the Mau Mau. In 1954, Colonel Gamal Abdel Nasser seized power and became premier of Egypt; the French garrison at Dien Bien Phu in North Vietnam was overrun. These events—and others—were part of the middle of the end for colonialism, the unstoppable onrush of human freedom that was being heard and seen and felt everywhere—in Africa, in Europe, in Southeast Asia, and here at home.

The 1954 *Brown* decision was also seen in an international context. The friend of the court brief filed by President Truman's Justice Department had argued that school desegregation was in the national interest because of foreign policy concerns. The brief, filed in December 1952 during the final weeks of the Truman administration, argued that "the United States is trying to prove to the people of the world, of every nationality, race, and color, that a free democracy is the most civilized and most secure form of government yet devised by man."

"Racial discrimination," the brief said, "furnishes grist for the Communist propaganda mills, and it raises doubts even among friendly nations as to the intensity of our devotion to the democratic faith."[2]

THE MIDDLE 1950s were the height of the McCarthy era, when US congressman Joseph McCarthy, joined by others in the federal government, promoted fear of Communism, holding hearings and making accusations against hundreds of individuals for being Communists or having Communist sympathies. Following World War II, American foreign policy had shifted from defeating Nazism and fascism to intense competition with the

Soviet Union. Preoccupation with Communism became a central feature of American political culture, and both foreign and domestic policies were evaluated, in part, by their effectiveness in combating Communism.

Thus, segregationists argued that integration was Communist inspired; integrationists argued that continued segregation weakened America's international posture; the NAACP, for example, described its efforts as part of the struggle against Communism. In the NAACP's magazine, *The Crisis*, in December 1951, Roy Wilkins wrote:

> The survival of the American democratic system in the present global conflict of ideologies, depends on the strength it can muster from the minds, hearts, and spiritual convictions of all its people. . . . The Negro wants change in order that he may be brought in line with the *American* standard . . . [which] must be done not only to preserve and strengthen that standard at home, but to guarantee its potency in the world struggle against dictatorship.

In 1951, the US Supreme Court upheld loyalty oaths, ruling that candidates for public office, teachers, and other public employees could be required to swear they had not belonged to organizations that sought or advocated the violent overthrow of the government. President Truman had required loyalty investigations for all persons entering employment in executive branch departments and agencies in 1947. That same year the attorney general issued a list of "fascist, Communist or subversive" organizations; past or present membership in any constituted disloyalty.[3]

This fervent anti-Communism permeated and colored the debate on civil rights: liberals claimed that racial progress would aid the United States in winning the Cold War; racists claimed an international Communist conspiracy was responsible for all civil rights agitation. Liberals embraced anti-Communism to prove their Americanism, their worthiness for civil rights. They engaged in witch hunts, expelling tainted members, fearful that racists would expose the "Red vipers" in their midst. In doing so, they helped to limit the permissible boundaries of political and economic debate, excluding critiques of the economic order and accepting a vision of America flawed only by racism, and not by built-in structural deficiencies such as our gross maldistribution of wealth. The 1960s movement that would follow would therefore look to Jesus and Gandhi and the Sermon on the Mount for inspiration rather than Marx, class struggle, or labor solidarity. The likelihood that the civil rights movement would develop a class analysis had been diminished. Finally, participation in red-baiting by civil rights forces weakened, divided, and isolated them, increasing the likelihood they would themselves be subject to attack. The NAACP, for example, by collaborating with anti-Communist purges, helped to remove and destroy organizations that had protected its left flank. Some of these had been interracial; their disappearance made it more difficult for the *Brown* decision to find a favorable audience.

DWIGHT DAVID EISENHOWER, the war hero who had become president in 1952, believed what most white Southerners believed: school segregation was a matter of ancient local custom, sanctioned by the Constitution, best eliminated over time through Black self-improvement, through which Blacks would gain the gradual acceptance of their white neighbors without interference from the federal government. Eisenhower never endorsed the *Brown* decision. Early in 1954, at a White House dinner whose guests included both Chief Justice Earl Warren and John W. Davis, the segregationist lawyer who argued *Brown* for the Southern states, the president had lobbied Warren, praised Davis, and raised the specter of interracial sex between Black boys and white girls in integrated schools.

THE 1956 PRESIDENTIAL ELECTION

In the 1956 presidential election, the popular Eisenhower would probably win again, but both Democrats and Republicans hoped Black votes would help their party to prevail. The party with the best civil rights record would be rewarded with Black votes. These votes could be crucial. In the congressional midterm elections of 1954, Blacks were more than 5 percent of the vote in seventy-two congressional districts outside the South and held the balance of power in sixty-one of those districts. In fourteen of these, Democrats were elected in 1954 with less than 55 percent of the vote; Republicans were elected in twenty-five districts with similar small majorities. Republicans needed to win fifteen seats in 1956 to control the House and two seats to control the Senate.

Unlike today, there was intense competition between the parties for Black votes, and unlike today, each political party offered some attraction to Black voters. These opportunities were evident to Attorney General Herbert Brownell. Brownell had seen New York governor Thomas Dewey lose in 1948 by losing sections of big cities where the African American vote was key. Truman had been elected president in 1948 by a slim margin, carrying Illinois by 33,000 votes, California by 17,000 votes, and Ohio by 7,000 votes. The Black vote in these states had helped to make the difference. Brownell had been horrified by the murders of Emmett Till and George Lee in Mississippi in 1953 and 1954; his more liberal attitude toward race and his party's need for Black votes galvanized him into action.

Blacks had given the Democrats a consistent majority of their votes since 1936. Before Roosevelt, Roy Wilkins told a reporter twenty years later, the Black vote had been just as solidly Republican. "I remember when I was young in Kansas City," Wilkins said, "the kids threw rocks at Negroes on our street who dared vote Democratic." To counter the Democrats' appeal, Republicans tried to emphasize their own civil rights record—the 1944 GOP platform plank on civil rights was stronger than the Democrats'. New York governor Tom Dewey endorsed his state's pioneering fair employment commission bill in 1945, and major Black newspapers endorsed presidential candidate Dewey in 1948. Blacks remained firmly Democratic, however, even while both parties continued the competition.

Eisenhower's civil rights record rested largely on executive orders rather than legislation; he had been lukewarm at best and hostile at worst to civil rights. A Southerner, as general, Eisenhower had opposed President Truman's integration of the armed services. In 1948, he told the Senate Armed Services Committee: "The Negro is less well educated than his brother citizen that is white, and if you make a complete amalgamation, what you are going to have is in every company the Negro is going to be relegated to the minor jobs, and he is never going to get his promotion . . . because the competition is too tough."[4]

As president, Eisenhower argued that gradualism, rather than legislation, would eliminate discrimination. Under pressure from the NAACP and Congressman Adam Clayton Powell, Eisenhower ordered the desegregation of naval installations at Norfolk and Charleston, convinced the heads of major movie studios to integrate their Washington theaters, and persuaded hotels in the capital to accept Black guests and municipal agencies in Washington to integrate their labor force. At best, Eisenhower was a benign racist who believed social change in race relations occurred only when men's hearts and minds were changed.

The civil rights community had failed to get action on its broad 1955 agenda; it decided instead to concentrate on the franchise. "Voting rights," Representative Richard Bolling (D-MO) told the NAACP's Washington lobbyist Clarence Mitchell, were "far less susceptible than school desegregation to inflammatory opposition by racists."[5]

On January 5, 1956, Eisenhower asked Congress to establish a bipartisan commission to study denials of the right to vote and make recommendations. The Montgomery bus boycott then was just thirty days old. That same day, Brownell, Assistant Attorney General William Rogers, executive assistant John Lindsay, and Solicitor General J. Lee Rankin met to discuss a more ambitious program than the president had proposed. On March 6, 1956, Brownell presented a four-part plan to the cabinet:

1. Title 1: Create a civil rights commission
2. Title 2: Elevate the Justice Department Civil Rights Section to a division
3. Title 3: Authorize the attorney general to seek injunctions against violations of civil rights
4. Title 4: Seek injunctions against voting discrimination in particular[6]

Brownell argued for civil rather than criminal sanctions and preventive rather than punitive measures, to avoid stirring up "ill feelings in the community" or causing "bad relations" between white state and local officials and the federal government. By "community," Brownell meant the white community. His solicitous concern for the passions of the violators was typical of the government's attitude then and later; his concern for maintaining good relationships between the segregationist South and the federal government was an acknowledgment that even the moderate reforms he was proposing could harm his party's future chances among white Southerners.

Thus, a Southern strategy was born. Eisenhower decided to support only Titles 1 and 2, but, speaking before Congress, Brownell gave the clear impression that Eisenhower and the cabinet supported the entire proposal. He then sent copies of Titles 3 and 4 to Representative Kenneth

Keating (R-NY) and Senator Everett Dirksen (R-IL), who promptly introduced them in Congress.

Brownell had clearly overstepped his mandate from Eisenhower and the cabinet. But he had given the GOP an important weapon for their election arsenal, a legislative program that would help GOP House and Senate candidates with Black voters. While HR 627 passed the House (168 Republicans joined 111 Democrats in voting yes), in the Senate, Judiciary Committee Chairman Senator James O. Eastland (D-MS), easily the most racist member of Congress, bottled HR 627 in his committee, where it died when Congress adjourned on July 26. The split vote among House Democrats on the bill and Eastland's role in squashing Senate consideration sent a signal to Black voters.

With the fall, the nation's attention turned to the upcoming elections. Both party platforms supported civil rights generally; the Democrats supported the "full right to vote," while the Republicans promised to work toward passage of the House-passed bill. Less than a month before the general election, New York congressman Adam Clayton Powell endorsed Republican Eisenhower, demonstrating the unease Black Democrats felt about their party's commitment to civil rights.

ADLAI STEVENSON, the Democratic nominee, equivocated in his support for the bill; a few days before the November election, Eisenhower endorsed the civil rights bill. When all the votes were counted, Eisenhower had done more than defeat Stevenson; he had increased his share of Black votes over his totals in 1952. The election results showed Republicans they could win through appeals to Black voters. The shift in Black votes gave civil rights an urgency for Democrats it had not had before. Although he eventually abandoned Title 3, to pass any civil rights measure through the Senate, Ike needed active support from the majority party, and he got it from Senator Lyndon Baines Johnson (D-TX), the majority leader.

Johnson had been a candidate for vice president in 1956; he wanted higher office in the future. To win it, he would have to shed his identity as a Southerner, a segregationist, an opponent of civil rights and become a national politician. As a congressman in 1945 and 1946, Johnson had voted with most Southerners against repeal of the poll tax and against anti-lynching bills. Now, as majority leader, he had a chance to reshape his national profile and to aim his sights at the White House. Johnson had been a fervent supporter of Franklin Roosevelt's New Deal as a young member of Congress; as senator, he had become more conservative. A complicated figure, he was described by one biographer as "driven, tyrannical, crude, insensitive, humorless, and petty . . . empathic, shy, sophisticated, self-critical, witty, and magnanimous."[7]

LYNDON BAINES JOHNSON

Lyndon Johnson was born in 1908 to Sam and Rebekah Johnson in a three-room shanty in Texas's Hill Country, where people lived as far from the twentieth century as anywhere in the United States. There was no indoor plumbing or electricity; all the Johnsons' neighbors were uneducated and barely literate. His father was active in local and state politics all his life; from both parents, and from his environment, where there was little difference between rich and poor, Johnson inherited a lifelong interest in the problems of others and a healthy identification with life's underdogs.

He interrupted his education at San Marcos College—where he was a hotshot campus politician—to teach three grades at a segregated school for Hispanic children in Cotulla, Texas. His students came to school, he said later, "most of them without any breakfast, most of them hungry, and all the time they seemed to be asking me, 'Why don't people like me? Why do they hate me because I am brown?' Most of them . . . were taught that the end of life is a beet row, a spinach field, or a cotton patch." He was determined to help "those poor little kids," saying, "I saw hunger in their eyes and pain in their bodies. Those little brown bodies had so little and needed so much. I was determined to spark something inside them, to fill their souls with ambition and interest and belief in the future."[8]

Black unemployment in the early 1930s was almost 50 percent; those employed saw their wages cut by as much as half. Forty percent of all Blacks who had jobs were farm laborers or tenant farmers; their income averaged less than $200 a year. Among Blacks older than twenty-five, 10 percent had not finished a single year in school; only one out of every hundred had a college degree. Many of the New Deal programs intended to help everyone gave little help to Blacks—the National Recovery Agency, called the NRA, was called by Blacks the "Negro Run-Around," "Negro Robbed Again," and "Negroes Ruined Again."[9] Some New Deal agencies, like the Civilian Conservation Corps (CCC), the Farm Security

Administration, and the Works Progress Administration (WPA), did help Blacks, however. Eleven percent of the CCC's enrollment was Black, the Farm Security Administration gave 23 percent of its assistance to Black farmers, and the proportion of Black workers in the WPA was higher than in the private construction industry.

The National Youth Administration (NYA), whose Texas organization Johnson headed, was among the most aggressive of New Deal agencies in helping Blacks. While it—like other New Deal agencies—followed the generally accepted pattern of segregation in the South, the NYA hired a disproportionate number of young Blacks for menial labor, hired Black administrators to supervise Blacks in every Southern state, refused to agree to either regional or racial wage differentials, had more Black administrators than any other New Deal program, and gave 20 percent of its annual budget to Black youngsters. Fifteen of twenty NYA college centers were reserved for Blacks. Twenty-four percent of Blacks eligible for help in Texas got NYA assistance, while only 14 percent of eligible whites were aided.[10]

Johnson left the NYA in 1937 to run for Congress and won, identifying strongly with FDR and the New Deal. Roosevelt had carried Johnson's congressional district in 1936 by nine to one. As a congressman, Johnson voted with the white South on civil rights and generally with Roosevelt on the New Deal. "There's nothing more useless than a dead liberal," he said to explain his voting record. After the election, Roosevelt met Johnson in Texas and told a friend: "In the next generation the balance of power would shift south and west" and "this boy [Johnson] could well be the first Southern President."[11] Johnson fought to see that Black farmers got equal—if segregated—treatment from the Farm Security Administration and worked quietly to keep federal school lunch money away from any state that didn't make an equitable distribution of the funds.

In an election in which Johnson successfully stole votes more efficiently than his opponent, he was elected to the US Senate in a bitterly contested runoff primary in 1948. On Election Day, Johnson was reported ahead of his opponent in one county 4,197 to 40. The next day, he got 425 more votes in that county and 203 more in another. Six days after the election, Johnson had twice as many votes in one county than had been cast in the first election. In the fight over those votes, Johnson's opponent brought in two former FBI agents, including the man who had tracked down Bonnie Parker and Clyde Barrow, while armed mobs faced each other in the streets. After much maneuvering and politicking and a final decision made by the state's Democratic Executive Committee and the Supreme Court, Johnson won the primary by eighty-seven votes, giving him the lifelong nickname "Landslide Lyndon." One observer said later: "They were stealin' votes in east Texas . . . . We were stealin' votes in south Texas. Only Jesus Christ could say who actually won it."[12]

His first Senate speech was against cloture—shutting off filibusters, the tactic the white South had used to defeat civil rights bills. Johnson argued that shutting off debate was an infringement on free speech. He announced he was for civil rights but against Truman's civil rights proposals. The Houston NAACP sent him a telegram reading: "Do not forget that you went to Washington by a small majority vote and that was because of the Negro vote. There will be another election and we will be remembering what you had to say today."[13]

He was elected majority whip in 1951, and when the Republicans took majority control of the Senate in the Eisenhower landslide in 1952, he was chosen minority leader. When *Brown v. Board of Education* was decided in 1954, he counseled that the ruling, however disagreeable, should be obeyed. Johnson was reelected in 1954; that election also gave the Democrats a majority in the Senate again, and Johnson became the youngest majority leader in Senate history. He had become the consummate politician and ran the Senate like he owned it. He had become the master of compromise—one friend said he was like a man with a bucket of bubbling acid on each shoulder—balancing each, not afraid that either would fall.

Despite strong support for a second nomination for Adlai Stevenson at the 1956 Democratic Convention, Johnson ran for the nomination as Texas's favorite son, with an eye toward running in 1960. He let it be known that he would accept the vice presidential position too. His ambitions for higher office, his desire to see the South move beyond race toward solutions of its economic problems and into national acceptance, and his conviction that unless the South relaxed its opposition to *any* civil rights legislation it would have an unpalatable law forced upon it, made him a natural champion of a compromise.[14]

Johnson's support of the 1957 Civil Rights Act had a price—the jury trial amendment and elimination of Title III. The jury trial amendment, which would provide protection for those who would deny people their civil rights, passed 51 to 42 (with John F. Kennedy one of five Democrats switching to side with Johnson). For Vice President Richard Nixon, then a civil rights supporter, "this was one of the saddest days in the history of the Senate because this was a vote against the right to vote."[15]

After slight modifications in the House, the bill passed 279 to 97 in the House and 60 to 15 in the Senate, the first time in the twentieth century the US Senate had voted on a civil rights bill. On September 9, 1957, Eisenhower signed HR 6122 into law. The 1957 Civil Rights Act and the debate that created it helped the ambitions of three politicians particularly. It did not help much to advance the right to vote.

Lyndon Johnson's role in passing the act helped him to shed his Southernness; he became a national politician and could comfortably aim his sights at the White House. It did, however, mean that civil rights laws *could* be passed through Congress, an important precedent for the years ahead. John F. Kennedy won favor with Southerners who had thought he was too liberal; his vote for the jury trial amendment moved him toward the center and enabled him to compete for future votes from the South he could not attract as a vice presidential candidate in 1956.

Richard Nixon's behavior helped him become a certified civil rights champion, a reputation that would help him almost win the presidency in 1960. Nixon had begun a warm relationship with King; his chairmanship of the president's committee to combat discrimination in government contracts gave him visibility as a defender of civil rights.

If Johnson, Kennedy, and Nixon won, Black Southerners lost. Within two years, the US Commission on Civil Rights, created by the bill that Johnson and Nixon had helped to pass and that Kennedy had tried to weaken, reported hundreds of instances of voter discrimination that the federal government could not or would not end. But a few days after the signing of the 1957 Civil Rights Act, another city would grab the national spotlight just as Montgomery had two years before. Headlines this time would be made not by peaceful Blacks marching in dignity but by violent white mobs and a recalcitrant governor, nine Black high school students, and a courageous and militant Black woman.

EIGHT

LITTLE ROCK, 1957

EMMETT TILL'S DEATH and the Black newspapers that came into my Pennsylvania home created a great vulnerability and fear of all things Southern in my teenaged mind. When my parents announced in 1957 that we were relocating to Atlanta, I was filled with dread. Emmett Till's death had frightened me. But in the fall of 1957, a group of Black teenagers encouraged me to put that fear aside. These young people—the nine young women and men who integrated Central High School in Little Rock, Arkansas—set a high standard of grace and courage under fire as they dared the white mobs that surrounded their school. Their names were Ernest Green, Elizabeth Eckford, Jefferson Thomas, Terrence Roberts, Melba Patillo, Carlotta Walls, Gloria Ray, Minnijean Brown, and Thelma Mothershed.

By the end of the 1956–57 school year, no schools in Alabama, Florida, Georgia, Louisiana, Mississippi, North Carolina, South Carolina, or Virginia had integrated. The Southern states had passed 130 pro-segregation school laws. An August 1957 Gallup poll showed a majority of Americans predicting race relations would get worse in the coming year; in the South, a two-to-one majority predicted the same.

President Eisenhower's vacillation on civil rights encouraged the resistant white South. They knew there would be no strong federal effort to protect Black voting rights or integrate schools or to punish those who illegally opposed civil rights. On July 17, 1957, Eisenhower said at a press conference: "I can't imagine any set of circumstances that would ever induce me to send federal troops . . . into any area to enforce the orders of a federal court." The president's desire to avoid direct involvement in school desegregation ended on September 24, 1957, in Little Rock, Arkansas.

Arkansas was an unlikely location for a showdown between federal and state authorities over school desegregation. In 1948, Arkansas became the first state to admit Black students to a state university without a court order. Immediately after *Brown* in 1954, the Little Rock school board announced a gradual plan that would begin integration with senior high schools in 1957, junior high schools in 1960, and elementary schools in 1963. The NAACP challenged the plan as too slow but lost, and the Little Rock school board announced integration would begin at Central High School in September 1957.

DAISY BATES

Daisy Lee Gatson Bates was born in Huttig, Arkansas, a town she described as a "sawmill plantation, for everyone worked for the mill, lived in houses owned by the mill, and traded at the general store run by the mill."[1] When she was eight, she discovered that the people she knew as her parents were, in fact, her parents' best friends. Her mother had been killed by three white men when she resisted their attempt at rape; her father, despondent, had left town, leaving young Daisy with friends. L. C. Bates, who would become her husband, was born in Mississippi and educated at Wilberforce College in Ohio. He worked for newspapers in Colorado, California, Missouri, and Tennessee before returning to selling insurance in Arkansas.

Shortly after their marriage, the Bateses moved to Little Rock and founded their own newspaper, the *State Press*, in 1941. Both joined the NAACP after they arrived in Little Rock. In 1957, Daisy Bates was elected president of the Little Rock NAACP. Tireless crusaders, the Bateses had vigorously supported the 1954 *Brown* decision; their activism earned them many enemies among Arkansas whites. Their credit was cut off, and both were threatened. They were convicted of contempt for criticizing a court trial; the Arkansas Supreme Court reversed their conviction. Mrs. Bates was elected president of the Arkansas State Conference of NAACP Branches in 1952.[2]

BY AUGUST 1957, local racists, supported by the Mother's League of Little Rock, stepped up their opposition to integrating the schools and persuaded school superintendent Virgil Blossom to delay the entrance of nine Black students to Central High School. On August 28, the Mother's League asked a county court to block desegregation. That same day, Arthur Caldwell of the US Department of Justice met with Arkansas governor Orval Faubus. Caldwell told Faubus the federal government wanted to avoid being involved in controversy over the integration of schools. Thus encouraged that he would not be restrained, Faubus began to move to prevent the schools from being integrated. On August 29, with Faubus arguing that gun sales were up and violence was therefore imminent, the county court issued a temporary injunction against desegregating Central High School. That same day, the final version of the 1957 Civil Rights Act passed both houses of Congress.

School officials, backed by Mrs. Bates and the NAACP, filed suit in federal court, asking for an injunction against anyone who interfered with integrating the schools. Federal judge Ronald Davies ordered the integration to proceed, and the school board announced that Central High School would open on September 3. On September 2, Faubus ordered the Arkansas National Guard to the school's grounds, and the school board told the nine students not to try to attend the school until the legal battle had been settled.

On September 4, the Black students tried to attend school, escorted by Daisy Bates and a group of Black ministers she had recruited. One of the nine, Elizabeth Eckford, had not gotten the instructions to meet at Bateses' home beforehand to go together. She went alone and met a mob. Guardsmen that Faubus had ordered to the school turned them away. In a court hearing, Judge Davies ordered the FBI to investigate the governor's claim that violence was imminent.

Three days later, on September 7, Judge Davies rejected a school board request for a delay, and on September 9 the judge asked the Department of Justice to file a petition for an injunction against the governor and two National Guard officers. Faubus was ordered to appear in court on September 20 to show why he should not be held in contempt. Faubus met with Eisenhower in Newport, Rhode Island, on September 14. Eisenhower thought he had obtained an agreement from Faubus to order the National Guard to admit the students; within two hours of the meeting Faubus changed his mind. On September 19, the day before his contempt hearing, Faubus's lawyers tried to disqualify Judge Davies. At the hearing, Judge

Davies issued an injunction barring Faubus and the National Guard from any further interference with the integration of Central High School. It had finally become clear to President Eisenhower and Attorney General Brownell that Faubus never had any intention of allowing integration to proceed.

Little Rock mayor Woodrow Wilson Mann asked Brownell to assign U.S marshals to the school. Brownell refused, saying that only the court could do so. Judge Davies refused in turn, saying he could not issue such an order without an official request from the Justice Department. Eisenhower was more worried about the harmful political consequences of the federal government forcing the integration of nine Black students and providing protection for them than the harmful violence that would result if he did not. Earlier, FBI director J. Edgar Hoover had refused to send FBI agents to Little Rock to police the school. The city only had 175 policemen; they had refused to escort the children to Central High School, and the Little Rock Fire Department refused to provide hoses for crowd control.

On September 23, the nine Black students entered Central High School through a side door. Daisy Bates had again arranged for them to meet at her home to go together for safety. A screaming mob of several thousand whites gathered, and the students were trapped in the school. Finally, through the plan of one police official, the nine were spirited safely out of the building in station wagons, ducked down so the massive crowd outside didn't see them. Daisy Bates issued a challenge to President Eisenhower: the students would not return until she had his word they would be protected. She had become the spokesperson for the students, their protector and defender.

Twenty-four hours later, US Army paratroopers from the 101st Airborne escorted the nine into the building and were stationed outside Central High School. The integration of Little Rock's public schools had begun. And that military protection would last the entire year—as would the harassment of the nine teenagers in the building.

The year before, Eisenhower had allowed school authorities and Texas governor Alan Shivers to defy a federal court order integrating schools in Mansfield, Texas. In 1957, in Little Rock, a reluctant president acted. National politics made the difference. Texas was a major prize for the Republicans in the 1956 presidential race, and Governor Shivers was a personal friend and political ally of Ike's. Arkansas was solidly Democratic; there was nothing political to be gained in Arkansas for Eisenhower by capitulating to Orval Faubus.

The Little Rock crisis energized American Blacks who watched the drama unfold on television. Unlike the Montgomery boycott of 1955 and 1956, the Little Rock school integration crisis in 1957 was told on television, as well as in daily national and international headlines. The Little Rock crisis had larger media elements than the Montgomery bus boycott. In Montgomery, the community fought primarily with local officials; in Little Rock, a governor fought with the president of the United States, and the president equivocated about protecting the safety and civil rights of nine young people against a white mob and hostile state government. In Little Rock, state troops were used to stop integration; federal troops were used to enforce it and to finally stop the white mob. Little Rock had rabid white mobs attacking defenseless teenagers, the eldest only sixteen years old, the youngest fourteen. Montgomery had an entire community, largely faceless, fighting a faceless evil—bus segregation. And unlike Montgomery, where Martin Luther King emerged as the dignified single spokesman for the entire community, the heroic figures in Little Rock were nine personable teenagers—selected from an eighty-student pool of applicants—and a middle-aged Black woman. The evil in Little Rock had a face—the screaming mobs that gathered outside Central High School every day and the wily, duplicitous governor.

THE MOST POPULAR teenagers in the US in the fall of 1957 were Arlene Sullivan, Kenny Rossi, Justine Corelli, and Bob Clayton. Five afternoons a week, after school, beginning in August 1957, with other high school students from South Philadelphia, they appeared on a new television program called *American Bandstand*. "Every kid in America was watching the show," said its host Dick Clark years later.[3] *Bandstand*'s regulars quickly developed fan clubs, becoming teenaged heroes and heroines. According to historian Richard Aquila, "The show became a live soap opera: would Carol be dancing with Joe today? Did you see Carmen's new sweater? Why aren't Bob and Justine dancing together? . . . Did you notice Pat's new dance step?"[4]

But then, in September 1957, another group of teenagers came into my life, and the ones on *American Bandstand* danced out of my life. For

Black young people, who had only one Black couple on *American Bandstand* to relate to, the Little Rock Nine quickly became heroes and heroines—a model for what a concerned Black teenager ought to be. Younger Blacks were especially thrilled by the courage of the Little Rock Nine who faced daily harassment from their white schoolmates. They were threatened, kicked, punched, spat upon—the objects of verbal and physical abuse—and set a high standard of grace and courage under pressure. Because their activities were so widely reported in both the Black and white press, and because the waiting world knew instantly when one was hurt or attacked, the personalities of each of the Little Rock nine became well known throughout Black America. They were the poster children of the modern civil rights movement.

Minnijean Brown was the "bad" girl who wouldn't take anything from anyone; when two white boys attacked her, she upset a bowl of chili on their heads. When a white girl called her "Black bitch," Minnijean called her "white trash" and said, "If you weren't white trash, you wouldn't bother me!" A few days later, a white student upset a bowl of hot soup on her head. Because of her refusal to suffer in silence, she was expelled and graduated from high school in New York. A generation of young Black people worried with Minnijean, were angry when she was provoked to answer taunts with other taunts, and at the same time proud when she refused to take punishment without retaliation. Elizabeth Eckford's courage and calm demeanor in facing the mob the first day the students tried to attend school won her fans around the world. Ernest Green, at sixteen, was the oldest of the nine and the most mature; he was looked upon as their leader.

Mrs. Bates showed a national audience that civil rights work was women's work too. A professional woman and business owner, her profession and part-time work with the NAACP were all-consuming. In her middle age, she showed that civil rights activism could be work that consumed a lifetime. Even before the school integration crisis, the Bateses had suffered incredible harassment: had their home attacked, their lives and livelihood threatened, their newspaper eventually strangled to death by an advertiser boycott. She argued with a governor and won. She gave the president of the United States an ultimatum, and he obeyed. Daisy Bates would not back down. Armed guards protected her home. She kept a .45 caliber automatic in her lap when she sat at home at night. Several of the women active in the early 1960s sit-ins said that Daisy Bates gave them a model of what a woman could be and should be—fierce in the face of opposition but a calm and reassuring presence to the nine Black students to whom she was surrogate parent and protector.[5]

Finally, the Little Rock crisis, unfolding in the days and weeks immediately after passage of the 1957 Civil Rights Act, showed how irrelevant to civil rights the bill actually was. When in March of 1956, 101 members of Congress signed the Southern Manifesto, they issued a prediction that violence would follow attempts to enforce the *Brown* decision. Common to mid-1950s school crises, whether in Little Rock or Prince Edward County, Virginia, were several themes. In Arkansas and Virginia, each state's political leadership—Governor Orval Faubus in Arkansas and Senator Harry Byrd in Virginia—seized the school integration issue to rally white support at a time when their political futures seemed insecure. In both states, the NAACP's reliance on the federal courts to enforce integration was turned on its head by segregationists, who knew that litigation could mean later, that later meant further delay, and that further delay might mean never. Without support from Eisenhower, only rarely could the courts overcome the mobilized white resistance. Defiance clothed in legalisms also encouraged extralegal, violent defiance.

COOPER V. AARON, 1958

On May 27, 1958, Ernest Green became the first Black student ever to graduate from Central High School. It was estimated that his diploma had cost the US taxpayers $5 million. But would he be the last? Or at best, the first for a long, long time? That same month, the Little Rock school board went back to federal court to ask that desegregation be postponed until January 1961—a delay of two and one-half years. This delay, the school board argued, was what the Supreme Court meant when it ordered desegregation to proceed "with all deliberate speed." Citing "pupil unrest, teacher unrest and parent unrest," they maintained: "The principle of integration runs counter to the ingrained attitudes of many of the residents of the District. For more than eighty years the schools have been operated on the basis of segregation. . . . The transition involved in the gradual plan of integration has created deep rooted and violent emotional disturbances."[6]

Their argument was that if Supreme Court decisions resulted in disagreement—or violence—then that violence should be rewarded by a stay (a delay of implementation) by the court. A trial was held before a federal district judge in early June; witnesses testified to "chaos, bedlam and turmoil," and the court granted the school board the relief they had sought, suspending school desegregation until January 1961. In August, the Eighth District Court of Appeals reversed this: "The time has not yet come in these United States when the order of a federal court must be whittled away, watered down, or shamefully withdrawn in the face of violent and unlawful acts of individual citizens in opposition thereto."[7] But the school board, having lost the constitutional battle, nevertheless won a temporary procedural war; the court stayed its own order, delaying desegregation until after the opening of school.

The lawyers for the Black children went to the US Supreme Court. On August 25, the court scheduled a special term and set a hearing for August 28. The Department of Justice lined up foursquare behind the Black petitioners, recognizing that behind the immediate issue of school desegregation the power of the federal courts was at stake. After hearing arguments on procedural points, the court announced it would consider the case on its merits and set arguments for September 11, 1958. The school opening date was delayed until September 15 to allow the legal drama to play out.

In *Cooper v. Aaron*, the justices firmly upheld judicial supremacy over state action. The *Brown* decision "is the supreme law of the land," they said. They expressed contempt for officials like Governor Faubus who waged "war against the Constitution." The war over school integration continued after the court's ruling. Little Rock officials refused to obey court orders and closed all high schools until 1959. Finally, parents and voters who cared more about education than segregation changed the school board. The integration of Little Rock schools resumed. The court's decision established an important precedent. But it did not end conflict over racial issues that have divided Americans since the time of slavery.

School segregation, a relic of that system, stubbornly refuses to go away. Judges can decide legal issues, but they can't change housing patterns or cultural attitudes. Since its unanimous decision in *Cooper v. Aaron*, the Supreme Court has split over cases dealing with school integration. *Brown* is still on the books, but the question remains: when will Black children in schools across the country receive the integrated and equal education the Constitution commands?

NINE

THE SOUTHERN CHRISTIAN LEADERSHIP CONFERENCE

IN DECEMBER 1956, Bayard Rustin introduced Martin Luther King Jr. to two friends, both white, who would play important roles in King's future and the future of the movement that was slowly growing beyond King himself. One was Harris Wofford, the first white twentieth-century graduate of the Howard University Law School, who had written a book on Gandhian nonviolence. The other was Stanley D. Levison, a forty-four-year-old New York lawyer active in a group called In Friendship, formed in 1956 to raise money for Southern activists; its other members included a Black woman named Ella Baker.

Rustin and Levison told King they had discussed with Baker an idea Rustin had for using the momentum generated by the Montgomery bus boycott's success to create other movements throughout the South. The numbers who had attended the Institute on Nonviolence in Montgomery proved there was wide interest, and now was the time to strike. Rustin and Levison had drafted a memorandum on the establishment of a "Southern Leadership Conference on Transportation." King agreed and promised to issue a call for the meeting, set for early January 1957 in Atlanta at King's father's church, Ebenezer Baptist.

Rustin, ever the organizer, drafted seven position papers. He later wrote, "In practical terms . . . the movement needed a sustaining mechanism that could translate what we had learned during the bus boycott into a broad strategy for protest in the South."[1] King, Rustin, Reverend K. C.

Steele, Reverend T. J. Jemison, and Reverend Fred Shuttlesworth issued a call for the "Southern Negro Leaders Conference on Transportation and Integration."

In his working papers circulated to the participants, Rustin argued: (1) The church is the base for a protest movement; (2) nonviolent action will be necessary; (3) an organized mass force must supplement the legal approach of the NAACP; and (4) Black clergymen and the masses must make up the movement.[2]

That the church would be expected to continue to play such an important role is not surprising. "The black church," Cornel West reminds us, "is the major institution created, sustained, and controlled by black people themselves; that is, it is the most visible and salient cultural product of black people in the United States."[3] The Black church represented both a separation imposed by whites and a refuge preferred by Blacks, both an accommodation to white prejudice and an assertion of Black independence and self-respect.

Despite denominational differences and differences in social class, Black churches shared many commonalities. They shared the role of attending to their congregations' spiritual needs. They sang the same songs, and all believed in contributing to church-endorsed causes. Their ministers were independent agents, free from dependence on the white world for sustenance, able to take leadership without the restraints imposed on most Blacks. And their ministers not only had weekly access to a built-in constituency but also had access to city, state, and nationwide networks; locally they shared membership in citywide denominational or interdenominational alliances.

The leadership elected at a second meeting of the group in New Orleans in February reflected the extent to which ministers would dominate the new organization and demonstrated how a newer generation of leadership was seizing control. King was chosen president; all of the executive officers were men, and all but two were clergymen. Reverend Kelly Miller Smith of Nashville was elected chaplain. All were Southerners educated at Southern Black colleges, and all but two were under forty. All had histories of past NAACP activism, demonstrating how important the NAACP was as an incubator for the more activist movement of the late 1950s. In New Orleans, a name was chosen; the group became the Southern Leadership Conference and later the Southern Christian Leadership Conference.

Rustin and Levison prepared drafts of speeches for King's "Give us the ballot" speech at the May 17 March on Washington, and Rustin prepped King for a meeting with Vice President Nixon on June 13. At the Nixon meeting, the vice president reported later, King and Abernathy said they had voted Republican in 1956.

Both Rustin and Levison would continue as speechwriters, critics, and editors of King's books; theorists; and confidants for years; Levison even prepared King's tax returns. Eventually, as Rustin's politics grew more conservative, he and King would drift apart, but Levison remained King's closest white friend until King died.

The new SCLC met for a third time in early August in Montgomery; a plan, prepared by Rustin, King, and Levison, for a "Crusade for Citizenship" was presented and adopted. This meeting heightened the tension already existing between King and the NAACP, tension that had begun in the early days of the boycott when the MIA adopted a "separate but equal" demand for bus seating; now King was planning to do what the NAACP did. Additionally, dynamic NAACP presidents in Atlanta, Tallahassee, and Nashville had become presidents of SCLC affiliates. Despite King's appearance at two NAACP conventions, Roy Wilkins remained wary of him and saw the new organization as a threat to the NAACP's emphasis on legal strategies—and a threat to the NAACP itself.

The SCLC met for a fourth time in early November in Memphis, and King announced plans to begin the Crusade for Citizenship, a South-wide voter registration drive, on January 20, 1958. With no director or other staff hired for the Crusade, no office secured, and with little money raised, King postponed the opening rallies until February 12, the birthday of Abraham Lincoln. In early January 1958, Rustin and Levison proposed that King hire the executive director of In Friendship, Ella Baker, to direct the Crusade; they would raise her salary so she would not cost the SCLC. She arrived in Atlanta, set up her headquarters in the Savoy Hotel on Auburn Avenue, and, as acting director, began work.[4]

ELLA JO BAKER

Ella Jo Baker was born on December 13, 1903. Her mother, Georgina Ross, was one of twelve or thirteen children born to parents themselves born in slavery. Her family moved to Littleton, North Carolina, in 1910. Her mother taught the children to read before they entered school. Ella attended Shaw University's high school in Raleigh in 1918, taking courses in English, Latin, French, math, science, history, home economics, and the Bible. She graduated as class valedictorian and in September 1923 entered Shaw as a college student.

While at Shaw she worked two jobs—waiting tables and supervising a chemistry laboratory. She began a lifetime of protest at Shaw too. Women students were not allowed to wear silk stockings to class; Baker couldn't afford them but thought those who could do so should have the right to wear them and spoke out. When she heard that Ella Jo Baker was questioning the school dress code, the dean of women fainted. And when the president of the university asked students if they would entertain visiting white Northerners by singing spirituals, Baker refused. In 1927, she graduated as valedictorian again, with enough credits to receive both a bachelor of arts and a bachelor of science degree.

She moved to New York in the summer of 1927 and took a job waiting tables at a New York University dormitory. Her free time was spent in the public library, listening to street corner speakers in Washington Square Park and attending plays and discussion forums at the Harlem YMCA at 135th Street. The Depression devastated Harlem, beginning in 1929; the misery she saw and the intellectual ferment she saw around her created a new understanding in Baker of social problems. She served on the editorial staff of the *American West Indian News* from 1929 to 1930 and in 1930 became office manager for the *Negro National News*. She went undercover to expose New York's "slave markets" where black women stood on street corners, waiting for jobs as maids. She wrote for several Black publications including *The Crisis*, the *New York News*, the *Amsterdam News*, and the *Pittsburgh Courier*.

In December 1930, she and other young Blacks organized the Young Negroes' Cooperative League. The league believed in democratic control; voting was based on one person, one vote, rather than a vote for each share you owned. In the co-op movement, Baker learned organizing techniques—taking all classes into an organization and using democracy as an organizing and managerial principle.

In the '30s, Baker worked at the 135th Street Branch of the New York Public Library, the center of Harlem's intellectual life, and as a consumer education teacher for the Committee on Negro Welfare for the Welfare Council of New York, sponsored by the Works Progress Administration.

In October 1936 she became assistant director for the Consumer Education Division of the WPA.

In 1941, she joined the staff of the NAACP as field secretary. The organization was then in the middle of internal strife—both personal and political—between executive director Walter White and *The Crisis* editor W. E. B. Du Bois. Baker took her first trip South for the NAACP in 1941, staying in members' homes rather than hotels. For the next three years she traveled six months out of every year, organizing NAACP chapters; in 1942, she attended 146 meetings and traveled 9,294 miles. In 1943, she was appointed director of branches and continued her whirlwind travel, beginning leadership training conferences the NAACP still employs today. By 1946, however, she resigned, frustrated at her inability to operate in the NAACP's hierarchical structure so dominated by Walter White.[5] She still served the NAACP as president of the New York branch, the first woman to hold that position, and also worked for the Young Women's Christian Association and the American Cancer Society.

In January 1958, Baker moved to Atlanta to assume her position as the first acting executive director of SCLC. With less than two months to pull together voter registration rallies across the South, Baker used her NAACP contacts as well as those furnished by SCLC. She put together a list of twenty-one cites where rallies would occur, gathered state registration laws, and produced and distributed literature. Again, there was tension with the NAACP. NAACP field secretary Medgar Evers, who had been ordered by Roy Wilkins to end his association with SCLC, reported to the NAACP's New York office that he had stopped plans for an SCLC rally in Jackson. This example of petty backbiting characterized too much of the NAACP's attitude toward newer civil rights groups. The NAACP's imperious attitude would do much to dislodge it from its position as the premier civil rights organization in the years ahead.

Only a dozen of the rallies actually occurred, few new voters were added to the rolls, and Baker went back to New York on February 16. She returned to Atlanta March 20. Knowing King had preferred a preacher for the job and had objected to hiring a woman, Baker sought out an old friend, Reverend John Tilley of Baltimore; on April 30, the SCLC board made Tilley executive director and Baker associate director. Fifteen months after it began, the SCLC finally had a staff.

ON JUNE 23, 1958, King, Randolph, Wilkins, and Lester Granger of the National Urban League met at the White House with Eisenhower and Attorney General William Rogers. This was the president's first meeting with Black leaders; he had been in office for five years. They asked the president to vocally support the 1954 *Brown* decision, to call a White House meeting to promote peaceful desegregation, to support stronger federal antidiscrimination laws, to recommend the extension of the Civil Rights Commission, and to order the Justice Department to become more active in fighting voting discrimination. Nothing resulted from this meeting. Randolph gathered the group to sponsor an October "Youth March for Integrated Schools" in Washington, DC, but after a deranged woman stabbed King in New York on September 17, he had to cancel his appearance there.

In the meantime, Tilley and Baker alone could do little toward making the SCLC into a viable organization. In April 1959, Tilley was dismissed as executive director, partly because the SCLC board was impatient with the organization's inaction and lack of focus. Baker stayed on as interim director.

A second Youth March on Washington, organized by Bayard Rustin, occurred in April. King, Wilkins, and Kenyan labor leader Tom Mboya, then visiting the United States, were the featured speakers; 26,000 gathered at the Washington Monument. Mboya also spoke at an SCLC-sponsored "African Freedom Dinner" in Atlanta. "I am absolutely convinced," King said there, "that there is no basic difference between colonialism and segregation. They are both based on contempt for life, and a tragic doctrine of white supremacy. So, our struggles are not only similar; they are in a real sense one."[6]

By the fall, it was clear that, after two and half years, SCLC had little program beyond the personality and pronouncements of its leader, Dr. King. Baker had begun to explore SCLC's adoption of citizenship training to overcome the illiteracy that kept many Southern Blacks from registering. She visited Highlander Folk School to see such a program in operation.

If King could devote more time to the organization, it might succeed. He decided to resign his pulpit at Dexter Avenue in Montgomery and return to Atlanta where he would become co-pastor of his father's church. He was coming home, but no one in Atlanta's Black leadership—beside his father—greeted him with open arms. Whites felt the same way. Governor Ernest Vandiver said: "He is not welcome to Georgia. Until now, we have had good relations between the races."[7] Since SCLC's founding in 1957, King had been unable to get the largely clerical board to do more than come to meetings, where much of the discussion consisted of praise for King. Baker was frustrated by her inability to get King's attention or resources to carry out any program.

That same year, students at South Carolina State College conducted a boycott of classes, and, in 1958, students in Nashville had begun training in nonviolence under the direction of a Vanderbilt University divinity student, James Lawson. These events, the two youth marches, and a 1959 Prayer Pilgrimage had been the major civil rights activity since SCLC's founding. None could be traced directly to SCLC, but each involved something more than boycotts or marches—for the first time, large numbers of young Black people were becoming involved. Civil rights activity was no longer something only older people could do.

TEN

THE SIT-INS AND
THE FOUNDING OF SNCC

KING'S FAREWELL APPEARANCE in Montgomery was on January 31, 1960. That same night, Joseph McNeil, a freshman at North Carolina A&T University, was returning to Greensboro. He entered the Greensboro bus station cafe and was told, "We don't serve Negroes here." McNeil returned to his dormitory room, where he discussed what had happened with three friends: Ezell Blair, Franklin McCain, and David Richmond.

Three of them had been raised in Greensboro and attended Dudley High School; McNeil was from Wilmington, North Carolina. Each of the four remembered high school teachers who had instilled them with racial pride. Two of the four were active in the Greensboro NAACP youth chapter. One worked in the A&T library with Eula Hudgens, who had participated in the 1947 CORE/FOR Freedom Ride that had sent Bayard Rustin to the chain gang. All remembered the Montgomery bus boycott, one calling it "a catalyst. It started a whole lot of things rolling."[1] Blair's father was an NAACP activist. The younger Blair heard Martin Luther King when he spoke at his high school in 1955 and at Bennett College in Greensboro in 1958 and remembered being moved by a television documentary on Gandhi's passive resistance. All of them held long conversations with Dr. George Simpkins, Greensboro NAACP president, and with Ralph Johns, a white store owner active in the NAACP. They were part of a protest community with deep roots in Greensboro's past.

MONDAY, FEBRUARY 1

The four students entered the Greensboro Woolworth's Department Store and, after buying school supplies, took seats at the segregated lunch counter. When they were refused service—by a Black waitress—Blair said, "I beg your pardon, but you just served us at [that] counter. Why can't we be served at the [food] counter here?"[2]

"You are stupid, ignorant. You're dumb!" the waitress said. "That's why we can't get anywhere today. You know you are supposed to eat at the other end."[3]

The store's manager tried to persuade them to leave, and when that failed, he told the employees to ignore them. The students said they would return the next day and every day until they were treated just like white customers.

McCain remembered, "We had the confidence of a Mack truck. I probably felt better that day than I've ever felt in my life. I felt as though I had gained my manhood."

"I felt that I had powers within me, a superhuman strength that would come forward," McNeil recalled.

When they left, they went by Dr. Simpkins's home, telling him they planned to go back tomorrow. A Greensboro radio station broadcast a story about the sit-in; the campus was in an uproar when the four returned. People wanted to join in. They contacted student leaders and began to coordinate transportation for the next day and discuss how to impose discipline on future demonstrators.

TUESDAY, FEBRUARY 2

They were joined by twenty-three A&T students and four young women from nearby Bennett College. Some of the men wore ROTC uniforms; others, coats and ties. The women wore dresses. All carried books and notebooks and used their time at the lunch counters to study. That night the Greensboro NAACP endorsed the students' sit-in and voted to give them legal assistance.

WEDNESDAY, FEBRUARY 3

Students took over sixty-three of the sixty-five seats in the store. A newly formed Student Executive Committee that included students from A&T

and Bennett College set strategy and recruited new demonstrators. "We did an hour-by-hour job," Richmond said. "We had students to take each other's place at the counters. We had a carpool to transport everybody. We had a place where everybody would come and register for the whole week."[4] North Carolina newspapers picked up the story, and the Associated Press and United Press International carried it across the country.

THURSDAY, FEBRUARY 4

Three white women from the Women's College of the University of North Carolina joined the protest. The protest overflowed the Woolworth's counter into S. H. Kress's down the street. And, for the first time, white teenaged thugs filled both stores' aisles and harassed the protesters.

FRIDAY, FEBRUARY 5

More than three hundred students were part of the protest. Three white men were arrested, one for setting fire to a Black student's coat as he sat at the lunch counter.

SATURDAY, FEBRUARY 6

Hundreds of students, including the A&T football team, flooded downtown Greensboro. They were met by white gangs waving Confederate flags. Carrying small American flags, the football team formed a flying wedge that broke through the gang and allowed new demonstrators to replace those already sitting in.

"Who do you think you are?" one of the whites asked.

A football player replied: "We are the Union Army."

Bomb scares closed both lunch counters. When the students marched back to campus chanting, "It's all over! It's all over!" the line they made was over two miles long.[5]

OF COURSE, IT was not over. The sit-in movement had only just begun. There had been sit-ins before. The Howard University NAACP had staged sit-ins at a Washington restaurant in 1943; there had been others sponsored by NAACP youth chapters in Kansas and North Carolina cities in the late 1950s. Suddenly one had caught fire, spreading from Greensboro through the Carolinas and into the Upper South.

The sit-in demonstrations, from Greensboro forward, provided a technique through which traditional patterns of white oppression could be attacked by ordinary people—not lawyers or ministers or social scientists. These were college students, most of them Southerners, the generation born during the Second World War, raised in segregation, educated at Black public schools and now attending Black colleges, knowing racism would frustrate the training they were receiving and would work to diminish the worth of their degrees. They had been frightened by Emmett Till's murder, encouraged by the 1954 *Brown* decision, thrilled by the marching feet in Montgomery, uplifted by the rhetoric of Martin Luther King (at thirty years old in 1960, he was closer to the students' age than the faraway figures of the civil rights establishment like Roy Wilkins, A. Philip Randolph, and Lester Granger), and given a strong dose of youthful courage by the Little Rock Nine. They were exposed to the movement for African independence, led by college-trained Africans only a few years older than they were, and the worldwide destruction of colonialism.

In 1952, a state of emergency was declared in Kenya following activity by freedom fighters called the Mau Mau, led by Jomo Kenyatta. In 1956, Sudan proclaimed its independence. Nasser became president of the United Arab Republic in 1958. In 1960, the Belgian Congo became independent. The future sit-inners attended college with Africans who chided their American classmates for their lack of aggression against American apartheid. "We are freeing our countries," the Africans would say, "When will you be free in America?"

Following the Friday demonstrations, the Greensboro students agreed to a two-week cooling-off period. On Saturday, 1,600 students rallied at A&T and agreed to let negotiations proceed.

MONDAY, FEBRUARY 8

That morning, a single Black college student conducted Winston-Salem's first sit-in; that afternoon, twenty-five others joined him. That same day, seventeen students from North Carolina College and four from Duke University staged a sit-in in Durham.

TUESDAY, FEBRUARY 9

Sit-ins were held in Charlotte.

WEDNESDAY, FEBRUARY 10

After a radio station in Raleigh announced that no sit-ins were planned there, forty-one students were arrested at Raleigh lunch counters. Students from Hampton Institute staged a sit-in in Hampton, Virginia, the first outside North Carolina since the movement started on February 1.

THURSDAY, FEBRUARY 11

Sit-ins were held in High Point, North Carolina, and Portsmouth, Virginia, where police dogs were used to disperse crowds.

WEDNESDAY, FEBRUARY 17

Seventy-six sit-in demonstrators were arrested in Nashville. James Lawson, a divinity student at Vanderbilt University and Southern field secretary for the Fellowship of Reconciliation, had been conducting nonviolence workshops for two years. The Nashville students—John Lewis, Diane Nash, Bernard Lafayette, Marion Barry, and others—trained by Lawson would become stalwarts of the movement that young people like them were creating, day by day, across the South.

MONDAY, FEBRUARY 22

Thirty-three students were arrested in Richmond, and demonstrations began in Petersburg, Newport News, and Arlington, Virginia.

TUESDAY, FEBRUARY 23

High school students sat in in Chattanooga; college students staged sit-ins in Knoxville, Memphis, and Oak Ridge, Tennessee.

WEDNESDAY, FEBRUARY 24

Sit-ins were held in Orangeburg, Sumpter, Columbia, and Rock Hill, South Carolina. In Montgomery, thirty-five students from Alabama State College sat in at the Montgomery County Courthouse snack shop. Alabama governor John Patterson ordered the president of the college to expel them. King spoke to a campus protest rally, where one thousand students pledged to quit school if anyone was expelled. Students from Texas Southern University sat in, in Houston; there were mass arrests of students in Marshall, Texas.

BETWEEN FEBRUARY 1960 and February 1962, thousands of lunch counters and other facilities in 150 Southern cities were integrated, either by nonviolent action or the threat of such action. Over seven thousand people eagerly went to jail, and over one hundred thousand people had actively participated in this new movement. Millions more were moved by mass media reports of the sit-ins.

WHAT THE SIT-INS MEANT

The sit-ins represented a tactical change from earlier boycotts and lawsuits, by their nature demanding and establishing equality at the same time. It was confrontational activity, creating an immediate contradiction for whites—between a new reality and the continuing myths upon which white fantasy rested. The region-wide inbred culture of white supremacy had long practiced automatic responses to Black transgressions against the color line, but the nonviolent nature of the sit-ins disarmed whites and rendered them impotent. The sit-ins challenged cherished beliefs most whites had embraced since birth and held dearly: that Blacks were satisfied with the Jim Crow system and had no desire to see it changed. These young people were clearly dissatisfied and unwilling to wait for any time to pass or hearts to change. They wanted action now!

College students were ideally situated to sponsor and spread the sit-in movement. They were young and had none of the responsibilities that come with maturity—a job, mortgage, car loan, or family. Many of them emerged from school networks such as fraternities and sororities, student governments, and other campus organizations. The sit-ins gave on-the-spot leadership training to a new, young generation and gave impetus to a new organization. The sit-ins struck at the notion expressed by whites in authority—mayors, governors, presidents—that racial troubles were caused by outsiders, by Northerners, by Communists, or the Supreme Court. These students were home-grown local products, raised, nurtured, and educated in the towns where they protested. There was not an outside agitator among them. The protests showed Blacks and whites that demonstrations by Blacks could be orderly and peaceful and skillfully organized, giving Black people a sense of their own power and ability in the face of overwhelming white power.

In the Black communities from whence these protests sprung, ancient conflicts between activists and accommodationists, between "go-slows" and "nows!" were exposed. The sit-ins upset traditional race relations in the South and upset the established way of negotiating racial progress: behind closed doors, through negotiations between powerful whites and Blacks often chosen by whites. They also upset the NAACP's nearly unchallenged dominance as the single organization that fought for racial progress.

Although they targeted lunch counter segregation, they were about much, much more. A Howard University student wrote years later: "I still carry with me the feeling of those days—black people in motion against white supremacy. White people never gave the sit-ins that definition, probably because the thought of that frightens them. They always talked about the sit-ins in terms of lunch counters, and desegregation, and civil rights bills."[6] If the 1954 *Brown* decision had theoretically ended segregation through court action, the hostile reaction to *Brown* had paradoxically begun to tilt the movement toward greater activism and away from dependence on the courts.

When the sit-ins began, in 1960, Mahatma Gandhi had been dead for only twelve years. First Montgomery and then the sit-ins gave new life to Gandhi's message. The sit-ins combined nonviolence and confrontation; for participants, they fused personal faith and social justice, peacefully demanding equality now, not from the courtroom or the pulpit but in the most public sphere, where everyone, Black and white, was witness.

Television had brought the sit-ins into American homes, as it had done with the Little Rock crisis in 1957. Ugly images of raging mobs threatening innocent schoolchildren and T-shirted thugs attacking suit-wearing college students brought naked racial hatred to new audiences. Even the segregationist editor of the *Richmond Times Dispatch* was dismayed—he called the white rowdies "a ragtail rabble, slack-jawed, black jacketed, grinning fit to kill."[7]

And for many of those witnesses who were white, the sit-ins created a conflict between belief and reality, a conflict that could only be resolved in two ways—a further retreat into Negrophobia or an acknowledgment, however reluctant, of the justice of the sit-in students' demands.

For the Southern white political leadership, the sit-ins called for an adjustment they had promised never to make, a reversal of deep-seated beliefs, an unexpected—and therefore all the more challenging—moral claim to extend fairness to everyone, not just to the racially favored caste. That the claim was cloaked in common Judeo-Christian principles made it all the more irresistible.

The sit-ins loosed a great moral energy, and their nonviolent nature confused and, in many cases, paralyzed the reaction. Moderate Southern whites whose previous silence had given sanction to the greatest brutality to punish real and imagined racial transgressions were moved by the sit-in students' willingness to absorb jail and summary punishment.

The civil rights movement, as it had existed until February 1960, would never be the same.

ELEVEN

THE STUDENT NONVIOLENT COORDINATING COMMITTEE

ELLA BAKER, like almost all other adults, was caught off guard by the sit-ins and their rapid spread. She knew, however, that few of the students thrust into leadership had any preparation or background for their new roles. With eight hundred dollars borrowed from SCLC, she secured space at her alma mater, Shaw University in Raleigh, North Carolina, for a conference of sit-in students to be held April 16–18, 1960. Highlander Folk School had hosted a conference of one hundred sit-in leaders from nineteen states during the first weekend in April; many of these students would attend the conference organized by Ella Baker two weeks later. An invitation, signed by Baker and Martin Luther King Jr., was sent to protest groups, asking them to send representatives to the Raleigh meeting.

The invitation, written by Baker, insured the students that they—and not adults—would be in charge. The conference, she wrote, would be "youth centered." She was a remarkable woman—and one of our adult advisors. We didn't trust older people. Miss Baker was in her late fifties and very much the distinguished lady. But we trusted her and always called her "Miss Baker." I know some of the women called her Ella, but I could never call her Ella. She was always "Miss Baker" to me.

The meeting was a success. More than 120 students from fifty-six colleges and high schools in twelve Southern states and the District of Columbia attended, as well as observers from a dozen liberal and student organizations and Northern colleges.[1] Helped by Ella Baker, the students resisted attempts to subsume their energies into existing, older organizations. They set up a Temporary Student Nonviolent Coordinating Committee (SNCC), adopted a statement of purpose that stressed nonviolent theory over a program for action, and elected a Fisk University student, Marion Barry, as SNCC's first chair.

SOME OF THE PEOPLE WHO MADE SNCC

Marion Barry

Marion Barry was a member of one of the largest delegations to Raleigh— the Nashville group. Most Nashville students had been attending James Lawson's workshops in nonviolence for over a year and had staged "hit-and-run" sit-in demonstrations in downtown Nashville in the fall of 1959. Barry, born to sharecropper parents in Itta Bena, Mississippi, had moved to Memphis when he was seven. He earned a BA degree from LeMoyne College in Memphis, where he was active in the campus NAACP. In Nashville he was working for an MA degree in chemistry and said of himself before his participation in the sit-ins: "I was not a free man. I was not a man at all. I was only part of a man, and I felt in order to be a whole man I must be an American citizen as anybody else."[2]

Diane Nash

Diane Nash was born in Chicago and was a runner-up in Chicago's Miss America pageant. She spent a year at Howard University and then transferred to Fisk. Nashville's segregated life depressed her after the freedoms she had experienced in Chicago; she could not understand why her fellow students had surrendered to it. Raised as a Catholic, she saw her protest activities as "applied religion."[3]

John Robert Lewis

John Lewis was born in March 1940, in rural Alabama near Troy, one of ten children in a family of tenant farmers. Deciding early to become a minister, he used to baptize chickens in his front yard and was the first member of his family to finish high school. He had heard King speak on the radio in 1955 and became enthralled with the notion of the social gospel. He enrolled in American Baptist Theological Seminary in Nashville in 1957, supporting himself by washing dishes, and traveled to Montgomery in 1959 to meet with King, Abernathy, and Gray to seek their support for a lawsuit to integrate Troy State College near his home. They persuaded him it was too dangerous, and Lewis returned to Nashville and Lawson's workshops.

His fellow students at ABT were Bernard Lafayette, James Bevel, and Paul Brooks. Bevel, like Barry, was from Itta Bena. He described himself as the perfect example of the "chicken-eating, liquor-drinking, woman-chasing, Baptist preacher."[4]

James Lawson

Most influential in the Nashville group was Lawson, a theology student at Vanderbilt University. A minister's son like Martin King, he attended Baldwin-Wallace College in Ohio. A conscientious objector, he went to prison in 1951 rather than enter the army; Bayard Rustin and Glen Smiley were his counselors in draft resistance. He was paroled to the Methodist Board of Missions and spent three years as a teacher and missionary in India, returning to the United States after spending a month in Africa, where he met leaders of independence movements. He met King at Oberlin College in 1957. In 1958, Lawson became a field secretary for the Fellowship of Reconciliation and began workshops in nonviolence for the Nashville Christian Leadership Conference. These workshops attracted Lewis, Barry, Nash, Lafayette, Bevel, and others, and now the Nashville students had the deepest grounding in nonviolence of any student protest group. On the third day of the Greensboro sit-ins, Douglas Moore, a Durham minister, called Lawson in Nashville to get him to step up his plans for sit-ins.

Lawson wrote SNCC's statement of purpose, which "expressed the religious underpinnings of nonviolent direct action." But his greater influence was in the students he trained and in the speech he gave at the Raleigh conference. Lawson described a role for the student sit-in leaders that set them apart from the rest of American society and the established views of civil rights. The issues they faced, he argued, were not legal or economic but spiritual and moral. They succeeded in stripping the white South of its greatest weapon: "the manipulation of law enforcement to keep the Negro in his place." The sit-ins, he said, were "a judgment upon middle-class, conventional, half-way efforts to deal with radical social evil." He named the NAACP as an example of this "half-way" thinking; it had failed, he said, to develop "our greatest resource, a people no longer the victims of racial evil who can act in a disciplined manner to implement the constitution." "All of Africa will be free," he lamented, "before the American Negro attains first class citizenship."[5] And he warned the students that the struggle they had entered would not be over soon. "Most of us will be grandparents before we can live normal lives."[6]

Next to Lawson, King's speech seemed ordinary, but he too said the sit-ins represented a revolt "against the apathy and complacency of adults in the Negro community, against Negroes in the middle class who indulge in buying cars and homes instead of taking on the great cause that will really solve their problems, against those who have become so afraid they have yielded to the system."[7]

Ella Baker's speech "More Than a Hamburger" was in the same vein. She said, "The younger generation is challenging you and me. They are asking us to forget our laziness and doubt and fear, and follow our dedication to truth to the bitter end." Keep the movement youthful and independent, she instructed. Change the whole society, she insisted, not just lunch counters.[8]

The students who formed SNCC clearly had the whole society—and even the world—in their sights. One of its workshops reported, "We identify ourselves with the African struggle as a concern for all mankind." SNCC Executive Committee member Charles Jones of Charlotte declared, "This movement will affect other areas beyond [lunch counter] services such as politics and economics."[9] At the conference's closing press conference, Chairman Barry attacked President Eisenhower's planned trip to Africa and linked American prestige overseas with racial unrest at home. Before going to Africa, Barry said, "the President should lend the prestige of his office to the solution of the racial problems in this country and thus he shall be even better prepared for his visit to Africa."[10]

Baker offered SNCC a corner in the Atlanta SCLC office and hired Jane Stembridge, a white Virginian, daughter of a Presbyterian minister and student at Union Theological Seminary, to run the office until a permanent executive secretary could be hired. Stembridge and volunteers printed the first issue of SNCC's paper, the *Student Voice*, in June 1960. The corner in the SCLC office provided little more than a desk. Connie Curry, director of the National Student Association Southern Regional

Office, offered the use of her mimeograph machine and her contacts on campuses across the South.

SNCC's name said it was a coordinating committee, but Baker and Stembridge had much more in mind than just that. In July, a New York schoolteacher named Robert Moses, who'd come South to do volunteer voter registration work for SCLC, discovered that no one at King's organization had prepared for his arrival. He gravitated to SNCC's corner desk.

Robert Parris Moses

Born in Harlem in 1935, Robert Moses graduated from Stuyvesant High School and Hamilton College. The summer after his junior year he worked in a European camp sponsored by the American Friends Service Committee; in the summer after his senior year he did similar work in Japan. In 1956, he entered Harvard University to begin work on a PhD in philosophy and received an MA degree in 1957. But his mother's death in 1958 interrupted his education, and he became a math teacher at Horace Mann High School in New York. Moses traveled with the doo-wop group Frankie Lymon & the Teenagers by bus to several cities as Lymon's private tutor. It was the first time, he said, despite growing up in Harlem that he realized there was an urban Black nation within the United States. He helped Rustin organize the second Youth March on Integrated Schools.

He was visiting an uncle in Newport News, Virginia, in 1960 when he joined a sit-in. That demonstration, he said later, gave him "a feeling of release." Before then, like so many others, he had accommodated himself to racial slights. "My whole reaction through life to such humiliation," he said, "was to avoid it, keep it down, hold it in, play it cool." He had volunteered in 1960 at the New York Office to Defend Martin Luther King, run by Bayard Rustin to raise money and political support for King's defense on Alabama charges of income tax evasion.

Rustin and Ella Baker recommended he go South to work for SCLC. He discovered that he and Jane Stembridge had a mutual interest in philosophy. She asked him to take a tour of Mississippi for SNCC to recruit students for a planned October 1960 conference in Atlanta; few students from the Deep South had attended the Raleigh conference. One of the people Moses met was Amzie Moore, the president of the NAACP branch in Cleveland, Mississippi.[11]

Amzie Moore

Moore was a veteran, like Medgar Evers, who had returned to Mississippi determined to fight at home for the freedoms for which he'd risked his life overseas. Born in Grenada, Mississippi, in 1912, he had been drafted in 1942. He served in Burma and India in the segregated army. When he returned to Mississippi in 1946, he helped to organize the Regional Council of Negro Leadership. Under their auspices, thirteen thousand Blacks had come to all-Black Mound Bayou, Mississippi, to hear Chicago congressman William Dawson (D-IL). The council brought NAACP chief counsel Thurgood Marshall to speak in Mound Bayou in 1952. In 1956, Moore began voter registration work. His job as a mailman gave him some protection from hostile local whites.

Moore agreed to come to the October 1960 SNCC meeting in Atlanta but made it clear to Moses that his main interest was voter registration, not sit-in demonstrations. He suggested SNCC send students to Mississippi to do registration work. Although not yet an official SNCC staff member, Moses had planted the seed of an idea that would shift the Southern movement—and the efforts of Black youth—away from integration and toward a direct challenge to Southern white power: voter registration in the most resistant state in the South.

IN JULY 1960, SNCC chair Marion Barry and other SNCC representatives appeared briefly before the platform committees of the Democratic and Republican Conventions. He told the platform writers to "stop playing political football with the civil rights of eighteen million Negro Americans" and to take immediate action to integrate public schools, expand job opportunities for Blacks in the federal government, and give home rule to Washington, DC.[12] In August 1960, Barry wrote members of Congress to explain what motivated Southern students. "We want all the rights, opportunities and responsibilities enjoyed by any other American, no more, no less, and we want these things now. . . . We call upon Congress to work to strengthen and implement the 1957 and 1960 voting legislation and to work toward a Constitutional Amendment that will encourage, rather than discourage, every qualified citizen to register and vote."[13]

Barry's letter to Congress and his testimony before the party platform committees demonstrated that the students were interested in more than lunch counter sit-ins. They saw themselves as the equal to other civil rights groups, capable of competing with them for the allegiance of the Black public, concerned about issues beyond those traditionally identified as "civil rights."

Also in August, Jane Stembridge spoke to the annual congress of the National Student Association. She told her audience that discrimination existed everywhere in America, not just in the South. SNCC, she said, would create "an unbroken chain" among students nationally that would "branch out with full force into broader areas, especially . . . into the political arena."[14] But the new organization had actually done very little to branch out, beyond Moses's trip to Mississippi and Barry's convention pronouncements. SNCC's organizers knew Southern Black college students had set free energies that would not be stilled; SNCC's job was to encourage a continuation of the spontaneity of the sit-ins and to direct it into fighting discrimination everywhere.

SNCC'S FALL CONFERENCE, OCTOBER 1960

SNCC had planned a fall conference for Atlanta from October 14 to 16. Its aims were to consolidate the still scattered and uncoordinated student protest movement and to define its goals and principles. The invitation sent to student groups said the meeting would be "action oriented" and declared,

> Truth comes from being involved and not from observation and specu-
> lation. We are further convinced that only mass action is strong enough
> to force all of America to assume responsibility and that nonviolent
> direct action alone is strong enough to enable all of America to under-
> stand the responsibility she must assume.

The student movement they had begun had national and international implications: "Students must look beyond the South, into the Pentagon, into Europe, and into Russia."[15]

The 1960 Democratic and Republican nominees for president, Massachusetts senator John F. Kennedy and Vice President Richard Nixon, were invited to attend. One hundred forty delegates and eighty observers from sympathetic groups—including the Socialist Party, the Young People's Socialist League, the Southern Conference Education Fund, the Highlander

Folk School, and a newly formed group, Students for a Democratic Society—and Northern campuses attended the conference. They participated in workshops led by students who had initiated sit-ins in their college communities.

Again, Martin Luther King spoke; again, James Lawson attracted the most attention. He scolded the students for losing their "finest hour" when they left jail on bail. Instead of having adults waste time looking for bail money, they should have spent their time changing the system that had put their children in jail. The protests, Lawson said, were the start of a "nonviolent revolution" to "destroy segregation, slavery, serfdom, paternalism [and] industrialization which preserves cheap labor and racial discrimination."[16] Ella Baker—in a speech called "After the Sit-ins, What?"—challenged the students to move beyond integrating lunch counters.

The meeting further solidified the feeling among many of the sit-in students that the protests they had begun barely six months before must not only continue but must enlarge their scope. They felt themselves moving toward even greater confrontation with the system of segregation, indeed with the United States itself. They saw themselves as part of a worldwide movement—against colonialism in Africa and racism and other forms of oppression at home.

Recommendations adopted by the conference demonstrate how rapidly and widely students' vision of their role had grown since the first sit-ins in February 1960. Embracing much more than integration of restaurants and movie theaters, they felt competent to issue opinions on the 1960 presidential election and the weaknesses of American democracy.

What had been the "Temporary Student Nonviolent Coordinating Committee" became more permanent at the Atlanta conference. The delegates approved a Coordinating Committee composed of one representative from each Southern state and the District of Columbia. Local groups—like the Atlanta Committee on Appeal for Human Rights (COAHR) and the Washington Nonviolent Action Group (NAG)—remained independent and autonomous. SNCC's only call to action was an appeal to its constituent groups to engage in Election Day protests demanding Nixon and Kennedy take positive steps on civil rights and to call attention to Southern violations of voting rights.

After King made his conference speech, leaders of the Atlanta sit-in group COAHR asked him to join them at a sit-in at Rich's Department

Store. Atlanta was his home, they argued, and Rich's the most important store. King could not make up his mind. The co-chairman of the Atlanta student sit-in group thought that if Martin Luther King could get arrested in Georgia this close to Election Day, the comments the candidates made—or refused to make—would demonstrate their commitment, or lack of it, to civil rights.

ATLANTA SIT-INS

The Atlanta sit-ins had begun much as they did in other Southern locales and reflected the character of the student leadership and the white opposition as much as they did the older, established patterns of race relations against which the sit-ins revolted. Atlanta had a history as a centerpiece of Black higher education. Its reputation rested more heavily, however, on its history as a center of Black capitalism, of Booker T. Washington's dream writ large. Spelman College students, largely at the urging of Professor Howard Zinn, had staged tentative sit-ins at the city auditorium using tickets for seats reserved for whites purchased in advance. The manager then designated their seats a "Negro section."

ON FEBRUARY 5, 1960, I was sitting in Yates and Milton's drugstore, an off-campus hangout for students at the Atlanta University Center schools. I was a Morehouse College junior, majoring in English, with only the vaguest career plans. An older student, Lonnie C. King Jr., whom I knew as a football player, approached me with that day's copy of Atlanta's Black daily newspaper, the *Atlanta Daily World*. King was a veteran who had been in Oklahoma in 1958 when NAACP youth chapters staged sit-ins there. He thought the Greensboro sit-in would soon become "another isolated incident in black history if others didn't join in to make it become something the kids ought to be doing."[17] A headline in the *World* read "Greensboro Students Sit-In for Third Day."

"Have you read this?" he asked.

"Yes," I replied. "I read the paper."

"What do you think about it?" he wanted to know.

"I think it's great," I replied.

"Don't you think it ought to happen here?" he asked.

"I'm sure it will," I replied. "Someone will make it happen here."

"Why don't *we* make it happen here," he insisted.

Before I could ask "What do you mean *we?*" he said, "You take this side of the drugstore, and I'll take the other, and we'll organize a meeting."

Within a few hours, we had organized twenty students. Over the next few days, with conscious attention to attracting representation from each school, the group grew larger. Atlanta University president Rufus Clement heard though the campus grapevine of our organizing efforts; he invited us to meet with him. We told Dr. Clement we intended to stage sit-in demonstrations; he convinced us to write a statement of grievances to tell the Atlanta community what we were protesting against.

Borrowing liberally from a pamphlet, *Atlanta: A Second Look*, published by a group of Black professionals called the Atlanta Council for Cooperative Action and written by Clark College professor M. Carl Holman and Atlanta University School of Social Work dean Whitney Young, another student, Roslyn Walker, and I wrote *An Appeal for Human Rights*. It began:

> We, the students from the six affiliated institutions forming the Atlanta University Center—Clark, Morehouse, Morris Brown and Spelman Colleges, Atlanta University and the Interdenominational Theological Center . . . pledge our unqualified support to those students in this nation who have recently been engaged in the significant movement to secure certain long-awaited rights and privileges. This protest, like the bus boycott in Montgomery, has shocked many people throughout the world. Why? Because they had not quite realized the unanimity of spirit and purpose which motivates the thinking and action of the great majority of the Negro people. The students who instigate and participate in these sit-down protests are dissatisfied, not only with the existing conditions, but with the snail-like speed at which they are being ameliorated. . . . We do not intend to wait placidly for those rights which are already legally and morally ours to be meted out to us one at a time. . . . We want to state clearly and unequivocally that we cannot tolerate, in a nation professing democracy and among a people professing Christianity, the discriminatory conditions under which the Negro is living today in Atlanta, Georgia—supposedly one of the most progressive cities in the South."

The *Appeal* listed seven areas of grievances: education, jobs, housing, voting, hospitals, law enforcement, and movies, concerts, and restaurants. It closed with a warning: "We must say in all candor that we plan to use every legal and non-violent means at our disposal to secure full citizenship rights as members of this great democracy of ours."[18]

Signed by representatives of the student governments at all six schools, and paid for with money solicited from novelist Lillian Smith by Dr. Clement, the *Appeal* was printed as a full-page ad in each of Atlanta's daily newspapers on March 9, 1960. The reaction was immediate. Georgia governor Ernest Vandiver said the *Appeal* sounded "as if it had been written in Moscow, if not Peking."

"Obviously, it was not written by students," Vandiver continued, adding, it was a "left-wing statement calculated to breed dissatisfaction, discontent, discord, and evil." But Atlanta mayor William B. Hartsfield said it represented "the legitimate aspirations of young people throughout the nation and the entire world."[19]

Six days later, in actions coordinated with split-second accuracy, two hundred students sat in at downtown restaurants and cafeterias—the Greyhound and Trailways bus stations, the train station, the city hall, county courthouse, and Georgia State Capitol cafeterias, and a cafeteria in a federal office building. Seventy-seven students were arrested under a new trespass law the legislature had passed on February 16 in anticipation of sit-ins in Georgia.

I led the group to the city hall. A large sign on the lawn outside announced "City Hall Cafeteria—the Public Is Welcome." When my group approached the cashier at the end of a steam-table buffet line, we were told the cafeteria was open to city hall employees only, despite the sign's invitation. "But," I protested, "you have a large sign outside that says 'City Hall Cafeteria—the Public Is Welcome.'"

"We don't mean it," she said and called the police who came and locked us up.

I was summoned to an arraignment hearing, representing the group arrested with me. My lawyers were Donald L. Hollowell and Austin T. Walden. Walden, the dean of Georgia's Black lawyers, was elderly; when the judge asked me how I pled to the charges, I turned to Walden—he was, it appeared, asleep on his feet. I turned frantically to Hollowell who whispered loudly, "Not guilty, you fool!"

I had the presence of mind to drop those last words. I said, "Not guilty." I was bound over to a grand jury and, with the others, released from jail about seven that night. We celebrated at Paschal's Restaurant with a chicken dinner—heroes on our campuses, proud to have joined the South-wide student revolt.

The first Atlanta sit-ins brought an immediate response, but no action, and proof of serious divisions over tactics and strategy among adult Black Atlantans. Most argued that the one-day sit-in had been enough and that the legal cases raised by the arrests would eventually result in integrating the public lunch counters where sit-ins had occurred. On the advice of sympathetic adults, the committee of Atlanta students decided to focus on winning improved employment for Blacks at stores with heavy Black patronage—two A&P grocery stores in Black neighborhoods were chosen. After fruitless negotiations, picketing began on April 22.

But student leaders were mindful that their colleagues across the South had done more than stage one sit-in for one day. They wanted an opportunity to further demonstrate their impatience and rally student support. It came when Lonnie King announced that students would march on the state capitol on May 17, the sixth anniversary of the 1954 Supreme Court *Brown* decision.

Governor Vandiver ordered state highway patrolmen, armed with sticks, fire hoses, and tear gas, to surround the capitol. If a demonstrator stepped on the capitol grounds, he warned, "appropriate action" would be taken. Mayor Hartsfield said, in contrast, "It is none of my business, probably, but if I were governor, I would invite them inside [the capitol] to see that wonderful museum." Two thousand students marched. A block from the capitol, they were turned away by Atlanta police chief Herbert Jenkins.

When the school term ended, most students left. The leadership of the committee, however, was Atlanta-based. They determined to continue their activity to win jobs for Blacks and to spend the summer soliciting support from an obviously divided Black community. We began printing a mimeographed leaflet for weekly Sunday distribution in churches; we convinced two radio stations serving Black Atlanta to donate time for weekly shows on the student movement. We created a presentation called "The Student Movement and You" and appeared before church, civic, and social clubs in Black Atlanta. We carried on a summer-long campaign against job discrimination at the two A&P stores; a frequent picketer was Robert Moses.

We decided to resume sit-in demonstrations, this time aimed not at safe targets like city hall or the bus and train stations. This time the target would be Rich's, the largest department store in the South. Black adults warned against choosing Rich's. It enjoyed a near-perfect relationship with its customers, white and Black. Its unofficial slogan was "the only thing you can't return to Rich's is your husband." It was the first Atlanta retail store to tell its clerks to call Black customers "Mr." and "Mrs.," the first to extend credit to Blacks, and the first to remove segregated drinking fountains. Large numbers of Blacks worked at Rich's—but none in sales, managerial, or other white-collar jobs.

The summer sit-ins at Rich's were hit-and-run, as students avoided being arrested. But on June 24, Lonnie King and sit-inners were picked up by police. Waiting for them at the police station was Richard Rich, the company's president. He told the students his Jewish origins made him sympathetic to their aspirations and also a special target for the wrath of local racists. If sit-ins in his store were stopped, he said, he would call together all the city's merchants to begin negotiations for an end to segregation at all the city's lunch counters and restaurants. The students refused. If Rich's integrated, the other stores would follow. As he left in anger, Rich said he didn't care if Blacks ever patronized his store.

When students returned in the fall, the "fall campaign" began, prompted at least in part by the knowledge that over one hundred cities had integrated lunch counters since the Greensboro protests began seven months before. On Wednesday, October 19, at exactly 11:00 a.m., there were large-scale demonstrations at Rich's and seven other downtown stores, demanding integration of everything—lunch counters, restrooms, restaurants, and changing rooms. Pickets surrounded Rich's, and students issued a plea for a boycott of the entire downtown area. The stores refused to negotiate—the students responded with harassment sit-ins, making the city call out hundreds of extra policemen and detectives. One of the people who would be arrested was Martin Luther King. His arrest would literally change history—by affecting the outcome of the 1960 presidential election.

KENNEDYS AND KINGS: THE BLUE BOMB

Two days after the Atlanta SNCC conference ended, on October 18, Lonnie King called his pastor, Martin Luther King, to ask him again to join the Atlanta students. "You are the spiritual leader of the movement, and you were born in Atlanta, Georgia," Lonnie King told him. "I think it might add tremendous impetus if you would go."[20]

"Where are you going tomorrow, L.C.?" Dr. King asked.

"I'm going to be on the bridge at Rich's," Lonnie answered.

"Well, I'll meet you on the bridge tomorrow at ten o'clock!" King said.[21]

Lonnie King, Martin Luther King, and thirty-three students sought service at a cafeteria on a pedestrian bridge separating two sides of Rich's. Failing to be arrested there, they took an elevator to the Magnolia Room, the store's best restaurant. There, on orders of the chairman of Rich's board, police arrested them under the newly passed anti-trespassing law.

At an arraignment hearing, Dr. King refused to post bond. "I cannot accept bond," he said. "I will stay in jail one year or ten years." All thirty-five were taken away for what would be Martin Luther King's first night in jail.[22] Once in jail, the students and King heard bulletins about how their arrest, especially King's, was shaking the city and the country.

On Thursday, October 20, over two thousand students picketed in downtown Atlanta; twenty-five more were arrested. Within two days, telegrams supporting and opposing were arriving at city hall by the bagful. Atlanta police were reporting increasing tension between Black picketers and white thugs in downtown Atlanta.

On Saturday, October 22, Harris Wofford, now a civil rights advisor in John F. Kennedy's presidential campaign, decided to do what he could, on his own, to get King released from jail. He began calling Atlantans he knew; one of them, attorney Morris Abram, agreed to call Mayor Hartsfield. Hartsfield was at that moment in negotiation with some members of the adult Black leadership and proposed an end to demonstrations and a beginning of negotiations. But King and the jailed students refused to be released on bail; they wanted all charges against them dropped. But Hartsfield didn't have the power to drop King's charge. King's charge could be dropped only by the state prosecutor or the complainant, Rich's Department Store. Richard Rich was in turmoil. He had cried when he learned his board chairman had caused Martin Luther King to be removed from his store in handcuffs. But he was afraid to drop the charges; if he did, Blacks would insist he integrate everything in the store, and angry white customers would go elsewhere.

But when Abram told Hartsfield he'd received a call from Wofford, Hartsfield decided he would announce that a truce had been reached, although none had, and that candidate Kennedy himself had called to inquire about freeing King. This announcement would not only associate Hartsfield's imaginary truce with Kennedy, making it appear more solid, but also help Kennedy in Northern states with large numbers of Black votes.

Wofford panicked, reminding Hartsfield he had acted alone, not for the candidate, and begged him to do nothing until Wofford had cleared it with Kennedy himself. Wofford could not reach him; neither could Hartsfield. Finally, the mayor announced to the Black delegation that Kennedy was supporting efforts to solve Atlanta's sit-in crisis and to free Martin Luther King. A reporter in the room sent the story of Kennedy's involvement out on the national wire. When Hartsfield told Wofford what he had done, Wofford panicked again; campaign officials angrily issued a statement that Kennedy had asked only that "an inquiry be made."

Hartsfield spent the rest of the day in negotiations; King and the jailed students continued to demand that charges against them be dropped before they agreed to leave jail. Finally, Hartsfield reached an agreement; he ordered that students held in the city jail be released unconditionally and promised that King and those held in the county jail would be out on Monday. There would be no demonstrations on Monday, the Black delegation agreed. Hartsfield intended to visit Richard Rich and the state prosecutor separately and tell each one that the other had agreed to drop the charges.[23]

But when a crowd gathered outside the county jail on Monday, October 24, to embrace the soon-to-be released prisoners, they met a shocking development instead. The past May, while Martin and Coretta had been driving author Lillian Smith from their home to Emory Hospital, he had been stopped by a policeman who charged King—for three months then a Georgia resident—with driving without a proper Georgia license. A DeKalb County judge had sentenced King to twelve months in jail, suspended, and fined him twenty-five dollars. Now the judge was asking Fulton County to hold King until a hearing was held on whether his arrest at Rich's violated the terms of his suspended sentence.

While another vigil waited outside the jail on Tuesday, King was taken to DeKalb County in leg irons and arm shackles. Nearly two hundred supporters crowded into the courtroom, including Roy Wilkins and four presidents from the Atlanta University schools. King's suspension was revoked. Ordered to spend four months at hard labor on a state road gang, his appeal bond was denied, and he was immediately taken away. Wyatt T. Walker began to work the phones, sure that once inside a Georgia prison, where men were killed for a pack of cigarettes, King's life was worthless.

In Washington, Harris Wofford drafted a protest statement for Kennedy to issue; the campaign talked to Governor Vandiver who agreed to release King only if Kennedy made no statement. So, when Mrs. King called Wofford for help, he could not tell her of the agreement with the Georgia governor. If it became public, Governor Vandiver would keep her husband in jail.[24] Over a beer after work, Wofford talked it over with campaign aide Louis Martin, a Black newspaper publisher from Chicago. If only someone important would call Mrs. King, they could privately put out the word in Black America. They considered Adlai Stevenson, but Stevenson refused to talk to her.

Later that night, King was rousted from his cell in the DeKalb County jail, handcuffed and shackled again, placed in a police car, and driven off into the night. When King's lawyer called the jail Friday evening bearing a writ of habeas corpus, he was told his client was gone, transferred in the night to Reidsville, Georgia's maximum-security prison. Wofford and Louis Martin conferred again, and Wofford called Sargent Shriver, Kennedy's brother-in-law and political advisor, and asked him to get Kennedy to call Mrs. King. "If the Senator would only call Mrs. King and wish her well," Wofford said, "it would reverberate through the Negro community in the United States. All he's got to do is say he's thinking about her and he hopes everything will be all right. . . . He can even say he doesn't have all the facts in the case."[25]

Shriver took Mrs. King's number and, when Kennedy's aides left the candidate alone, told him he ought to make the call. "What the hell," Kennedy said. "That's a decent thing to do. Why not? Get her on the phone." Shriver did, and when Mrs. King answered the phone, he said, "Just a minute, Mrs. King, for Senator Kennedy."

Kennedy said, "I know this must be very hard for you. I understand that you are expecting a baby, and I just wanted you to know that I was thinking about you and Dr. King. If there is anything I can do to help, please feel free to call on me."[26]

At Reidsville, King was held in solitary confinement, standard procedure for a new prisoner undergoing processing. Black prisoners sent him messages that they were going to stage a hunger strike in his support. He discouraged it.

When Robert Kennedy discovered reporters were inquiring about his brother's phone call, he cursed Louis Martin and Wofford and accused them of losing the campaign. He ordered them to do nothing—no literature, no press conferences, nothing that would attract attention. When Senator Kennedy landed in New York that night, a reporter asked him about the call. "She is a friend of mine," he said of Mrs. King, whom he had never met and never would meet, "and I was concerned about the situation."[27] The election was nine days away.

In Atlanta that morning, King's lawyer Albert Hollowell had convinced the judge to change his mind and release King on a two-thousand-dollar bond. Hollowell didn't know Robert Kennedy had called the judge too. A band of supporters flew to Reidsville in four private planes. After eight days, in three different jails, King was free.

One hundred well-wishers met King's car caravan on the highway leading from the Fulton County airport where he landed; they tumbled out of their cars into the road and sang "We Shall Overcome." At a welcome-home celebration at Ebenezer Baptist Church, King's father delivered the words he had promised to Wofford.

"I had expected to vote against Senator Kennedy because of his religion," he said to a standing-room-only crowd. "But now he can be my president, Catholic or whatever he is. It took courage to call my daughter-in-law at a time like this. He has the moral courage to stand up for what he knows is right. I've got all my votes and I've got a suitcase, and I'm going to take them up there and dump them in his lap." Abernathy told the crowd it was time "to take off [their] Nixon buttons."[28]

When Wofford was asked about reports that "a brother" of Senator Kennedy had called the judge to secure King's release, Wofford angrily denied the story. Robert Kennedy's assistant John Seigenthaler did too. That night Seigenthaler told Robert Kennedy about the rumor and denial. Kennedy said, "You'd better retract it."[29] It turns out Robert Kennedy had called the judge from a New York telephone booth to say any decent American judge would free King by sundown.

The *New York Times* carried a two-inch story on page 22 saying Kennedy had called Mrs. King; Nixon had no response to King's jailing.

Wofford and Louis Martin had what they wanted: a news item reflecting favorably on their candidate that had passed by white America almost unnoticed.

The next day Martin and Wofford told Shriver that the news—forgotten in the white press—was causing a major shift in Black voter sentiment. Martin and Wofford would have to trumpet the two Kennedy telephone calls to Black America without letting white America know—or reminding those few who did know. Black newspapers—all but two of them weeklies—could not reach the voters in time. They set up a phony committee of Black clergymen, the Freedom Crusade Committee, to avoid any linkage to the Kennedy campaign, as sponsors of a pamphlet, printed in blue, which read "'No Comment Nixon' Versus a Candidate with a Heart, Senator Kennedy" and highlighting Kennedy's call to Mrs. King. Martin Luther King Jr. had not endorsed Kennedy, only saying that he was "deeply indebted to Senator Kennedy, who served as a great force in making my release possible." By Sunday, October 30, over fifty thousand copies of the "blue bomb" were already printed.[30]

Louis Martin began calling Black newspapers. The front page of the *Washington Afro-American* newspaper read: "King Freed After Kennedy Intervention." On Tuesday, November 1, Shriver ordered 250,000 more pamphlets printed and then 250,000 more printed for distribution in Illinois alone. At dawn on Sunday, November 6, another large shipment was sent by Greyhound bus to Virginia and North and South Carolina for distribution in Black churches.

JOHN F. KENNEDY WINS

When Eisenhower had been reelected president in 1956, about 40 percent of Black voters supported the Republican ticket. Four years later, in a thirty-point shift, Black votes went Democratic roughly 70–30, a percentage greater than Kennedy's margin in Michigan, New Jersey, Pennsylvania, Illinois, and North and South Carolina. In the Memphis bellwether Black Ward Five, the Democratic vote rose from 36 to 67 percent; in eight Atlanta Black precincts, it rose from 14 to 29 percent. Nixon won only 10 to 12 percent of the Black vote, compared to the 39 percent Eisenhower had won four years earlier.

Kennedy had employed an "association" strategy—creating the impression that he was a committed civil rights activist. His narrow victory taught him that this minimalist civil rights strategy, bolstered by high-profile appointments to his campaign staff, was endorsement of a prescription for presidential moderation on civil rights. He liked to quote Thomas Jefferson: "Great innovation should never be imposed on slender majorities."[31] On the day after the election, the Republican Party chair said the GOP had taken Black votes for granted. President Eisenhower later remarked that "a couple of phone calls" had lost Nixon the election; Nixon blamed the Eisenhower White House for not releasing a statement on King's arrest and jailing.

The final outcome was the supreme irony. Nixon had entered the race against Kennedy as the civil rights favorite; Kennedy was the Democrat civil rights supporters least wanted to win the nomination. He had voted for the jury trial amendment to the 1957 Civil Rights Law, weakening the possibility of winning convictions of racists who blocked the right to vote, and had named Lyndon Johnson his vice presidential running mate, frightening many civil rights supporters who saw Johnson as a Southerner, not the Westerner he eventually transformed himself into. Nixon had a credible civil rights record. As vice president, he used his chairmanship of the President's Committee on Government Contract Compliance to win jobs for Blacks in the nation's capital, and he had fought for passage of a stronger 1957 Civil Rights Act. Unlike Kennedy, Nixon had a personal relationship with Martin Luther King; they had met together in the White House. Nixon expressed regret over Eisenhower's failure to issue a statement; Kennedy, on the other hand, was worried that confirmation of his dependence on Black votes for his victory might alienate racist whites, making governing more difficult. As a result, he let it be known that the Kennedy administration didn't anticipate any changes in the filibuster rule or introducing any new civil rights legislation.

Two telephone calls had shifted an election and elected a president. That the two calls originated in a Southern anti-segregation protest and that the most prominent protest leader was the subject of the call showed the power the protest movement had, even at this early stage. That two telephone calls could achieve this, demonstrated that Black America was an identifiably separate political culture that marched to a different rhythm, spoke its own language, and—at least on November 8, 1960—saw its fate tied to the fortunes of the Southern civil rights movement personified by the Reverend Dr. Martin Luther King Jr.

And the movement in Atlanta continued on.

ATLANTA SIT-INS CONCLUDE

Atlanta lunch counters integrated on September 28, 1961, eighteen months after the sit-ins there began. As elsewhere, the Atlanta sit-ins were a mild challenge to the established racial order. *An Appeal for Human Rights*, published in the daily papers on March 9, defied Atlanta to live up to its reputation, to dare to join the modern world whose Southern capital it aspired to be. By announcing "unqualified support" for the new sit-in movement sweeping the Upper South, the *Appeal* instantly differentiated the students from the strategy of legal action and polite cross-racial negotiations employed by Black and white elites. It placed racial issues in a moral context—asserting that segregation was intolerable "in a nation professing democracy and among a people professing Christianity."

Black objection to Atlanta's apartheid was nothing new. What was new was the strength of the language used. The *Appeal* placed the struggle in an international context, charging, "America is fast losing the respect of other nations by the poor example which she sets in the area of race relations." It issued a call to action: "We must say in all candor that we plan to use every legal and non-violent means at our disposal."

We knew this was going to be a longer struggle. The world out there was segregated, and we could use what we'd done in this instance to attack it in those instances too. In employing these broad terms, and promising to adopt new means, the Atlanta students were joining, perhaps unknowingly, a larger and older Black tradition of issuing petitions of appeal dating back to David Walker's "Appeal to the Colored Citizens of the World" in 1829 and to the 1952 petition by W. E. B. Du Bois, William Patterson, and Paul Robeson called "We Charge Genocide: The Crime of Government against the Negro People."

The Atlanta students' *Appeal* did not match these earlier efforts in stridency or scope, but it did place the discussion of civil rights under a broader rubric of "human rights." "We felt that 'civil rights' was too limited," Lonnie King said. "When you talk about 'human rights' you're talking about not just the right to go to a lunch counter. You're talking about other kinds of things. In fact, you're bordering on natural rights that should be granted to you just by virtue of your having been created and in this world."[32]

THE ATLANTA SIT-IN MOVEMENT ended with more of a whimper than a bang. As was true of other sit-in locales, students whose sit-ins had predicted a departure from the standard behind-the-scenes negotiations between Black leaders and powerful whites soon found that when their action precipitated negotiations, the Black seats on the negotiating table that followed were filled by the very figures their actions had seemingly replaced.

Black adults and white leaders agreed on March 7, 1961—almost a year to the date from the sit-in's initiation—that the sit-in protests would stop, but lunch counters wouldn't integrate until several months later.

On Monday night, March 10, 1961, a tumultuous mass meeting was held at a local church as leaders who had agreed to the delayed schedule for integrating lunch counters tried to placate a community angry that their year-long sacrifices would not be rewarded for nearly half a year more. "The sit-in revealed their limitations as an ongoing strategy," historian William Chafe wrote. "Once the demonstrations ended, control over negotiations reverted to those who exercised power in the first place. They set the rules. They determined the framework for discussion."[33] On September 28, 1961, seventy-five Atlanta stores integrated their lunch counters. Atlanta became the 104th city to integrate lunch counters since the sit-ins began in Greensboro on February 1, 1960.

NEW PERSONALITIES JOIN THE MOVEMENT

Some new personalities, meanwhile, were joining the movement. On August 1, 1960, the Reverend Wyatt Tee Walker replaced Ella Baker as executive secretary of SCLC. As a New Jersey high school student in the 1940s, he had joined the Young Communist League. He became the pastor of a church in Petersburg, Virginia, in 1952 and led the successful Prayer Pilgrimage in Richmond in 1959. Walker commanded respect from the ministers who ran SCLC that Ella Baker could not. He was one of them;

he was a minister—*and he was a man*. Baker had been critical—publicly and privately—of King's leadership, arguing that deifying King stunted the growth of grassroots leadership. Walker rejected *any* criticism of King and referred to him as "leader."[34]

In November 1960, Marion Barry resigned as SNCC chairman to return to school. Elected in his place was a student from South Carolina State College, Charles McDew. Born in Massillon, Ohio, McDew was one of the few sit-in leaders not native to the South. After Black students were refused admission to various Christian churches during a "church-in" in Orangeburg, South Carolina, and then were admitted to a synagogue, McDew converted to Judaism. His election was the result of internal tensions within SNCC in which various factions were pitted against each other. The divisions were generally these: The Atlantans, led by Lonnie King, believed segregation could be nickel-and-dimed to death; economic boycotts would force white racists to do what they did not want to. They had won the fight to have the SNCC office located in Atlanta. The Nashville students, heavily influenced by the radical pacifism and nonviolence of James Lawson, believed Christian love and redemptive suffering would conquer evil. They had won the fight to choose the chairman. McDew won and served as chair until 1963.

ROCK HILL, SOUTH CAROLINA, STUDENTS

Students from Friendship Junior College in Rock Hill, South Carolina, had joined the sit-in movement eleven days after the first Greensboro sit-in. Within a month, seventy students had been arrested. A boycott of segregated establishments followed and continued through the summer and the fall. Most of the students were members of the local CORE or NAACP chapter. While attending a CORE workshop in December 1960 they adopted the idea of staying in jail without posting bond—the "jail, no bail" plan that Lawson had suggested at the first SNCC conference. But so far, only a few students from Florida A&M, and the Atlanta students who had vowed to stay in jail until Mayor Hartsfield's machinations released them, had followed this strategy.

On January 31, 1961, the eve of the anniversary of the Greensboro sit-in, nine students and CORE field secretary Tom Gaither sat in at a segregated lunch counter. Found guilty the next day, they were sentenced to thirty days in jail or a $100 fine. Gaither and eight students refused to pay.

CORE sent out an appeal for help. At a SNCC meeting in early February, the fifteen students present voted unanimously to support the Rock Hill students. Mary Ann Smith, a student at Morris Brown College in Atlanta, suggested they send students to join them and volunteered to be one of the four who would go, but she was talked out of going by her younger sister, Ruby Doris.

Ruby Doris Smith Robinson
Ruby Doris Smith was born in Atlanta on April 25, 1942, the second oldest in a family of seven children. Her family home was attached to a beauty shop—run by her mother—and a store, run by her father. When Ruby Doris was in high school her father became a Baptist minister. She was a debutante in 1958 and a majorette with the Price High School marching band. In 1959, she entered Spelman College; the Greensboro sit-ins began in the second semester of her freshman year. Her older sister, Mary Ann, was an early member of the Committee on Appeal for Human Rights; she signed the *Appeal*, published in the Atlanta newspapers, as secretary of the Morris Brown Student Government Association. Ruby Doris later told Howard Zinn:

> I began to think right away about it happening in Atlanta, but I wasn't ready to act on my own. . . . I told my older sister, who was on the Student Council at Morris Brown College, to put me on the list. And when two hundred students were selected for the first demonstration [March 15], I was among them. I went through the food line in the restaurant at the State Capitol with six other students, but when we got to the cashier, she wouldn't take our money. She ran upstairs to get the Governor. The Lieutenant-Governor came down and told us to leave. We didn't, and went to the county jail.[35]

BY THE FALL, Ruby Doris had become an important leader in the Atlanta student movement and the newly developing SNCC. She was joined on the trip to Rock Hill by Diane Nash, Charles Jones of Johnson C. Smith University in Charlotte, and Charles Sherrod of Virginia Union. They were arrested and spent the next thirty days in jail.

SNCC's first experience with "jail-no-bail" was a failure; no students joined them. But the jail experience itself served to give them a chance to reinforce their commitment to the movement and make plans for the future. They had all made a break with their lives as students; free to devote full time to the movement, they spent their jail time discussing what that movement would be. "You get ideas in jail," Charles Sherrod said. "You talk with other young people you've never seen. Right away we recognize each other. . . . We're up all night, sharing creativity, planning action. You learn the truth in prison, you learn wholeness. You find out the difference between being dead and alive."[36]

TWELVE

THE FREEDOM RIDES

JAMES FARMER

James Farmer was born in Marshall, Texas, on January 12, 1920. In 1941, he graduated from Howard University's theological school and became the race relations secretary for the Fellowship of Reconciliation (FOR). While living in the interracial Fellowship House in Chicago with other pacifists, Farmer organized sit-ins at a segregated skating rink and restaurants in Chicago in 1942. FOR authorized Farmer to begin an anti-segregation group in Chicago in April 1942.

"We began," Farmer said, "what I believe to be the first organized civil rights sit in in American history." It was successful. Twenty-eight Blacks and whites sat-in at the Jack Sprat Coffee House in May 1942; the police were called but refused to make arrests, and the protesters were served.

That anti-segregation group FOR had authorized Farmer to start, in part to keep more confrontational tactics away from the organization, what would become the Congress of Racial Equality. CORE's founders were four whites and two Blacks, Farmer and another young African American leader, Bayard Rustin. All were pacifists, all active in the student pacifist movement, and all believed discrimination must be challenged directly. Three had served jail terms as conscientious objectors.

FOR created a race relations department in the fall of 1942 and hired Farmer and Bayard Rustin. As they traveled, they set up CORE groups— in Denver, Syracuse, Colorado Springs, New York, and elsewhere. By 1947, there were thirteen affiliated groups, none of them in the South.

———

ON JULY 16, 1944, Irene Morgan boarded a Greyhound bus bound for Baltimore, in Hayes Store, Virginia. She stood up at first but in Saluda, Virginia, took a seat three rows from the back, in front of a white couple. Another white couple boarded, and the driver asked her to move. She asked if she could change seats with a white passenger behind her. The driver refused and fetched the Middlesex County sheriff and a deputy. They dragged her off the bus.

"He touched me," she said. "That's when I kicked him in a very bad place. He hobbled off, and another one came on. He was trying to put his hands on me to get me off. I was going to bite him, but he was dirty, so I clawed him instead. I ripped his shirt. We were both pulling at each other. He said he'd use his nightstick. I said, 'We'll whip each other!'"[1]

In court, Morgan represented herself. She pled guilty to resisting arrest and paid a hundred-dollar fine but refused to pay ten dollars and court costs on the charge she had violated segregation laws. She was an interstate passenger, she said. Virginia's segregation laws did not apply to her.

Plessy v. Ferguson had validated Louisiana's segregation laws in 1896. In 1910, with Ku Klux Klansman Edward White sitting as chief justice, the Supreme Court ruled in *Chiles v. Chesapeake and Ohio Railway* that segregation laws applied to interstate travelers. The NAACP took Morgan's appeal to Virginia's Supreme Court, lost, and appealed to the US Supreme Court—and on June 3, 1949, Irene Morgan won![2] In December 1958, a Howard University student named Bruce Boynton was arrested at the white-only bus terminal in Richmond and subsequently convicted on a trespassing charge. Two years later, in *Boynton v. Virginia*, the US Supreme Court overturned his conviction, extending the *Morgan v. Virginia* decision, ruling that state laws segregating lunch counters, waiting rooms, and restrooms that served interstate travelers were unconstitutional.

IN JUNE 1943, Farmer became national chairman of CORE. CORE married pacifism and civil rights, using Gandhian tactics to achieve social change. Farmer moved to New York in 1943 and in 1945 resigned from FOR and spent the next two years working as a union organizer in Virginia, North Carolina, Ohio, and Illinois. Fired in 1947, he became student field secretary for the League for Industrial Democracy, a socialist organization, and was active in the New York CORE chapter. In 1955, he worked for the American Federation of State, County and Municipal Employees (AFSCME) in New York, and in 1959 was hired by Roy Wilkins as director of the youth department of the NAACP.

In 1946, while Farmer was a union organizer, CORE mounted a "Journey of Reconciliation" through the Upper South to test the Supreme Court's decision in *Boynton v. Virginia.* One of CORE's founders, George Houser, and Bayard Rustin toured the Upper South to scout a route for the early Freedom Ride; NAACP branches offered them and their future riders lodging and meeting places. On April 9, 1947, sixteen men left Washington, DC, on the ride—half white, half Black—en route to fifteen cities in the upper South: North Carolina, Kentucky, Virginia, and Tennessee. They met some violence in Chapel Hill; some were arrested in Ashville, North Carolina, and Culpeper and Amherst, Virginia; and Rustin and two others eventually served thirty-day sentences on a North Carolina chain gang. The ride received some publicity in Black newspapers and gave CORE a visibility it had not had.

From 1947 to 1954, CORE held a series of annual summer "Action Institutes," training participants in nonviolent action. Baltimore CORE—with students from Morgan State—integrated restaurants in downtown Baltimore in 1954. With seventeen chapters in 1951, CORE chapters in Chicago, Omaha, Wichita, Los Angeles, and Berkeley concentrated on employment, but in the late 1950s, the organization began to decline. By 1957, there were only seven groups affiliated with CORE. Only seven people attended the 1957 CORE convention: four national officers and three delegates. The organization tried to rebuild; its field representatives had been Black, but its membership base almost exclusively white. Martin Luther King agreed to sign a fundraising letter, and the organization's finances began to improve. In 1958, Gordon Carey, who spent a year in jail as a draft resister, was hired, and in 1959 Marvin Rich became community relations director.

When the Greensboro sit-ins began, on February 1, 1960, the four students had approached NAACP president Dr. George Simpkins for help; he had called the CORE national office, which sent Gordon Carey to Greensboro. In 1960, Tom Gaither joined the CORE staff. In early 1961 James Farmer left the NAACP to return to CORE as its national director. Farmer said that when he told Roy Wilkins he was leaving, Wilkins told him, "You're going to be riding a mustang pony—while I'm riding a dinosaur."[3]

Farmer's first day on the job was February 1, 1961, the first anniversary of the Greensboro sit-ins. CORE field secretary Tom Gaither was being sentenced to thirty days in jail in Rock Hill that day, but the organization had no visibility and little actual presence throughout the South. The movement was moving, and CORE was not moving with it. Gordon Carey suggested a second Journey of Reconciliation, like the first one in 1947. Farmer said, "Let's call it a Freedom Ride!"

THE FREEDOM RIDES

For Farmer, the Freedom Rides were to be a continuation of the sit-ins— "putting the movement on wheels." They would leave Washington May 4, traveling south through Virginia, the Carolinas, Georgia, Alabama, and Mississippi, planning to arrive in New Orleans on May 17 for the seventh anniversary of the 1954 Supreme Court *Brown* decision. In April 1961, Farmer sent letters outlining CORE's plans to test the new Supreme Court decision to President Kennedy, Attorney General Robert Kennedy, the FBI, and the Greyhound and Trailways bus companies. He received no replies.

The Freedom Riders included seven whites and six Blacks. They were Farmer; a white couple, sixty-year-old Dr. Walter Bergman and his wife, Frances Bergman; James Peck, a veteran white pacifist who had been on the 1947 ride and heir to the Peck & Peck fortune; the Reverend Elton B. Cox; Charlotte DeVries, a white writer from New York; white World War II navy captain Albert Bigelow; Henry Thomas, a Howard University senior from St. Augustine, Florida; Jimmy McDonald, a part-time CORE staffer and folksinger; John Lewis; a white CORE field secretary Genevieve Hughes; Joe Perkins, a CORE staffer; and Ed Blankenheim, a white CORE activist. Farmer was the captain of the Greyhound bus group; Peck, for the Trailways group.

Simeon Booker, the Washington correspondent for *Ebony* and *Jet*, also went along. The ride proceeded without much difficulty until May 8, when Perkins was arrested in Charlotte for sitting in a white shoeshine chair; he was acquitted on May 10. In Rock Hill on May 9, Lewis and Bigelow were beaten. Lewis described what happened. He and Bigelow entered the terminal and saw young white men lounging in the lobby.

"Other side, nigger," one said.

Lewis replied, "I have a right to go in there on the grounds of the Supreme Court in the *Boynton* case."

"Shit on that," one of them said.

"The next thing I knew, a fist smashed the right side of my head. Then another hit me square in the face. As I fell to the floor I could feel feet kicking me so hard in the sides. I could taste blood in my mouth."[4] Both Lewis and Bigelow refused to press charges, and no one was arrested.

That night, Lewis left the Freedom Ride temporarily for a scholarship interview in Philadelphia—to live and work in India; James Lawson had won the same scholarship in 1954. Jim Peck and Henry Thomas were arrested in Winnsboro, South Carolina, but the riders had no difficulty in Sumpter or Camden, South Carolina, or in Augusta or Athens, Georgia.

They arrived in Atlanta on May 13. Met by a large group of students, they had dinner that evening with Martin Luther King. King told them he was proud of them and proud to be a member of CORE's Action Council. During the meal, King whispered to *Jet*'s Simeon Booker, "You will never make it through Alabama."[5]

That night, Farmer's mother called to say that his father died.

On Sunday, May 14—Mother's Day—Farmer left for the funeral. He was replaced by Perkins as the leader of the riders on the Greyhound bus. After stops in Tallapoosa and Heflin, Alabama, the driver told Perkins a mob was waiting for them in Anniston. In Anniston, the Greyhound riders were met by a large mob of white men carrying clubs, bricks, iron pipes, and knives who shouted for the riders to come out. Two undercover Alabama state investigators ran to the front of the bus to keep the door from being forced open while the mob began to slash the tires and pound on the windows with iron pipes. The Freedom Riders shouted for the driver to pull away before the bus was disabled; he left Anniston at a high rate of speed, with fifty carloads in hot pursuit. As the tires went flat, the driver pulled to the side of the road, and the mob surrounded the bus.

The mob used bricks and an axe to smash the windows one by one, scattering broken glass on the terrified Freedom Riders inside. They broke open the luggage compartment underneath and again tried to force open the door. One threw a firebomb through a broken-out window; seats caught on fire, and as the Freedom Riders moved toward the door in the front, the mob barricaded it shut from the outside. Finally, Alabama state investigator E. L. Cowling pulled out his revolver and waved it at the mob, and they fell back. He got the door open, and Albert Bigelow herded the passengers through the door away from the flames and smoke as the mob took wild swings at those escaping. Henry Thomas fell to the ground from a head blow. Attacks on the others continued until Alabama state policemen finally arrived and fired shots into the air. The mob retreated, and the policemen took the beaten and bruised passengers to Anniston Hospital.

Meanwhile, the Trailways bus pulled into Anniston an hour behind the Greyhound bus. Jim Peck led the Freedom Riders into a silent terminal and the whites-only restaurant. They reboarded the bus with their sandwiches. Two students who had joined the ride in Atlanta, Charles Person, a Morehouse College freshman, and Herbert Harris, a Morris Brown College sophomore, sat in front. The driver left the bus and talked with a group of rough-looking white men. Eight of them jumped on the bus; the driver announced through the microphone, "We have received word that a bus has been burned to the ground and the passengers are being carried to the hospital by the carloads. A mob is waiting for our bus and will do the same to us unless we get these niggers off the front seats."[6]

One of the Freedom Riders said they were all interstate passengers; they could sit wherever they pleased. Before he could finish, one of the mob hit Person in the head; another hit Harris. They pulled the two students into the aisle, kicking and beating them. Peck and Walter Bergman ran from their back seats to the front to protest. One of the white men hit Peck so hard he was knocked backward over two seats, and the mob turned on the two whites. Some held Peck while others beat his face; others stomped on Bergman's chest.

When Mrs. Bergman screamed "Don't beat him anymore! He's my husband!" members of the mob called her a "nigger lover."[7] Bergman was unconscious on the floor; some members of the mob warned others not to kill him. They then dragged Person and Harris back through the aisle and threw them in the back, on top of other passengers. They threw Peck on top of them, dragged Bergman into the back, and then took seats to ensure the racial line would not be crossed again.

The driver boarded the bus with a policeman, who inspected the bloody scene and got off. The driver sped away, taking back roads to the next stop: Birmingham. An FBI informant active in Klavern Palace 13 (the KKK's local units came to be called Klaverns), Gary Thomas Rowe, had told the FBI that the Birmingham police commissioner, "Bull" Connor, had agreed in late April to give the KKK fifteen minutes alone to beat the Freedom Riders; if Klan members were arrested, Connor promised them light sentences. The report had been sent to FBI headquarters in Washington several times. The Birmingham police—part of the conspiracy—had also been warned five times. The FBI special agent in charge told FBI director J. Edgar Hoover that he had given his last warning on Sunday, May 14, to Birmingham detective Tom Cook, an active collaborator with the Klan. Even Birmingham minister and civil rights activist Fred Shuttlesworth knew that the Freedom Riders would be met by the Klan.

Anticipation was so strong that half a dozen reporters, television crews, and photographers were gathered near the downtown bus stations. At the Greyhound bus station, FBI informer and Klansman Rowe learned from the police that the Trailways bus would arrive first; he alerted the mob to move the four blocks to the Trailways terminal. As it parked, the eight white members of the Anniston mob got off first; Charles Person and Jim Peck, covered with blood, stepped off next. "Let's go!" Person said and began to walk through a mob of Klansmen into the white waiting room, with Peck, Bergman, and the others following behind.

A Klansman shouted that they should kill Person, who was Black, because they mistakenly believed Person had hurt the bleeding Peck, a white man. When Peck said Person was not to be harmed, the mob became enraged. Three Klansmen began to beat Person; when Peck came to his defense, a dozen Klansmen beat them both with fists and iron pipes. Rowe joined in the beating.

The other Freedom Riders tried to retreat, but other Klansmen stopped them. Simeon Booker saw Walter Bergman on his hands and knees, trying to find his way through the legs of the men who were beating him. Booker punched a hole through a newspaper for a peephole and, holding it over his face, walked to a Black cab and sped away to the Reverend Shuttlesworth's home.

A white Birmingham man, innocent of the day's events and not connected with the riders or the Klan, came out of the bathroom and was beaten badly enough to be hospitalized. A Black man who had come to pick up his girlfriend was beaten, as was a white photographer from the *Birmingham Post-Herald*. A white radio reporter, broadcasting live from his car, had the car trashed. Fifteen minutes had gone by; the Klansmen dispersed. Two Klansmen driving away came across two Black men talking on a street corner and beat them too.

One by one, the Freedom Riders straggled into Fred Shuttlesworth's home. Part of the mob that had beaten the Freedom Riders on the Greyhound bus had followed them to the hospital; hospital personnel ordered the Freedom Riders to leave. Shuttlesworth sent out a call for volunteer drivers to travel the sixty miles to Anniston and back. "No weapons will be allowed," he said, "not even a toothpick."[8] Soon, eight cars driven by Black clergymen, bristling with rifles and shotguns, pulled away to rescue the embattled Freedom Riders in Anniston.

Back at Shuttlesworth's home, Simeon Booker finally reached John Seigenthaler, special assistant to Attorney General Robert Kennedy. Seigenthaler told Booker that the Justice Department would make sure the right to travel was protected and suggested the job would be easier if the story wasn't widely reported. That would be impossible, Booker said. There were too many reporters there; some of them had been beaten themselves.

The ambulance carrying Jim Peck was turned away from one hospital; at another, he needed fifty-three stitches to close his wounds. From the emergency room operating table, he told reporters, "The going is getting rougher, but I'll be on that bus tomorrow heading for Montgomery." He was discharged from the hospital at 2:00 a.m. and spent the rest of the night on Shuttlesworth's living room couch. In Nashville on Sunday night, members of the Nashville student movement—including John Lewis, en route from Philadelphia to rejoin the CORE Freedom Riders—heard about the Birmingham violence and began to make plans for continuing the Freedom Ride.

ON MONDAY, MAY 15, pictures of the burned-out Greyhound bus, surrounded by the bloodied bodies of beaten Freedom Riders, appeared on the front pages of newspapers around the world. Back in Birmingham, police commissioner Connor explained that his men had been unable to stop the beatings: "It happened on a Sunday, Mother's Day," he explained. "We try to let off as many of our policemen as possible so they can spend Mother's Day with their families."[9]

Robert Kennedy called the Shuttlesworth home at ten on Monday morning. Shuttlesworth told him the Freedom Riders were going to take the 3:00 p.m. bus to Montgomery and would go forward to Jackson, Mississippi. They needed federal protection at least as far as the Alabama state line.

Shuttlesworth took eighteen Freedom Riders into the Greyhound bus terminal to wait for the 3:00 p.m. bus; while on the way, car radio bulletins issued periodic reports on their location, described the mobs waiting for them at the station, and said groups of angry white men were lining the highway to Montgomery. At the station, no driver would take them; after the terrible beating most had received, they decided to continue their trip to New Orleans by plane. As they began to leave the bus station, the radio reported their change in plans, and the mob reached the airport ahead of them.

In Nashville, news that the original group of CORE Freedom Riders was abandoning the bus trip ended the debate over whether the Nashville group should join the Freedom Ride. Now they intended to replace the original Freedom Riders. Diane Nash managed to call James Farmer in Washington attending his father's funeral. Would CORE object, she asked, if the Nashville students went to Birmingham to take up the Freedom Ride where it had ended? Farmer gave his consent.

From Washington, Robert Kennedy dispatched John Seigenthaler to Birmingham. Seigenthaler met the Freedom Riders at the airport, unable to leave because of bomb threats. "Some of them had given way to paranoid ranting and had to be restrained by their companions," according to historian Taylor Branch.[10] With the airport manager and police, Seigenthaler concocted a scheme to divert the mob's attention; just before midnight, the Freedom Riders left Birmingham on a plane bound for New Orleans.

Early Tuesday morning, May 16, Seigenthaler was awakened in his New Orleans hotel room with news that the Nashville students were going to continue the ride.

With eight hundred dollars in hand, donated by the Nashville Christian Leadership Conference, Diane Nash called Shuttlesworth to tell him a new group of Freedom Riders was on the way. "Young lady," he said, "do you know that the Freedom Riders were almost killed here?"

"Yes," she said. "That's exactly why the ride must not be stopped. If they stop us with violence, the movement is dead. We're coming. We just want to know if you can meet us."[11]

James Bevel selected ten people to make the ride from Nashville to Birmingham: John Lewis as leader, five other Black males, two Black females, and a white man and woman—all veterans of what he called a "nonviolent standing army." They left early Wednesday, May 17, and experienced no trouble until they reached the Birmingham outskirts. There, police boarded the bus and arrested an integrated pair of men for violating Alabama's segregation law. With officers on board, police escorted the bus to the station. Newspapers were taped over every window, and every passenger's ticket was examined. Those who had boarded the bus in Nashville with tickets to New Orleans by way of Montgomery and Jackson were identified as Freedom Riders and told to stay on the bus.

Finally allowed to leave the bus, they found themselves protected from a hostile mob by a thin line of Birmingham policemen, who asked them not to engage in interracial mingling. As they prepared to board the 5:00 p.m. bus for Montgomery, Commissioner Connor himself appeared and ordered his men to arrest them; they were taken to the Birmingham jail.

On Thursday, May 18, seven riders (a white woman rider's father had flown to Birmingham to take her home; the two arrested on the bus had been separately released) were dragged from the Birmingham jail, driven in two cars—one driven by Bull Connor—one hundred miles north to the Alabama-Tennessee state line, dumped at the side of the road next to railroad tracks, and told to take a train back to Nashville. It was early Friday morning, before dawn, May 19.

A call to Nash in Nashville revealed that eleven other Freedom Riders were on their way to Birmingham. The seven stranded riders walked down the railroad tracks until they found a Black home, where, after much pleading, they were taken in. Their hosts, an elderly Black couple, bought breakfast food at several neighborhood stores to avoid suspicion. John Lewis called Diane Nash to say the seven were ready to go back to Birmingham. Nash sent a car to drive them back to Fred Shuttlesworth's home.

There they met the eleven who had arrived before them; one was Ruby Doris Smith, known to them all as a survivor of the "jail-no-bail" crusade in Rock Hill, South Carolina. Together they headed downtown to catch the 5:00 p.m. Greyhound bus to Montgomery. The company canceled the trip; no driver would drive the bus. One driver said, "I don't have but one life to give. I don't intend to give it to CORE or the NAACP."[12]

Finally, at 8:30 a.m. on Saturday, May 20, after intense negotiations between President Kennedy, the attorney general, and Alabama governor John Patterson, the Freedom Riders were herded onto a bus guarded by Alabama state patrolmen in cars and an airplane, and then, watched by FBI observers and trailed by carloads of journalists, they took off for Montgomery at ninety miles an hour.

In Montgomery, the FBI's special agent in charge told his Washington office that he did not believe the promises made by Montgomery police commissioner L. B. Sullivan that the Freedom Riders would be protected. Sullivan assured the FBI there were sufficient police at the bus station. But when the bus arrived a few minutes later, the police were gone. The Alabama state patrolmen had dropped off at the city limits.

John Lewis stepped off the bus first into a nearly empty terminal, except for a small army of journalists. He had begun to answer a question when he saw a mob of angry white men armed with baseball bats, bottles, and lead pipes coming at him. They beat the reporters and destroyed their equipment. Some of the Freedom Riders jumped off a loading platform onto the roofs of cars parked below. A dozen men surrounded Jim Zwerg and beat him to the ground, knocking out his teeth, as others held their children up so they could see. John Lewis was knocked unconscious with a blow from a wooden Coca-Cola crate. His schoolmate William Barbee was knocked out and was being kicked by a mob when Floyd Mann, Alabama public safety director, drew his revolver and forced them away from Barbee's body. John Seigenthaler, trying to rescue two white female Freedom Riders, was knocked unconscious with a lead pipe. Freedom Riders who jumped into Black taxis found the exits blocked, the taxis overrun and destroyed. Over one thousand people gathered at the scene even after the Freedom Riders were dispersed. The mob burned the Freedom Riders' luggage in a bonfire in the streets and attacked two Black teenagers, breaking one's leg and setting the other on fire with kerosene.

At the Federal Building nearby, John Doar of the Justice Department described the action to Burke Marshall in Washington. "Oh, there are fists, punching! A bunch of men led by a guy with a bleeding face are beating them! There are no cops. It's terrible! It's terrible! There's not a cop in sight. People are yelling, 'There those niggers are! Get 'em, get 'em!' It's awful!"[13] As John Lewis lay unconscious on the ground, Commissioner Sullivan and Alabama attorney general MacDonald Gallion read him an injunction enjoining CORE and its followers from further Freedom Rides.

The Freedom Riders, with Diane Nash coordinating from Nashville, regrouped at the home of Reverend Solomon Seay. John Lewis arrived from the hospital. From his bed in Montgomery's St. Jude Catholic Hospital, William Barbee said, "As soon as we've recovered from this, we'll start again." From the white section one floor above, Jim Zwerg had recovered enough to say, "We will continue our journey one way or another. We are prepared to die!"[14]

That afternoon, Attorney General Kennedy ordered US marshals into Montgomery, under the direction of Assistant Attorney General Byron White.[15]

On Sunday, May 21, James Farmer, Martin Luther King, and a host of others began to converge on Montgomery. By now, the Freedom Riders were hiding in the basement of Ralph Abernathy's church. By night, 1,500 people had gathered inside, about a dozen US marshals stood guard, and more than 3,000 whites surrounded the church. Latecomers reported that the mob was ugly, breaking out car windows, daring the people inside the church to leave. At 8:00 p.m. the mob overturned and burned a car and began to throw rocks at the church. The marshals fired tear gas at the mob, and the mob responded with Molotov cocktails. Some inside the church took out hidden knives and guns. As some members of the mob reached the church's front door, King called Attorney General Kennedy. While the two were talking, reinforcements arrived. A pitched battle in the street followed; at one point the marshals had to push rioters out of the church with nightsticks. Attorney General Kennedy placed army units at Fort Benning, Georgia, on alert. From his command post at Maxwell Air Force Base, Byron White told Kennedy his marshals might not be able to repulse another charge from the mob.

"That's it!" Kennedy said, but, before he could act, Governor Patterson had proclaimed martial law. Alabama National Guardsmen and Montgomery policemen replaced the marshals and the siege of the First Baptist Church was over.[16] The guardsmen who kept the mob out and drove it away would not let the people leave the church until 4:30 a.m.

The Freedom Riders relocated again, this time in the home of Montgomery pharmacist Richard Harris, whose drugstore had served as a dispatch point for the bus boycott. By Monday evening, May 22, Wyatt

Walker, King, Farmer, Diane Nash, James Bevel, and others met to plan the future. Diane Nash asked King to come with them as the Freedom Ride continued; King said he was still on probation from his 1960 traffic arrest in Georgia and could not go. "I think I should choose the time and place of my Golgotha," he said.[17] Many of the students were themselves on probation and could not understand King's reluctance.

For John and Robert Kennedy, the prospect of the Freedom Ride continuing raised important political questions. Alabama governor John Patterson had transformed himself into a martyr for those who opposed federal power; further use of marshals would allow him to portray himself as the victim of a second Reconstruction. Robert Kennedy agreed through daylong negotiations with Mississippi senator James O. Eastland that the State of Mississippi could *illegally* arrest Freedom Riders for attempting to integrate interstate facilities. The Supreme Court had ruled segregation in those facilities illegal just six months before. Kennedy agreed that Mississippi could continue to enforce the now-illegal segregation laws; Eastland agreed that the only violence against the Freedom Riders would be violence to their civil rights, not their persons.

TUESDAY, MAY 23

More Freedom Riding recruits arrived, including a Howard University student named Stokely Carmichael.

WEDNESDAY, MAY 24

At dawn, the Freedom Riders approached the Greyhound station again; this time, one hundred Alabama guardsmen held the crowd a block away. With King and Abernathy, the Freedom Riders integrated the bus station lunch counter. When they approached their bus, they discovered that guardsmen had not permitted anyone except journalists and Freedom Riders into the terminal. Sixteen reporters and twelve Freedom Riders, led by James Lawson, boarded and were escorted away by a protective ring of fifty-two police vehicles, supported by FBI cars, helicopter escorts, and US Border Patrol airplanes. There would be no rest stops for seven hours until the bus reached Jackson except for a stop at the Alabama-Mississippi state line for an even larger contingent of Mississippi law enforcement officers to replace the Alabama forces.

Another group of fourteen Freedom Riders, including Henry Thomas from the original ride, presented themselves at the Montgomery Greyhound station with tickets for the 11:25 a.m. bus to Jackson.

As James Farmer shook hands with the departing riders, one of them, Doris Castle, said, "You're coming with us, aren't you Jim?" He shouted, "Get my luggage! Put it on the bus! I'm going!"[18]

Robert Kennedy announced that no federal marshals would protect this second group. His brother, the president, would soon leave for a European trip. "Whatever we do in the United States at this time which brings or causes discredit on our country can be harmful to his mission," the attorney general said.[19] To John and Robert Kennedy, the Freedom Riders were causing discredit to our country, apparently by provoking white mobs to attack them. Using federal power to protect the Freedom Riders and put down the mobs was politically embarrassing, threatening the administration's political stature in the South and its international stature overseas.

Shortly after the second group of Freedom Riders departed, a bus pulled into the Montgomery station from Atlanta, bringing with it a new crew of Freedom Riders, including the Yale chaplain, William Sloane Coffin, and Charles Jones, who had been testing bus facilities at every stop. National Guardsmen had to clear a way through the rock-throwing mob before Abernathy could drive them away. As he drove away, a reporter asked him about the attorney general's statement that the Freedom Ride should be stopped because it was embarrassing the United States.

"Doesn't the Attorney General know that we've been embarrassed all our lives?" he replied.[20] The first and second group of Freedom Riders were quickly arrested as they walked into the Jackson bus terminal. All refused to post bail and announced they would stay in jail after they were convicted.

FRIDAY, MAY 26

King presided over the newly formed Freedom Ride Coordinating Committee. Representatives of CORE, SCLC, SNCC, and the National Student Association promised to intensify the rides and fill the jails, and to seek a ruling from the Interstate Commerce Commission establishing the rights of interstate travelers. Three weeks before, the first Freedom Riders had left Washington in obscurity. Now the country knew a new term, "Freedom Riders," and a new organization, CORE.

BY LATE JULY, over four hundred Freedom Riders had been arrested in Jackson. On September 22, 1961, the Interstate Commerce Commission issued an order banning segregation in all interstate terminal facilities.

WHAT THE FREEDOM RIDES MEANT

Historian Eric Foner writes, "The Freedom Rides revealed the pathology of the South. This was a society not simply of violent mobs but of judges who flagrantly disregarded the Constitution, police officers who . . . refused to treat the injured. Southern newspapers almost universally condemned the riders as 'hate mongers' and outside agitators (even though about half had been born and raised in the South)."[21]

Like the 1960 sit-ins, which began with four participants and escalated into thousands, the Freedom Rides began with thirteen participants and exploded into a broad-based movement involving hundreds. Like the sit-ins, the Freedom Rides transcended the traditional legal approach to civil rights, taking it from the courtroom to the streets. Nothing seemed to deter them—not widespread disapproval, not political pressure, not arrests and imprisonment, not even the threat of death. Instead, these hardships seemed to stiffen their resolve, confounding their antagonists and testing the patience of those sympathetic to their cause. At every instance when they seemed to face defeat or retreat, or when compromise beckoned, they found the courage to go on. Every intimidation served to reinvigorate them and brought new comrades to their cause. The Freedom Riders invited the invocation of federal supremacy over state law and custom.

The rides meant much more than the introduction of a new organization to the top ranks of civil rights leadership; they meant that the activist CORE joined SNCC on the movement's militant wing. The rides demonstrated that there was much more at stake than a hamburger, as Ella Baker had put it.

In contrast to the sit-ins, whose participants were mostly Black college students, the Freedom Rides had greater participation by whites, non-Southerners, and clergy and academics. These were truly the "outsiders" the white South had demonized, but one had to be an "outsider" from somewhere else to use interstate transportation. In addition to expanding participation, the rides expanded the movement's geography, making it interregional, pushing it deeper into the Deep South, where no sit-ins had occurred. Crossing state lines to challenge segregation was a highly provocative act. In the early '60s in Georgia, outside Atlanta, and in all of Mississippi and Alabama, a myth of invincibility existed—segregation was thought to be so entrenched in these areas it could not be challenged from the inside. The rides challenged it and won.

As the rides challenged the invincibility of the wall of racism in the Deep South, they also exposed cracks in that wall—following the violence in Anniston, Birmingham, and Montgomery, white moderates were heard from for the first time. In Montgomery, the Ministerial Association, the Rotary Club, the chamber of commerce, and the Alabama Press Association condemned the failure of police and the breakdown of law and order. The *Birmingham News* said, "We the people—the newspaper people, the lawyers, the bankers, the executives, the labor leaders, the clergy and the average householders . . . permitted intolerance and brutality to take over. We . . . have let gangs of vicious men ride this state now for months."[22]

The rides—and the bus boycott and sit-ins that preceded them—revealed that what many whites thought of as "normal" interracial communication in their communities was profoundly unequal communication between individuals of unequal status. For many whites, the protest movement had destroyed what Gunnar Myrdal called the "convenience of ignorance." Rather than dividing a previously harmonious community as many whites charged, the demonstrations tried to create a new consensus on basic American values—individual dignity and equal opportunity. The Freedom Rides' hooligans and thugs, and the politicians who encouraged them, were outside that consensus. Many Americans gave these opponents of civil rights vigorous support, while others silently acquiesced to their tactics. But Americans generally supported the unifying values around which the civil rights movement was organized.

The Freedom Rides represented a transition from the largely spontaneous, unconnected protests of the sit-ins to a tactic that was well-coordinated and more dangerous, aimed at larger targets than separate, segregated lunch counters in Southern towns. The rides demanded a degree of organizational cooperation that had not existed—or was not really needed—before and created a temporary halt in conflict among civil rights groups. Instead, they mobilized people, money, legal assistance, and publicity in record time between the Alabama violence and Mississippi arrests. While this cooperation was short-lived, it did demonstrate the capacity for cooperation in a crisis.

Unlike the sit-ins, the Freedom Rides hoped to change both local policy and federal enforcement. And they did so. They challenged and engaged the federal government as the sit-ins had not and could not. The government responded—first by trying to stop the rides, then by negotiating the riders' civil rights away, and then finally by acting to remove the discrimination that had prompted the rides to be held. And the government was moved by the publicity about the rides to try to turn the movement away from confrontation and toward voter registration.

The Freedom Rides resulted in the "nationalization" of the civil rights movement, at first through news accounts that broadcast the violence of the mob and the courage of the riders around the nation and the world, and then through the support—financial as well as in actual participation in the rides—that grew from the first violence in Alabama. The day after Farmer was arrested in Jackson, the New York CORE office reported that contributions were pouring in and that one hundred people had volunteered to go south on a Freedom Ride. On the eve of the Freedom Rides, CORE had twenty-six thousand contributors; two years later, it had sixty-three thousand.

The Freedom Rides continued and enlarged the process begun earlier in the year in the jail in Rock Hill, South Carolina. Freedom Riders served thirty days of their sentences, posting bail at the last possible opportunity. The thirty days gave the riders a chance to meet and know each other, to deepen their commitment to the movement, and to plan strategy for their release. One effect was the creation of "professional" civil rights workers from people who had been college students only a few months before. "There were [a] lot of little movements going into Parchman [prison]," Ruby Doris Smith said, "but one big one coming out!"[23]

The Freedom Riders demonstrated a commitment to nonviolence that went far beyond the less harmful beatings some had received at lunch counter sit-ins in 1961. Their refusal to concede to Attorney General Kennedy's request for a "cooling-off" period showed a new eagerness to press forward, regardless of political considerations. The riders were saying to the racist white South: "The cost of violence to you is greater than the cost of violence to us; we can take more violence than you can dish out!"

The rides created the opportunity for new voices to be heard. While no one would challenge King's position as spokesman for the Southern movement, there now were others who had earned the right to speak through their courage and their suffering. Despite increased interorganizational cooperation, the rides increased the gap between Martin Luther King Jr. and the students. His refusal to join the ride in Montgomery, his support of the cooling-off period, and his indecisiveness during the Montgomery crisis—all this widened a breach between King and the students.

The deal made by Robert Kennedy with Senator Eastland set a pattern for race relations for the next several years: behind-the-scenes negotiations with, and accommodations to, the resistant white South and little face-to-face contact with the civil rights movement. Even worse, it demonstrated a cynicism that argued that civil rights were politically negotiable, expendable in the interest of a legislative program or a reelection campaign. The *Washington Post* quoted a high government source—probably Robert Kennedy himself—saying, "The Attorney General does not feel that the Department of Justice can . . . side with one group or another in disputes over constitutional rights." Les Dunbar of the Southern Regional Council noted, "There was a great reluctance [by the federal government] to accept the fact that you have to be on somebody's side in the South."[24]

JAMES FARMER CALLED the Freedom Rides the sit-ins on wheels, but there were also key differences between these actions. Assaults on the Freedom Riders were more vicious and brutal than attacks on the sit-ins; great harm was intended, and great harm was done. One Klansman, Gary Thomas Rowe, had become an FBI informant in April 1960. On Mother's Day, he was head of what the Klan called an "action squad." He had diligently reported all the plans for this day—and for many other acts of Klan brutality he participated in—to his FBI controller. He reported the time, the place, the assailants, their choice of weapons—and the FBI did nothing to stop it.[25]

Rejection of the government's "cooling-off" period reflected a greater commitment to nonviolence and an acknowledgment that giving in to violence gave the opposition an effective weapon they would not hesitate to use. Lunch counter sit-ins almost never immediately achieved their goal. Greensboro didn't integrate its lunch counters until six months after the protests began; in Charlotte it wasn't until 1961, and in Alabama and Mississippi it took the 1964 Civil Rights Act to integrate public facilities. The Freedom Rides began May 4, 1961; by September 22, the Interstate Commerce Commission ordered all interstate travel facilities integrated, and most complied. The ICC's involvement marked another difference; the Freedom Rides managed to invoke federal authority, while sit-inners bargained with mayors and local merchants.

And, much more than the sit-ins, the Freedom Rides exposed the racial passions that underlay Southern white society and exhibited the complicity of Southern political leaders with the brutality of the mob. The sit-ins made confronting segregation look somewhat easy; the Freedom Rides gave clear evidence of how dangerous and difficult it could become.

The Montgomery bus boycott, the sit-ins, and the Freedom Rides all democratized the movement, taking it away from lawyers and scholars and placing it in the hands and hearts of students, the unskilled, and the unlettered. The sit-ins and Freedom Rides gave encouragement to those who favored direct action. Montgomery's buses were integrated by court order; lunch counters were integrated by the power of protest and by boycotts; the ICC integrated interstate travel, but it took the Freedom Riders' movement to make the government move.

The Freedom Rides occurred at the same time as the botched Bay of Pigs invasion, and President Kennedy's upcoming summit in Vienna with Soviet premier Nikita Khrushchev, and figured in the president's thinking about both. The rides forced the Kennedy administration to devise a strategy to take the civil rights movement out of the headlines and into activity that would reinforce Kennedy's political and reelection prospects.

THIRTEEN

KENNEDY AND CIVIL RIGHTS, 1961

R ICHARD NIXON AND John F. Kennedy had competed with each other as presidential candidates to see who could attract the most votes from Blacks and liberals. Each had some reasonable expectation of winning those votes. As chair of President Eisenhower's Committee on Federal Contract Compliance, Nixon had won high marks. He was a card-carrying member of the NAACP, had been praised by Martin Luther King for his help in passing the 1957 Civil Rights Act, which created the Civil Rights Commission, and had received thanks from Roy Wilkins for supporting reform of the filibuster rules in the Senate. He had fought for a stronger civil rights plank at the 1960 Republican Convention.

The Democrats matched and passed the Republicans in platform rhetoric. They endorsed the sit-in demonstrations and called for equal access to "voting booths, schoolrooms, jobs, housing, and public facilities" and asked that the attorney general be given the power to file discrimination suits for individuals—the power that conservatives in both parties had refused to keep in the 1957 Civil Rights Act and that Lyndon Johnson had kept out of the Civil Rights Act of 1960. The Democrats also called for a permanent, statutory Fair Employment Practices Commission—a dream of the civil rights community since the Roosevelt presidency and the March on Washington movement.[1]

Both parties' platforms were more liberal than the legislators who represented them in Congress, and both Nixon and Kennedy continued to try to win civil rights points as the campaign continued. Kennedy attacked Nixon for having only brought two successful discrimination actions against contractors in seven years. Nixon countered by saying the Congress should give the committee statutory authority—something to which Kennedy, who needed Southern support, could never agree. And Nixon attacked Kennedy's running mate, Lyndon Johnson, as "a man who had voted against most of these proposals and a man who opposes them at the present time."[2] Kennedy's telephone call to Coretta Scott King—and his brother Robert's telephone call to the judge who had sent Martin Luther King to jail—was a grab for Black votes that Nixon would not make; Kennedy won the election.

Once the election was won, civil rights quickly receded as an issue for the new president; civil rights could not be made to disappear, however. The energy and expectation set loose in the South by the sit-ins and then the Freedom Rides was too great to be contained, but the new administration thought it might be redirected away from confrontational activity that inspired worldwide headlines and toward less visible efforts that would help not only Black Southerners but would aid the Kennedy administration politically. At least the Kennedys aimed to try to channel these young activists into areas that would do no harm.

VOTER REGISTRATION

One kind of activity that would fit that prescription—no political harm for the president or embarrassment for the nation and great political gain for his reelection chances—was increased voter registration in the South.

Increased registration and the removal of the barriers to registration and voting had long been a demand of Black Americans. At the end of Reconstruction, slavery had returned to the South in all but name. Intimidation and murder drove many Blacks who had been elected to office away from their posts; others were frightened away from the polls. Beginning in Mississippi in 1890, the Southern states imposed anti-Black codes, including poll taxes, grandfather clauses, white primaries, and literacy tests.

For most of the first half of the twentieth century, progress toward regaining the franchise was slow. In 1927 and in 1944, two Texas cases decided by the Supreme Court weakened the white primary. One of the ways Blacks had been kept out of the political process was by whites operating the primary as a private political club that Blacks could not enter (in most

Southern states, till the 1960s, the Democratic Party was in complete control, so the primary was the only election that mattered). As late as 1944, however, Gunnar Myrdal estimated that fewer than 225,000 Blacks, less than 5 percent of the adult Black population, had voted in the South in the previous five years. In 1945, in *King v. Chapman*, a federal district court struck down Georgia's white primary; in 1947, South Carolina's all-white election system met the same fate. By 1947, Southern Black registration had jumped to 775,000, an increase of 500,000.

But the end of the white primary only meant that the next barriers needed to be attacked: the arcane process to register to vote and the poll tax that required a payment before a citizen could vote. In 1939, the income of working Southerners, white and Black, averaged $5.60 a week, less than the amount required for food and shelter. Additionally, the states of Virginia, Alabama, Georgia, and Mississippi aggregated poll taxes, requiring a would-be voter to pay for past years when they did not vote before they could cast a ballot in the future.

Here's how Virginia Durr, an Alabama-born white woman, described attempting to register to vote. The Durrs lived in Alexandria, Virginia, during the Second World War. Clifford Durr was an official of the Roosevelt administration; Virginia Durr had just been elected president of the all-white Northern Virginia PTA. Her new position required that she become a registered voter in Virginia, so she called the county courthouse and asked for the registrar. He lived in the rural countryside. Mrs. Durr obtained directions to his house. "'Does he have a telephone?' I asked. 'No.' 'How will I know he's going to be there?' 'You'll just have to take your chances.'"

She writes:

Now this was during the war, and gasoline was rationed, but I was allowed five gallons to go to the registrar to vote. I drove out an old road and came to an old country farmhouse. I asked the old lady who answered my knock on the door if I could see the registrar. I said I wanted to register to vote. She said he wasn't there and she didn't know when he would be back. I waited and waited, but dark came on and I had to go home. I went back a second time and he wasn't there. The third time, he was in and said he would be delighted to register me. Like most Virginians, he had nice manners.

He said to his wife, "Mamie, where is the poll book?" . . . So she went up in the attic and rustled around for a while, and finally came back with the poll book. . . . The registrar asked me for identification and then he asked me to sign the book.

"Don't you have a pen?" I asked. "No, don't you?" "No, I don't. I have a pencil." . . . "Well, let's see if we can find a pen," I said. So the old lady began looking around, and she finally found an old rusty pen. Then he said, "We don't have any ink."

"You don't have a pen and you don't have any ink?" . . . I asked his wife if she knew of anything we could use for ink. She said, "Well, I've got some Mercurochrome. Let's mix it up with a little soot and see if we can't make some ink out of it." And she did. . . . It made a kind of pale red-blue ink. I signed the book and got my receipt to show I had registered.

Next she had to go to the Fairfax County courthouse to pay her poll taxes. The State of Virginia required two years back poll taxes plus the current year. She paid $4.50 and presented herself at the polls on Election Day. But her name was not on the list; an election official explained to her that she had not paid the interest on the poll taxes. Before she could cast a vote, she had to return to the courthouse and pay twenty-seven cents before her name was inscribed on the registration books.[3]

Remember, this is the experience of a college-educated, Alabama-born, white woman; think what the experience of an educated Black man or woman or an uneducated Black person might have been.

In 1938, Roosevelt had made some tentative moves toward supporting a federal prohibition on the poll tax, but when white voters in Georgia and South Carolina rejected his candidates in favor of anti–New Deal Democratic incumbents, he backed away. The battle was waged largely by the Civil Rights Committee of the Southern Conference for Human Welfare; Mrs. Durr was an active member. After *Smith v. Allwright* in 1944 struck down the white primary, white Southern fears made repeal of the poll tax impossible.

Like Roosevelt, Truman mouthed opposition to the poll tax but did little, initially, to achieve repeal. Repeal would not have meant a flood of Black votes; like the white primary, the poll tax was only one of several methods used to keep Blacks from voting. With the white primary gone, however, removal of the poll tax would have allowed the use of these other devices to have been exposed to public examination. The white South could not tolerate this exposure; the rest of the country did not have the courage to insist.

Nevertheless, the registration battle in the South continued. Led largely by the NAACP, but including a variety of other groups as well, spurred by returning veterans, voters' leagues flourished across the South, and registration drives became regular events in many communities. While adding few names, these efforts made voting—or even attempting to register—an acceptable, even desirable activity in the Black South. By 1954, over one million Southern Blacks were registered, twice as many as in 1946. But in twenty-four majority-Black counties in five Southern states, not a single Black voter was registered.

In the 1920s, 1930s, and 1940s, over two and one-half million Blacks had migrated from the South, settling fortuitously in areas of the North and West where their votes would be felt the most, in seven states that cast 197 electoral votes. In 1954, Blacks made up more than 5 percent of the electorate in seventy-two congressional districts outside the South. This was enough to tip the balance in sixty-one of these districts. A shift of Black votes from Democrats to Republicans gave the Republicans control of the House of Representatives in 1956. Black votes were important in 1960 too, giving Kennedy the election over Nixon. That lesson was not lost on Kennedy administration officials in early 1961.

ON MAY 15, 1961, the day after the May 14 Mother's Day bus burning in Anniston, Alabama, and the beatings in Birmingham, NAACP executive director Roy Wilkins met with Attorney General Robert Kennedy and Assistant Attorney General Burke Marshall. Wilkins was there to seek federal protection for the Freedom Riders. Wilkins noted that the attorney general was shocked at the bare-knuckled brutality of the Alabama mobs but was more concerned with the foreign policy ramifications of American racial violence on the president's upcoming European trip. For the Kennedy brothers, the timing of the Freedom Rider violence could not have been worse. The rides began less than a month after the Bay of Pigs disaster and weeks before the president would meet with Nikita Khrushchev, who would be sure to highlight America's racial problems. Kennedy took advantage of the meeting with Wilkins to stress the administration's interest in voter registration. Burke Marshall also began talks with Harold Fleming, former executive director of the Southern Regional Council, about possible funding sources for Southern voter registration drives. He had also met with foundations to plan setting up a privately funded, nonpartisan, region-wide voter registration organization that would coordinate the activities of all the civil rights organizations.

On June 16, 1961, representatives of the Freedom Ride Coordinating Committee—SNCC, SCLC, CORE, and the National Student Association—met with Robert Kennedy. The Freedom Rides were counterproductive, Kennedy told them. More could be done for civil rights by registering voters, and he suggested a government-promoted registration drive. The attorney general promised that the government would protect voter registration workers and hinted that protection from the military draft could be arranged too. If they focused on registration, he said, they would receive support and protection; if they persisted with protests, the federal reaction would be very different.[4]

Winning agreement from the NAACP and SCLC was easy; registration was already an important part of these groups' agenda, although Roy Wilkins was against registration activity in the deep, rural South. He thought it would be unproductive and not worth the effort or money it would consume. He also wanted to make sure the NAACP would not be seen to have abandoned its commitment to integrating Southern schools. Convincing CORE and SNCC would be hard. CORE was at the height of its greatest glory—the Freedom Rides. SNCC was torn between the administration's offer and continuing its present course—direct action, taking the challenge directly to the resistant white South. Tim Jenkins, the representative to SNCC's Coordinating Committee from the National Student Association, argued for a shift to voter registration work; Marion Barry and Diane Nash argued for nonviolent direct action. They assumed correctly that voter registration was simply an attempt to take the movement out of the headlines and to aim it toward President Kennedy's 1964 reelection.

On June 27, Harry Belafonte, a personal and political supporter of the Kennedys, met with SNCC representatives. Some SNCC members left the meeting determined to press the issue of voter registration and convinced that money to support it would be forthcoming.[5] SNCC had hired its first field secretary in June: Charles Sherrod, a student sit-in leader from Virginia Union and former Freedom Rider. Sherrod and Bob Moses had visited Cleveland, Mississippi, in April. Both were convinced that SNCC should devote its energies to registration work and that a good beginning spot for student volunteers was Cleveland, in the Mississippi Delta. When no housing could be arranged in Cleveland, Moses accepted an invitation from C. C. Bryant, president of the NAACP in McComb, a town of thirteen thousand in the southwest corner of the state.

SNCC's Coordinating Committee met in Baltimore July 14–16. Charles Jones, a student sit-in leader from Charlotte and a Freedom Rider, recommended that SNCC establish a voter registration project, but the others were still unsure. Part of the uncertainty came from the resignation of executive secretary Ed King, who had left to return to school; there was no one in the Atlanta office to hold things together. Even those who favored voter registration were reluctant to begin fieldwork without strong headquarters support. Jones was asked to put his recommendations forward again at the September meeting, but the balance had already begun to tip in favor of registration over direct action. Moses ended his nebulous affiliation with SCLC and became a volunteer field secretary for SNCC in Mississippi. SNCC sent two students to work with him. Even before SNCC had given its official approval to a voter registration plan, it had taken actions that committed it to registration activity in Mississippi.

On July 28, representatives of the NAACP, SCLC, NSA, Urban League, and SNCC met with the Southern Regional Council and officials of the Taconic Foundation and the Field Foundation in New York. Again the civil rights groups were assured that the Justice Department would protect their workers. The exact nature of this protection was not spelled out and would be a source of controversy, charges of betrayal, and countercharges for years to come.

With money he obtained from the Field Foundation, Tim Jenkins gathered SNCC's leadership together for a three-week seminar in Nashville beginning July 30 titled "Understanding the Nature of Social Change." Jenkins said, "We made a calculated attempt to pull the best people out of the movement and give them a solid academic approach to understanding the movement. What we needed now was information, not inspiration."[6] Teacher-consultants for the three-week seminar were the Justice Department's John Doar and scholars Kenneth Clark, E. Harland Randolph, E.

Franklin Frazier, C. Eric Lincoln, Rayford Logan, and Herbert Hill. For Jenkins, the meeting was intended to conquer the students' "lack of comprehension of the institutional world and the way in which their programs had to plug in and manipulate those forces in the institutional world in order to succeed." Jenkins also wanted the SNCC activists to see there were sympathetic forces in the Justice Department.[7]

At a SNCC staff meeting in August, James Forman, visiting the new organization, argued that "voter registration in the deep South *is* direct action." Any voter registration activity in the resistant South would provoke retaliation from whites and "create more exposure, more consciousness."[8] At that meeting, Ella Baker proposed that SNCC adopt two divisions—a direct action wing, led by Diane Nash, and a voter registration division, headed by Charles Jones. This was a crucial decision for SNCC and the movement—they had weathered their first internal debate. By supporting a voter registration division, they had also approved the creation of a cadre of locally based, full-time, grassroots organizers. If successful, this would be the first time many indigenous activists in many parts of the deepest South would have day-to-day organizational assistance.

In September, the objections of SNCC members who opposed having a strong organizational hand in control of the office were overcome. The Coordinating Committee agreed to hire James Forman.

JAMES RUFUS FORMAN

James Forman was born in Chicago in 1928 but spent most of his youth on his grandmother's farm in Mississippi. After serving four years in the air force, he entered the University of Southern California in September 1952. He transferred to Chicago's Roosevelt University in September 1954 and was elected student body president. He graduated from Roosevelt in 1957. In 1958, Forman covered the integration of Central High School in Little Rock as a reporter for the *Chicago Defender*. He had written an unpublished novel about an interracial corps of students who had created a nonviolent movement for social change.

In 1960, while teaching school in Chicago, he became active in the Emergency Relief Committee (ERC), an affiliate of the Chicago CORE chapter. The ERC gathered and distributed food and clothing to Black residents of Fayette County, Tennessee, who were victims of white harassment, including eviction, because of their voter registration activity.

Forman visited Monroe, North Carolina, where Monroe NAACP president Robert Williams was engaged in meeting Ku Klux Klan attacks with
armed self-defense. Forman was arrested in Monroe and sentenced to six
months for inciting to riot. He went to Atlanta to work for SNCC, and in
September 1961 he became its executive director.

In the early days, I dropped by SNCC's office and found Forman
sweeping the floor. I thought he was the janitor. He immediately began
to ask me what I could do. Before I knew it, I had become the publicity
director of the organization, editor of the newsletter, and the person who
wrote the press releases. Because Forman made me do it. He had a compelling personality.

IN SEPTEMBER 1961, CORE, like SNCC, approved Deep South voter registration work with some reluctance. SNCC and CORE were leery of involvement in Democratic Party politics; they saw themselves primarily as
direct action groups, not political organizers. Each also feared folding its
organizational identity into a coordinated effort with less militant groups.

While SNCC was debating its future course and changing its operations, and the Kennedy administration was building the organizational
structure and arranging the financing that would serve its purposes, other
civil rights organizations were making personnel and organizational
changes that would prepare them for greater future demands.

SEPTIMA POINSETTE CLARK

In March 1961, SCLC hired Septima Poinsette Clark. Born in 1898, Clark
was the daughter of Henry Poinsette, who had been born a slave to the
family that developed the poinsettia, and Victoria Warren Anderson. Her
mother had grown up in Haiti and boasted of having never been a slave,
telling her daughter, "I never gave a white woman a drink of water." Clark
began teaching on John's Island, off Charleston, South Carolina's coast, after finishing the twelfth grade at Avery Normal Institute 1916. "In that two-
teacher school," she said, "we had 132 children. . . . Across the road from
where I worked was a white schoolhouse [with] three children attending
that with one teacher. That teacher received $85 a month for her teaching
and living. . . . [At our school] I was the teaching principal so I got $35 and

the assistant $25 [with 132 children] . . . [compared] to the one teacher who made $85 for three children."[9] She stayed on John's Island for three years, becoming a crusader for equal salaries and a leader in the fight to win the right for Black teachers to teach in Charleston's public schools.

In 1919, she returned to Charleston to teach at Avery Institute and began to work with the NAACP. She went door-to-door, circulating petitions for Black teachers. Over ten thousand were collected, and in 1920 the South Carolina legislature permitted Black teachers in public schools. "We had been victorious," she said later, "in this my first effort to establish for Negro citizens what I sincerely believed to be their God given right."[10]

As a young girl, she remembered being filled with racial pride when she saw ships from Marcus Garvey's Black Star Line docking in Charleston Harbor. Later, in 1937, while a student at Atlanta University, she took a course from Dr. W. E. B. Du Bois, who influenced her lifelong commitment to document the events of her struggle. In 1920, she married a seaman and settled in Columbia, South Carolina, where she lived until 1947, receiving a BA from Benedict College and an MA from Hampton Institute.

It was in Columbia that she began her work in adult education, working in a program at Camp Jackson to educate illiterate Black soldiers. She also became involved in a lawsuit to equalize teachers' pay—Thurgood Marshall argued her case, which was won in 1945. She taught in Charleston's public schools from 1947 until 1956; she was active with the YWCA and local civil rights efforts and attended workshops at Highlander Folk School.

In 1956, in the racist anti-NAACP hysteria that swept South Carolina and the rest of the South in the wake of the 1954 *Brown* decision, her NAACP membership cost her her job. In April 1956, South Carolina passed a law stipulating that no city or state employee could be affiliated with a civil rights organization. Refusing to hide her NAACP membership—she was fifty-eight years old—she not only lost her job of forty years but also her retirement benefits. In 1976, Republican governor James Edward wrote to tell her she had been unjustly fired and was entitled to her pension.[11]

Unable to find work in South Carolina, she joined the staff of the Highlander Folk School as director of education and brought Esau Jenkins, a

farmer and bus driver, to Highlander. He had attended Highlander workshops as early as 1954 and had asked Highlander's cofounder and director,
Myles Horton, to help him teach illiterate Sea Island Blacks to read and
write enough to register to vote.[12]

With Bernice Robinson, a beautician and NAACP activist as teacher,
they set up an adult night school on John's Island in January 1957 with
fourteen illiterate students; three months later, eight of them passed their
final exam, the South Carolina voter's test. Other schools, soon known as
Citizenship Schools, were established on other Sea Islands, following the
formula that had proven so successful on John's Island. There would be no
"professional" teachers trained in education; instead, anyone who could
read and write and recruit students could teach. Of equal importance, no
whites would be allowed to teach. Horton thought whites would dominate
the schools by force of habit, reinforcing white supremacy. Teachers were
paid thirty dollars a month.

Trained teachers had followed a "See Jane run" curriculum, foreign
to most of the students. Robinson would begin by asking students why
they wanted to learn to read; for many, it was a chance to read the Bible or
write their sons in the military or read the letters written back to them. For
some, it was to fill out money orders. Robinson began teaching how to do
these simple tasks. Robinson and Septima Clark devised a handbook—a
sample question was "Ten students were arrested in the sit-in movement
and were fined $75 apiece. How much fine was paid?"[13]

Soon the demand for schools and training teachers became too great a
task for Robinson; teacher training was moved to Highlander. The staff at
Highlander had always thought of the school as an initiator—not an admin-
istrator—of programs and wanted someone else to take over the Citizenship
Schools program. Ella Baker had visited the school in 1959 and reported
back to SCLC on her meeting with Septima Clark. By 1961, with Highlander
near extinction after raids by the State of Tennessee, SCLC took over the Citizenship Schools program. Clark and Robinson joined the SCLC staff, and a
young minister named Andrew Young was hired as director.

By 1963, it was estimated that the Citizenship Schools had held four
hundred sessions attended by sixty-five thousand students who, in turn,
had taught twenty-six thousand to read and write well enough to register to vote. After the schools were transferred to SCLC, an estimated
seven hundred teachers and fifty thousand new voters were traced to the

Citizenship Schools by 1963.[14] But the schools did more than teach people how to become voters; they also taught them how to become leaders in their communities.

ANDREW JACKSON YOUNG

Andrew Jackson Young was born in New Orleans on March 12, 1932. Young's grandfather was a successful businessman in Franklin, Louisiana, who owned a drugstore and a saloon; his father was a New Orleans dentist and his mother, a Sunday school teacher. Young entered the first grade at four and graduated from private Gilbert Academy in 1947. After attending Dillard University for a year, he entered Howard University in Washington and graduated at nineteen in 1951 with a major in biology. That same year, Young decided to become a missionary in Africa and enrolled in Hartford Seminary in Connecticut. There he was exposed to Gandhi for the first time. Sent to a summer pastorate at the Congregational church in Marion, Alabama, in 1952, he met Jean Childs, a graduate of Marion's Lincoln School. They married in May 1954. They had made plans to go to Angola as missionaries in 1954, but when the Portuguese began expelling foreign missionaries, charging that they were making the natives restless, they settled on pastoring two small rural churches in Thomasville and Beachton, Georgia. In Thomasville, Young worked with the Thomasville County Business and Civic League on voter registration campaigns. Because Coretta Scott King was also a Marion native, the Youngs had occasionally stopped in Montgomery to visit the Kings.

In late 1957, Andrew Young accepted a job in New York as associate director of the Department of Youth of the National Council of Churches, the only nonwhite staff member. In late 1961, he became Director of a Voter Registration project of the United Church of Christ, funded by the Field Foundation. The Field grant was to have gone to SCLC, but they had no tax exemption, a legal necessity for receiving tax-exempt foundation funds, so the United Church of Christ served as a conduit for the money. Young would direct the Citizenship Schools, teaching Southern Blacks how to teach others to read and therefore pass the literacy test Southern states used to keep Black registration low. He would be paid by the Field Foundation.[15] Dorothy Cotton, an SCLC staffer brought to Atlanta from Petersburg, Virginia, by Wyatt Tee Walker, would recruit students, and Septima Clark and Bernice Robinson would teach.

DAVE DENNIS

In the fall of 1961, CORE hired Dave Dennis as their Mississippi voter registration director. Dennis had grown up as the son of sharecroppers in Omega, Louisiana, and attended Southern University in Baton Rouge, where he had led sit-ins. He had been a Freedom Rider and a veteran of the New Orleans CORE chapter, which was deeply steeped in nonviolence.[16]

THE ADDITION OF new personnel at SNCC, SCLC, and CORE meant that a new group of activists was poised to attack segregation at ballot boxes in the most resistant and violent part of the South. At SNCC and CORE, most new workers were veterans of the Freedom Rides. Most had spent a month in Parchman state penitentiary, using their stay, like the Rock Hill "jail, no bail" protesters had done before them, to learn about each other and argue whether radical Christianity and radical nonviolence were compatible with or antagonistic to the process of larger social change. Many of the Freedom Riders had attended the three-week-long seminar in Nashville and had received a quick education in how the American social order worked and where its weak spots and pressure points were. All of them had argued long and hard—in prison and out—about the course they were about to take. They were no longer students, tied to campus and home. They were independent activists, tied together less by organizational history than by common experience, daring to try to organize a rural, isolated community in Southwest Mississippi, away from the spotlight and protective publicity of the sit-ins and Freedom Rides.

SNCC IN MCCOMB, MISSISSIPPI

Robert Moses arrived in McComb, Mississippi in July 1961 and began lining up housing for the student volunteers he expected even before he became a member of the SNCC staff. When John Hardy and Reginald Robinson joined him, they opened a voter registration school to teach Black residents of McComb how to take and pass Mississippi's registration test. Their first few students were unable to pass, but residents of nearby counties—Amite and Walthall—asked that schools be set up for them. Amite County had one registered Black voter out of twenty-five hundred eligible Blacks; Walthall County had none. Two hundred of Pike County's eight thousand eligible Blacks were registered. Moses knew that resistance in the two more rural counties would be greater but accepted the invitation. SNCC had to demonstrate it was willing to go anywhere if it was to gain the confidence of local people.

On August 15, 1961, Moses took three Black applicants to the Amite County Courthouse in Liberty. While driving away, he was arrested by police and charged with interfering with their duties. He placed several calls to the Justice Department, deliberately speaking loudly, to protest this harassment, but was convicted, given a ninety-day suspended sentence, and fined five dollars; he spent two days in jail before the NAACP posted an appeal bond.[17] While Moses was in jail, nearly a dozen Freedom Riders and SNCC members had come to town, including Ruby Doris Smith, Charles Sherrod, Marion Barry, and Charles Jones. They began recruiting high school students to help in door-to-door canvassing.

On August 29, after another registration attempt, Moses was attacked and beaten by Billy Jack Caston, the sheriff's cousin. Moses pressed charges against Caston, something no Black person had ever done. The sheriff advised him to leave town before the innocent verdict came in.

On September 5, Moses and SNCC worker and Freedom Rider Travis Britt took four Blacks to the registrar's office in Liberty. A white man beat Britt, and they left town with no one added to the voters' list.

On September 7 John Hardy took two people to the Tylertown registrar's office. The registrar ordered Hardy—at gunpoint—to leave his office and then hit Hardy on his head with the pistol. The sheriff, instead of arresting the registrar for assault, arrested Hardy for disorderly conduct.[18] The charge, we joked, was striking the registrar's pistol with his head.

In the first instance of promised federal protection, the Justice Department moved to block Hardy's prosecution, which was set for September 22. Not only were they challenging the right of a state to bring criminal prosecutions under its own law; they were supporting the testimony of a Black man against a white elected official. The case was heard before the first judge appointed by President Kennedy in the South. Federal judge Harold Cox, who later called Blacks "baboons" from the bench, refused to grant an injunction, and the Justice Department appealed to a three-judge panel from the Fifth Circuit Court of Appeals. There the two judges appointed by President Eisenhower supported an injunction against the state's prosecution of Hardy; the Democratic appointee voted no.[19]

On September 24, John Doar met with Bob Moses and McComb farmer E. W. Steptoe. They told Doar that Herbert Lee, a nearby Black farmer, feared reprisals from local whites—especially from state representative E. H. Hurst, the father-in-law of the man who had beaten Moses. Lee had used his car to drive registration workers around and had attended registration classes. Doar tried to see him, but he was away. When Doar returned to his office in Washington the next day—September 25—he received a message that Representative Hurst had shot and killed Herbert Lee at a cotton gin in Liberty.

Hurst had approached Lee's truck with a gun in his hand. Lee told Hurst he wouldn't talk until the gun was put up. Hurst put the gun away, and Lee stepped out of his truck. Hurst ran around the front and shot Lee in the head. The body lay on the ground for two hours in the dirt. Two eyewitnesses reported that Lee had menaced Hurst with a tire iron; a coroner's jury ruled the killing justifiable homicide later that day.

One of the witnesses was Louis Allen. He later told Moses he had lied at the inquest. On February 23, 1963, I met Louis Allen at E. W. Steptoe's farm; Allen repeated to me that he had lied for fear of his life. Less than a year later, on January 31, 1964, Louis Allen was assassinated in his driveway. No one was ever arrested.[20]

While Moses had occupied himself with voter registration, some of the other SNCC workers—James Bevel, Marion Barry, Charles Sherrod, Charles Jones, and Diane Nash—had been conducting workshops in nonviolence for McComb's teenagers, who were tired of the unexciting, dusty work of door-to-door canvassing for voters among the fearful Black population. Barry encouraged them to demonstrate against the white-only library; on August 26 two students, Curtis Hayes and Hollis Watkins, were arrested at a Woolworth's store. A few days later, three students—including sixteen-year-old Brenda Travis—were arrested for sitting-in at the Greyhound bus station lunch counter. On October 4, the principal of McComb's Black high school, Burglund High, refused to admit two of the students—over one hundred walked out to protest his refusal and the killing of Herbert Lee. Led by Moses, Charles McDew, and SNCC's first white field secretary, Bob Zellner, they paused for prayers in front of the city hall, where a mob attacked them; the SNCC workers and 119 students were arrested.

They were released on bond, the students charged with disturbing the peace, the SNCC workers with contributing to the delinquency of a minor.

Brenda Travis, who was on probation, spent six months in a juvenile detention center. On October 31, they were sentenced to terms of four to six months, if they also had a sit-in arrest, in jail. While in jail, Moses wrote a letter that was later reprinted over and over—it was a message to supporters that, despite beatings and harassment, the movement would continue:

> We are smuggling this note from the drunk tank of the county jail in Magnolia, Mississippi. Twelve of us are here, sprawled out along the concrete bunker; Curtis Hayes, Hollis Watkins, Ike Lewis and Robert Talbert, four veterans of the bunker, are sitting up talking—mostly about girls. . . . Later on, Hollis will lead out with a clear tenor into a freedom song. Talbert and Lewis will supply jokes, and McDew will discourse on the history of the black man and the Jew. . . . To Judge Brumfield, we are cold calculators, leading sheep to the slaughter. . . . This is Mississippi, the middle of the iceberg. . . . This is a tremor in the middle of the iceberg—from a stone that the builders rejected.[21]

Jail officials brought tour groups from Magnolia to look at the twelve "communists." When a young girl asked McDew to "say something in Communist," he said, "Kiss mir tuchus."

When they were released from jail after thirty-seven days on December 6, Moses found a dispirited community. Although McComb's Black adults had rallied to the defense of their arrested children, the threats, beatings, jailings, and Herbert Lee's death had taken their toll. Their meeting place at the Masonic Temple was closed to them; someone just missed John Hardy with a shotgun blast into his bedroom. No one would come to registration classes. With Hardy, Curtis Hayes, and Hollis Watkins, Moses left McComb for Amzie Moore's house in the Delta. SNCC's first attempt at establishing a voter registration project in Mississippi was over.

The McComb experience helped to further shape SNCC from the coordinating committee it had intended to be into a staff-directed organization. The student-directed sit-in movement SNCC had been formed to coordinate was in decline, but SNCC, despite the McComb defeat, was on the ascendancy. The direct actionists had learned a valuable lesson in McComb: voter registration *was* direct action in small-town Mississippi. The split between the "direct action" and "voter registration" wings became meaningless. In the future, SNCC's direction would be determined by actions taken and work done, not by titles and divisions. McComb helped to refine SNCC's organizing techniques. Dependence on local leadership coupled with militancy might not have succeeded in McComb, but it could be tried again elsewhere with greater success.

The addition of Bob Zellner to SNCC's staff made it interracial, but Zellner's presence meant more than that. He was hired with a grant to SNCC from the Southern Conference Education Fund (SCEF), an interracial organization formed in the 1930s. Like many interracial organizations, SCEF was a target of Southern red-baiters, especially after a field secretary, Carl Braden, refused to answer questions before the House Un-American Activities Committee and was sentenced to a year in prison for contempt of Congress. Braden and his wife, Anne, developed close ties with SNCC. SCEF's newspaper, the *Southern Patriot*, printed articles about SNCC's efforts and philosophy when the mainstream press and other liberal organizations ignored them. And the Bradens understood—more than most whites—the proper role of whites in a Black-led movement. Southern Blacks, she said, did not "want the participation of white people if they are to be a drag on [the] movement" or if including whites meant "the old pattern that has often prevailed even in liberal interracial organizations—that of white domination."[22] SNCC's easy acceptance of Anne and Carl Braden, who were persona non grata to every other civil rights organization, marked the beginning of a political openness in SNCC that distinguished it from the rest of the civil rights pack.

The SCEF grant was to be used to hire a white student to recruit on white campuses; John Robert Zellner was the student hired. Born in southern Alabama, the son of a Methodist preacher, he attended high school in Mobile and Huntingdon College in Montgomery. He became interested in the protest movement through a class assignment—he met Black students involved in protests and saw a workshop in nonviolence at a Black church. This activity drew him to the attention of school authorities and Alabama's attorney general, MacDonald Gallion, who had served the unconscious John Lewis with an injunction after the Freedom Riders were beaten in Montgomery. Calling them into his office, Attorney General Gallion told Zellner and his schoolmates they were in danger of associating with Communists. "Are there Communists in Alabama?" they asked. "No," said the attorney general, there were none there, but they did pass through.

The McComb project brought SNCC face to face with the flimsiness of the promises made months earlier by Robert Kennedy when he encouraged a turn toward voter registration. Protection had been offered to keep the state from prosecuting John Hardy, but none was forthcoming for Herbert Lee. SNCC could not count on the federal government for protection for their voting rights work and the white violence that would ensue.

McComb had been a detour before SNCC's entry into Albany.

FOURTEEN

ALBANY, GEORGIA, 1961

WHILE MOSES, ROBINSON, and Hardy were setting up shop in McComb, Charles Sherrod and Cordell Reagon were beginning SNCC's second field operation in Southwest Georgia. Sherrod had originally planned to conduct the same kind of voter registration activity in rural Terrell County, but local Blacks were too frightened to let him spend the night; he settled on Albany, the region's largest town, instead. The sheriff of Terrell County, Zeke T. Matthews, had told a *Washington Post* reporter in 1959: "A man who knows the nigger can tell when dissatisfaction is brewing. Niggers up late at night are suspicious. You know, Cap, there's nothing like fear to keep niggers in line."[1]

Both Sherrod and Reagon had been Freedom Riders and spent the summer in Mississippi. Both had been arrested in McComb. Reagon was only eighteen and had been active as a high school student in the Nashville protests. Sherrod was twenty-two, a native of Petersburg, Virginia, born in poverty to a fourteen-year-old mother. Educated at Virginia Union, where he received a BA in 1958 and a bachelor's of divinity in 1961, he intended—like John Lewis, James Bevel, Bernard Lafayette, and others—to become a minister. He saw in King's articulation of the social gospel an alternative to the passive style of leadership most Black ministers represented. At Virginia Union, he was cochair of the Social Action Committee, which ran Petersburg's sit-ins, and had been the first representative from Virginia to SNCC's Coordinating Committee. He had been arrested during a Richmond sit-in and at a Charlotte, North Carolina, theater stand-in.

Mass meetings, such as this one in Danville, Virginia, provided sustenance throughout the movement.

SNCC staffers sit in at a Toddle House in Atlanta in 1963.

Willie Ricks, one of the first to verbalize "black power," speaks in Atlanta.

Brave citizens of Greenwood, Mississippi, try to register to vote, having been organized by SNCC workers.

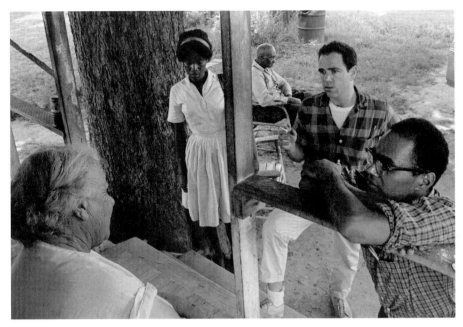

SNCC workers Martha Prescott, Mike Miller, and Bob Moses encourage residents in rural areas of Mississippi to register.

The bomb that killed four young girls at the Sixteenth Street Baptist Church in Birmingham in 1963 blew out these windows.

Jimmy Hicks, Julian Bond, John Lewis, and Jeremiah X survey the damage after the church bombing.

Some of the Selma, Alabama, high school students who helped start their hometown's movement.

SNCC organized "Freedom Day" in 1964 to register Selma voters and brought in author James Baldwin to help.

Martin Luther King Jr. in Selma in 1965.

"Freedom Day" in Hattiesburg, Mississippi, in 1964 is overseen by a large police presence.

Students at a "Freedom School" in Ruleville, Mississippi, one of many set up by SNCC during Freedom Summer 1964.

The Freedom Choir, featuring high school students in Selma in 1964, was just one example of the important role music played throughout the movement.

SNCC members (including Julian Bond at far right) even sang in their office.

Singing at the March on Washington in 1963.

Not all the singers were amateurs. Here is Bob Dylan in Greenwood, Mississippi, in 1963.

He was one of the four SNCC representatives who spent thirty days in the Rock Hill jail.

First Reagon and Sherrod slept in parked cars or front porches and then at the homes of Dr. E. D. Hamilton, a dentist and the local NAACP president, and C. B. King, a local lawyer. They began attracting young people by playing basketball and through Reagon's tales of adventure from the Freedom Rides and Parchman penitentiary. A minister allowed them to use a church room to hold nonviolence workshops; their aim was to test the Interstate Commerce Commission ruling integrating interstate transportation, which Robert Kennedy had extracted after the Freedom Rides.

The plan was simple: Reagon and Sherrod would arrive by bus from Mississippi, where they had gone to attend the trials of those arrested in the Burglund High School demonstration in McComb; local Black youth would meet them in another test of the station's facilities. But word had leaked to the Albany police, directed by Laurie Pritchett. Pritchett had studied police responses to the Freedom Rides and decided that Alabama's mistake had been to allow violence to occur where it could be seen and photographed, thereby inviting federal action. His men would keep the races separate without nightsticks and billy clubs. He told the city commissioners that, if demonstrations occurred, his men would not make arrests under the segregation laws; these were vulnerable to court attack. Instead, they would use the laws protecting public order. Pritchett also developed a system of informers inside the Albany Movement; two newsmen, one an out-of-town reporter and another from the Associated Press, regularly informed police on the movement's plans. The FBI employed paid informers—in the movement and the Ku Klux Klan and from the *Albany Herald*—as well.[2]

The local NAACP was unsure about the protest, but enough young people and then older people and then a few ministers flocked to the meetings Sherrod and Reagon held. Fearful that young people would begin protests without them, the adult leaders created an umbrella organization to plan further action—on November 16, 1961, the Albany Movement was born. Dr. William G. Anderson was elected president. Marion Page, a retired railroad postman, was elected secretary. The NAACP president, Dr. Hamilton, said he could not join; permission would have to come from regional director Ruby Hurley and state field secretary Vernon Jordan.

Hurley had relocated her office to Atlanta after Alabama outlawed the NAACP. Hurley and Jordan told Hamilton the NAACP should take the lead in testing the ICC ruling, lest the SNCC workers' appeal to youth become too attractive. They also hinted to Anderson that he could become the president of the local NAACP, replacing Dr. Hamilton, if he would play down the Albany Movement.

Five days later, on November 22, three members of the Albany NAACP Youth Council were arrested at the bus station. That same afternoon, the local Black college, Albany State, closed for Thanksgiving vacation, and hundreds of students descended on the bus station to take rides home. The earlier trouble had prompted the dean of students to accompany them; he stood at the outside door directing students into the "colored" waiting room. All but two—Blanton Hall and Bertha Gober—obeyed; they had attended Sherrod's workshops and decided to enter the white waiting room. There, Chief Pritchett arrested them—not for violating the segregation laws, which they had done, but for disturbing the peace, which they had not done. They remained in jail through Thanksgiving night, and, as in McComb, their presence galvanized the Black community. Until then, there had been hopes among many that Albany's racial problems could be solved through negotiation; the arrests made it clear this would not be the case. The Albany Movement decided to call its first mass meeting. Before it could be held, and even before they were tried or released from jail, Albany State College suspended the two students, further adding to the community's anger.

At the mass meeting, something occurred that distinguished the Albany Movement from the others that grew and passed across the South, as much as Chief Pritchett's discovery that hidden violence attracted no attention. Cordell Reagon had discovered in the SNCC workshops two gifted young women, ministers' daughters, studying voice in hope of becoming opera stars. That night Bernice Johnson and Rutha Mae Harris sang freedom songs with him and began using that night in Albany's largest mass meeting a technique that effective singers have always known: human voices raised together can convey emotion and passion more powerfully than the spoken word. More than five hundred people gathered outside the courthouse on Monday, November 28, for the trial; the five students were sentenced to fifteen days probation and a hundred-dollar fine. Charles Jones, who had recently arrived in Albany, led the crowd to

Union Baptist Church, where four hundred signed a petition asking the president of Albany State to readmit the expelled students, and then to the campus, where the president refused to see them.

On November 30, 1961, Dr. Anderson, representing the newly formed Albany Movement, met with the city commissioners and asked for a response to the movement's request for desegregation of the city's facilities. The commissioners told him no. That same night Sherrod was arrested on a trespass warrant sworn out by the president of Albany State.

Sherrod, Reagon, and Jones called SNCC's new executive secretary, James Forman, and asked him to organize a Freedom Ride to test integration of train facilities between Atlanta and Albany. On Sunday, December 10, an integrated group of nine Freedom Riders arrived in Albany. Chief Pritchett had sealed off the station and ordered them out of the white waiting room. When they complied, they were met on the street by a joyous crowd of several hundred, assembled by the Albany Movement. The crowd threw the chief off stride. He arrested the nine Freedom Riders— mistakenly letting one go and arresting an Albany State student instead— plus Bertha Gober and Charles Jones.

On Monday, December 11, a small group praying outside Albany's jail were arrested; one of them was Marion King, the wife of Slater King, a respected, middle-class figure in Black Albany. Her arrest added more fuel to the fire in Black Albany, and that night's mass meeting overflowed one church into another across the street. That night Sherrod began to lay plans to fill Albany's jails. When Reagon doubted if even that tactic would break segregation, Sherrod said, "My uncle always told me that enough pressure can make a monkey eat pepper!"[3]

On that same day, two US Army helicopters arrived in South Vietnam, the first overt American involvement in a war between the South Vietnamese government and Viet Minh guerrillas.

Four hundred Blacks marched behind Sherrod in the rain to the courthouse the next morning in Albany. Chief Pritchett ordered them all arrested. Two hundred sixty-seven were arrested. About one hundred posted bond; those remaining overflowed Albany's thirty-person jail and the county jail and were farmed out to jails in the surrounding counties. Two hundred two were arrested the next day. Four hundred seventy-one people were now being held in various jails.

Sporadic attempts at negotiations between the Albany Movement and the city sputtered and failed; the city simply would not agree to integrate anything or to meet to discuss integrating anything. On Tuesday, December 12, Dr. Anderson asked Ralph Abernathy if he and Martin Luther King could come to Albany; King said he would if he was officially invited, and Anderson fired off a telegram of invitation. The news that King had been invited without consultation prompted invitations to heads of other civil rights organizations. SNCC, however, and Marion Page thought the movement could proceed without outside help from any quarter; the local community had leaders aplenty, and King's presence meant local leadership—and local goals—would take a backseat.

On Wednesday, December 13, Albany mayor Asa Kelley and Georgia governor Ernest Vandiver conferred by telephone with Attorney General Robert Kennedy; the two Georgians assured the attorney general that race relations in Albany were excellent, except for a few incidents stirred up by the outsiders from SNCC. Assistant Attorney General Marshall also talked with Marion Page.

Fifteen hundred people waited in two churches on Friday night, December 15, for Martin Luther King. That night, Anderson sent the mayor a telegram, asking for a response by 10:00 a.m. on December 16, Saturday morning. No one received the telegram until just before the deadline; without a response from the mayor, 260 protesters, led by King, Abernathy, and Anderson, marched to city hall, where they were arrested by Chief Pritchett. King was jailed over the weekend in Americus, Dr. Anderson's hometown. Inside prison walls, his mental condition began to deteriorate; King told Wyatt Tee Walker they had to get him out of jail.

Back in Albany, Marion Page held an angry press conference, prompted by SNCC, to announce that Wyatt Tee Walker was not in charge of the Albany Movement; local people were. And in Washington, the attorney general was saying he would not intervene but was willing to offer advice to both sides.

On Monday, December 18, an agreement was reached between city and movement leaders: all local citizens of Albany would be released without bail. The outsiders—mostly from SNCC—would have to pay high bail. The demonstrations would end. The city would hear requests for a biracial committee and integration of the bus and train stations. And Martin

Luther King would leave town. Robert Kennedy called Mayor Kelley with congratulations.

The truce marked the end of the beginning of the first phase of the protest movement in Albany. The truce without victory was immediately portrayed as a defeat for King; the weak settlement was described as the outcome of serious infighting between civil rights organizations. Integration of the bus and train stations involved no more than compliance with federal law. Hearing requests for the establishment of a biracial committee didn't mean they would be granted or that the committee, if established, would accomplish much. Those jailed were released, but the charges against them remained in place.

ALBANY, 1962

The movement in Albany—momentarily without Martin Luther King—struggled on. The January 12, 1962, arrest of an Albany State freshman, Ola Mae Quarterman, for refusing to give up her seat on a local bus precipitated a boycott, with SNCC workers organizing a carpool. Within three weeks, the bus company suspended operations. It finally agreed to integrate its seating, but when the city would not agree to honor integrated seating, the bus company went out of business. A successful boycott of the city's stores was begun.

In January negotiations between the city and the Albany Movement, the city denied it had agreed to any concessions the previous December. King had vowed to stay in jail when he had been arrested in Albany in December 1961. His failure to stay behind bars had become the subject of much movement criticism.

On April 30, 1962, Diane Nash, now married to James Bevel and pregnant with their first child, announced she would drop her appeal of a McComb conviction, for contributing to the delinquency of minors by organizing high school demonstrations there in 1961, and instead serve her sentence. "Since my child will be a black child, born in Mississippi, whether I am in jail or not, he will be born in prison," she said. "I believe that if I go to jail now it may help hasten that day when my child and all children will be free—not only on the day of their birth but for all their lives."[4]

Her plans were frustrated by the judge, who suspended her sentence, but she wrote a widely circulated memo that was critical of movement leaders, especially King. She wrote: "I believe the time has come . . . when each of us must make up his mind, when arrested on unjust charges, to serve his sentence and stop posting bonds. . . .We in the nonviolent movement have been talking about jail without bail for two years or more. It is time for us to mean what we say."[5]

After further skirmishes and unsuccessful negotiations, an Albany judge sentenced King and Abernathy on July 10 to pay a $178 fine or serve forty-five days in jail. They chose to go to jail. King's presence in the Albany jail had begun to attract attention from the Kennedy administration. Robert Kennedy met with an Albany lawyer and told him King's jailing "was an embarrassment to Albany, to the Kennedys, to Georgia, and to the United States in the court of world opinion . . . it must be terminated by any means necessary."[6] The next day the lawyer paid the fines for King and Abernathy, and they were released.

The leaders of white Albany who agreed to this plan also agreed to lie about it. For years, Chief Pritchett said a well-dressed Black man had paid the fine. They had to lie. Admitting they had first jailed and then freed King would hold them up to ridicule and contempt in white Georgia. Doing nothing and allowing the Kennedy administration to release him through court action would force them to admit defeat at other hands. Neither choice would do. But King had to be freed; in jail, he was a martyr; freed, he was subject once again to Pritchett's masterful use of nonviolence to counter the movement's search for photographable violence. The Kennedy administration wanted him released. In jail, his presence was an indictment of their inaction; freed, he was just another petitioner, with Albany's whites, for the administration's ear. But they could not act to free him; that would mean taking sides with Blacks against Albany's whites.

On July 21, Albany Movement leaders were served by federal marshals with an injunction issued by federal judge Robert Elliot, a segregationist Kennedy appointee. Elliot had ruled that segregation was not a denial of Albany Blacks' rights to equal protection; he ruled instead that Albany's white people were denied equal protection by having police services diverted by protests seeking integration. Leaders of the movement were ordered to cease and desist their protests.

The order put the government against the movement and King in a shouting telephone confrontation with Robert Kennedy. Reluctantly, King hesitated to break a federal injunction and decided to obey the order until it could be overturned.

While waiting for the movement's leaders to decide what to say to a mass meeting crowd of over seven hundred, the Reverend Charles Wells had had enough. "I've heard about an injunction," he shouted, "but I haven't seen one. I heard a few names, but my name hasn't been called. But I do know where my name is being called. My name is being called on the road to freedom! I can hear the blood of Emmett Till as it calls from the ground!"[7] Over two hundred people followed him out of the church, down the street, and into jail. "They can stop the leaders," King said from the sidelines, "but they can't stop the people.[8]

The order was vacated a few days later by federal judge Elbert Tuttle, an Eisenhower appointee. But Black Albany was angry with the news that sheriff's deputies in Mitchell County had beaten Mrs. Marion King, six months pregnant, to her knees, knocking her daughter from her arms onto the ground. She had gone to the jail to visit her maid's daughter. A nighttime march through the Black neighborhood exploded in violence, and the movement's leaders called a two-day halt of protests in penance.

SOUTHWEST GEORGIA VOTER REGISTRATION, 1962

Charles Sherrod, meanwhile, picked up where the protests of 1961 had stopped him, organizing in the rural counties outside Albany and Dougherty County. SNCC workers arrived in Lee and Terrell Counties in June 1962. Terrell County was called "terrible Terrell" by local Blacks; they outnumbered whites two to one, but out of 2,858 voters, only 48 were Black. In both places, SNCC accepted invitations from women activists—Mama Dolly Raines in Lee County, and Caroline Daniels in Terrell—to live in their homes. "There is always a 'Mama,'" Sherrod wrote in a field report. "She is usually a militant woman in the community, outspoken, understanding and willing to catch hell, having already caught her share."[9]

Sherrod wanted his project to be integrated. Southern Blacks would lose their fear of whites, he believed, if young whites lived in their home, shared their food, and took upon themselves the risks of being a liberal white in a society where all other whites were hostile, some of them violently so. Seeing whites and Blacks working together, he said, would "strike at the very root of segregation . . . the idea that white is superior. That idea has eaten into the minds of the people, black and white. We have to break this image. We can only do this if they see black and white working together, side by side, the white man no more and no less than his black brother, but human beings together."[10]

The night of Albany's violence, July 25, 1962, Charles Sherrod had driven to a mass meeting in Terrell County at Mount Olive Baptist Church. Sheriff Z. T. Matthews, smoking a cigar, and several armed deputies burst into the church. Sherrod recited "The Lord's Prayer," and then parishioners began to sing "We Are Climbing Jacob's Ladder" when Sheriff Matthews interrupted. Terrell County's whites, he said, were "a little fed up with the registration business. . . . Niggers down here have been happy for a hundred years."[11]

Matthews had not known before he entered that three reporters, including Claude Sitton, were in the church. But had they not been present, more than angry words would have been heard. A front-page story in the *New York Times* two days later explained what happened. The *Times* story prompted Robert Kennedy to act swiftly; in two weeks the Justice Department had filed a complaint against the sheriff.

Back in Albany, Martin Luther King had managed to get arrested again, while praying for negotiations on the steps of the city hall. On July 28, when attorney C. B. King presented himself at the county jail to see white SNCC worker William Hansen, who had been beaten by other white prisoners, Sheriff D. C. "Cull" Campbell beat King with a heavy cane. "Yeah," I beat him," Campbell told the FBI. "I told the son of a bitch to get out of my office, and he didn't get out."[12]

Finally, President Kennedy spoke out about events in Albany: "Let me say that I find it wholly inexplicable why the city council of Albany will not sit down with the citizens of Albany, who may be Negroes, and attempt to secure them, in a peaceful way, their rights. The United States government is involved in sitting down at Geneva with the Soviet Union. I can't understand why the government of Albany . . . cannot do the same for American citizens."[13]

Kennedy's plea was not answered. On August 8, the Justice Department made its first move in the Albany protests, filing a brief in support of the Albany Movement's opposition to the injunction. After three weeks in jail, King and Abernathy were finally tried, convicted, and sentenced to sixty-day terms, suspended on the condition that they did not break any segregation laws.

On August 14, arsonists burned Shady Grove Baptist Church in Lee County; SNCC had used the church for a voter registration mass meeting just four days before. On August 31, someone fired shots into a Lee County home where SNCC workers slept. On September 4, shots were fired into a Terrell County home; a white student was wounded, and two others slightly grazed. On September 9, two churches SNCC had used for registration meetings in Terrell County were burned to the ground. On September 17, another church was burned; the four arsonists had stayed to watch the blaze and were arrested on the spot. Although they confessed to the FBI, the Justice Department declined to prosecute them, reasoning that they burned the church because they hated Blacks, and *not* because they wanted to intimidate Blacks from voting. They were tried and convicted in state court, the only convictions resulting from a rash of church burnings that summer. By September 26, four more churches were burned. In Albany, the movement sputtered on, but for Martin Luther King, the Albany Movement was over.

WE CAN'T WIN BY SINGING, BUT WE CAN'T WIN IF WE DON'T SING!

For both King and SNCC, Albany taught important lessons. They learned that nonviolent suffering and jail-packing alone could not win against law enforcement that suspended the First Amendment and a federal government that did not notice or did not care. They learned the federal government would not intervene when violence was hidden from public view.

This was SNCC's first effort in a community larger than McComb and a first experience in dealing with a multiplicity of local organizations. Local NAACP leadership had been supportive in Southwest Mississippi, but the NAACP was cautious in Albany, and everyone's efforts were undercut by the actions of the NAACP's national staff. But SNCC learned how to ingratiate itself with most local leadership by refusing to dictate to them. SNCC had helped develop and organize the protest movement in Albany; they didn't arrive after the movement began, as did King and representatives from SCLC. SNCC had helped to create the Albany Movement that invited King; he had come to a community where SNCC had already earned some respect. SNCC learned to develop new leadership and support existing ones; it learned it succeeded best when it sublimated its identity in a community effort. It learned that local Blacks were already poised on the edge of revolt, were ready to go to jail for the movement's goals if the opportunity was presented to them.

Both SNCC and Martin Luther King learned that a movement can be hurt or helped by media coverage. The national media's depiction of the Albany Movement as a failure suggested that it was over in December 1961; in fact, it continued onward for several years. Martin Luther King learned that his brand of nonviolent witness and persuasion had proven ineffective. In Birmingham he would be better organized, and there would be no competition from the NAACP or SNCC. In Birmingham, he would move toward coercive nonviolence. If Albany had failed, the next time there would be clear success.

As had the Freedom Rides, Albany established SNCC as a partner able to sit as equals with SCLC and the NAACP. SNCC workers learned in Albany and Southwest Georgia that music, always a part of Black culture and community, could be an important weapon in the movement too. In the Albany Movement, music became part of the movement's arsenal. It inspired; it created community; it told stories better than speakers could and some stories speakers could not tell. The music issued challenges to the white opposition. It tied the movement's experiences—a march, a boycott, a clash with white authority—to the tradition of the Black church. And it took from the tradition of Black church songs, substituting words and names to create new songs, applying old songs with biblical messages to the current movement. Bernice Johnson—who became Bernice Reagon—said, "This music was like an instrument, like holding a tool in your hand."

SNCC field secretary Charles Sherrod described in a field report how the music helped the movement when he wrote about the Albany Movement's first mass meeting in November 1961:

> The church was packed before eight o'clock. People were everywhere in the aisles, sitting and standing in the choir stands, hanging over the railing of the balcony upstairs, sitting in trees outside near windows.... When the last speaker among the students, Bertha Gober, had finished, there was nothing left to say. Tears filled the eyes of hard, grown men who had known personally and seen with their own eyes merciless

atrocities committed. . . . And when we rose to sing "We Shall Overcome," nobody could imagine what kept the top of the church on its four walls. . . . I threw my head back and . . . sang with my whole body.[14]

These songs served many purposes. They helped to rally community spirit. They helped the community to say things in song they might not dare to say in conversation. Most of them were congregational, sung by everyone in the mass meeting. When everyone sang, everyone shared in the emotion and everyone shared in the spirit expressed in the song. Each community also had song leaders who served as galvanizers and selected the right song for the right moment.[15]

One of the most known is the movement anthem, "We Shall Overcome." The documentary maker George Stoney has produced a marvelous film on this song, tracing its development from an old church song, "I'll Overcome Someday." In 1945, members of the Food and Tobacco Workers Union in Charleston, South Carolina, adopted it for use during a strike and brought it with them to Highlander Folk School. Zilphia Horton, the wife of Highlander's founder, used it at union meetings all over the South and taught it to folksinger Pete Seeger. Seeger and Horton added verses appropriate to labor, peace, and integration movements. In 1959, Guy Carawan was hired as Highlander's music director. He sang it at SNCC's organizational meeting in Raleigh on Easter weekend, 1960. That was the first time many of us had heard it. It quickly became the movement's anthem.

I have seen Israeli and Palestinian women holding hands and singing it; it was sung as the Berlin Wall came down. I heard it sung in Tiananmen Square. During the pro-immigration protest marches by Latinos, I heard it sung in Spanish in Jackson, Mississippi.

In July 1963, Robert Shelton, the music critic of the *New York Times*, wrote:

"We Shall Overcome" has been called "The Marseillaise" of the integration movement. It has passed by word of mouth with great speed despite the fact that no single disk of the song has been issued and no sheet music will be available in stores next month.[16]

FIFTEEN

MISSISSIPPI VOTER REGISTRATION

IN 1963, MOVEMENT activity cascaded and grew in three states. As the conflict in Albany continued, Bob Moses was organizing an assault on Mississippi. This time he began in the Delta counties in the northwest portion of the state, assembling a staff drawn largely from Mississippi. Unlike Sherrod's project in Southwest Georgia, Moses's effort in Mississippi would be all Black.

A 1963 SNCC report said it was "too dangerous for whites to participate in the project in Mississippi—too dangerous for them and too dangerous for the Negroes who would be working with them."[1] When whites were involved, it was too difficult to secure meeting places or places to live; the presence of whites brought extra attention from law enforcement officials and a community's white residents, already hostile to the idea of registering Black voters.

Moses wanted young Black Mississippians who "identified with SNCC . . . [and] with each other in terms . . . of being from Mississippi and more or less thinking that their job, and even their life's work, would be to make some sense out of living in Mississippi." Unlike older Blacks, younger Mississippians, he believed, "would not be responsible economically to any sector of the white community and . . . would be able to act as free agents."[2] He dispatched Hollis Watkins and Curtis Hayes, two McComb students arrested in the fall 1961 Hattiesburg demonstrations and expelled from school. Sam Block, a college student from Cleveland,

Mississippi, began a voter registration drive in Greenwood, where he was soon joined by a Rust College graduate, Willie Peacock. Charles McLaurin opened an office in Ruleville, the home of Senator James O. Eastland. By the spring of 1962 there were six offices with twenty field secretaries—only two were not Mississippians—Moses and Charles Cobb, a minister's son from Springfield, Massachusetts, who had dropped out of Howard University to come south.

In June 1962, Moses took his staff to Highlander Folk School for a week's retreat. They decided to use the campaigns of two Black ministers in Delta districts to spur interest in registration. Neither candidate was expected to win, and their running at all was such a novelty that whites were not expected to harass them. The campaigns could be used as cover for registration and education work. Moses became the campaign manager for one, and Bevel managed the other.

On the same Saturday that the Albany Movement experienced its false expectation of victory, Moses and Sam Block took twenty-five Blacks to the Leflore County Courthouse in Greenwood; two days later, three white men beat Block on a downtown street. On August 14, while Shady Grove Baptist Church was burning in Lee County, Georgia, a mob attacked the SNCC office in Greenwood. Block and two other workers escaped through an upstairs window. The Greenwood raid triggered a meeting in Clarksdale between Wiley Branton, the director of the Voter Education Project, and registration forces in the state.

THE VOTER EDUCATION PROJECT

In March 1962, the Voter Education Project (VEP) was formally born. It had its origins in talks Robert Kennedy and his aides held in 1961 with civil rights leaders and foundation officials as the Freedom Rides had claimed national and international attention. The administration wanted the civil rights movement out of the headlines, and its energies turned toward activity that would both help the administration and advance the cause of civil rights. Voting rights fit both these criteria; it also had the advantage of being difficult to oppose. Even the most ardent segregationist congressman found it hard to defend denying Black people the right to vote.

Funded with foundation money channeled through the Southern Regional Council, the VEP pretended to be a research project, an investigation into Southern Black voting. If its real purposes were hidden, its

sponsorship made them obvious; the national committees of both political parties endorsed it and Attorney General Robert Kennedy personally
intervened with Mortimer Kaplan, the commissioner of internal revenue,
to obtain its tax exemption.[3] The director was attorney Wiley A. Branton,
a thirty-eight-year-old lawyer from Pine Bluff, Arkansas, who had been
counsel to the Little Rock Nine. His job, ostensibly, was to coordinate the
voter registration activities of SNCC, CORE, NAACP, and SCLC. In practice, Branton's job was to see that the organizations honestly conducted
separate voter registration drives in distinct sections of the South, with
little actual cooperation among them.

Despite Branton's fairness, inevitable clashes occurred. One problem was Mississippi itself. Roy Wilkins of the NAACP thought spending
money on voter registration there was a mistake; the state was too difficult,
and the gains would be too small to justify the danger or the expense of a
voter registration drive. If money was to be spent on voting drives, however, he thought it should go to the NAACP. Mississippi was an NAACP
state; his organization's long history and considerable sacrifice there gave
him first call on any funds to be spent there. Wilkins also disliked SNCC.
He thought the organization was irresponsible and foolishly militant, interested in headlines, while the NAACP did the important, less glamor-
ous work.

After the raid on the Greenwood SNCC office, Branton called a meeting in Clarksdale of groups working in Mississippi. James Bevel, now
an SCLC staffer, represented his organization. Dave Dennis represented
CORE. Aaron Henry and Amzie Moore represented the NAACP, and
James Forman, Bob Moses, and his organizers represented SNCC.

Wilkins's objections might have meant that no VEP money would be
spent in Mississippi, but Branton constructed an alternative. He knew that
if any work toward registration was to be done, it was the young people
of SNCC who would do it. He agreed to set up a front organization, an
umbrella like that used in Montgomery and in Albany. This one would
be called the Council of Federated Organizations (COFO). Aaron Henry,
head of the Mississippi State Conference of NAACP Branches, was chosen
president; Moses became director of voter registration. Henry, a long-time
NAACP activist, offered his reputation and NAACP associations as cover;
Moses brought the activists and organizers from SNCC. Dennis would

provide some workers from CORE. SCLC provided a small number of workers; VEP would provide the money.

Wilkins was right about the difficulty of working in Mississippi. As they left the Clarksdale meeting, Forman's car was stopped, and he was ordered to leave the county. Dave Dennis was arrested for a traffic violation; Sam Block and five others were arrested for loitering—in a moving car—and rearrested with Moses and five others the next day for distributing literature without a permit.

In August 1962, SNCC workers—still called Freedom Riders by local Blacks—came to Sunflower County, the home of Senator James O. Eastland, chairman of the Senate Judiciary Committee. A vigorous opponent of civil rights laws, Eastland was the chief reason why so many of the Kennedy appointees to the federal bench were racists. The county's reputation for racial violence stretched back to a lynching involving the Eastland family in Doddsville in 1904. Eastland's uncle had an argument with a Black man; shots were exchanged, and the uncle was killed. A lynch mob of two hundred whites with two packs of bloodhounds chased the killer and his wife into a swamp, killing two innocent Blacks on the way. The accused were tied to stakes before a mob of one thousand. As the funeral pyre was being prepared, their fingers and ears were cut off and distributed as souvenirs. The man was beaten, and one of his eyes knocked out. According to one newspaper account, a large corkscrew was "bored into the flesh of the man and woman, in the arms, legs and body, and then pulled out, the spirals tearing out big pieces of raw, quivering flesh every time it was withdrawn." They were then burned to death.[4]

In 1929, an escaped Black prisoner from Parchman penitentiary was captured, chained to a log, and burned to death in Sunflower County. "Now and then," the *Memphis Press-Scimitar* reported, "someone would step forward and throw a little gasoline on the blaze. The whole burning took a little more than an hour. The Negro was alive and screaming 40 minutes of that time."[5]

Senator Eastland had been appointed to the Senate in 1941 to fill a vacancy; he was reelected without difficulty thereafter. A champion red- and race-baiter, he said the 1954 *Brown* decision aimed at "the mongrelization of the white race." He had held up Thurgood Marshall's appointment to a federal judgeship until President Kennedy agreed to nominate W. Harold

Cox to the US district court in Mississippi. He told Robert Kennedy, "Tell your brother that if he gives me Harold Cox, I will give him the nigger."[6]

Mrs. Mary Tucker, a Ruleville Black woman in her late sixties, let some "Freedom Riders" stay in her home. Their days were spent walking from house to house in Ruleville or riding from plantation to plantation, recruiting potential voter applicants. Mrs. Tucker thought about a friend of hers. "I said, 'Lord, I believe I'll go out in the country and get Fannie Lou. I want her to come in here and hear this because I believe it would mean something to her.'"[7]

FANNIE LOU TOWNSEND HAMER

Fannie Lou Townsend was born on October 6, 1917, in Montgomery County, Mississippi, the youngest of twenty children. Her birth was a benefit to her family; the plantation owner paid her father fifty dollars for producing a future field hand. In 1919, they moved to Sunflower County, part of a larger internal migration by Mississippi Blacks. While many moved to Chicago, others moved within Mississippi, relocating to the Delta counties to take the places of those who had left.

Sunflower County's largest town—then and now—was Indianola; the Townsends lived near Ruleville. When she was six years old, Mrs. Hamer remembered, "I was playing beside the road and this plantation owner drove up to me and asked me 'Could I pick cotton?' I told him I didn't know, and he said, 'Yes, you can. I will give you things that you want from the commissary store,' and he mentioned things like crackerjacks and sardines. So I picked the 30 pounds of cotton that week, but I found out that actually he was trapping me into beginning the work I was to keep doing and I never did get out of his debt again."[8] The next week, she had to pick sixty pounds.

The large Townsend family managed to put money aside; Mr. Townsend bought three mules, two cows, farm implements, and a car. While they were away one night, local whites poisoned the animals, and the family was reduced to the sharecropping system again.

Mrs. Townsend was protective of her children, once attacking a white man who had slapped her youngest boy. The Townsends earned extra money by "scrapping cotton," or picking fields clean. Mrs. Townsend would help kill hogs and be rewarded with the intestines, feet, and head, but sometimes the family had little more to eat than bread and onions.

Young Fannie Lou noticed the discrepancy between the life her family led and that of the whites whose land they worked. She asked, "Mother, how come we are not white? Because white people have clothes, they can have food to eat, and we work all the time and we don't have anything."

"She said, 'I don't ever want to hear you say that again, honey.' . . . She said, 'You respect yourself as a little child, a little black child. And as you grow older, respect yourself as a black woman. Then one day, other people will respect you.'"[9]

When Fannie Lou was eight, she learned about a white mob that had come to get a Black man who had shot back at a white man, killing him. "I ain't never heard of no one white man going to get a Negro," she later recalled.

> They're the most cowardly people I ever heard of. The mob came to get Mr. Pullum, but he was waiting for them and every time a white man would peep out, he busted him. Before they finally got him, he'd killed 13 and wounded 26. The way they finally got him was to pour gasoline on the water of the bayou and set it afire. When it burned to the hollowed-out stump, he crawled out. . . . They dragged him by his heels on the back of a car and paraded about with that man for all the Negroes to see. They cut his ear off and for the longest time it was kept in a jar of alcohol in a showcase in a store window in Drew.[10]

She left school after the sixth grade to help support her family but took advantage of the whites' homes she lived in to continue reading. Her father died in 1939; an accident with an axe began to take her mother's eyesight. As older brothers and sisters left home to find a better life, she stayed home to care for her mother, who died in 1961.

In 1944, at the age of twenty-seven, she married thirty-two-year-old Perry Hamer, known as Pap. They lived in a small house on the Marlow Plantation with running cold water and a broken indoor toilet. Mrs. Hamer remembered not minding the broken toilet until one day she worked for a white family and was told that a second bathroom didn't have to be cleaned too well. "It's just Old Honey's," she was told. Old Honey was the dog. "I just couldn't get over that dog having a bathroom when [the white man] wouldn't even have the toilet fixed for us. But then, Negroes in Mississippi are treated *worse* than dogs."[11]

The plantation routine followed the cotton season. Planted in April, it had to be chopped—or weeded—from May onward. "You get up before sunrise and go in the kitchen and get some breakfast. You fixes what you had, and about sun-up we were in the fields, choppin' cotton." There would be a respite at the end of August; then picking began. To get a five-hundred-pound bale, fifteen hundred pounds had to be picked; the seeds, removed during ginning, added to the weight. "We picked from Monday morning until Saturday night," a plantation worker remembered.[12]

In 1961, Mrs. Hamer entered a hospital to have a small uterine tumor removed. Without her knowledge or consent, the doctor performed a hysterectomy. "I went to the doctor who did that to me and I asked him, 'Why? Why had he done that to me?' He didn't have to say nothing—and he didn't."[13]

In August 1962, Mary Tucker called on Fannie Lou Hamer. "'Fannie Lou, I want you to come to my home.' She said, 'What for, Tuck?' I said, 'I want you to come to a meeting. We're having a civil rights meeting . . . We're learning how to register to vote so you can be a citizen.'"[14] Mrs. Hamer went to her first civil rights meeting at Williams Chapel Church in Ruleville; James Bevel was the main speaker. James Forman told the small gathering that each one of them had the right to register to vote.

"It made so much sense to me because right then, you see," Mrs. Hamer said later, "the man who was our night policeman here in Ruleville was a brother to J. W. Milam, which was one of the guys helped to lynched this kid Emmett Till. . . . Then they asked who would go down there Friday and try to become a registered voter. I was one of the persons that held up my hand."[15]

Two weeks before, SNCC worker Charles McLaurin had taken three elderly Black women to Ruleville to register to vote. "I learned then," he said, "that a faithful few are better than an uncertain ten." They found the clerk's office locked.

On August 31, 1962, Mrs. Hamer and seventeen others went to Indianola in a rented bus to register to vote. Once there, McLaurin said, the people milled about; the courthouse was a symbol of white power and a source of Black fear. All were hesitant about entering it. "Then this one little stocky lady just stepped off the bus and went right on up to the courthouse and into the circuit clerk's office. I didn't know this was Fannie Lou Hamer."[16]

Mrs. Hamer remembered that first trip: "It was so many people down there, you know, white people, and some of them looked like the Beverly Hillbillies . . . but they wasn't kidding down there; they had on, you know, cowboy hats and they had guns, they had dogs."

Applicants had to fill out a long questionnaire, including listing their employer's name, and interpret a section of the state constitution. The registrar asked Mrs. Hamer to interpret Section 16 of the constitution. It dealt, she said later, "with facto laws and I knowed as much about a facto law as a horse knows about Christmas Day."[17] She failed the test.

On the way back to Ruleville, the bus was stopped and the driver arrested; the bus was too yellow and, according to the officer, could be mistaken for a school bus. The stranded passengers were "restless and afraid." McLaurin remembered: "In the midst of all this grumbling about the problems, a voice, a song, a church song just kind of smoothly came out of the group. 'Down By The Riverside.' Or 'Ain't Gonna Let Nobody Turn Me Around.' 'This Little Light of Mine.' And that voice was Fannie Lou Hamer, and it seemed to calm everybody on the bus."[18] They scraped together the money for the driver's fine and were finally allowed to return home.

When Mrs. Hamer returned to the Marlow Plantation where she had lived for eighteen years, the owner had already been there, asking for her, and had told Pap Hamer she had gone to Indianola to register. "We ain't gonna have that now," he said. He told Pap Hamer she would have to take her name off the registration book if she wanted to stay on his plantation. Since she had failed the test, her name wasn't there. When her husband asked what she was going to do, Mrs. Hamer replied, "I didn't go down there to register for Mr. Marlow. I went down to register for myself."[19] She repeated this to Mr. Marlow. The next morning, she left and moved in with Mrs. Tucker and, for safety, later moved in with friends in Tallahatchie County.

Bob Moses asked Charles McLaurin to find the woman who had tried to register to vote, sung on the bus, and been evicted from her home. He finally found her. McLaurin told her Moses had asked her to join the movement. He wanted her to become a part of the SNCC staff, to go to Tougaloo College, and then to a meeting of Mississippi registration workers in Nashville. "And she said, 'I'll be ready in a minute.'"[20]

Another person who was ready was Hartman Turnbow. I remember him. Dressed like the farmer he was, in coveralls, boots, and an old hat,

Mr. Turnbow carried a briefcase. When he opened the briefcase, there was nothing in it but an automatic.

In April 1963, Mr. Turnbow went with a group of other Black farmers in Holmes County, Mississippi, to try to register to vote. When the sheriff asked "Who'll be the first?," no one moved. Then Mr. Turnbow said, "Me, Hartman Turnbow, I came here to die to vote. I'm the first."[21] Four days later, the Klan firebombed his home and fired multiple shots into the living room. Mr. Turnbow fired back. Then the sheriff charged him with arson, accusing him of setting fire to his own uninsured home.

SNCC's projects in Southwest Georgia experienced a wave of terror, including arson and night-rider shootings in August and September 1962. At the same time, violence increased in Mississippi. On September 11, night riders fired into two of the three homes that provided shelter for SNCC volunteers in Ruleville; two young girls were wounded, one of them seriously.

The two-state violence prompted an unusually strong statement of condemnation from President Kennedy on September 13. In response to a press conference question, he said: "I don't know any more outrageous action which I've seen occur in this country than the burning of a church—two churches—because of the effort, made by Negroes, to be registered to vote." He called the Ruleville shootings "cowardly as well as outrageous."[22]

"I commend those who are making the effort to register every citizen. They deserve the protection of the United States government, the protection of the states. . . . And if it requires extra legislation, and extra force, we shall do that."[23]

Three nights later, the I Hope Baptist Church in Terrell County, Georgia, was burned; the arsonists were arrested on the spot, drinking beer. Four more Georgia churches were burned within two weeks.

The president's rhetoric had not been able to stop church burnings—and the president's Justice Department was becoming more timid rather than more aggressive in its pursuit of voting rights. It faced the hostility of segregationist federal judges, many of them Kennedy appointees. In September, Burke Marshall admitted the difficulties they faced and warned a delegation of civil rights leaders that they could not expect "protection guarantees" for registration workers, despite the president's statement and the department's earlier promises to civil rights groups.

SIXTEEN

BIRMINGHAM

M ARTIN LUTHER KING'S SCLC staff met in Dorchester, Georgia, in early January 1963 to plan a major assault on segregation in Birmingham, Alabama. After the criticisms he had received in Albany, King and SCLC were determined that their next target would be more carefully chosen. Birmingham seemed perfect in every way. It was frequently described as the most segregated city in America, and its segregation laws were as comprehensive and harsh as those in any Southern city. The NAACP was still outlawed in Alabama, and SNCC had little presence there. There would be none of the sniping and backbiting that had drawn unwelcome media attention to divisions in the movement in Albany. SCLC's affiliate, the Alabama Christian Movement for Human Rights, had issued the invitation to King and SCLC to come to Birmingham. Reverend Fred Shuttlesworth's organization enjoyed community support and had held mass meetings every Monday night for seven years. Birmingham, more than Albany, was a town whose economy was ruled by outside financial interests in the North that SCLC supporters could pressure. Forty percent of its population of eighty thousand was Black, but there were fewer than ten thousand Black voters. There were fifty cross burnings and eighteen bombings in Birmingham between 1957 and 1963.

A 1961 *New York Times* story described Birmingham's race relations: "Every channel of communication, every medium of mutual interest, every reasoned approach, every inch of middle ground has been fragmented by the emotional dynamite of racism, enforced by the whip, the razor, the gun, the bomb, the torch, the club, the knife, the mob, the police and many branches of the state's apparatus."[1]

Theophilus "Bull" Connor had been Birmingham's police commissioner in the late 1930s and again in the early 1950s. Born in Selma, Alabama, in 1897, Connor became the play-by-play announcer for Birmingham's baseball team, the Birmingham Barons, in 1925. The job gave him his nickname "Bull" and a loyal following throughout the city.

As a politician, he fiercely opposed what he described as the Communist-integrationist conspiracy and promised to use his authority to drive these scoundrels from Birmingham. He courted and won blue-collar white votes by declaring himself the friend of the working man, aligned with them against the unions and the owners; in truth, he was the best friend the owners ever had. In 1938, he and his policemen invaded a convention of the interracial Southern Conference for Human Welfare at the city auditorium to enforce the city's segregation ordinance; he made Blacks and whites sit on opposite sides of the auditorium. In 1948, waving the Alabama Standard flag, he led the walkout of Southern delegations from the Democratic National Convention in Philadelphia; a week later, back in Birmingham's Municipal Auditorium, he helped to create the Dixiecrat Party that challenged President Truman in the 1948 election. In 1950, he ran unsuccessfully for governor of Alabama as an outspoken segregationist.

By then, Birmingham's business elite had tired of him; his bullyboy actions as police commissioner had given the city a bad name and hurt its attempts to attract industry. In February 1952, a citizens' investigating committee sponsored by the city's economic and social powers attacked his direction of the police department—especially his failure to solve a series of bombings in a Black section called Smithfield, more popularly known as Dynamite Hill. The criticism and a scandal forced him from office.

With Connor gone, Birmingham began to make moderate racial progress, spurred by a biracial committee formed over Connor's objections in 1951. Birmingham's first Black hospital was built in 1954. Plans were made to admit Black doctors to the all-white Jefferson County Medical Society. Segregation in downtown elevators was eliminated and taxi drivers pressured to carry all passengers. In January 1954, the city commission repealed the ordinances mandating segregated athletic events, mainly to allow the Birmingham Barons to play against teams that had hired Black players. Segregationists put the matter to a referendum that overwhelmingly lost.

In July 1955, a Black minister named Fred Shuttlesworth appeared before the commission to ask them to hire Black police. One commissioner said yes; another said no; the third said such a move should be delayed because of tensions aroused by the *Brown* decision. Plans to integrate the police force were put on a back burner as racial tensions rose across Alabama.

In December 1955, the Montgomery bus boycott began. In February 1956, there was rioting over the integration of the University of Alabama. After pressure, both from organized racist groups and from segregationist businessmen, Birmingham's biracial committee was disbanded. Connor ran unsuccessfully for sheriff in 1955 and in 1956 lost a special election for a commission seat. He denounced Shuttlesworth's attempts to integrate buses and parks. In 1957, he regained the office of police commissioner by 108 votes, running as an ardent segregationist who would do more to protect white privilege than the more genteel segregationists who ran the city. Riding the anti-Black sentiment unleashed by the 1954 *Brown* decision, he quickly consolidated his power and directed a reign of terror at both white and Black citizens who dared challenge segregation, even in the slightest way. His policemen raided a meeting of Birmingham's only interracial organization, the Alabama Council on Human Relations, taking the names of all in attendance. Shortly afterward, neighbors and business associates of the whites in attendance received a notice of their membership in this biracial organization. Most resigned. Connor closed city parks to avoid integration.

In addition to rigid segregation and a police chief much less sophisticated than Albany's chief, Laurie Pritchett, Birmingham had, like other Southern cities, a history of protest and an ongoing movement. The NAACP had agitated for equal rights in Birmingham for years. The Communist Party had organized boycotts, marches, and other protests in Birmingham and across Alabama in the 1930s and 1940s. A boycott begun by students at Miles College in March 1962 had already cut business for some merchants in half. And Birmingham had the Reverend Fred W. Shuttlesworth.

FRED SHUTTLESWORTH

Fred Shuttlesworth was membership chairman of the Birmingham NAACP until the organization was outlawed in June 1956 by Alabama attorney general John Patterson; within four days Shuttlesworth started a new organization, the Alabama Christian Movement for Human Rights.

Following the Montgomery bus boycott, Shuttlesworth announced he would lead a group to integrate Birmingham's buses on Christmas Day, 1956; on Christmas Eve, fifteen sticks of dynamite blew up his parsonage. The next day, he led two hundred of his followers onto city buses, where most of them were arrested. In January 1957, he filed suit against bus segregation in Birmingham. When he won, the city commission passed a law requiring passengers to sit where drivers placed them. In November 1958, he filed suit against the new bus seating law, a suit that eventually—in 1962—integrated Birmingham's buses. In August 1957, Shuttlesworth applied to have his children transferred to a white school. When they were rejected, he filed suit. When the law was declared unconstitutional, he tried to enter them again. When they were refused, he filed suit again. His suit integrated the schools in 1963. In 1959, he filed suit to integrate the city's parks.

When Bull Connor halted Freedom Riders in Birmingham, Shuttlesworth was arrested twice. When a mob surrounded a church in Montgomery during the Freedom Rides, Shuttlesworth boldly made his way through, so surprising the mob that they were unable to attack him. When the sit-ins began in February 1960 from Greensboro to High Point, North Carolina, Shuttlesworth was there as a visiting preacher. After he watched the students, he called Ella Baker to tell her, "You must tell Martin that we must get with this."[2] In 1961, Shuttlesworth moved to Cincinnati to pastor at Revelation Baptist Church but remained connected to the struggle in Birmingham, coming back often.

SINCE THE FREEDOM RIDER violence in Birmingham in 1961, Birmingham's business leaders and moderate whites had been trying to devise a plan to get rid of Bull Connor. Matters came to a head in November 1961, when a federal judge ruled in Fred Shuttlesworth's suit that the city's parks would have to integrate. Connor and the other two commissioners voted instead to close them. To the business community, interested in attracting new industry into the city, the idea of a city without parks, playgrounds, and pools was unthinkable. The city's business leadership organized a drive to reverse the park closings but failed.

Harming the city's economic interest was the last straw. Unable to defeat Bull Connor at the polls, business leaders decided to try to change

Birmingham's form of government from the three-member commission system that gave Connor control of the police department to the standard mayor and council system in place in Atlanta, Birmingham's successful rival. Their plan would keep anyone from having to campaign directly against Connor; that way lay real risk. Instead, they could campaign for good government, and, if successful, a mayor might be elected with more polish and sophistication than the dangerous Connor. Their efforts were at least partially successful; a referendum to change the system won in November 1962, requiring election of new city office-holders—a mayor and council members—in March 1963. What they had not counted on was that Connor decided to run for mayor.

Meanwhile, word that King and SCLC were coming to Birmingham was no secret. SCLC held its annual convention in Birmingham in September 1962, and hints were dropped then that something "big" would hit the city early the next year. Supporters of the change in government were sure King's presence and any civil rights demands would solidify Connor's support, resulting in his election as mayor. Desperately, they sought an audience with King, who referred them to Shuttlesworth. This was the first time Shuttlesworth had been invited to sit down with the city's economic leadership. One merchant offered to integrate water fountains. "We passed water a long time ago," Shuttlesworth said. "We have to have toilets." The merchants agreed to integrate the public facilities—toilets and water fountains—in five downtown stores, and Shuttlesworth advised King to call off the protests he was planning.

But Connor torpedoed this plan; by the time the SCLC convention was over, he threatened to prosecute the stores, and the "white" and "colored" signs reappeared. King and Shuttlesworth agreed to reschedule the demonstrations for the Easter shopping season in 1963. Businesses would be especially vulnerable to a boycott then. Any longer delay might mean facing a new administration, and SCLC wanted to face Bull Connor.

A two-day retreat at Dorchester Academy in Midway, Georgia, was intended to ensure that mistakes made in Albany would not be repeated in Birmingham. SCLC believed that if the movement could create a large, national demand for action, the federal government would respond. There, in Midway, Wyatt Tee Walker laid out the four-step plan he had been working on for months. He called it Project C—for "confrontation." First, small-stage sit-in demonstrations would draw attention to the movement's demands, while community spirit was built up through nightly mass meetings. Next, the boycott of downtown stores would be stepped up, and demonstrations would grow progressively larger. Third, they would engage in mass marches, both to enforce the boycott and to fill the jails. Finally, if they were needed, outsiders would be solicited to cripple the city under the combined pressure of the boycott, publicity, and jails crowded to overflowing.

The Birmingham movement had to build steadily from smaller to larger confrontations, Walker said; it must always be larger than the Albany protests because it would inevitably be compared with it. At least one thousand people would have to be in jail at any one time; each person would have to stay for five or six days before being bailed out. When members of the SCLC staff left Dorchester in January 1963, King warned that some of them might not leave Birmingham alive. "There are eleven people here assessing the type of enemy we're going to face," he said. "I have to tell you that in my judgment, some of the people sitting here today will not come back alive from this campaign. And I want you to think about it."[3]

In early 1963, King met with Attorney General Robert Kennedy and talked by telephone with President John Kennedy, asking if the 1963 State of the Union Address couldn't contain the promise of new civil rights legislation—the promise candidate Kennedy had made three years before. President Kennedy demurred, telling King he could do more good through executive orders and appointments, rather than sending legislation that could not pass to Congress—where, he did not add, it might endanger the rest of his legislative program.

On January 23, 1963, SCLC's staff met in Atlanta to confirm their decision. They would begin demonstrations in Birmingham for three reasons: first, local Blacks wanted action; second, there had already been a successful boycott; and, finally, the Albany experience had taught them valuable lessons that they would apply in Birmingham. In Birmingham, a victory could be won. The protests would start on March 14.

One lesson learned in Albany was the need for regular consultation with local leadership. In early February, King and Walker met with the board of the ACMHR to finalize their plans. Shuttlesworth provided an entree into Black Birmingham, but, despite Shuttlesworth's personal popularity, not every Black minister would support the movement. Connor's penchant for brutality was a double-edged sword: violence could attract outside attention and federal intervention, but it could also crush the movement. As a steel company union buster in the 1930s, he had broken the labor movement in Birmingham, which was more powerful than the civil rights movement was in 1963.[4]

Walker laid detailed plans for the Birmingham protests. He collected the names and addresses of three hundred people who had promised to go to jail and a larger number of volunteers who would help in other ways. He established telephone, transportation, food, and jail visitation committees. And he selected his targets carefully. In Albany, the movement had demanded an end to all segregation; in Birmingham, the target would be lunch counters. While court orders had integrated buses, the lunch counters were a daily reminder to all Blacks who passed through downtown stores that while their money was welcomed, their presence wasn't. Secondary targets in the federal building and city hall were scouted.

Unlike Albany, the Birmingham protests focused on specific goals: (1) desegregation of store facilities; (2) fair hiring in all stores; (3) dismissal of all charges from previous protests; (4) equal opportunity hiring in city government; (5) the reopening of Birmingham's closed parks and swimming pools on an integrated basis; and (6) establishment of a biracial commission.

James Lawson began a regular commute from his church in Memphis to conduct nonviolence workshops in Birmingham. While King continued a national fund-raising tour, Harry Belafonte began to solicit rich donors in New York and Los Angeles who could provide bail bond money. SCLC affiliates in the North held rallies to raise money as well. SCLC's man in Washington, the Reverend Walter Fauntroy, began to recruit Northern clergymen who would answer a call to come to Birmingham at a moment's notice.

Meanwhile, the election for mayor was held on March 5, 1963. When no candidate won a majority and a runoff was set between Connor and Albert Boutwell, SCLC's plans to begin protests in March were delayed. A new date was set for April 3, the day after the runoff. On April 2, Boutwell defeated Connor by eight thousand votes. The new government was scheduled to take office on April 15. Two Klansmen and then the incumbent commissioners sued to invalidate the referendum and election, and for the next two months Birmingham had two city governments—one headed by the newly elected mayor, Albert Boutwell, the other by segregationist commissioner Art Hanes, a Connor ally. Both mayors' names appeared on city checks. Both had city hall offices. If you wanted to see the mayor, you'd be asked, "Which one?" A local movement joke was that Birmingham was the only city with two mayors, a King, and daily parades.

ON APRIL 3, 1963, the Birmingham campaign began with sit-in demonstrations at downtown Birmingham stores. Twenty-one were arrested, most of them students from nearby Miles College. On the next day, April 4, only four went to jail. A march on Sunday, April 7, resulted in the first use of police dogs in Birmingham; as the marchers were arrested, a crowd gathered, and a Black bystander attacked a dog with a knife. He was instantly subdued by other policemen with dogs. That was the precipitating confrontational event Walker needed to make Project C a success.

But more work was needed to secure the support of Black Birmingham. Despite the careful work SCLC had done in preparing the community, they were taken aback by the opposition the first days' protests raised among Birmingham's Black middle class, who were fearful that King's movement would upset the transition from racist wild man Connor to the more sophisticated segregationist Boutwell. Election of a more moderate government meant the protests could be postponed again, they reasoned, just as they had once been postponed allowing the moderate to win. Middle-class Blacks and many Black ministers were also unprepared to follow Shuttlesworth's autocratic leadership.

King and SCLC countered these rumblings with continued mass meetings on Monday and Tuesday, April 8 and 9, to encourage the public, and with private meetings to still hostility among the city's Black elites. These meetings paid off—the nightly mass meeting crowds grew larger, and support among the middle class grew stronger.

On Wednesday, April 10, a state judge issued an injunction barring all marches and other protests. A similar injunction, King thought, had helped to cripple the Albany Movement; this one would have to be broken. By Thursday, April 11, only 160 people had been arrested in the entire campaign. King would have to go to jail himself to give the movement new momentum. On Good Friday, April 12, King, Abernathy, and fifty others were arrested and taken to jail.

That same day, April 12, a group of Birmingham's most liberal clergymen—eight Christian ministers and a rabbi—had issued an open letter that attacked King for "unwise and untimely" demonstrations and praised the police for "the calm manner" in which the protests had been restrained. Over the next several days, on toilet paper and around the edges of newspaper pages, King wrote a twenty-page letter now known as "Letter from Birmingham Jail."[5]

"LETTER FROM BIRMINGHAM JAIL"

As he had from Montgomery forward, King aimed in his letter to connect the justice of the movement's demands and the nonviolent nature of its tactics to the common religious heritage Black and white Southerners shared. To the charge made by Birmingham's white clergy that he was fomenting violence, King responded that this was like blaming Jesus for his own crucifixion.

King's "Letter from Birmingham Jail" describes who he is and where he thinks he fits on the continuum of Black leadership, from militant to moderate to accommodationist. He tells why he is in Birmingham, why he does what he does, and who he thinks the real enemies of Black progress are. He is in Birmingham, he writes, because he has been invited there; he has organizational ties there. But he is also there because injustice is there.

He spends a fair amount of time arguing for the correctness of the nonviolent campaign he has launched. He outlines the basic steps he follows and tells why Birmingham has been selected, and he refutes the idea that he has not tried to negotiate before demonstrations began. And he explains why his methods—sit-ins, marches, demonstrations—are necessary. Then he explains who he thinks the real enemy is. It isn't the Ku Klux Klanner or the White Citizens' Council member, he writes, but the white moderate, "who is more devoted to 'order' than to justice; who prefers a negative peace which is the absence of tension to a positive peace which is the presence of justice; who constantly says 'I agree with you in the goal you seek but I can't agree with your methods . . .'; who paternalistically feels he can set the timetable for another man's freedom; who lives by the myth of time and who constantly advises the Negro to wait until a 'more convenient season.'"

And in a masterful passage he writes: "Shallow understanding from people of good will is more frustrating than absolute misunderstanding from people of ill will. Lukewarm acceptance is much more bewildering than outright rejection." Then he explains that, on the scale of Negro opinion, he stands in the center, not the extremes. He refuses to compromise with segregation, but he hasn't given up on America, as others have. And he next argues that the protests are beneficial in themselves and an alternative to violence. "This is not a threat," he writes. "It is a fact of history." He closes with a condemnation of the white clergymen who denounce his actions but never condemn segregation, who are preaching an "otherworldly" religion.

GREENWOOD, MISSISSIPPI

As King and SCLC were inching toward beginning demonstrations in Birmingham through the spring of 1963, Bob Moses had dispersed seventeen SNCC workers across six counties in the Mississippi Delta. The Mississippi legislature had added two new laws to the already difficult and dangerous job of registering to vote. One required that every applicant's name be published in a local newspaper for two weeks before registration became final; another allowed current voters to object to the "moral" qualifications of applicants.

The previous December, 1962, Moses had said there were three ingredients needed for change in Mississippi: (1) stopping the control the White Citizens' Council exercised over politics; (2) getting the Justice Department to guarantee safe registration by Blacks, and (3) a mass uprising of Blacks demanding the right to vote. The small staff he had gathered would have to try to achieve these goals. On January 1, 1963, Moses and other SNCC workers had filed suit against Robert Kennedy and J. Edgar Hoover, asking a federal court in Washington to order them to enforce sections of the federal code that made it illegal to harass or intimidate potential voters or those who helped them. The suit cited incident after incident of attacks on registration workers. Attorney General Kennedy's staff had argued that the law prevented them from defending people who wanted to vote; Moses wanted to prove that the law required them to act. Kennedy's lawyers were successful in blocking the suit.

While federal authorities did nothing, state officials moved ruthlessly—they cut off distribution of federal food surpluses in two counties, Sunflower and Leflore. Sunflower was the home of Senator Eastland, the headquarters of the White Citizens' Council, and the home of Mrs.

Hamer. In Leflore, the cutoff affected twenty-two thousand people, almost all Black, half the county's population, one-third of whom had annual incomes of less than five hundred dollars. COFO workers sent out a national appeal for help.

In early February, Harry Belafonte and the Albany Freedom Singers held a concert at Carnegie Hall. Dick Gregory announced he was paying for a chartered plane to transport seven tons of food to Mississippi. Six thousand people lined up to receive the food in Greenwood. COFO workers were quick to make the connection between the registration attempts and the food cutoff: "Don't let the white man do to your children as he has done to you," James Bevel told a mass meeting crowd on February 11.[6]

On February 12, the Civil Rights Commission met with President Kennedy to let him know they were beginning an investigation of racial conditions in Mississippi. In its five-year history, the commission had never held hearings or conducted investigations in the one state that cried out for it most. Indeed, the Justice Department had tried to keep the commission out of the state. Now the president told the commission chair, Michigan State University president John Hannah, that hearings would do no good; they might, in fact, hurt the Justice Department's chances of success at county-by-county litigation.

White officials remained adamantly opposed to Black registration. A white man told the *New York Times*, "We killed two-month old Indian babies to take this country, and now they want to give it away to the niggers."[7] On February 20, four Black businesses near the Greenwood SNCC offices were burned. When SNCC worker Sam Block said the arson was a bungled attempt to burn his office, he was arrested for "statements calculated to breach the peace." He had lived in Greenwood for nine months and had been arrested seven times; he had taken would-be voters to the courthouse in ones and twos, braving a line of hostile whites, civilians, and policemen. He had led the singing at mass meetings where the numbers in the pulpit were as great as those in the congregation. Now, an extraordinary one hundred Greenwood Blacks crowded into police court for his trial. The judge offered to suspend his fine and sentence if he would leave town; he refused and was sentenced to six months in jail and a five-hundred-dollar fine.

The next day, February 26, the lines at the courthouse swelled—more than two hundred of the poorest Blacks in Greenwood tried to register to vote the Monday after Block's arrest. On February 28, Randolph Blackwell, the Voter Education Project's field director, held a meeting with COFO staff members in Greenwood. SNCC worker Jimmy Travis warned that cars of whites—without license plates—were circling in front of the office. As Blackwell and Moses drove away from Greenwood that night with Jimmy Travis at the wheel, a Buick pulled up, firing .45 caliber shots into the SNCC car. Travis was hit twice, once in the neck.

Travis's shooting galvanized the SNCC staff; they descended on Greenwood from across the South. The SCLC sent staff members to establish a citizenship training school. Voter Education Project director Wiley Branton sent appeals to the Civil Rights Commission and to Attorney General Kennedy. The commission began preparing its report on Mississippi, and the attorney general sent Justice Department lawyers to Greenwood to investigate the surplus food cutoff.

On March 6, night riders fired into a car carrying Sam Block and Willie Peacock. Greenwood's mayor said SNCC had shot at its own workers to generate publicity. On March 24, the SNCC office was destroyed by fire. On March 26, a night rider fired a shotgun at Dewey Greene Sr., a popular Greenwood native who was a constant volunteer in the registration campaign. In response, a large crowd gathered at a Greenwood church on March 27. Moses suggested a march to protest the shooting, and 150 filed out of the church behind him. At city hall, a police dog bit Moses's leg and bit a Black minister so badly he had to be hospitalized. The crowd broke and ran as a policeman shouted, "Kennedy is your God!"[8] Back at the church, Moses and seven others were arrested and decided to stay in jail, forcing the government to act to have them released. News of the police dog attack drew reporters to Greenwood—first, Claude Sitton of the *New York Times*, followed by those reporters who needed Sitton to point out news for them. Their travels were rewarded the next day.

On March 28, almost one hundred policemen, most recruited from surrounding counties, watched a small march of forty-two Blacks walk back to the church from the courthouse. As whites in the crowd yelled "Sic 'em, sic 'em!" a police dog bit the church's pastor, drawing blood. Pictures of the charging dog—followed by charging policemen—appeared in newspapers across the country the next day.

The picture was embarrassing for the Kennedy administration; it appeared with the news that Republicans, critical of Kennedy's inaction, were pushing their own civil rights legislation. The Justice Department threatened to file suit seeking an injunction against further persecutions of potential voters, but they knew such a suit would be heard by a Kennedy-appointed judge who was an ardent segregationist.

By April 2, Dick Gregory was in town himself. His constant badgering of white officials, his ceaseless sarcasm, made even more embarrassing news. He told the mayor, "You really took your nigger pills last night, didn't you?" He shouted to newsmen: "There's your story—guns and sticks for old women who want to register!" "Look at them," he said, pointing at the policemen. "A bunch of illiterate whites who couldn't even pass the test themselves!"[9]

The continuing news story of police attacks on peaceful would-be voters proved to be too much. On April 3, John Doar visited the eight jailed SNCC workers. He told them he was going to ask Judge Claude Clayton for an injunction voiding their convictions, preventing further harassment, and requiring police protection. On April 4, the city of Greenwood caved—and suspended their sentences. All eight were free.

Their freedom meant the Justice Department would not proceed with its injunction. The conditions that put them in jail on March 27 were still in effect. In exchange for putting leashes on their police dogs, Greenwood officials were able to keep the lid on their registration lists. The federal government had negotiated for peace and order over justice. As in the Freedom Rides two years before, ending racial confrontation was more important than ending racism. Over the next six months, COFO workers in Leflore County brought fifteen hundred Blacks to the county courthouse; only fifty were able to register to vote.

On April 4, when Moses and the other seven SNCC workers were freed, the Birmingham demonstrations were beginning their second day.

BIRMINGHAM CONTINUES

In early April 1963, Bull Connor invited Albany police chief Laurie Pritchett to Birmingham for consultation on how to handle King. Pritchett told Connor to give King protection at all times, but Connor never followed Pritchett's advice.

One initial hope SCLC had about the Birmingham protests was that they would involve the Kennedy administration, which had done little in Albany except issue statements from afar. Burke Marshall—at the instigation of a white, Birmingham businessman—had called King as the demonstrations were beginning to ask him to call them off, but until King was jailed on April 12 the administration had not said or done anything. King was held overnight in solitary confinement; a lawyer was unable to see him alone. Seizing the moment, Wyatt Tee Walker called Burke Marshall at home and sent a telegram to President Kennedy asking him to insure safe and humane treatment for King in jail. Walker then pressed Coretta King to call the president herself. Marshall told Kennedy—as he had told reporters—that there were no grounds for federal action or involvement in Birmingham. After several false starts, Robert Kennedy called Mrs. King to assure her he would make inquiries about King's confinement and condition. Little else was forthcoming from the president.

THE ALBANY NINE, 1963

While King and Abernathy were in jail in Birmingham trying to interest the federal government in intervening there, and Bob Moses was discovering in Greenwood that the Justice Department was more interested in preserving segregated order than demanding integrated justice, events in Albany were leading many in the civil rights movement to ask which side the federal government was really on.

On the Fourth of July, 1961, an annual barbecue was held in rural Southwest Georgia for the Blacks who worked on the plantation owned by Robert Woodruff, board chairman of the Coca-Cola Company. Three thousand Blacks attended the 1961 party; one of them, a field hand named Charlie Ware, flirted with the Black mistress of the plantation overseer. The overseer complained to the Baker County sheriff, L. Warren "Gator" Johnson, who drove to Ware's home, beat his wife until Ware came home, beat Ware, arrested him, and drove to Newton. Parked outside the jail, with Ware handcuffed in the seat beside him, he picked up his radio microphone and said, "This nigger's coming at me with a knife! I'm gonna have to shoot him." After firing two .32 caliber bullets into Ware's neck, he yelled, "He's still coming on! I'm gonna have to shoot him again!" and shot Ware again.[10]

An FBI investigation fully supported Ware's version of events, but a Baker County grand jury indicted Ware for felonious assault on the sheriff. A civil suit filed on Ware's behalf by Albany attorney C. B. King came to trial in Columbus, Georgia. On April 12, Good Friday, King's first day in the Birmingham jail, an all-white jury, after deliberating for ninety minutes, found Sheriff Johnson innocent of violating Charlie Ware's civil rights. One member of the jury was Carl Smith, who owned one of the three white-owned stores in Harlem, Albany's Black commercial district. On April 20, the Albany Movement began another picket line at Smith's store; as usual, they were arrested within an hour.

B. C. Gardner, the white Albany lawyer who had secretly paid Martin Luther King's fine in Albany on July 12, 1962, filed a suit for Smith against the Albany Movement, charging he had been the victim of an illegal boycott. He also asked the local bar association, the FBI, and Burke Marshall to investigate the picketing, charging that Smith had been persecuted for his role on the jury in the Ware case. Ten days after the picket line, a report on the incident was on Robert Kennedy's desk. More than thirty FBI agents investigated, interviewing dozens of Albany Blacks and serving nearly sixty subpoenas.

On August 9, 1963, Attorney General Robert Kennedy held a press conference to announce federal criminal indictments for perjury against nine members of the Albany Movement. Two were alleged to have conspired against Carl Smith and only one alleged to have actually picketed the store; the others, seemingly included for political reasons. The only white person indicted was SNCC worker Joni Rabinowitz. Her father was Victor Rabinowitz, a New York lawyer who represented the government of Cuba, and she fit the sexual and racial paranoia of local whites. Some FBI agents believed that whites—not Blacks—directed the movement, and that those whites were directed from Moscow. The *Washington Star* congratulated Kennedy for demonstrating that he did not stand "with the Negro against the white man."[11]

There had been no indictments against Sheriff Johnson for beating and shooting Charlie Ware, nor against the police officer who had knocked Slater King to the ground, nor the police officer who had beaten pregnant Marion King to her knees. There had been no indictments to punish numerous other instances of brutality and denials of the most basic civil rights: the right to peacefully assemble, to petition the government— which had occurred repeatedly during the Albany Movement. None of the numerous complaints of police brutality ever received the attention or massive FBI presence the grocery-store picketing received. Instead, when given a questionable opportunity to side with whites against Blacks in a racial conflict, the Kennedy administration had sided with whites.

BACK IN BIRMINGHAM

Back in Birmingham, national news outlets—so crucial to the movement's success—reported that the Birmingham movement had been poorly timed and suggested King should let the new city administration have a chance to succeed. King and Connor were both extremists, this view seemed to suggest; left to themselves, local people would solve Birmingham's problems.

King, depressed over local and national attacks on his leadership, left jail on April 20, 1963; the movement had almost come to a standstill during his stay in jail. James Bevel, who had left Mississippi for Birmingham on King's orders, had been conducting afternoon workshops, training young people in nonviolence. By the start of King's trial on April 22, the workshops were larger than the evening mass meetings. On April 24, when King made the daily appeal for volunteers to go to jail, most of those who responded were high school and elementary school students. King told them he hoped their example would help their parents to make up their minds; the children, he said, were too young.

On April 25, Robert Kennedy came to Montgomery for a meeting with Governor George Wallace. On April 26, King and others who had violated the injunction were found guilty. To recoup the ground lost during the week of the trial, the movement planned a mass protest march for May 2 and asked for a permit. The city denied permission on April 30.

Mass meeting crowds were producing even fewer adult volunteers; King and others debated using teenagers. Local adults were vigorously opposed; these were their children, after all. Walker and Bevel argued that the youth had to be used; the press was losing interest in the movement, the number of adults willing to go to jail was falling. Without agreeing to their use, King approved inviting interested students to a mass meeting at noon on Thursday, May 2. By noon that day, hundreds of teenagers had gathered outside the Sixteenth Street Baptist Church.

Bull Connor deployed his men at a park across the street which actually and symbolically divided Black and white Birmingham. Just after noon, the first wave of fifty youngsters left the church. Some were as young as six. When they were arrested, another wave followed, and then a third. At Walker's direction, they began to take circuitous routes toward the white downtown, to take the protests to white shoppers. By 4:00 p.m., the first day of protest was over and more than six hundred young people had gone to jail.

At the mass meeting that night, Bevel shouted: "There ain't gonna be no meeting Monday night because every Negro is gonna be in jail by Sunday night!"[12] On Friday, May 3, curious crowds of Blacks surrounded and filled the park, waiting to see if the previous day's events would be repeated. Police sealed the downtown side with fire engines, school buses, and police cars. Once again, the children marched. Police stopped the first group of sixty singing children, unwilling to arrest them. Birmingham's jails were already filled, and, unlike in Albany, no plans had been made to use facilities in neighboring towns. A policeman told them to disperse "or you're gonna get wet!" As the students continued to sing, the fire hoses were turned on. Connor shouted, "I wanna see the dogs work! Look at those niggers run!"[13]

The water came through two hoses coupled to one nozzle mounted on a tripod, a monitor gun used for fighting long-range fires, capable of knocking bricks loose from buildings and stripping bark from trees. It tore the clothes from some of the children's backs. As he watched from his office building overlooking the park, Black millionaire A. G. Gaston, a moderate who had tried to delay the demonstrations and who wanted King to leave town, became an instant convert to the movement. Placing a call to David Vann, a white lawyer, Gaston said, "Lawyer Vann, they've turned the fire hoses on a little black girl! And they're rolling that girl right down the middle of the street!"[14]

The crowd scattered, but because the nozzle required the hoses to be fixed in place, they could not be easily moved. Other young people escaped from the church and headed downtown. The police needed a more dangerous weapon—eight K-9 units entered the park and began attacking the people gathered there. Some challenged the dogs with shirts like bull fighters; others threw rocks at the dogs and the policemen who handled them. Three teenagers were bitten badly enough to be hospitalized. By 3:00 p.m., 250 had been arrested; the dogs and hoses had cleared the park. But fewer than half of the students had actually left the church; another 500 were ready to march the next day.

Criticism of King for using children was immediate—from Mayor Boutwell to Robert Kennedy to Malcolm X. King answered the critics with a question: Where were you, he asked, when these children's lives were being crushed by segregation? Where were you then?[15] The rock throwing had prompted two calls from Burke Marshall to King to say he was coming to Birmingham and asking for a halt in the demonstrations; King refused. But he knew that the calls and the visit were evidence of pressure building on the Kennedy administration; the concern about children was a defensive reaction, a confession of the wrongness of a system that put even children in jail.

That night's mass meeting was so crowded that it took an hour to pass the collection plate. King announced, "Now yesterday was D-Day, and tomorrow will be Double D-Day!"[16] The marches would continue over the weekend.

Marshall began shuttle diplomacy—traveling back and forth between separate groups of Blacks and whites. White merchants, who had been feeling the boycott's pinch, had begun to meet daily. Now Marshall began to take messages from white businessmen to local Black negotiators. The whites wanted the protests to end but refused to accept the movement's demands. For the Birmingham movement, the protests would not end until their demands were met.

With over two thousand in jail, Marshall met with King on Monday, May 6, arguing that if demonstrations would stop, negotiations would start. No, said King; when integration begins, then demonstrations will end. Over ten thousand people attended Monday night's mass meetings at four churches; there were twenty-five hundred people in jail.

On Tuesday, May 7, as Birmingham's biggest business leaders met with Burke Marshall to argue about negotiations, dozens of demonstrators broke through police lines and entered the downtown area. That afternoon, police were waiting—fire hoses were used again, and again the crowds nearby reacted with bricks and stones. Shuttlesworth was knocked into a wall by a fire hose; he was taken away in an ambulance. Connor said he was sorry he hadn't been taken away in a hearse.

President Kennedy and members of his cabinet began making telephone calls to Birmingham's businessmen, while telling newsmen they were not involved in the Birmingham negotiations. That night, the businessmen agreed to negotiate directly with the Black community and later that night with King himself. On May 8, President Kennedy told a press conference that he hoped for a final settlement in Birmingham within a day. Many in the movement objected—Shuttlesworth particularly. He had been hospitalized while the negotiations proceeded and now objected that he had not been consulted. Only a telephone call from Robert Kennedy kept him from breaking the truce. Left unresolved, while smaller details were being negotiated, were the charges against all those arrested and freeing those still in jail.

King extended the truce deadline twice, while arguments continued about freeing the jailed demonstrators. President Kennedy had raised $60 million to ransom the twelve hundred prisoners captured in the Bay of Pigs invasion of Cuba in 1961; he could raise $250,000 to free Americans imprisoned in Birmingham. Robert Kennedy raised the money: $80,000 came from AFL-CIO president George Meany; $40,000 from the United Steelworkers; $50,000 in a black satchel was hand-delivered to Harry Belafonte from the New York Transport Workers Union. An SCLC lawyer signed a receipt promising to repay cash he was given from the Chase Manhattan Bank by New York governor Nelson Rockefeller's assistant. After the lawyer flew to Birmingham to deliver the money and returned home, he found a receipt saying the money had been repaid in full.[17]

The final agreement said that within three days after the demonstrations ended, department store fitting rooms would integrate; within thirty days after the courts sorted out the legal battle between Boutwell and Connor, toilets and drinking fountains would be integrated; sixty days after a city government was in place, lunch counters would be integrated and at least one Black salesperson or cashier per downtown store would be hired. Fifteen days after demonstrations were over, a biracial committee would be established.

On Friday, May 8, King announced the settlement in general terms. The white businessmen were afraid that announcing the details would subject them to recriminations from Connor and other racists.

Late Saturday, May 9, with King safely back in Atlanta, bombs hit the Birmingham home of his brother, Reverend A. D. King; over two thousand angry Blacks gathered at the scene. Another bomb exploded at the Gaston Motel where King had stayed during the demonstrations. A crowd quickly gathered there as well, and rock and bottle throwing followed, then arson, then looting. Ministers and policemen had nearly convinced the crowds to disperse when Alabama State Patrol colonel Al Lingo and 250 troopers arrived, dispatched by Governor George Wallace; their savage and unprovoked attacks triggered more retaliation by Blacks—by morning, six businesses, several stores, and an apartment building were burned to the ground.

In Washington, on Sunday, May 10, John and Robert Kennedy conferred. Obviously, the Wallace-Connor forces had tried to sabotage the Birmingham agreement by intimidating the businessmen who had agreed to it, provoking Birmingham's Blacks to violence and forcing federal intervention. Sending in troops would mean that the administration was declaring the state troopers were a threat to public order and would put the federal government squarely on the side of the demonstrations and Martin Luther King.

To the Kennedys, King was the key; they believed he could halt the violence with a word. But they also thought the Birmingham violence would spread to other cities unless some action was taken to demonstrate the government stood with justice as well as peace. President Kennedy also thought SNCC to be a disruptive force, as revealed in Oval Office recordings from September 23, 1963, when he called SNCC "sons of bitches."[18]

Kennedy finally federalized units of the Alabama National Guard. Two weeks later, the Alabama Supreme Court ruled that Boutwell would be mayor of Birmingham; Connor and his forces were ordered to vacate their offices. Within days of Connor's leaving office, the new city council authorized Mayor Boutwell to appoint a "Commission on Community Affairs." The members were named in mid-July. In June, signs on segregated water fountains came down. On July 23, the council repealed the city's segregation laws. On July 30, lunch counters formally desegregated. The Birmingham movement was over.

News reports of the initial settlement were necessarily vague. The white businessmen wanted details and their names kept secret; King and the movement agreed to vagueness to win the agreement. But the lack of specificity led to charges that little had been won. Nonetheless, the Birmingham drama—fire hoses, police dogs, small children singing on their way to jail—had firmly fixed King and civil rights in the nation's consciousness. King spent the last weeks in May traveling across the country to a series of rallies and fundraisers; the crowds and cash collected showed him that the movement had moved onto a higher plane. One lesson King took from Birmingham was the need for additional civil rights legislation. Kennedy's actions in Birmingham, he said, had been "inadequate."[19]

For John and Robert Kennedy, Birmingham was a lesson in the volatility of Black America, even if they did not clearly understand it. Chicago mayor Richard Daley had told Robert Kennedy, "The Negroes are all mad for no reason at all."[20] They did understand, however, that the violence in Birmingham could easily be duplicated anywhere in urban America. Perhaps legislation was the answer to the threat of Black violence. The administration's narrow reading of federal law limiting its ability to intervene in places like Birmingham meant that new laws were required if the federal government was to play any role beyond behind-the-scenes negotiator.

When the Birmingham protests were beginning in early April, Robert Kennedy had convened a group to draft a new civil rights bill. By June, the administration's proposals were ready. Another Alabama crisis presented the opportunity to put them forward.

On June 11, Governor George Wallace stood in the door of a building at the University of Alabama to block the admission of two Black students. Kennedy federalized the Alabama National Guard, and later that afternoon the students were admitted. That night, Kennedy made a dramatic television address:

> We are confronted primarily with a moral issue. It is as old as the scriptures and is as clear as the American Constitution. The heart of the question is whether all Americans are to be afforded equal rights and equal opportunities, whether we are going to treat our fellow Americans as we want to be treated. If an American, because his skin is dark, cannot eat lunch in a restaurant open to the public, if he cannot send his children to the best public school available, if he cannot vote for the public officials who will represent him, if, in short, he cannot enjoy the full and free life which all of us want, then who among us would be content to have the color of his skin changed and stand in his place? Who among us would then be content with the counsels of patience and delay? One hundred years of delay have passed since President Lincoln freed the slaves, yet their heirs, their grandsons, are not fully free.... We preach freedom around the world, and we mean it, and we cherish our freedom here at home, but are we to say to the world, and much more importantly, to each other that this is the land of the free except for the

Negroes; that we have no second-class citizens except Negroes; that we have no class or caste system, no ghettoes, no master race except with respect to Negroes? . . . A great change is at hand, and our task, our obligation, is to make that revolution, that change, peaceful and constructive for all. Those who do nothing are inviting shame as well as violence. Those who act boldly are recognizing right as well as reality. Next week I shall ask the Congress of the United States to act, to make a commitment it has not fully made in this century to the proposition that race has no place in American life or law.[21]

He said details of his new civil rights proposals would be sent to Congress the next week.

SEVENTEEN

MISSISSIPPI, MEDGAR EVERS, AND THE CIVIL RIGHTS BILL

J UST HOURS AFTER Kennedy's speech, Mississippi NAACP field secretary Medgar Evers was shot to death from ambush in his driveway. Evers had been leading a movement, like Birmingham's, in Jackson for weeks. By June 1, 1963, more than six hundred Blacks were in jail, and Roy Wilkins, who had condemned the sit-ins just two years before, flew to Jackson to join them. The Jackson movement sputtered and stopped and started. It was only one of several flash points across the South. In Tallahassee, Florida, 257 demonstrators were tear-gassed and arrested. Forty Black soldiers in Newfoundland protested segregation at a restaurant near their base, and there were demonstrations in a half-dozen North Carolina cities. On June 6, 278 students from North Carolina A&T University were arrested, including the student body president, Jesse Jackson.[1] Between the settlement in Birmingham and Evers's murder, there had been 758 racial demonstrations and 14,733 arrests in 186 cities.

Four days before Evers was shot, Mrs. Fannie Lou Hamer was returning to Greenwood, Mississippi, from a Citizenship School session in Charleston, South Carolina, with sixteen-year-old June Johnson, SCLC's Annelle Ponder, and three others. Thirty miles away at a rest stop in Winona, Mississippi, Ponder entered the bus station's white waiting room. Police arrived and threw her out. As she stood on the sidewalk writing down the license numbers of the police cars, she was arrested.

At the station, Ponder was beaten by three policemen with blackjacks for ten minutes when she refused to say "Sir" to the policemen, who called her a "nigger bitch." The policemen then beat June Johnson; Mrs. Hamer was next. She was taken into the jail's bullpen where two Black inmates waited. A policeman gave one a blackjack, and Mrs. Hamer remembered him being told, "I want you to make that bitch wish she was dead." The inmate told Mrs. Hamer to lie down on a bed. She asked him, "You mean you would do this to your own race?" She described what happened next.[2]

> I had to get over there on the bed flat on my stomach, and that man beat me—that man beat me until he give out. And by me screamin', it made one of the other ones—plainclothes fellow . . . , he didn't have nothing on like a uniform—he got so hot and worked up off it, he just run . . . there, you know, and start hitting on the back of my head. Well, my hand, I was trying to guard some of the licks . . . you see—and my hands, they beat my hands till they turned blue, and . . . quite naturally, being beaten like that, my clothes come up, and I tried to pull them down, you know. . . . One of the other white fellows—just taken my clothes and just snatched them up, and this Negro, when he had just beat me until I know he was just [about to] give out, well, then, this state patrolman told the other Negro to take it. So he taken over from there. . . . I had to hug around the mattress to keep the sound from coming out.[3]

By this time, the SNCC office in Greenwood knew where the women were. Lawrence Guyot went to Winona to see what had happened to them. When he refused to say "Sir" to a policeman in front of the jail, he too was arrested and beaten. A young law student, Eleanor Holmes, also visited the jail.[4] Finally, on June 12, SCLC's Andrew Young posted their bail, and they were released. They learned that President John Kennedy had made a stirring civil rights speech the night before, and that a few hours after the speech Medgar Evers had been murdered.

BIRMINGHAM'S EFFECTS
Before the Birmingham movement began on Easter weekend 1963, active opposition to the city's segregation system seemed limited to a small cadre

of liberal whites and members of Shuttlesworth's organization, but these numbers were too small to effect any significant change. Only the intervention of outside forces obliged Birmingham to confront segregation. Using nonviolent techniques refined in the sit-ins, the Freedom Rides, and Albany, King's SCLC drew some previously uninvolved local Blacks into the protest movement but was never able to attract sizeable numbers of the city's Black middle class.

Birmingham's white community reacted in two ways. Initially, Bull Connor and the police he directed tried to meet nonviolence with nonviolence, as Chief Laurie Pritchett had done in Albany, but, as the protests grew larger, Connor brutally unleashed the full force of the police. The newly elected mayor and council did not make the city's racial problems worse, but they took no positive steps to make them better. Only when they agreed to meet and negotiate secretly with the protest leaders did they separate themselves from the prevailing view of the city's former political leadership.

It was the city's business leadership, rather than political leaders, who brokered the deal that ended segregation and ended the demonstrations. The federal government, drawn unwillingly into Birmingham by the sympathetic reaction nationally to televised fire hoses and police dogs, sent Assistant Attorney General Burke Marshall to facilitate negotiations. Desegregation of downtown stores, employment opportunities for Blacks, establishment of a permanent biracial committee, the release of jailed demonstrators on low bail—all were achieved within three months.

These victories for Blacks stimulated heightened resistance among antagonistic whites; after initially preparing to accept limited school integration, the Birmingham school board used the post-protest riots as an excuse to close the integrated schools, and, when they reopened, Governor George Wallace used state troopers to prevent Black children from attending. Only when President Kennedy federalized the Alabama National Guard to ensure the children's safety were the schools integrated.

But the primary impact of the Birmingham demonstrations was national, rather than local. Birmingham's six weeks of demonstrations were followed by an explosion of protests. *Time* magazine called it a "feverish, fragmented, spasmodic, almost uncontrollable revolution."[5] Across the South, Blacks asserted their right to use facilities that had been whites-only two months earlier—parks, playgrounds, beaches, libraries, theaters, restaurants, and hotels. They marched and boycotted and sat in.

The post-Birmingham protests were like the 1960 sit-ins—disconnected and spontaneous but much more widespread, involving many more people of all ages and backgrounds. There were 930 demonstrations in 115 cities. In a single three-week period after Birmingham, 143 cities agreed to some degree of integration; by the year's end, over 300 had done so. Birmingham's inspiration meant that maintaining segregation had become untenable. Segregation had depended on everyday acceptance by Blacks, but the civil rights movement in six short weeks had defeated the beast in its most entrenched locale, against an opposition led by violence-prone racists.

Like the Freedom Rides before them but on a much greater scale, the Birmingham protests nationalized the civil rights movement, bringing televised images of dogs and fire hoses into American homes. At the most basic level, the protests galvanized Northern political opinion against the excesses of defiant Southern whites. President Kennedy said it best: "The civil rights movement should thank God for Bull Connor. He's helped it as much as Abraham Lincoln."[6] The Birmingham protests caused the Kennedy administration to rethink its civil rights strategies. Its civil rights program had been developed in response to crises—federal protection for the Freedom Riders in 1961 and for James Meredith at Ole Miss in 1962.

After the Birmingham protests, it was obvious that a basic tenet of nonviolent theory had been found wanting: unmerited suffering by peaceful protesters would not soften the hearts or change the minds of the most resistant whites. More was required—the economic squeeze that a boycott of stores could provide and national and worldwide publicity created by dramatic confrontations. For many in the movement, power replaced love and Christianity. Rather than converting white opponents and arguing the moral righteousness of their cause, they could force change through mass disruption.

Birmingham's images of young people facing down dogs and fire hoses goaded thousands nationwide into activism. If children in Birmingham could do this, how could their elders say no? Historian Adam Fairclough described the catalytic effect of the movement: "The SCLC's protests electrified black Southerners. They were thrilled when hundreds of black schoolchildren marched out of Sixteenth Street Baptist Church and into lines of waiting policemen, taunting them and singing as police vans hauled them off to jail. They were incensed when blacks were chased by police dogs, then drenched and pounded by high-pressure fire hoses. Above all they were inspired by the sheer audacity of it all—and moved to action."[7]

"The sound of the explosion in Birmingham," King said, "reached all the way to Washington."[8] Across the country, Blacks awakened to a new sense of power. If America's most segregated city, led by the most intransigent whites, could be forced to yield, then any city could be brought to heel by an awakened Black insurgency.

Birmingham drew into the racial struggle the previously torpid, poorest Blacks, a population with little interest in the symbolic and status gains motivating college students, professionals, and religious middle-class Blacks. As the racial struggle's demographics became more democratic and massive and encompassed more lower-class participation, impatience multiplied, disobedience became less civil, and nonviolence became more and more a mere tactic.

Birmingham also heightened the militancy of civil rights organizations, even those that played no role in the Birmingham protests, presenting greater demands on civil rights leadership. The national mood changed too. Polls and surveys in 1963 showed large majorities favoring Black voting rights, job opportunities, good housing, and desegregated schools and public accommodations.[9]

White supremacists, perhaps realizing that Birmingham represented a great shift in the national mood signaling an end to their way of life, under attack by an alliance of civil rights agitators and the federal government, felt embattled, endangered, and desperate and increasingly turned to terrorism and murder.

KENNEDY'S CIVIL RIGHTS BILL

The centerpiece of the bill Kennedy sent to Congress on June 19, 1963, was Title II, the section on public accommodations, which allowed individuals to file suit against discriminatory establishments and permitted the attorney general to file suit under limited conditions. There was no Title III, the disputed section of the 1957 bill that would have given the attorney general authority to sue over the violation of any citizen's rights. The school desegregation section would give the attorney general limited authority to sue local school boards or public colleges that refused to integrate.

The Kennedy administration found the constitutional authority for the public accommodations section in a controversial place: the interstate commerce clause of the Constitution, which gives Congress the power to regulate the nation's economic life, rather than in the Fourteenth Amendment, which guarantees equal protection. This choice was as much political as it was legal—the use of the Fourteenth Amendment would send the legislation to the Senate Judiciary Committee, chaired by bigoted Senator James O. Eastland. The commerce clause meant it would be considered by the Senate Commerce Committee, chaired by much more liberal Senator Warren Magnuson (D-WA).

The school desegregation section posed potential political problems too. Northerners of both parties agreed that segregated schools were bad—in the South. Those in their own backyards were another matter. A behind-the-scenes bipartisan coalition quickly arose to focus the school desegregation bill on Southern segregation, away from requiring that the segregation found in the North and West also be addressed.[10]

To the administration's surprise, Title VI of the bill found bipartisan, non-Southern support as well. It called for a single, comprehensive ban on federal funding of racially discriminatory programs. Also not included was a title on job discrimination. Kennedy had asked Congress to make the President's Committee on Equal Employment Opportunity, headed by Vice President Lyndon Johnson, permanent.

By the time Kennedy introduced his bill, on June 19, other members of Congress had introduced several versions of their own, including the small band of Northern, liberal Republicans in the House. When hearings began, there were 168 bills on the House Judiciary Committee's calendar. May 8 was the same day King announced the Birmingham settlement. The administration's strategy was to pass a bill through the liberal House Judiciary Committee, chaired by Emanuel Celler (D-NY), to overwhelm the reactionary Rules Committee, chaired by Howard Smith (D-VA), and to pass the bill to the House floor, where national outrage over the Birmingham brutality would send it to the Senate.

The biggest opponent on the Judiciary Committee was not the chair, Senator Eastland; rather, it was a member from North Carolina, Senator

Sam Erwin (D-NC). Ten years later, Americans would think of Erwin as a hero as he demolished the Nixon administration's attempts to justify its break-in and cover-up in the Watergate scandal. In 1963, however, he conducted a "committee filibuster" against the civil rights bill, which dragged the hearings into September.

On a separate track, another piece of civil rights legislation was moving through the tortuously slow processes in the House. When Representative Adam Clayton Powell became chair of the Education and Labor Committee in 1961, he created a Subcommittee on Labor, which held hearings across the North and West in 1961 and 1962 on racial discrimination in employment, to demonstrate the need for a strong federal law like the Fair Employment Practices Committee, which civil rights forces had been trying to establish for years. In the 1962 hearings, another committee looked quickly into including age and gender discrimination in such a law. It found great enthusiasm for making age discrimination illegal but little for the prospect of adding gender.

The Powell committee's legislation was introduced in 1963 and reported to the full House on July 22. It made it illegal for an employer, labor union, or employment agency "to fail or refuse to hire or to discharge any individual, or otherwise to discriminate against any individual with respect to his compensation, terms, conditions, or privileges of employment because of such individuals' race, religion, color, national origin, or ancestry."

There was no mention of gender discrimination, although age was added, with seniority systems excepted. The mechanism that enforced this new law would be a five-member Equal Employment Opportunity Commission (EEOC), modeled on state fair employment practices commissions. After investigation and attempts at conciliation, the commission could order an offender to "cease and desist from such unlawful employment practice and to take such *affirmative action* . . . as will effectuate the policies of the Act."[11]

On August 5, the House Judiciary Committee had completed twenty-two days of hearings on the administration's bill, compiled 1,742 pages of printed testimony, and begun private sessions to mark up the bill. President Kennedy asked Chairman Celler to delay the markup sessions; he was afraid that the seven Southern committee chairs would use progress on the civil rights bill to threaten the president's tax cut bill, which had higher priority for him. Congress recessed for the Labor Day weekend on August 28, 1963.[12]

That day, August 28, President Kennedy was host at the White House to the leaders of that day's successful March on Washington—only male leaders; no women were included. It had been the largest gathering of civil rights supporters in the nation's history.

EIGHTEEN

THE MARCH ON WASHINGTON

A. PHILIP RANDOLPH and his associates had been planning a march on Washington since late 1962. In late January 1963, Bayard Rustin, Norman Hill, and Tom Kahn gave Randolph a memo describing a "mass descent" on Washington for May 1963. They envisioned one hundred thousand people coming to Washington for two days of protests, including blocking all legislative business in Washington and presenting Congress and the president with a legislative agenda to draw attention to "the economic subordination of the American Negro" and the need for creating "more jobs for all Americans."[1] Integrating schools, housing, transportation, lunch counters, and restaurants would be of little use, the document said, as long as "fundamental economic inequality along racial lines persists." The second day of the protest would be devoted to a mass rally.

Randolph approved the plan; target dates of June 13 and 14 were selected. Now the plans were to have one day of legislative lobbying and one day featuring a mass procession down Pennsylvania Avenue, ending at a rally at the Lincoln Memorial that the president would be invited to address. Randolph's organization, the Negro American Labor Council (NALC), approved the plan on March 23. Randolph then approached Roy Wilkins of the NAACP and Whitney Young of the Urban League. Both were cool to the idea, and King expressed little interest—he was in the middle of the Birmingham campaign.

In early June 1963, given Kennedy's inadequate leadership during the Birmingham crisis, King was ready to discuss the idea. The civil rights movement should sponsor an interracial March on Washington that could include sit-ins on Capitol Hill. On June 11, King's New York representatives announced that a protest, using disruptive tactics, would be held later that summer if the federal government didn't move quickly to help Black Americans. But given President Kennedy's speech later that day embracing civil rights on national television, King decided that the march's focus should be on Congress, not the president.

Representatives from SCLC, CORE, SNCC, and the NALC decided that the march would be held sometime between August 10 and 24, and that each organization should name one person to a coordinating committee to plan the details. At the suggestion of Steven Currier, a wealthy New York philanthropist, the civil rights leadership agreed to establish the Council for United Civil Rights Leadership to serve as a clearinghouse for soliciting and dividing large contributions.

Back in Birmingham on a weekly visit to monitor the agreement on June 20, 1963, King announced the March on Washington at a mass meeting. Kennedy had sent his civil rights bill to Congress the day before. "As soon as they start to filibuster," King said, "I think we should march on Washington with a quarter of a million people."[2] In New York City the next day, the march was formally announced. It would focus on jobs and Black unemployment, not just on the need for new civil rights laws.

Within hours, Kennedy had invited the civil rights leadership to a White House meeting the next day, June 21, 1963. The March on Washington might hurt more than it would help, the president claimed. "It seemed to me a great mistake to announce a March on Washington before the bill was even in committee," the president said. "The only effect is to create an atmosphere of intimidation—and this may give some members of Congress an out."[3] Vice President Johnson said the same thing: "We have to be careful not to do anything which would give those who are privately opposed a public excuse to appear as martyrs."

James Farmer of CORE and King objected. The march was an alternative to violence, King argued. "It may seem ill-timed. Frankly, I have never engaged in any direct action movement which did not seem ill-timed. Some people thought Birmingham ill-timed."

"Including the Attorney General," the president replied.[4]

THE FBI AND COMMUNISTS IN THE MOVEMENT

When the meeting broke up, Kennedy invited King into a private meeting in the White House Rose Garden. Once they were alone, the president repeated a warning King had already been given twice that day. Just before the civil rights leadership met with President Kennedy, Burke Marshall had taken King aside to warn him that two of his associates, Jack O'Dell and Stanley Levison, were agents of the Communist Party. Levison, Burke Marshall said, was a Communist Party functionary who had "planted" O'Dell inside SCLC to influence the civil rights movement. There must be some confusion, King said; there was a difference between a person who was sympathetic to Marxism and a Communist Party member. No, Marshall said. Stanley Levison was "a paid agent of the Soviet Communist apparatus." When King asked for proof, Marshall said security considerations prevented him from saying any more. Seeing that King was not convinced, Marshall gave way to Attorney General Robert Kennedy. Kennedy repeated the charges, and again King asked for proof. Many people in the South thought Kennedy was a Communist, King argued; everyone in the movement had been called a Communist for years. Kennedy told King this was different; Levison was even more sinister than Kennedy was permitted to say. The information about him came from the highest ranks of American espionage.[5]

Now the president of the United States walked King through the Rose Garden, as if he himself was afraid of secret surveillance. O'Dell and Levison were Communists, the president told King. O'Dell was a ranking member of the American Communist Party. Stanley Levison's position was so highly classified that it could not be revealed to a man outside the secret world. Levison was O'Dell's "handler," the president said. O'Dell was "the number five Communist in the United States." "I don't know if he's got time to do that," King said, trying to make a joke. "He's got two jobs with me!" Kennedy didn't think that was funny. "If they shoot you down, they'll shoot us down too," Kennedy said. "So we're asking you to be careful."[6]

Three nights later, on June 24, King met with Jack O'Dell, Andrew Young, and others in a New York hotel room. Stanley Levison could not join them; he was on vacation. Some of them joked about the Communist agent being absent, just when the masses had the capitalists on the run. O'Dell was almost too angry to talk. The issue here, he said, wasn't himself.

He was proud of his associations with Communists; most of the people in the room knew them. They were important people to the movement. O'Dell had never done anything to hurt the movement. "J. Edgar Hoover can kiss my ass," he said.[7]

Others agreed. This was a purge that started with Levison and O'Dell; who knew where it might end? The movement couldn't allow a witch hunt—it would self-destruct, bit by bit. King agreed. The government wanted them to sacrifice one set of principles—freedom of association and loyalty—to achieve another—the civil rights bill. "You know," King said, "it's one thing to have the head of the Civil Rights Division of the Justice Department come down on you. I can handle that. And even the Attorney General. But when Burke Marshall, the Attorney General, *and* the President of the United States all come down on you in *one day,* you have to consider that. You have to give it some weight."[8]

The information about Jack O'Dell and Stanley Levison came, of course, from J. Edgar Hoover, director of the FBI since 1924. Hoover had long made it his business to stay informed about what he called "racial matters." During the Montgomery bus boycott, the Mobile FBI office had gathered a few bits of information about King and the Montgomery Improvement Association, but the FBI's interest in Black America dated to 1917. For the FBI, Blacks were second-class citizens who naturally had second-class loyalties. By 1919, FBI offices across the country regularly solicited information about "the Negro question," recruiting "reliable" informants who reported on anyone who preached "social equality" or "equal rights." They infiltrated groups as moderate as the NAACP and as radical as the African Blood Brotherhood, an organization founded in 1919 that advocated armed self-defense against white attacks and coalesced with the Communist Party USA.[9]

As the twenty-four-year-old director of the FBI's General Intelligence Division, Hoover had concluded that "the Reds have done a vast amount of evil damage by carrying doctrines of race revolt and the poison of Bolshevism to the Negroes."[10] A life-long bachelor, Hoover's sexual anxieties were reflected in the special interest he developed in the sex lives of those he investigated; he thought oversexed Black men posed a special threat to white women. He used four Black men to infiltrate Marcus Garvey's Universal Negro Improvement Association (UNIA), accusing Garvey of "pro-Negroism." He investigated the Black press for promoting "sex equality" and unsafe ideas about "the Negro's fitness for self-government." When Hoover became FBI director, he weeded out all but two of the handful of Black agents in the FBI; there were never more than a handful of Black agents until after he died in 1972.

Hoover's FBI, encouraged by President Roosevelt, gathered intelligence reports on radicals, including Communists and Nazis; information on Blacks was collected under special categories called "Negroes" and "Negro trends." In 1942, Hoover launched his most aggressive "Negro Question" investigation, asking his agents to discover "why particularly Negroes or groups of Negroes . . . evidenced sentiments for other 'dark races' (mainly Japanese)."[11] He investigated Black-owned newspapers, recruited Black informants, wiretapped the offices of civil rights groups, and sent derogatory information about the NAACP and Urban League to their contributors. He was particularly interested in rumors about Black domestic servants joining "Eleanor Clubs," named after First Lady Eleanor Roosevelt; the rumor reported that their slogan was "A White Woman in the Kitchen by Christmas."[12]

During the 1943 riots that swept Detroit and other cities, Hoover's FBI probed unsuccessfully for proof that Communists had incited the riots. His men did find that Black attitudes were shifting. The Richmond, Virginia, office reported "a definite change in the attitude of some Negroes," saying, "A number of them appear to have become more disrespectful, more assertive of their rights and more discontented with their station in life."[13]

In 1939, the FBI's ability to protect the civil rights of Black Americans was expanded when the Civil Liberties Unit was established in the Justice Department's Criminal Division. The FBI would serve as investigators of civil rights complaints, but Hoover was reluctant to enter into aggressive civil rights investigations, especially of police brutality complaints, where his men would have to investigate the police officers they worked closely with in other cases; the Justice Department waxed and waned in its enthusiasm.

In 1947, the bureau had three Black agents: one worked in Hoover's office, taking hats and coats from visitors, and one wore a chauffeur's cap and drove the director around. Hoover appointed these two special agents to keep them from being drafted and exempted them from civil service protection. The third, who had helped to investigate Marcus Garvey, supervised the weapons in the New York office.

When President Harry Truman's Committee on Civil Rights called Hoover to testify, Hoover secretly investigated the committee. During the Eisenhower presidency, Hoover managed to rescind a Truman-era directive allowing the FBI to investigate civil rights complaints on its own; now the FBI would have to be ordered to do so by the attorney general.

In 1956, Hoover developed a counterintelligence program, COINTEL-PRO. It conducted burglaries and break-ins in a widespread program of illegal harassment of Communists and any others that Hoover thought were subversive. By 1959, there were four hundred agents in New York assigned to monitor subversive activities; four were assigned to organized crime.

Hoover called the killing of Emmett Till an "alleged lynching," began wiretapping the Nation of Islam in 1957, briefed Eisenhower and Supreme Court chief justice Earl Warren on the 1957 Prayer Pilgrimage for Freedom, maintained secret dossiers on thousands, and secretly supplied information on the private lives and political associations of thousands of Americans to presidents, sympathetic members of Congress, and dozens of newspaper columnists and writers. Hoover's agents tried to get Martin Luther King to commit suicide. The list of lives destroyed and careers ruined by Hoover and the FBI will never be fully known.

Interest in Martin Luther King had increased when the New York FBI office opened a King file in 1958. In October 1960, an informant reported on that year's SCLC convention. In December 1960, federal judge Irving Kaufman told the New York bureau that King and the NAACP were supporting the Committee for Secure Justice for Morton Sobell, who had been convicted of espionage. But when, in a February 1961 article in *The Nation*, King called for more Blacks in federal employment, including the FBI, bureau interest increased.[14]

The Freedom Rides in 1961 quickened the FBI's interest. Hoover asked for information on King and other leaders of the rides. The report he received said King had contact with "subversive" groups, going back as far as 1948 when young Martin Luther King attended a Progressive Party meeting at Morehouse College.

Little other information was reported about King or SCLC until January 8, 1962, when Hoover wrote to Attorney General Robert Kennedy that Stanley Levison, "a member of the Communist Party, USA," was "allegedly a close advisor to the Reverend Martin Luther King Jr."[15] Hoover said that an FBI informant within the Communist Party had reported that Levison had written a speech King had delivered to an AFL-CIO conference in Miami in December 1961.

Levison and King had actually known each other for more than two years. They had been introduced in December 1956 by Bayard Rustin. With Rustin, Randolph, and Ella Baker, Levison had formed a New York group called In Friendship, to raise money for the victims of Southern vigilantes. It sponsored a May 1956 rally at Madison Square Garden to raise funds for the Montgomery Improvement Association.

Levison was a lawyer and businessman. Born in 1912 in New York, he was a University of Michigan graduate who had received a law degree from St. John's University Law School in 1939. Levison had made his money from real estate investments and a car dealership. He had been active in the American Jewish Congress and had raised money for a variety of liberal and progressive causes.

He became inactive in the Communist Party in 1955. He wanted to use his skills to help King where King was weak—in complicated financial and legal matters, and in writing and editing his books and speeches. He had helped Rustin prepare the working papers for the meeting in 1957 that created SCLC. He helped King draft and edit his first book, *Stride Toward Freedom*, and helped to negotiate the contract with the publisher. He met Coretta at the airport after King was stabbed in New York. He helped SCLC set up formal fund-raising procedures, and he advised King on SCLC's staff and personnel, interviewing Wyatt Tee Walker for the executive director's job and a young man—King couldn't remember his name—for the job of citizenship director. The young man's name was Andrew J. Young.

The FBI had long thought Levison was still an active member of the Communist Party. In 1959, following the second Youth March on Washington, Hoover noticed that A. Philip Randolph thanked Stanley Levison for helping arrange the demonstration. Documents at the FBI noted that Levison was close to King; Hoover concluded that Levison had been placed by the CPUSA to influence King and the civil rights movement.

The FBI had followed Levison and wiretapped his telephone since 1954 and had broken into his office in New York twenty-nine times between 1954 and 1964. In 1961, an FBI informant reported that Levison was writing speeches for King and advising him. Robert Kennedy authorized a legal wiretap on Levison's telephone, and members of the administration who knew King—Burke Marshall, John Seigenthaler, the attorney general himself, and Harris Wofford, who knew both men—would be asked to warn King about Levison and Jack O'Dell, who had formerly been a party member too.[16]

On several occasions, King was warned by administration officials about both men; on each occasion, he asked for proof and said Levison's service and friendship bound them together. After receiving warnings from Seigenthaler and Wofford, King and other SCLC officials met with Robert Kennedy at a Washington hotel to discuss voter registration. Wofford asked Kennedy if he knew the name of the man who had sat beside him. "That was Stanley Levison," Wofford said.

In June 1961, those privy to the wiretap heard King tell Levison he wanted to hire Jack O'Dell as an administrative aide; Levison warned that O'Dell's past might hurt King. King said his past didn't matter; if he would say his party membership was in the past, that was all King required. O'Dell stayed in the New York office, but the FBI reported to Kennedy that O'Dell remained in the party. He had, they said, been elected to the party's national committee under a false name three years earlier. O'Dell had been an organizer for the Communist Party USA in the late 1940s and early 1950s in New Orleans. In 1963, pressure from the administration about O'Dell and Levison continued on King. Meanwhile, Levison met with party members in March to tell them he was formally ending his ties with the party.

The information about Stanley Levison came largely from two brothers, Jack and Morris Childs, party members and FBI informants since 1952. The Childs brothers were conduits for money from the Soviet Union to the Communist Party USA. Morris also traveled around the world, meeting with top figures in the world Communist movement, as a representative of the American party. He and his brothers were prizes for the FBI; their code name was SOLO. Each of the presidents from Kennedy through Carter knew about SOLO.

Hoover, who loved to curry favor with power, mentioned the FBI's interest in Levison to Senator Eastland; Eastland subpoenaed Levison to appear before the Senate Internal Security Committee on April 30, 1962. Represented by William Kunstler, Levison denied that he was or ever had been a member of the Communist Party and took the Fifth Amendment in response to all other questions. To his great surprise, King's name never came up. On the same day the subpoena had been issued, the Atlanta FBI office sent a thirty-seven-page report to FBI headquarters stating that no significant Communist influence was exerted on King or SCLC. Headquarters told Atlanta the statement was incorrect; they were ordered to produce a revised report.

At the same time the FBI ordered its New York office to increase surveillance on Levison and O'Dell, King's name was added to the second rank of the FBI's enemies list—one step below the top, where Levison was listed. There were twelve thousand names in Levison's group—all supposedly members of the CPUSA or similar groups. King's listing was for lesser offenders. Both lists were intended to make it easier to detain and arrest those listed in case of a presidentially declared national emergency. The Atlanta office was told to add King to the pickup list. In June 1962, information from the New York office on O'Dell and Levison was sent to Atlanta; they were told to reevaluate their earlier report clearing King and SCLC of Communist influence.

After repeated prodding from the New York and Washington FBI offices, the Atlanta office produced a ten-page report detailing all of the possible Communist influences on King and SCLC. The office advised that a COMINFIL—"Communist infiltration"—investigation of King be undertaken. Under the COINTELPRO program, the FBI sent stories to newspapers in New Orleans, Augusta, Birmingham, St. Louis, and Long Island about O'Dell's background and association with SCLC. On November 1, 1962, King issued a statement attacking the stories and defending O'Dell but announcing that O'Dell would resign. The resignation was purely cosmetic. He continued his work in the New York office.

Then an incident occurred that stirred J. Edgar Hoover into retribution against Martin Luther King. The Southern Regional Council had published a report on the Albany Movement, critical of the federal government, written by Spelman College professor Howard Zinn. King was asked if he agreed with it; he said he did and charged that the FBI's Southern agents were white Southerners who favored segregation. Hoover was irate. He issued a statement correcting King—four of the five agents in Albany were from outside the South. Only one was a native Southerner—Marion Cheeks. Other agents agreed Cheeks was a racist. He had instructed other agents to ignore Blacks' complaints; he edited reports of complaints against local policemen to water them down.

The FBI asked Kennedy to approve a wiretap on Levison's home; he gave permission on November 20, 1962. In late December 1962, final reports from the Atlanta and New York offices were complete. The Atlanta office described SCLC as harmless; the New York report said Communists have "infiltrated SCLC." Hoover ordered New York to take over the COMINFIL investigation.

During the spring of 1963, the FBI kept Attorney General Kennedy informed about conversations between King and Levison they overheard on the Levison wiretaps. With the administration preparing its civil rights bill, Robert Kennedy wanted to know as much as he could about what King was thinking and what kind of advice he was receiving from the "Soviet agent" Levison. Hoover's fixation with Communism and his certain conviction that Communists were everywhere helped fuel a massive American anti-Communist movement, and the movement fed Hoover's fixation.

King had tried to hide his association with O'Dell, and the FBI had twice exposed him as a liar with planted newspaper stories. Now Stanley Levison took steps to break his relationship with King before the FBI could launch a further attack, telling King in July 1963 that they should end their interaction.

In mid-July, Clarence Jones, a young lawyer who'd helped King fight his income tax evasion case in Alabama and served as manager of the Gandhi Society, was sent by King to the Justice Department to talk to Burke Marshall. He told Marshall that King was afraid to talk to Stanley Levison on the telephone, apparently referring to a possible tap on the phone. King, he said, would stop talking to Levison to protect the administration from having King and Levison linked. He would talk to him through Jones. Jones was asking Marshall—and the federal government—to conspire with him to deceive the FBI.

On July 22, Robert Kennedy ordered wiretaps on King's and Clarence Jones's home and office telephones. He backed off the King wiretaps, but the Jones wiretaps were installed. King and his family stayed with the Jones family in suburban New York in early August; the wiretaps soon gave the FBI their first information that Jones would be a conduit to Levison. They also began to hear of King's private life, information that was quickly sent to Robert Kennedy, who passed it to the president. Soon afterward, Hoover approached Robert Kennedy with another request to wiretap King; this time Kennedy felt increasing pressure to say yes. A Senate investigation into corruption in the majority leader's office threatened to reveal that President Kennedy had an affair with a German woman married to an American military man. Robert Kennedy had the woman deported. Hoover knew all about the affair. He had long kept private files on the private lives of important people; presidents were no exception. Hoover's latest request for wiretap authority came at a time when Kennedy needed Hoover to suppress news of the president's affair. The March on Washington had also shown King's influence and reach; the FBI described him as "demagogic" and "the most dangerous . . . to the Nation . . . from the standpoint . . . of national security."[17] Attorney General Kennedy agreed that the FBI could wiretap Martin Luther King's telephone—at any "address" where King happened to be—his home, office, or hotel room.

THE MARCH ON WASHINGTON

On July 2, 1963, the heads of the sponsoring organizations gathered in New York to discuss the March on Washington—Roy Wilkins of the NAACP, A. Philip Randolph of the Brotherhood of Sleeping Car Porters, James Farmer of CORE, John Lewis of SNCC (who had succeeded Charles McDew), and Whitney Young of the Urban League. After arguing whether Rustin's sexuality and politics made him a potential source of danger, they agreed that Randolph would be the march's official leader; Rustin, its organizer. They announced that no sit-ins or civil disobedience would be a part of the march; it had already begun to lose the militant edge Rustin had first envisioned.

In August 1963, the six-member Black leadership team of the march was joined by four whites: Walter Reuther, president of the United Auto Workers; Protestant clergyman Eugene Carson Blake; Rabbi Joachim Prinz; and Catholic layman Mathew Ahmann. Randolph emphasized that whites were welcome. An organizing manual for the march, written by Rustin, emphasized that "totalitarian or subversive" groups were not welcome.[18] Across the country, labor unions, church groups, and civil rights organizations mobilized their membership and supporters for the march.

Within SNCC, support for the march was mixed. Most community organizers—SNCC's field workers—thought the march was a diversion from their work. Others, like chairman Lewis, thought it would apply the necessary pressure to Congress to pass civil rights legislation, even though the president's bill was unsatisfactory.

Back in Southwest Georgia, the federal government took sides against the civil rights movement for a second time. On August 9, a federal grand jury had indicted nine members of the Albany Movement for perjury and conspiring to injure a juror. On August 8, SNCC workers in Americus became involved in a demonstration that resulted in the indictments—on capital charges—of four civil rights workers. The federal government refused to intervene. The August 8 demonstration followed sit-in protests by local teenagers throughout July; over one hundred were in jail. A mass meeting on August 8 became a march of two hundred people that was attacked by local police. Seven policemen and twenty-eight demonstrators were wounded; one protester's leg was broken and another was shot in the back and killed. Seventy-seven went to jail. The local prosecutor brought sedition charges against three SNCC workers and a CORE field secretary. The charge carried the death penalty, and on August 13, Attorney General Robert Kennedy announced that his office had found no evidence of police brutality. The federal government would not intervene in the prosecutions of the four civil rights workers. They remained in jail under high bail until mid-November.

The Albany Nine indictments and the government's refusal to aid the workers facing the death penalty heightened SNCC's hostility toward the government and the Kennedy administration. That hostility appeared in John Lewis's March on Washington speech and created conflicts between SNCC and the other, more moderate groups cosponsoring the march.

THE MARCH SCHEDULE called for all of the speakers to have advance copies of their remarks for press distribution the day before. King didn't but SNCC chairman John Lewis did, and what he'd prepared raised objections from Robert Kennedy. The original text said SNCC could not support the administration's civil rights bill. "It is too little and too late," Lewis planned to say. His language was objectionable to some other march leaders as well.

> We are now involved in a serious revolution. This nation is still a place
> of cheap political leaders who build their careers on immoral compro-

mises and ally themselves with open forms of political, economic and social exploitation. . . . The nonviolent revolution is saying, "We will not wait. . . . we will take matters into our own hands and create a source of power, outside any national structure, that could and would assure us a victory." . . . We all recognize . . . that if any radical social, political and economic changes are to take place in our society, the people, the masses, must bring them about. . . . We will march through the South, through the heart of Dixie, the way Sherman did. We shall pursue our own "scorched earth" policy and burn Jim Crow to the ground—non-violently. We shall fragment the South into a thousand pieces and put them back together in the image of democracy.[19]

Lewis attacked the Albany indictments and compared them with the government's failure to protect civil rights workers. He attacked the administration's appointing "racist judges." "Which side," he asked, "is the federal government on?"

Robert Kennedy and Burke Marshall spoke to Cardinal Patrick O'Boyle, the archbishop of Washington, who was to deliver the march's invocation. Boyle, acting for the administration, raised objections to Lewis's speech among other leaders of the march. At a meeting late on the night before the march, Lewis refused to change a word. The controversy continued on to the Lincoln Memorial the next day; Boyle threatened to boycott the march, saying he would not appear unless he had Lewis's changed speech in his hands ten minutes before the program began. After hasty consultations in a room behind Lincoln's statue and a personal appeal by Randolph, Lewis agreed to the changes.

I was the junior member of the public relation corps assembled from the civil rights groups; the NAACP's PR director Henry Lee Moon was the senior. His contribution seemed to me to be walking around making pronouncements. My main job consisted of fetching Coca-Colas for the movie stars. I had already distributed copies of Lewis's original text to the packs of journalists gathered in front of the speaker's platform. As I did so, I asked them to note the differences between what was written and what Lewis would actually say. Lewis was the only speaker that day to say "Black people" instead of "Negroes," but Lewis had to remove criticisms of Kennedy's civil rights bill as "too little and too late," the word "revolution," and the question "Which side is the federal government on?"

The sole woman on the march coordinating committee was longtime Black activist Anna Arnold Hedgeman. Hedgeman had worked for the FEPC, served as dean at Howard University, and then was hired to work with the Commission of Race and Religion for the National Council of Churches. Through her job with the National Council of Churches, Hedgeman helped bring many white Christians, including white clergy, into the civil rights struggle and to the march. Hedgeman also facilitated many of the day's logistics, including Operation Sandwich, in which she commanded a huge volunteer group to produce eighty thousand box lunches for the marchers.[20]

Hedgeman objected to the lack of women on the march program except as entertainers. Black lawyer Pauli Murray did too. Facing criticisms, Randolph agreed to a compromise. He would present a "Tribute to Women"—Rosa Parks, Daisy Bates, Gloria Richardson, and others were recognized, stood, and received applause.[21] Joan Baez sang as the march was beginning; Mahalia Jackson sang just before King spoke.

When King was introduced, ABC and NBC joined the live coverage by CBS. For the first time, Americans who had never known what it was to sit in a hot, cramped church in the middle of a campaign for lunch counter integration or the right to vote would have—through television—some small notion of that feeling. The closing moments of his speech—the "I have a dream" passages—had been used by King often before, but almost none of the people watching had heard more than a few seconds' sound bite from Martin Luther King or any other Black person.

King began by laying out how America had given Black people a "bad check" and how the country had "defaulted on this promissory note insofar as her citizens of color are concerned." They had come to Washington that day because "we refuse to believe that the bank of justice is bankrupt. . . . And so we have come to cash this check, a check that will give us upon demand the riches of freedom and the security of justice."

He answered critics of the movement who claimed that Black people would never be satisfied:

> We can never be satisfied as long as the Negro is the victim of the unspeakable horrors of police brutality; we can never be satisfied as long as our bodies, heavy with the fatigue of travel, cannot gain lodging in the motels of the highways and the hotels of the cities; we cannot be

satisfied as long as the Negro's basic mobility is from a smaller ghetto to a larger one; we can never be satisfied as long as our children are stripped of their selfhood and robbed of their dignity by signs stating "For Whites Only"; we cannot be satisfied as long as the Negro in Mississippi cannot vote, and the Negro in New York believes he has nothing for which to vote.

And he ended with a call for hope in the face of the "valley of despair. . . . I say to you today, my friends, so even though we face the difficulties of today and tomorrow, I still have a dream. It is a dream deeply rooted in the American dream. I have a dream that one day this nation will rise up and live out the true meaning of its creed, 'We hold these truths to be self-evident, that all men are created equal.'"

King's Black critics seized on the "dream" sequences; while King dreamed, Black America had nightmares, they said. Malcolm X said of the march in a speech in Detroit two months later: "Whoever heard of a revolution where they lock arms . . . singing 'We Shall Overcome'? . . . You don't do any singing, you're too busy swinging!" He called the march "a picnic" and "a circus" with "white clowns and black clowns"; it was "a sellout . . . a takeover"; "they controlled it so tight—they told those Negroes what time to hit town, how to come, where to stop, what signs to carry, what song to sing, what speech they could make, and what speech they couldn't make, and then told them to get out town by sundown. And every one of those Toms was out of town by sundown."[22]

In preparation for the potential riots and disasters federal officials feared from the march, all elective surgery in the area's hospitals was canceled, freeing 350 beds for riot-related emergencies; 1,900 of Washington's 2,900 police officers worked eighteen-hour overtime shifts, instead of their normal eight hours. Police plotted seventy-two potential disaster scenarios and planned a response to each one.

In the event of a riot, a policeman or National Guardsman would be stationed on every street corner in downtown Washington's business district to guard against looters. They deployed two hundred scout cars, eighty-six motorcycles, twenty jeeps, several police helicopters, and twenty-three cranes to move broken down or disabled buses. Local judges were placed on round-the-clock standby, and 350 inmates were evacuated from DC jails to create space for disruptive protesters. Twenty-four hundred National Guardsmen were sworn in as "special officers" and given temporary arrest powers. The National Guard made over one hundred doctors and nurses available. Government offices were shut down. Liquor sales were banned for the first time since Prohibition.

On the day of the march, the District of Columbia was placed under virtual martial law. President Kennedy ordered the biggest peacetime military buildup in American history. Five military bases on the capital's outskirts were bursting with activity—and a heavily armed, four-thousand-strong task force prepared for deployment. At Fort Meyer, Fort Belvoir, Fort Meade, Quantico Marine Base, and the Anacostia Naval Station, thirty helicopters were flown in to provide airlift capacity. At Fort Bragg, North Carolina, fifteen thousand Special Forces troops were placed on stand-by. One hundred fifty FBI agents were assigned to mingle with the crowds.[23]

Missing from this human and mechanical arsenal were police dogs. Washington's sixty-nine police dogs remained in their kennels on the orders of Robert Kennedy to avoid a repetition of the ugly images of Birmingham. Washington also canceled its long-standing policy of allowing white officers to bar Black policemen from their squad cars.

And the administration stationed an official just at the right of the Lincoln Memorial with a cutoff switch and a record turntable—if militant protesters overran the speakers' platform, the sound feed to the loudspeakers would be cut off and replaced by a recording of Mahalia Jackson singing "He's Got the Whole World in His Hands."

Sitting in the White House watching the march on television, President Kennedy said of Martin Luther King's speech: "He's damn good!" When Kennedy met with the march's male leadership after the march, the discussions focused on making the president's civil rights bill stronger. He made no promises.[24]

WHAT DID THE MARCH ON WASHINGTON MEAN?

For most Americans, and probably for most marchers in the March for Jobs and Freedom, "freedom" came first, and "jobs," if considered at all, lacked the symbolic status supplied by brave Southern protesters and stereotypical Southern sheriffs. Although the movement's leadership had long linked racism's economic and psychological dimensions, blatant forms of petty apartheid seemed more immediate, and also seemed more immediately susceptible to a solution. The demands of the Birmingham movement earlier in 1963, for integration of lunch counters and changing rooms had been linked to Black employment in downtown stores. In 1955, the Montgomery bus boycott had from the first asked for integrating the pool of bus drivers. But Bayard Rustin's desire to have the movement sharpen its economic focus was lost at the March on Washington.

The march demonstrated that hundreds of thousands of Americans, white and Black, supported civil rights. The leaders—and the thousands who had joined them in Washington—now had to find ways to intensify and enlarge that support. The march was the crowning moment of a summer-long national preoccupation with racial justice, during which demonstrations seemed to happen constantly in some new place. The march gave the civil rights movement the appearance of unity and responsibility. After all, at least 250,000 people, most of them Black, had gathered in Washington without violence. The presence of whites and the march's integrated leadership showed the nation that civil rights was everyone's concern. The march showed the nation how determined the movement was—some of the people in attendance, obviously poor, had come from great distances, at great sacrifices. These were a people not easily discouraged. Bayard Rustin said the march was "not a climax but a new beginning."[25]

Author James Baldwin wrote: "That day, for a moment, it almost seemed that we stood on a height, and could see our inheritance; perhaps we could make the Kingdom real, perhaps the beloved community would not forever remain that dream one dreamed in agony."[26]

King's speech made the movement more understandable and more palatable to white Americans, but it did little to advance Kennedy's bill. King's vision of a movement rooted in American justice forced the public and media to accept the rationale for the march and the movement that produced it. The speech strengthened the biracial coalition that the march's Black leadership believed was required if the movement was to succeed. King's speech not only said non-Blacks were welcome; it said racial justice was both a religious and secular concern and therefore the participation of whites was their obligation.

The speech was crucial for the Kennedy administration. JFK had done all he could, short of a direct appeal to cancel the march, to get it called off. He did not give it his cautious endorsement until early August, ensuring that the march's targets would be opponents of his civil rights bill and not the president himself. King's speech redeemed this strategy, and the peacefulness of the occasion reaffirmed the wisdom of the president's choice. But the speech also helpfully obscured, at least for a moment, divisions among the march's leadership and organizational disputes.

Women had little public visibility in the March on Washington's program, except as entertainers—though many worked behind the scenes to ensure the day's success. Even in the movement that one feminist scholar called "strikingly egalitarian," the absence of women in leadership roles was noticeable.[27] No woman was part of the delegation of civil rights leaders that met Kennedy after the march. But for the second time in American history the struggle against white supremacy would be midwife to a feminist movement. In the abolitionist movement of the 1830s and 1840s, women working for racial equality began to migrate from individual expressions of discontent toward a social movement on their own behalf. In the 1960s, the movement for racial justice again gave women experience in organizing and collective action and instructed them in an ideology that condemned an oppression similar to their own—a belief in human rights they could also claim for themselves.

LESS THAN THREE WEEKS after the March on Washington, on September 15, 1963, Klansmen planted a dynamite bomb that exploded at the Sixteenth Street Baptist Church, killing four young Black Sunday School students, all girls. This was the twenty-ninth bombing of Black property in Birmingham stretching back to 1947; the previous twenty-eight were all unsolved.[28]

I flew to Birmingham with John Lewis that afternoon and stood outside the bombed church.[29] For many in the movement, the Birmingham church bombing exploded whatever idealism they had maintained over the years. The deaths of four children seemed a last straw. Few movement activists had ever been committed pacifists. The bombing confirmed the ineffectiveness of nonviolence for many and relegated it to tactical use alone for many more, rather than a way of life. And it underscored the need for political power.

But even the church bombing did not strengthen Kennedy's lukewarm acceptance of the movement's goals. In a meeting with Birmingham's white businessmen a week later, he revealed how sympathetic he was to white objections to integration of lower schools and compared the hypocrisy of his liberal critics with their own actions.

Two months and seven days after the Birmingham bombing, on November 22, 1963, President John F. Kennedy was shot and killed in Dallas, Texas, by Lee Harvey Oswald. When it was announced that Kennedy was dead, King told his wife, "This is what is going to happen to me. This is such a sick society."[30]

NINETEEN

THE CIVIL RIGHTS ACT

T HE FIRST MODERN Civil Rights Act, enacted in 1957, was a weak and ultimately unsuccessful attempt at enforcing voting rights. The Civil Rights Act of 1960, which contained some voting rights provisions and criminal penalties for violent acts, was equally weak. The first major modern piece of civil rights legislation, which remains a viable force in all our lives today, was the Civil Rights Act of 1964.

These bills owe their existence to Lyndon B. Johnson. As a US representative and senator, Johnson voted against six civil rights bills. As the Senate majority leader, he led the Senate fight for the Civil Rights Act of 1957, forging the compromise that included jury trials for offenders against the act as a bow to Southern sentiments. He admitted, "We obtained only half a loaf in that fight, but it was an essential half-loaf, the first civil rights legislation in eighty-two years. . . . Once this first guarantee was on the books, the path was opened for later legislation extending federal protection into every area of civil rights."[1]

Upon assuming the presidency following President Kennedy's assassination, Johnson, during his first two weeks in office, met separately with the NAACP's Roy Wilkins and Clarence Mitchell, SCLC's Martin Luther King, CORE's James Farmer, and labor leader A. Philip Randolph. Johnson told them that "John Kennedy's dream of equality had not died with him" and that he "was going to press for the civil rights bill with every ounce of energy I possessed."[2] The civil rights bill, along with other social legislation proposed by President Kennedy, had been bottled up in committee for months. In October 1963, just before the assassination, columnist

Walter Lippman had written: "There are two great measures before Congress, and in all probability Senator [Barry] Goldwater was right when he said the other day that 'the President has to make up his mind whether he wants the civil rights bill or a tax cut, because he cannot get them both.'"[3]

The first ten months of Johnson's presidency witnessed the passage not only of the tax bill and the civil rights bill but also the Food Stamp Act, the War on Poverty, the Urban Mass Transit Act, the Housing Act, the Wilderness Areas Act, the Fire Island National Seashore Act, and the Nurse Training Act.

At this point in his career, Johnson saw civil rights as "a moral issue . . . [that] could not be avoided regardless of the outcome."[4] Comparing his situation to that of a poker player, he said, "I decided to shove in all my stack on this vital measure."[5] When told by his advisors that he "should not lay the prestige of the Presidency on the line" over civil rights, Johnson replied, "What's it for if it's not to be laid on the line?"[6] At a White House press conference, Johnson was asked why he had thrown his support so strongly behind the Civil Rights Act after opposing civil rights bills earlier. He said, "Some people get a chance late in life to correct the sins of their youth and very few get a chance as big as the White House."[7]

Johnson's strategy regarding the Civil Rights Act of 1964 was simple: no compromise: "It would be a fight to total victory or total defeat without appeasement or attrition," he wrote.[8] Everett Dirksen, Republican of Illinois and Senate minority leader, was known as a man who would put principle above party. Senator Dirksen held the key to obtaining cloture, the legislative device that sets a time limit on debate, thereby precluding a filibuster. Moderate Republicans, like Dirksen, would have to join Democrats in order to achieve the two-thirds vote necessary for cloture.

The liberals, with Minnesota senator Hubert Humphrey as floor manager, were, in Johnson's words, "organized as never before"—and perhaps never since![9] Southern legislators, led by Senator Richard Russell Jr. (D-GA), promised "to fight these discriminatory proposals to the last ditch."[10] In late March and early April, SCLC-sponsored demonstrations in St. Augustine, Florida, captured headlines as policemen let Ku Klux Klansmen attack and beat nonviolent protesters.

As the congressional debate continued through the spring of 1964, Governor George Wallace of Alabama entered Democratic presidential primaries in Indiana, Maryland, and Wisconsin, campaigning vigorously in opposition to civil rights. Analysts predicted that Wallace would win about 10 percent of the vote; he more than tripled their predictions. Although the Wallace showing stiffened Southerners' resolve to continue fighting against the civil rights measure, it also unified support.

On June 10, 1964, Senator Dirksen took the Senate floor to say: "The time has come for equality of opportunity, in sharing in government, in education, and in employment. It will not be stayed or denied. It is here . . . America grows. America changes. And on the civil rights issue we must rise with the occasion. That calls for cloture and for the enactment of a civil rights bill."[11]

The Senate, for the first time ever on a civil rights bill, voted cloture by a margin of 71 to 29. The fight was over. One by one, debilitating amendments proposed by Southerners were voted down on the floor, some votes coming as the search for Andrew Goodman, Mickey Schwerner, and James Cheney spread through Mississippi's swamps. Three weeks later Congress passed the Civil Rights Act of 1964. President Johnson signed it on July 2, 1964. The next day he told a friend in the White House: "We had to do it and I'm glad we did it, but I think we just delivered the South to the Republican Party for your lifetime."[12]

The bill contained eleven titles, the most important of which are Title II, prohibiting discrimination on the basis of race, color, religion, or national origin in places of public accommodation; Title VI, prohibiting discrimination on the basis of race, color, or national origin in any program receiving federal funds; and Title VII, prohibiting discrimination in employment on the basis of race, color, religion, sex, or national origin.

How did sex or gender discrimination come to be prohibited by the Civil Rights Act of 1964, a bill that clearly was directed at issues of *race* discrimination? Was it because an enlightened majority recognized the problems of gender discrimination and vowed to also make their elimination a national priority?

No. It was because Howard W. Smith (D-VA) offered an amendment to add "sex" to the bill's coverage, confident that it would sink the bill. To explain his "chivalrous" action, Smith read from a letter he said he had just received from a "lady": "I suggest that you might also favor an amendment . . . to correct the present 'imbalance' which exists between males and females in the United States. . . . The Census of 1960 shows that we had 88,331,000 males living in this country and 90,992,000 females, which leaves the country with an 'imbalance' of 2,661,000 females. . . . I am sure you will agree that this is a grave injustice to womankind." If all women weren't going to be able to get husbands, Smith argued, they at least should get jobs with equal pay.[13]

Suddenly, in a spontaneous spirit of sisterhood, a bipartisan coalition of congresswomen arose in support of Smith's amendment. Katherine St. George (R-NY) proclaimed to her bewildered male colleagues, "I can think of nothing more logical than this amendment at this point." Women "do not need any special privileges," she said. "We outlast you—we outlive you—we nag you to death, . . . [but] we are entitled to this little crumb of equality. The addition of that little, terrifying word 's-e-x' will not hurt this legislation in any way."[14] The amendment passed by a vote of 168 to 133. In the Senate, Maine's Margaret Chase Smith fought to retain the "sex" amendment. With the help of the broad new constituency that Howard Smith had inadvertently created, Senator Margaret Chase Smith succeeded. Even some of the supporters feared that the inclusion of "sex" in Title VII's prohibited categories of discrimination would lead to revolutionary changes in the male-dominated world. They were right.

Today the Civil Rights Act of 1964 stands as the centerpiece of antidiscrimination legislation. Its provisions prohibit discrimination not only against Blacks. When Black people faced violence and arrest in Southern towns and cities three decades ago, the law their bodies wrote also protects Jews, Muslims, and Christians from religious discrimination and women from employment discrimination based on gender.

TWENTY

MISSISSIPPI FREEDOM
SUMMER, 1964

B Y THE FALL OF 1963, few additional Blacks had been registered to vote in Mississippi, despite the best efforts of the COFO staff—most of them from SNCC. The Greenwood registration drives had produced little; after some initial publicity, the press had moved elsewhere. The federal government had intervened when violence seemed imminent but made no move to help get Blacks registered to vote.

SNCC's Bob Moses had begun discussing the idea of a "Freedom Vote" campaign for the fall. Mississippi's unregistered Blacks would be asked to cast "Freedom Votes" in a mock election that paralleled the statewide election in Mississippi that fall. For Moses and other COFO workers, the Freedom Vote was both an organizing tool and a chance to demonstrate that Blacks in Mississippi did want to vote.

Freelance social activist Allard Lowenstein suggested to Bob Moses that he be allowed to recruit white students for the fall Freedom Vote campaign; they would provide needed manpower, and their white skins could provoke interest from the news media that Black skins could not produce. Lowenstein recruited one hundred Yale and Stanford students to come to Mississippi between late October and November 4; they worked with the COFO staff to turn out Black citizens for a mock Freedom Vote in which Dr. Aaron Henry and Tougaloo chaplain Ed King were candidates for governor and lieutenant governor. Their platform was radically different from the usual Mississippi candidates—they called for school desegregation, fair employment, a $1.25 minimum wage. Over eighty thousand Blacks cast Freedom Votes while journalists flocked to interview the white students, and FBI agents appeared where none had been before.

During a SNCC staff meeting in Greenville in mid-November, the idea of more white students coming to Mississippi for a longer time was considered. While no decision was made, several noted that the white students did bring publicity and an increased federal presence. Others worried of the disruption of local leadership and potential dominating effect of white volunteers.[1] By the December COFO meeting, the idea was discussed again. There were suggestions that the number of whites be limited to one hundred. In late December, the SNCC Executive Committee approved the idea and sent SNCC staff to COFO's January 1964 meeting to lobby for approval. The COFO staff gave its approval.

Moses had argued, "These students bring the rest of the country with them. They're from good schools and their parents are influential."[2] Later, Forman wrote, "We made a conscious attempt . . . to recruit from some of the Ivy League schools . . . to consciously recruit a counter power-elite."[3]

For the Summer Project, COFO divided Mississippi along the lines of its congressional districts—CORE would work in the Fourth District; SNCC had the other three. From the very first, there were political differences SNCC had to overcome. Lowenstein had reportedly told Stanford students they would work during the summer under his direction, as had Boston recruiter Barney Frank.[4] Lowenstein further wanted the summer's work directed from New York. SNCC and COFO would not allow him to dominate. At Moses's insistence, SNCC moved its national headquarters from Atlanta to Greenwood.

SNCC's traditional poverty controlled its recruiting—the volunteers would have to be self-supporting, limiting the number of Blacks, few of whom could afford to spend a summer without salary working in Mississippi. It also meant that volunteers would be older than typical college students. Most recruitment was done by Friends of SNCC groups that SNCC had already established to provide funds and political support. Other civil rights groups with campus chapters—especially CORE—did recruiting too. To avoid control by Lowenstein or other outsiders, applications were sent directly to the COFO office in Jackson.

The applicants were hardly typical Americans. Average median family income in the United States in 1960 was $5,660; the Freedom Summer applicants' family income was nearly 50 percent higher—$8,417. Median income for a Mississippi Black family was only $1,444. Thus, the poorest people in the United States would play hosts for the summer for the children of the most privileged. Applications came from 233 schools, but the highest-ranking public and private schools provided more than half of the applicant pool. Forty percent came from Harvard, Yale, Stanford, and Princeton alone; 145 others came from elite public schools—Berkeley, Michigan, Wisconsin. They were also the children of the powerful, if not the rich. The children of historian Arthur Schlesinger and Representative Donald Edwards (D-CA) were volunteers.[5]

Of the applicants, 10 percent were married, usually to another potential volunteer. Fewer than 2 percent were parents. Ninety percent of the applicants were white, a figure not as surprising as it may seem. Along with the requirement that volunteers be self-supporting, during the 1961–62 school year, Blacks were only 2.9 percent of all college students in America. Forty-nine percent of the applicants were female, a higher number than the percentage of women in college; in 1964, women were only 39 percent of undergraduate students in the United States.

Most of the students came from the Great Lakes, Mid-Atlantic, and Far West. Almost half—46.3 percent—came from Illinois, New York, and California. Only 11 percent were from the South; most of these were Black.

The financial requirement set their average age at twenty-three. Twenty percent had completed their undergraduate education, and seniors and juniors outnumbered freshmen and sophomores by two to one. Twenty-two percent had full-time jobs; seventy percent of those who did were teachers.

Before the project began, the volunteers described themselves as optimistic and idealistic, religiously motivated, patriotic, and as conventional leftists, generally socialists. Of those, 48 percent belonged to a civil rights group, 21 percent to a church or religious group, 14 percent to a socialist or leftist organization, 13 percent to an affiliate of the Democratic or Republican Parties, 13 percent to an academic organization, and 10 percent to a teacher's organization. Half belonged to a CORE chapter or a Friends of SNCC organization, 90 percent had some kind of civil rights experience, and 25 percent of the volunteers knew another volunteer.

All those under twenty-one had to have parental permission. Most were interviewed on campus by a Friends of SNCC organization. Seventy were rejected—most because they were underage or applied too late; 25 percent of the applicants were no-shows. When interviewed later, 25 percent of the no-shows said their parents had convinced them not to go.[6]

In preparation for the summer, the city of Jackson, Mississippi, increased its police force from 390 to 450, adding two horses, six dogs, and two hundred new shotguns, stockpiling tear gas, and issuing a gas mask to every policeman. They added three canvas-topped troop carriers, two half-ton searchlight trucks, and three giant trailer trucks to haul demonstrators to two large detention compounds at the state fairgrounds. The city's pride was "Thompson's Tank," named after the mayor, a thirteen-thousand-pound armored battle wagon built to the city's specifications at one dollar a pound.

The Mississippi that summer volunteers would enter had long relied on non-mechanized cotton farming. In 1960, 68 percent of all Mississippi Blacks lived in rural areas, compared to 38 percent of Blacks nationally. Median nonwhite income was the lowest in the United States; 86 percent of all nonwhite families in Mississippi lived under the federal poverty level. In 1960, the median number of years of school finished by Mississippi Blacks over twenty-five was the sixth grade. For whites, it was the eleventh grade. Forty-two percent of whites had finished twelve years of school; only 7 percent of Blacks had gone that far. In 1964, Mississippi spent $21.77 per Black child and $81.86 per white child on education. In Holly Bluff, Mississippi, education expenditures were $191.70 for each white child and $1.26 for each Black child.[7]

Infant mortality rates for Blacks were twice as high as for whites. Two-thirds of all Black housing was "deteriorated" or "dilapidated." Half of all Black housing had no piped water; two-thirds of all Black housing had no flush toilets.

In 1960, only 7 percent of Mississippi Blacks old enough to register had registered to vote. Five counties had Black population majorities and no Black voters. In Coahoma County, 95 percent of the eligible whites were registered to vote.

Through the National Council of Churches, SNCC and COFO arranged for two weeklong training sessions for the summer volunteers to be held at Oxford College for Women in Miami, Ohio, from June 14 to 20. The Justice Department's John Doar spoke and told them not to expect federal protection: "Maintaining law and order is a state responsibility."[8]

The volunteers attracted a great deal of media attention. They were white, young, attractive, heading into potential danger, and willing to spend a summer living in primitive circumstances, the exact stuff from which media interest is born. Two hundred fifty of them left Oxford College in Ohio for Mississippi on June 20 and 21.

On the 21st, Bob Moses spoke to the volunteers. "Yesterday," he said, "three of our people left Meridian, Mississippi, to investigate a church burning in Neshoba County. They haven't come back, and we haven't had any word from them."[9] The three missing were Mickey Schwerner, a white CORE worker from New York; James Cheney, a Black volunteer from Meridian, Mississippi; and Andrew Goodman, a white volunteer from New York. They were already dead when Moses made his announcement.

The summer's original 550 volunteers were supplemented over the summer by 400 to 450 more; there were never more than 600 in the state at one time. There were originally thirty-two COFO projects spread out through the state, but by the summer's end, COFO had established forty-four projects. The safest area proved to be the Gulf Coast—a tourist area more progressive than the rest of the state, where illegal gambling and drinking had long been tolerated. The most dangerous was the Third District in Southwest Mississippi, where SNCC had begun its voter registration in Amite County four years before. Two-thirds of the summer's bomb attacks happened in the Third District.

The volunteers were divided between voter registration work in forty-two of the forty-four projects, Freedom Schools in thirty of the projects, and community centers in twenty-three projects.

WORKERS FROM SNCC and COFO had helped to found the Mississippi Freedom Democratic Party (MFDP)—an alternative to the racist all-white state Democratic Party—in April 1964. In June 1964, the MFDP fielded candidates in Mississippi's primaries for the US House and Senate elections: John Houston, John Cameron, Victoria Gray, and Fannie Lou Hamer. All four lost but decided to run as independents in the November elections. The state board of elections kept them off the ballot. They decided to run another Freedom Vote campaign like the previous fall, to dramatize the extent of voter disfranchisement in the state. Many of the summer volunteers spent their time preparing for the Freedom Vote as well as in regular registration work and in documenting the delays, obstructions, harassment, and terror that could become the evidence for lawsuits, the MFDP's convention challenge, and a congressional challenge in the fall.

Volunteers also helped to organize the complicated steps—from precinct conventions to county conventions to district conventions to state conventions—to establish the MFDP as a bona fide party. On August 6, sixty-eight delegates, sixty-four Blacks and four whites, were elected to represent the party at the Democratic Convention in Atlantic City. In the process of the summer's work, many of the volunteers learned organizing skills they would take with them into what would become the New Left.

Other volunteers worked in Freedom Schools. Conceived by Charlie Cobb, the schools, his proposal laid out, would "provide an educational experience for students which will make it possible for them to challenge the myths of our society, to perceive more clearly its realities, and to find alternatives, and ultimately, new directions for action."[10] In March 1964, the National Council of Churches sponsored a meeting to develop a curriculum: it consisted of remedial education, to make up for the meager education Black children had received from the public schools; leadership development, to find future leaders for Black Mississippi through study of the civil rights movement and Black history; and contemporary issues, to attempt to relate local, national, and world affairs to the children's current condition. A nonacademic curriculum included arts and crafts, poetry, playwriting, and establishing a student newspaper. Staughton Lynd, a Spelman College history professor, was the director of the Freedom Schools program. Over thirty-five hundred students attended.

At the summer's end, four project workers had been killed, four people critically wounded, eighty workers beaten, thirty-seven churches bombed or burned, thirty Black businesses or homes burned, and over one thousand people arrested.[11] Eighty of the volunteers decided to stay after the summer was over, the majority of whom were white women.

While Freedom Summer actually registered few voters, it built community centers, widened the horizons of some Mississippi schoolchildren, and invited America into Mississippi through the eyes and experiences of the summer volunteers. It established the MFDP, which would play an important role in Mississippi politics for years to come. The MFDP's lawsuits against the state's continual attempts to gerrymander, block, and otherwise interfere with the right to vote established important legal principles that had a widespread effect on reapportionment and voting rights throughout the nation. SNCC wanted to do more than challenge segregation in the Deep South. At the Democratic Convention in Atlantic City, it intended to challenge the Democratic Party itself. As the Mississippi staff prepared for the Atlantic City challenge and slowed down from Freedom Summer, the SNCC staff in Selma, in Central Alabama, was heating up.

TWENTY-ONE

SELMA, ALABAMA, AND THE
1965 VOTING RIGHTS ACT

SELMA, LIKE MONTGOMERY, had a powerful white political machine that dominated its politics. The first Alabama chapter of the White Citizens' Council was established in Selma. It quickly grew to thirteen hundred members and established a close relationship with the Selma city government, the county Democratic Party, and state and county elected officials. By 1958, the party chairman boasted that since the White Citizens' Council had been established, only one nonmember had been elected to office. Able to stifle all dissent among whites—if indeed there was any— it had not been able to keep Blacks from complaining about, or acting to improve, the conditions under which they lived.

In November 1955, Alabama governor James Folsom named James G. Clark sheriff in Dallas County to fill a vacancy caused by the death of the elected sheriff. Wilson Baker, a South Carolina native and charter member of the Selma White Citizens' Council, joined the Selma police force in 1940 and worked his way up to captain. Clark was just the sort of political appointee that Baker resented—one with no training or experience. When Clark ran for election in 1958, Baker resigned from the police force to run against him. In a runoff, Clark portrayed Baker as the tool of the city machine—and easily won.

Joseph Smitherman, who had grown up in a poor white section of the city, was elected to the council in 1960 and, in 1964, successfully ran for mayor. Only about two hundred of Selma's six thousand voters were Black;

he carried nearly every one. The most significant act he performed after the election was to name Wilson Baker to the newly created position of director of public safety.

The White Citizens' Council dominated Selma politics, and tilted it to the right. Allowing for such a tilt, Smitherman and Baker represented moderation; Clark was a racial extremist. In 1961, the Department of Justice had filed a lawsuit against the Dallas County registration board. Only 0.9 percent of the eligible Blacks in Selma were registered to vote. That suit had little success. In 1963, the Justice Department filed suit against Sheriff Clark and the local registration board to keep them from threatening and intimidating would-be voters. A conservative federal judge dismissed the suit.

In the winter of 1962–63, local Black leaders formed the Dallas County Voters' League. Two women—Marie P. Foster and Amelia Boynton—were among the league's founders. When her husband died suddenly in 1963, Amelia Boynton took over the civil rights work he had pioneered. "A voteless people is a hopeless people," she believed. She asked both SCLC and SNCC to help the Voters' League's efforts. SCLC decided against it because of their heavy investment in their Birmingham campaign, but SNCC was interested in the kind of long-term organizing effort the Voters' League wanted.

In February 1963, Bernard and Colia Lafayette came to Selma in a 1948 Chevrolet someone had given SNCC. Lafayette, a native of Tampa, Florida, was twenty-two. He had been a participant in James Lawson's 1959 nonviolence workshops in Nashville, active in the Nashville sit-ins, and a Freedom Rider who had served time in Parchman penitentiary. Preparing to go to Selma, he said, "The first struggle will be against Black fear, not against white resistance."[1]

Lafayette first met with the Black ministers' organization. One minister told him Blacks in Selma had no problems: "We know how to get what we want from white people. You just have to know how to get it."[2] He fell to his knees and held out his hand.

In contrast, Lafayette reported, the Voters' League members were "stand-up people." The Lafayettes and the Voters' League spent the spring and summer trying to persuade potential voters to come to a registration school or to go to the courthouse to register to vote. Although their focus was on voter registration, the presence of the SNCC workers spurred

Selma's youth into militant action. Inspired by the promise of the 1964 Civil Rights Act desegregating public accommodations, five students were arrested in lunch counter sit-ins on September 15, and one hundred young people marched in protest on the courthouse. They were arrested and jailed.

Ten days later, SNCC chairman John Lewis and twenty-five others were arrested for picketing the county courthouse demanding the right to vote; they were sentenced to one hundred days in jail. Two days later, comedian Dick Gregory and his wife, Lillian, came to town; she was arrested. James Forman wrote in his autobiography about the trap they were building for Clark: "My first objective was to turn the demonstrations and the whole climate of protest into a thrust for the right to vote and against Jim Clark. . . . Our strategy was to force the US government to intervene if there were arrests. If they did not intervene, that inaction would once again prove that the government was not on our side and intensify the development of a mass consciousness among blacks."[3]

On October 7, SNCC sponsored a "Freedom Day," and over two hundred Blacks came to the courthouse to try to register to vote. SNCC workers who tried to feed or bring water to those waiting in line were arrested and beaten. Earlier that year, in July 1964, in response to Black desegregation protests, a circuit court judge, James Hare, issued an injunction that suspended the First Amendment in Dallas County, and civil rights activity was declared illegal. The momentum SNCC had created was being dissipated.

In November 1964, Mrs. Boynton spoke to an SCLC staff retreat in Birmingham. She told them SNCC had nearly run out of steam in Selma. The judge's injunction had throttled all protest. But the division between city hall and the courthouse where Sheriff Clark ruled could be exploited to create a successful movement in Selma.

It was easy for SCLC to choose Selma. Voter registration was the main issue there; registration was an issue SCLC wanted to focus on, now that the Civil Rights Act had been passed. Two million more Blacks had voted in the 1964 election than had voted four years before; 94 percent had voted for the Democrats. President Johnson had carried every state except Arizona, Alabama, Georgia, Louisiana, Mississippi, and South Carolina. Fewer than 45 percent of eligible Blacks were registered in the Southern states Johnson lost. Black votes helped Johnson carry Arkansas, Florida,

Tennessee, and Virginia. Clearly, effective registration drives would influ-ence American politics. Already the 1964 election—in addition to elect-ing Johnson president—had upset the old coalition between Republicans and conservative Southern Democrats. Now the Democrats had convinc-ing majorities in both houses of Congress. But by 1964's election, only 335 Blacks were registered in Dallas County.

Sheriff Clark was another attraction. A clone of Birmingham's Bull Connor, he could be counted on to provide the violence required to create national revulsion. SCLC's director of affiliates, the Reverend C. T. Vivian, met with the Dallas County Voters' League. Selma is a good spot, he re-ported. The only negative was SNCC's presence. SCLC set January 2, 1965, as the date of a mass meeting in Selma to announce the beginning of its entry into the city, kick off its drive for the right to vote, and test Judge Hare's injunction.[4]

In the meantime, as in Birmingham, a split in Selma's white politics temporarily opened an opportunity for local Blacks to seek change. The powerful white political machine that had run Selma so successfully for so long was in decline, enabling the new, more moderate Selma government to try to distance itself from the racially radical government in the county. In 1963 and in 1964, Sheriff Clark had been responsible for most of the civil rights arrests in Selma, drawing unwelcome attention from the news me-dia and the federal government, embarrassing the industry-seeking city government, exactly as civil rights forces had hoped.

Clark and Baker came to an agreement; the city police under Baker would handle all law enforcement in the city's limits. Any offenses com-mitted at the courthouse would be handled entirely by Sheriff Clark. By restricting Clark to the courthouse, Selma's whites hoped to diminish his role in fueling the movement. In fact, the opposite happened. Clark's role in the protests actually expanded. The civil rights community in Selma wanted to be arrested by Jim Clark at the courthouse, not by Wilson Baker on the way there. Under the new arrangement, Baker protected marchers until they arrived at the courthouse door, where Clark could unleash his ugliest behavior.

King kicked off the SCLC campaign at the January mass meeting. Even before the SCLC campaign began, Lyndon Johnson was considering new legislation to protect the right to vote.

GENESIS: THE 1965 VOTING RIGHTS ACT

As expected, the 1964 Democratic Convention at Atlantic City had nominated Lyndon Johnson and Minnesota senator Hubert Humphrey for president and vice president. Winning the vice presidential spot, Johnson let it be known, depended on Hubert Humphrey's ability to peacefully settle the challenge posed by the Mississippi Freedom Democratic Party's delegation to the all-white Democratic regulars, who had kept Blacks from any participation in party activity.

The MFDP, while overwhelmingly Black, was open to all Mississippians. The white regular Mississippi Democrats opposed Johnson's domestic programs, which the MFDP supported. The MFDP supported the Democratic Party and expected to support Johnson; many of the regular Mississippi Democrats supported the Republican, Barry Goldwater. Through SNCC's contacts, the MFDP had lined up support from nine state delegations and twenty-five Democratic congressmen. Most important for the president, however, was avoiding any action that would alienate Southern whites. On August 22, 1964, at the Democratic National Convention in Atlantic City, the MFDP presented its case to the Credentials Committee; Fannie Lou Hamer was the most important witness. She was in the middle of a harrowing description of the beating she had received in Winona, Mississippi, when President Johnson hastily called a press conference, knocking Mrs. Hamer off national television.

The Johnson forces then offered a compromise: MFDP delegates could participate in the convention but would not be allowed to vote. When the MFDP rejected this resolution, Johnson's forces turned up the pressure. Johnson had instructed the FBI to keep tabs on the MFDP, so they knew the delegates supporting the MFDP challenge and began to strong-arm them.[5] Support for the MFDP began to erode. Another compromise was offered: the MFDP would be given two at-large seats that would be filled by MFDP members Aaron Henry and Edwin King. The Johnson administration specified the acceptable MFDP delegates, unwilling to let the MFDP choose who would fill the two seats; Johnson explicitly did not want Hamer. The other members of the delegation would be "guests" of the convention.

By August 25, Johnson had been successful in cutting away the MFDP's support. The choice they now faced was two seats or none. Civil liberties lawyer Joe Rauh, Martin Luther King, Bayard Rustin, Hubert Humphrey, Walter Mondale, and others urged the MFDP delegates to take the compromise; in the end, the delegates overwhelmingly rejected it. "We've been treated like beasts in Mississippi. . . . We risk our lives coming up here," Annie Devine explained.[6] "We didn't come all this way for no two seats," Mrs. Hamer said, "because all of us is tired!"[7]

The MFDP's defeat in Atlantic City at the hands of the Democratic Party's perfidious liberals further widened the gulf between SNCC and the national liberal community. For the Democratic Party, the offer of two seats seemed a reasonable compromise; for the MFDP and SNCC, two seats filled by representatives chosen by others was an insult, a continuation of the tokenism and condescension with which whites had been treating Blacks for years. "Them people had not been even talking to us poor folks," Unita Blackwell explained. "The big niggers talked to the big niggers . . . but the little folks told them no, they wasn't going to take it and they meant business."[8] For many SNCC workers, the MFDP's experience showed how weak white liberals *and* Black Democratic office-holders were, and how little they could be depended upon. Confronted by a reporter about the compromise, Moses angrily replied, "We are here for the people and the people want to represent themselves. They don't want symbolic token votes."[9]

What Blacks needed, many decided, was Black power, Black people electing *and* controlling their own representatives. SNCC had demonstrated its ability to organize and mobilize; but when it tried to win power, its allies fled. More and more, SNCC would look away from established politics and coalitions and toward creating Black power for Black people. As historian Steven Lawson observed, the MFDP served "as a prototype for the model of Black Power advocated and popularized by Stokely Carmichael."[10]

The MFDP's legal efforts against white resistance to political equality proved important to Black political efforts across the South. An MFDP-directed lawsuit resulted in the Supreme Court's landmark 1969 decision in *Allen v. [Virginia] State Board of Elections*, which said that all changes to state voting rights laws were subject to review under the Voting Rights Act. The decision was "critical to continuing Black political progress throughout the South," a scholar wrote. "For the first time, . . . the Supreme Court recognized and applied the principle of minority vote dilution—that the black vote can be affected as much by dilution as by an absolute prohibition on casting a ballot."[11]

The MFDP wasn't the only organization SNCC helped build that survived the demise of the parent. In 1964, SNCC encouraged a group of New York progressive health professionals to form a group to provide health care to workers in the Freedom Summer campaign. Most were veterans of past attempts to organize physicians to push to integrate the American Medical Association's segregated Southern affiliates and of sporadic attempts to win support for national health insurance. They called their new organization the Medical Committee for Human Rights (MCHR). "Wherever there was a demonstration or confrontation," historian John Dittmer writes, "be it at the Edmund Pettus Bridge outside Selma or on the Meredith March in the South, in Resurrection City with the Poor People's Campaign, at Columbia University during the student rebellion, in the streets of Chicago outside the Democratic National Convention in 1968 or at Wounded Knee with the American Indian Movement, men and women in white coats and Red Cross armbands were on the scene, providing 'medical presence' and assistance to the people who were putting themselves at risk." Seeing US health care as racist, unjust, and inadequate, Dittmer writes, "MCHR members established free health clinics in inner cities and . . . campaigned for a national health service that would provide quality health care for everyone."[12]

THE STRUGGLE FOR VOTING RIGHTS CONTINUES

Johnson was elected president on November 3, 1964. Blacks had voted nine to one for the Democrats. Black votes had been the victory margin for the Democrats in Arkansas, Florida, Tennessee, Virginia, and North Carolina. The MFDP had supported Johnson, even as most of the regular Democratic Party in Mississippi was campaigning—and carrying the state—for Barry Goldwater. Johnson won with a staggering sixteen-million-vote margin, carrying forty-four states. Goldwater won six—his home state, Arizona, and Alabama, Georgia, Louisiana, Mississippi, and South Carolina. But the Goldwater coattails added five new Republican congressmen in Alabama and one each in Georgia and Mississippi, the first GOP House and Senate members from those states since Reconstruction. Everywhere in the South that Blacks could vote, Johnson won; everywhere Blacks could not vote, he lost.

On November 4, the day after his election, Johnson asked Attorney General Nicholas Katzenbach to draft "the next civil rights bill—legislation to secure, for once and for all, equal voting rights."[13] The voting rights provisions of the Civil Rights Acts of 1957, 1960, and even 1964 had been hamstrung with onerous judicial procedures; the federal government had to go case by case, county by county, through a judicial swamp where hostile local officials and hostile federal judges made each case several years' work. As soon as one tortuous barrier to Black registration was beaten down after a long court battle, local officials erected another. Where provisions written in local law were not sufficient, terror and economic intimidation served to keep the number of registered Blacks low. The Mississippi Freedom Summer of 1964 had shown that hostile whites in Mississippi would spare no effort to block voter registration; Johnson knew something else was required if Blacks were ever to be able to vote.

Katzenbach turned to Harold Greene, a lawyer in the Civil Rights Division of the Department of Justice. Greene developed three alternative ways of guaranteeing the right to vote for Blacks. Katzenbach presented them to Johnson. First was a constitutional amendment that would prevent *all* states from imposing *any* requirement on voters except on the basis of age, residency, criminal record, or psychiatric institutionalization. This would eliminate the state literacy tests that Blacks failed while illiterate whites passed, and state poll taxes, which kept Blacks from voting in state and local elections. This way would be slow; thirteen states could kill it—such an amendment requires ratification by three-fourths of the states, thirty-eight of fifty, and it would be vulnerable to attack as federal interference with states' rights. The second option was the creation of a new federal commission with the power to appoint federal registrars for federal elections. This would leave state elections unaffected. Or finally, they could empower an existing agency to assume direct control of federal and state election registration in any area where the percentage of registered Blacks was low. This offered the quickest method and was therefore the one best able to take advantage of the national mood favorable to civil rights legislation brought about in part by Kennedy's death.[14]

In Johnson's State of the Union message on January 4, 1965, he promised legislation ending "every obstacle to the right and the opportunity to vote," but he set no timetable. Johnson's eventual plan applied in those states where fewer than 50 percent of voters had registered or voted in the 1964 presidential election and that employed a literacy test—Alabama, Georgia, Louisiana, Mississippi, South Carolina, Virginia, and sections of North Carolina. It suspended literacy tests, authorized the attorney general to dispatch federal registrars and observers to resistant counties, and empowered the Justice Department to require affected states to preclear changes in election law. Martin Luther King had arrived in Selma to kick off SCLC's campaign just two days before. Events there—and the personality of Jim Clark—would soon help the president and Congress see that the time was now!

SELMA, 1965

The Selma that King visited in January 1965 had been thoroughly prepared for increased movement activity by generations of Black activists and the patient work begun two years before by Bernard and Colia Lafayette. One measure of the Lafayettes' success was a surge in Black militancy and a willingness to confront Selma's white officialdom, which made King's movement possible. Bernard Lafayette had patiently earned the trust of Selma's Black community, following a pattern of walking, talking, and listening that had become SNCC's hallmark organizing style. He and his wife had begun regular meetings with the Dallas County Voters' League, conducted registration clinics, and established contacts among area activists in nearby counties.

In June 1963, a white man beat Lafayette; a few days later, Selma police arrested Lafayette for vagrancy. But he organized a series of mass meetings and invited speakers from outside Selma, including SCLC's James Bevel and Ella Baker. The numbers attending these gatherings slowly grew larger. Before King's arrival, Bevel had met in Selma with SNCC staffers and local Blacks to organize a coordinated campaign. No one wanted a repeat of the sniping that had characterized the Albany Movement in 1961 and 1962. Bevel announced that local Blacks would make all decisions.

In the middle of SCLC's planning for the Selma campaign, J. Edgar Hoover stepped up his attacks on King. At an FBI briefing for women reporters, Hoover called King "the most notorious liar in the country"—later charging that SCLC was "spearheaded by Communists and moral degenerates."[15] This attack followed King's criticism of FBI inaction in Albany two years before. It also came from Hoover's access, via phone tapping, to King's private life and his continuing relationship with Stanley Levison.

Hoover had circulated throughout the executive branch reports of King's philandering. As King was preparing to go to Norway to accept the 1964 Nobel Peace Prize, James Farmer told him he had heard three rumors about King: (1) King was guilty of financial misconduct; (2) he was the tool of Communists; and (3) he had participated in sexual orgies. If Farmer, a leader of the movement who was himself subjected to FBI suspicion and surveillance, had heard these charges, they were surely widespread within the Johnson administration. The FBI offered them to White House journalists and to church and labor leaders who might support King's efforts in the South. Other friends of King had heard the rumors and warned him about his behavior. Some supporters argued that womanizing was the Black pastor's prerogative, others that King simply reflected a prevailing male chauvinism. Bernard Lee said, "He believed that the wife should stay home and take care of the babies while he'd be out there in the streets."[16] Others argued that the entire movement was sexually promiscuous and that King's behavior was no different from the behavior of many others—men and women. But King was the best-known person in the movement, expected to set a high standard of public and private behavior. The FBI knew its threats and leaks and rumors would have an effect on King and hoped they would also affect the movement he led.

Women in the movement like Ella Baker and Septima Clark, as well as his own wife, had been critical of King's attitude toward women's roles and leadership.[17] Dorothy Cotton said after his death, "He would have had a lot to learn and a lot of growing to do" about women's rights. She remembered she was "always asked to take notes . . . always asked to go fix Dr. King some coffee." "I did it too," she added, while recognizing the chauvinism in the movement. "They were sexist male preachers [who] grew up in a sexist culture. . . . I really loved Dr. King but I know that streak was in him also."[18]

King and Hoover finally met on December 1, 1964; their meeting was nonproductive, with King withdrawing most of his criticism and Hoover defending the FBI's efforts in the South. But even while they met, FBI agents were offering material on King's sex life to newsmen waiting outside the FBI director's office for King to appear. Two days after King appeared in Selma, Mrs. King opened a box that had arrived at the SCLC office a month before. It contained a reel of tape and a letter. The tape contained King's voice and the voices of others, telling sexual jokes, and the sounds of people engaging in sex.

An unsigned letter mailed separately told King, "You know you are a complete fraud and a great liability to all of us Negroes. . . . Clearly, you don't believe in any personal moral principles. . . . The American public . . . will know you for what you are—an evil, abnormal beast." The letter invited King to kill himself before the news of his moral degeneracy became public. "There is one thing left for you to do. You know what this is. . . . There is but one way out for you. You better take it before your filthy, abnormal, fraudulent self is bared to the nation."[19] King correctly guessed that the letter and tape came straight from J. Edgar Hoover and the FBI. It had been ordered two days after Hoover attacked King in November. FBI assistant director William Sullivan wrote the letter and sent an FBI agent to Miami to mail it to help disguise its origins.[20]

The January 2, 1965, mass meeting where King kicked off the Selma movement was a test of the movement's ability to break Judge Hare's 1964 injunction and a test of white Selma's ability to deal with the movement. Selma's whites had two choices: to follow Sheriff Jim Clark's bluster or Wilson Baker's quieter law enforcement. Clark would guarantee headlines and would invite international attention; Baker might be able to counter the movement and quietly squash it as Chief Laurie Pritchett had done in Albany in 1961 and 1962. The day before King arrived, Baker announced he would not arrest anyone for attending the meeting.

King's mass meeting speech, delivered one hundred and two years after the Emancipation Proclamation was issued, laid down the challenge: "Selma has become a symbol of bitter-end resistance to the civil rights movement. We will dramatize the situation to arouse the federal government by marching in the thousands to the place of registration. We are not asking, we are demanding the ballot." If Selma didn't respond, King said, "We will appeal to Governor Wallace. If he refuses to listen, we will appeal to the legislature. If they don't listen, we will appeal to the conscience of the Congress in another dramatic march on Washington!"[21]

Demonstrations began anew in Selma on January 18, 1965. King and SNCC's John Lewis led four hundred Blacks from Brown's Chapel AME Church to the Dallas County Courthouse. Sheriff Clark made marchers— all of them potential voters—line up in an alley adjacent to the courthouse while they waited for one voter per hour to take the registration test. At discussions after the day's events, SCLC staff members were disturbed and disappointed that Clark had behaved in such a mild manner toward the marchers. There had been no incident, no beating, and no occasion for the newsmen present to send a signal to the world that brutality had been directed against peaceful citizens who wanted the most basic right—the right to vote. They discussed taking their protests outside Selma, into Marion or Camden, if they didn't get a better response from Sheriff Clark.

On January 19, the marchers decided they would not enter the courthouse alley; this was an SCLC strategy to provoke Clark, and, as if on cue, he responded. He grabbed Mrs. Boynton by the coat collar and roughly pushed her the length of a city block to a patrol car. Sixty of the marchers were arrested. Watching from the sidelines, King told newsmen, "That is one of the most brutal and unlawful acts I have ever seen an officer commit."[22] "Jim Clark," an SCLC staff member said, "is another Bull Connor. We should put him on the staff."[23]

Lyndon B. Johnson was sworn in as president the next day. As he celebrated his inauguration, three waves of marchers descended on the Dallas County Courthouse, and, when they refused to obey the sheriff's orders to go to the alley, he arrested them; 226 were now in jail. On January 22, Frederick Reese, one of the founders of the Voters' League and an unsuccessful candidate for the city council in the 1960 elections, led a march of more than one hundred Black teachers to the courthouse. That these ordinarily cautious public employees, the backbone of Selma's Black middle class, were marching to the courthouse was proof that a new militancy had been awakened in Black Selma. If teachers were marching, anything could happen! This was a result of the Lafayettes' patient work and a signal that Selma's Blacks thought the differences between Baker and Clark were large enough to encourage actions they had not dared to take before.

For the first time, some small cracks began to appear in the solid front that Selma's Blacks, SCLC, and SNCC had erected. Local Blacks in the Dallas County Voters' League wanted primarily to win the right to vote for themselves. SNCC hoped to develop a Black political movement in Selma. SCLC saw Selma as the staging ground for a protest movement that would win the right to vote throughout the South. King had a quick, national agenda. SNCC had a long-term strategy. Selma Blacks had a local, limited plan.

Over the weekend after the teachers' march, US federal judge Daniel Thomas issued a temporary restraining order barring Selma and Dallas County officials from hindering registration applicants, as they had since the drive began. But on Monday, January 25, Sheriff Clark was back on the job, harassing the demonstrators. After he pushed several of them, fifty-three-year-old Annie Lee Cooper gave the sheriff a powerful punch to the head. Three deputies jumped on her and wrestled her to the ground. As Clark stood over her with his billy club raised, she said, "I wish you would hit me, you scum!"[24] The sound his club made hitting her head could be heard across the street. A wire service picture of Mrs. Cooper on the ground with Clark standing over her was flashed around the world.

King went back to Atlanta for a dinner by city notables honoring him for winning the Nobel Peace Prize. Hoover had tried to disrupt this dinner, offering *Atlanta Constitution* editor Eugene Patterson and the Catholic archbishop information about King's sex life. Both men had refused and remained sponsors of the dinner.

The SCLC staff decided that King had to go to jail to further focus attention on Selma, and on February 1, he led 260 marchers to the courthouse, where all were arrested. Later that day, another 700 were arrested, and 600 marched to the courthouse in nearby Perry County. King and Ralph Abernathy shared a cell with white SCLC staff member Charles Fager. King and Fager talked about how difficult it would be—regardless of the success they were sure to have in Selma—to win true freedom for America's Blacks. King said to Fager: "If we are going to achieve real equality, the United States will have to adopt a modified form of socialism."[25] King wrote a "Letter from the Selma Jail" intended to echo his Birmingham jail letter. Appearing as a full-page ad in the *New York Times*, it said, "THERE ARE MORE NEGROES IN JAIL WITH ME THAN THERE ARE ON THE VOTING ROLLS."[26]

Judge Thomas issued another order on February 4, telling the Dallas County registrars to stop using Alabama's difficult registration test, to stop rejecting applicants for minor errors, to make monthly reports to the judge, and to process one hundred applicants each day. That same day, Lyndon Johnson issued a statement saying: "All Americans should be indignant when one American is denied the right to vote. The loss of that right to a single citizen undermines the freedom of every citizen. . . . I intend to see that that right is secured for all our citizens!"[27]

Malcolm X came to Selma that day too. He had been invited to speak at nearby Tuskegee Institute, and SNCC workers asked him to come to Selma. Speaking at Brown's Chapel, he said Blacks should stress the international nature of their struggle by taking their case to the United Nations and should use "any means necessary" to get the vote. Later, in a private meeting with Coretta Scott King, he told her, "If the white people realize what the alternative is, perhaps they will be more willing to hear Dr. King."[28]

More were arrested in Selma and in Perry County. On Friday, February 5, King left the Dallas County jail. The next day, in the first official announcement that new legislation was in the offing, presidential press secretary George Reedy told newsmen that LBJ would make "a strong recommendation" to Congress on voting rights in the near future.[29] King flew to Washington on February 9 where he met with Vice President Humphrey and President Johnson. On February 10, Sheriff Clark and his mounted posse used cattle prods to drive 165 protesters into the country on a forced march at top speed.

That night's mass meeting overflowed two churches. It would take months for Johnson's voting rights bill to go through Congress; how could SCLC keep the pressure on? Selma's Black population could not sustain many more months of demonstrations, beatings, and jail. They would have to take the movement elsewhere, but first they needed to win some sort of victory for the people of Selma. Nearby Lowndes County might be better for winning a victory than Selma, some SCLC staffers thought. It lay in the federal judicial district presided over by liberal federal judge Frank M. Johnson Jr. Judge Johnson was sure to give the movement rulings better than those handed down by Judge Thomas.

Tension among SCLC, SNCC, and local Blacks continued. SNCC workers objected, as did local Blacks, to the SCLC staff's high-handed ways. They made and announced decisions without consultation. On February 13, local whites met with representatives of the Community Relations Service and the Dallas County Voters' League; the whites agreed to ease registration requirements. It was becoming clear that Selma's Blacks would agree to a truce in Selma's racial war if local registration requirements were eased. What SCLC wanted, however, wasn't just the right to vote in Selma; they wanted it guaranteed by federal law everywhere. If Selma's whites accommodated *local* Black demands, and local

Blacks agreed, SCLC would have to move elsewhere to keep the pressure on for national relief.

As part of that strategy, King led a march in Selma on February 15; he then watched a march in Camden, in Wilcox County, and then spoke in Marion, in Perry County. On February 16, King told a reporter, "We are considering the possibility of a large group from throughout the state going to Montgomery," and he told a mass meeting crowd that the time had come for nighttime marches.[30] SCLC had used nighttime marches in St. Augustine, Florida, in 1964. They had succeeded in bringing out the most lawless elements among white supremacists, producing spectacular, violent clashes, and unplanned retaliation from some Blacks. Nighttime marches in Alabama might well produce the same result.

On February 18, C. T. Vivian led a nighttime march toward the Perry County Courthouse. State troopers stopped the marchers a block from the church where they had begun and ordered them to turn around. Suddenly the streetlights went out, and the troopers and other lawmen began attacking the crowd with their clubs. In a cafe a block away, a trooper mortally wounded a young Black man, Jimmie Lee Jackson, who was trying to protect his mother from the officers' beating.

IN THE MIDST of the Selma movement, on February 21, at the Audubon Ballroom in New York, Malcolm X was assassinated. One of the ironies of his life was that he never practiced the violence his earlier rhetoric had threatened. He criticized the Southern movement but never offered an alternative. He criticized the movement's passivity but never actively opposed segregation himself. King, on the other hand, preached nonviolence but courted violence to advance the cause of civil rights. King and Malcolm X met only once—almost a year before in Washington when King had been there to lobby for the 1964 Civil Rights Bill—and had spoken for less than a minute.

Malcolm X had broken with Elijah Muhammad and the Nation of Islam and was searching to find a place for himself in the Black movement that had escalated from the South to every part of the nation so quickly. The Muslims—and Malcolm X—had stood apart from this movement, approaching it only as critics, warning that its tactics were wrong, unmanly, and that its reliance on white allies could only end in betrayal. Muslims were forbidden to even register to vote.

After breaking with the Nation of Islam, Malcolm X had begun to support some of the orthodox civil rights strategies he had previously condemned. "The campaign that they have in Mississippi for voter registration is a good campaign," he said at the second rally of the Organization for Afro-American Unity (OAAU). "If our people down there are risking their lives so that they can register . . . what do you and I look like in New York City, with the registration booth only a few blocks away, and we haven't been in it? . . . It's a sin for you and me not to be registered so we can vote in New York City and in New York State, or throughout the North."[31]

In December 1964, Malcolm spoke at a Harlem rally for the Mississippi Freedom Democratic Party, appearing with Fannie Lou Hamer. He invited her to speak to an OAAU rally the next day. "Since I've gotten involved," he said, "I am surprised at how militant some of these integrationists are sounding. Man, sometimes they put me to shame." He also criticized the Nation of Islam. It "took no part in nothing that black people in this country were doing," he said, "to correct conditions in our community, other than it had moral force—that it stopped our people from getting drunk and taking drugs and things of that sort. Which is not enough—after you sober up, you're still poor."[32]

The Nation of Islam was fiercely reactionary, never challenging the nation's racial status quo, its members forbidden from registering and voting and from participation in civil life. Elijah Muhammad believed Africa and Africans to be uncivilized, embraced American capitalism without question or criticism, and flirted with fascist and white racist groups. Even as the Nation cursed white people as "devils," they were not beyond dealing with that same demon. But following the demise of Marcus Garvey's UNIA, no other group had promoted combining economic self-help, cultural redefinition, and moral living more vigorously than the Nation of Islam.

Malcolm X increasingly realized that not playing a direct role in the battle for Black rights was really taking sides against the civil rights movement; the militant rhetoric of the Nation of Islam concealed its essential conservatism. After his break with Elijah Muhammad, Malcolm X, in part through founding the Organization of Afro-American Unity, began trying to build bridges between Black Nationalists and the civil rights movement he had scorned.

After his death, the movement he had tried to build degenerated into posturing and revolutionary bombast, romanticizing revolutionary violence. Unlike the nonviolent civil rights movement that it held in contempt, Nation of Islam leaders created no mass movement, made no sustained institutional challenge, and, through the fantasy of separatism, isolated themselves away from building political strength. Their greatest effect was intellectual and cultural, not political.

FIVE DAYS AFTER Malcolm X was assassinated, Jimmie Lee Jackson died. On March 3, King returned to Marion to preach at Jackson's funeral. Two days later, King was back in Washington to meet with President Johnson. The president told King that he had managed to win the crucial support of Senator Everett Dirksen for the voting rights bill. Back in Selma, James Bevel announced that the planned drive to Montgomery had been converted to a march in Jimmie Lee Jackson's memory; it would begin on March 7.

While King was away, Alabama governor George Wallace was trying to decide how to deal with the planned march. Wallace reasoned that the marchers would not be prepared to go the fifty-four miles to the state capitol; if his officers let the marchers proceed, they would soon have to turn back, making them "the laughing stock of the nation."[33] State troopers were told to let it proceed. But the state representative from Lowndes County warned Wallace that his constituents would meet the marchers with guns and explosives; to protect the marchers and to protect Alabama from the unfavorable publicity of more attacks on nonviolent protesters, the marchers would have to be stopped. Wallace sent word to Al Lingo, the commander of the state troopers, to stop the marchers. Selma's mayor, Smitherman, was told the troopers wouldn't use violence as they had in Marion.

Within the Student Nonviolent Coordinating Committee, the march was both supported and opposed. SNCC chairman John Lewis, also an SCLC board member, argued that local people supported it and they should therefore continue to provide assistance.[34] Other SNCC workers argued that SCLC's dependence on marches and showy tactics killed local leadership. Finally it was decided that SNCC workers could march.

On Sunday, March 7, six hundred people gathered for the march. With King in Atlanta, SCLC's Hosea Williams telephoned Abernathy—who was also in Atlanta—to ask for directions, and, after consulting with King, Abernathy gave the go-ahead. A coin toss gave Williams the right to lead the march, and the six hundred filed out of the Brown Chapel Church.[35] Selma public safety director, Wilson Baker, was certain the march would end in bloodshed and declared—under threat of resignation—that his men would not take part in it. He was encouraged that Sheriff Clark was out of town, and Alabama state patrol commander Al Lingo would be in Montgomery.

When Lewis and Williams reached the crest of the Edmund Pettus Bridge, they could see state troopers waiting three hundred yards ahead. Flanking both sides of the road were members of Clark's armed and mounted posse. The marchers pulled to fifty feet of the line of troopers and were met by troop commander Major John Cloud. "This is an unlawful assembly," Cloud bellowed through a bullhorn. "Your march is not conducive to public safety. You are ordered to disperse and to go back to your church and your homes." Williams and Lewis asked if they could have a word with him. "There is no word to be had," Cloud replied. They repeated this exchange twice. Then Cloud announced: "You have two minutes to turn around and go back to your church." A moment later, Cloud gave the order: "Troopers, advance."

One witness reported:

> The troopers rushed forward, their blue uniforms and white helmets blurring into a flying wedge as they moved. The wedge moved with such force that it seemed to pass over the waiting column instead of through it. The first 10 or 20 Negroes were swept to the ground screaming, arms and legs flying, and packs and bags went skittering across the grassy divider strip onto the pavement on both sides. Those still on their feet retreated. The troopers continued pushing, using both the force of their bodies and the prodding of their nightsticks. A cheer went up from the white spectators lining the south side of the highway. The mounted possemen spurred their horses and rode at a run into the retreating mass.

The Negroes cried out as they crowded together for protection, and the whites on the sidelines whooped and cheered. The Negroes paused in their retreat for perhaps a minute, still screaming and huddling together. Suddenly there was a report like gunshot and a grey cloud spewed over the troopers and the Negroes. "Tear gas!" someone yelled.[36]

Protected by gas masks, the troopers continued their attack. John Lewis went down. Mrs. Boynton was knocked unconscious. Mounted policemen chased the marchers as they ran back across the bridge. Eighty people were treated for injuries; seventeen were admitted to the local hospital.

Across the country, many television viewers were watching the ABC-TV movie of the week, *Judgment at Nuremberg*, about the Nazi war crimes trials. When the movie was interrupted to show what had happened on the bridge in Selma, many thought they were still looking at the movie, seeing scenes of Nazi terror. Many felt drawn by the violence to Selma. One was a Harvard law student named Bruce Babbitt, who caught the first plane he could and stayed in Selma for a week.[37]

A hasty conference call between King and others concluded with a decision to send out the word for a national convergence on Selma and to coordinate an avalanche of telegrams and calls to the White House and Congress pressing for the voting rights legislation. A second attempt at the march was set for Tuesday, March 9, but King let it be known that meaningful federal intervention could cancel it. Movement lawyers—led by Fred Gray—asked federal judge Frank Johnson to issue an order demanding protection for future marchers. Instead Johnson ordered the planned march postponed until he could hold a hearing on March 11.

Again King was faced with the dilemma of violating an injunction from a federal judge. Hosea Williams and SNCC's Forman argued that the march should go on, no matter what Judge Johnson or President Johnson did. King told a mass meeting that the planned March 9 march would go on. In the meantime, SCLC's lawyers told Judge Johnson that King would *not* march; John Doar met with King late that night to try to persuade him to call the march off. President Johnson woke up former Florida governor Leroy Collins, now head of the Community Relations Service, and sent him to Selma to try to stop King and the marchers. Collins persuaded

King to make a *symbolic* march from the church to the spot where the troopers had begun their attack on March 7. There they would stop and return to the church. If Collins could get Clark and Lingo to agree, King said he would do it.

Collins got Clark and Lingo to agree, and on March 9, King took two thousand marchers out of the Brown Chapel Church—including some of the hundreds of outsiders who had begun to stream into Selma—back through the route that had led to bloody Sunday two days before. On the Selma side of the bridge, a US marshal read Judge Johnson's order to King, forbidding the march. King listened—and then led the column forward. Fifty feet from the troopers, King halted, and a brief prayer service was held. Then King turned and began walking back across the bridge toward Selma. As he did, the line of troopers blocking the road parted, leaving the path to Montgomery open and clear.

Obviously, Governor Wallace had ordered the troopers to clear the road, hoping to embarrass King just as he turned away. Back at the church, King faced other criticism, from SNCC and even from those who had been drawn to Selma following the terrible beating on Sunday night. The mood before the march had been optimistic, even cheerful; the movement was on the move. Now they had been turned back, not by beatings but through some secret agreement known only to King and a few leaders.

Despite the disappointments in Selma, sympathy was building across the country. Marches were held in Detroit, Chicago, Boston, New York, and other cities; six hundred picketers surrounded the White House demanding federal action.

That evening, on March 9, a gang of whites attacked a group of three white ministers from Massachusetts in downtown Selma; one of them, the Reverend James Reeb, was severely injured. The next day, Wednesday, anger at King—especially from SNCC—was mounting. SNCC's Forman announced that the organization would shift its operations to Montgomery, and protests at the Alabama State Capitol were organized with students from Tuskegee Institute. Judge Johnson held hearings on Thursday, Friday, and Saturday. On Thursday evening, James Reeb died of his injuries. His death generated much more protest than Jimmie Lee Jackson's. White clergymen from around the country were activated, and President Johnson and Vice President Humphrey called his widow.

On Sunday, Wallace flew to Washington to meet with President Johnson. King was the problem in Alabama, Wallace said, not the denial of the right to vote. He had hoped to reason with the president, just as Arkansas governor Orval Faubus had when he had flown to Newport in 1957 to meet with President Eisenhower over the Little Rock school integration crisis. But unlike Eisenhower, Johnson would not be taken in by another crafty Southern politician.

President Johnson reminded Wallace of his populist beginnings and said: "You came into office a liberal—you spent all your life trying to do things for the poor. Now, why are you working on this? Why are you off on this Negro thing? . . . What do you want left after you, when you die? Do you want a great big marble monument that reads "George Wallace—He Built." Or do you want a little piece of pine board lying across that harsh caliche soil that reads, 'George Wallace—He Hated.'"[38]

With one thousand protesters marching around the White House, Johnson told Wallace that he, Wallace, was wrong and later told a press conference:

> What happened in Selma was an American tragedy. The blows that were received, the blood that was shed, the life of the good man that was lost, must strengthen the determination of each of us to bring full and equal and exact justice to all of our people. This is not just the policy of your government or your President. It is in the heart and the purpose and the meaning of America itself. We all know how complex and how difficult it is to bring about basic social change in a democracy, but this complexity must not obscure the clear and simple moral issues. It is wrong to do violence to peaceful citizens in the streets of their town. It is wrong to deny Americans the right to vote. It is wrong to deny any person full equality because of the color of his skin.[39]

On Monday night, after King had spoken in Selma at a memorial service for James Reeb on the Dallas County Courthouse steps, Johnson spoke to Congress. He repeated much of what he had said at the White House on Sunday; he spoke of Selma. It was, he said, like Lexington, and Concord, and Appomattox, where "history and fate meet at a single time in a single place to shape a turning point in man's unending search for freedom." And he closed his speech with the movement's slogan, "We Shall Overcome!"[40]

In a living room in Black Selma, Martin Luther King cried.

On Wednesday, Judge Johnson handed down a decision. In this case, he said, "The wrongs are enormous. The extent of the right to demonstrate against these wrongs should be determined accordingly."[41] He approved a proposal made by SCLC lawyers to allow three hundred marchers to use sections of Highway 80 from Selma to Montgomery and enjoined Alabama authorities from failing to assist them. The federal government, Judge Johnson said, would provide whatever assistance Alabama needed. SCLC announced the march would begin on March 21.

On March 17, President Johnson's voting rights legislation was unveiled. It would empower the attorney general to suspend literacy tests and appoint federal registrars in any state or county where fewer than 50 percent of the voting age population was registered or cast ballots for president on November 1, 1964. It would cover Louisiana, Mississippi, Alabama, Georgia, South Carolina, Virginia, and North Carolina but not Texas, Florida, or Tennessee.

Frank Soracco, a former SNCC staff member who had joined SCLC's staff, was given the task of choosing three hundred marchers; he picked local people who had been to jail or been beaten and thirty-six outsiders. Once again, SCLC's Hosea Williams was in charge. Nineteen hundred Alabama National Guardsmen, two thousand army personnel, and US marshals accompanied and protected the marchers.

Approved by a federal court, escorted by federalized troops, protected by federal marshals and FBI agents—the Selma-to-Montgomery march enjoyed federal co-sponsorship as had no civil rights effort in the past. It would be the final defeat of the diehard, segregationist South.

As the marchers passed through Lowndes County, Stokely Carmichael established contacts he would later use to create the Lowndes County Freedom Party—or, as it was popularly known, the Black Panther Party. It would become—over time—a potent political force in that majority-Black county.

At the march's climax in Montgomery on March 25, twenty-five thousand people heard King, Rosa Parks, and others speak. King stood on the steps of the Alabama State Capitol, a few feet from the gold star that marks the spot where Jefferson Davis was sworn in as president of the

Confederacy. "We are on the move now," he said, "and no wave of racism can stop us."[42]

A hundred-plus yards before him he could see the Dexter Avenue Baptist Church, where his civil rights leadership had begun ten years earlier. It had taken King and the movement ten years to travel those hundred yards—a longer period than movement supporters had wished for, but a shorter period than most had dreamed. Governor Wallace watched the proceedings from inside the capitol.

Later that night, Viola Liuzzo, a white mother of five from Detroit, was shot and killed as she ferried marchers from Montgomery back to Selma. Liuzzo had answered the call after "Bloody Sunday" for volunteers to come down to Selma to support the movement. Four suspects were arrested the next day—one of them was FBI informant Gary Thomas Rowe, who had warned the FBI that Freedom Rider beatings would occur in Montgomery in 1961 and had then taken part in them.

THE VOTING RIGHTS ACT OF 1965

The 1965 Voting Rights Act was signed into law by President Johnson on August 6, 1965. Five days later, federal examiners began registering voters in Dallas, Hale, Marengo, and Lowndes Counties in Alabama; Leflore and Madison Counties in Mississippi; and East Carroll, East Feliciana, and Plaquemine Parishes in Louisiana. In one day, 1,144 Blacks had registered; overcrowding forced many to be turned away. The next day, 1,733 more were registered.

The right to vote, once restricted to white male property owners, had technically been extended to all men twenty-one and older by the Fourteenth Amendment, supposedly to African Americans by the Fifteenth Amendment, to women by the Nineteenth Amendment, to persons too poor to pay poll taxes by the Twenty-Fourth, and to everyone eighteen or older by the Twenty-Sixth.

The 1957 Civil Rights Act had been the first instance of modern federal interest in Southern Black voters. It created the Civil Rights Commission and a new Civil Rights Division in the Department of Justice and gave the attorney general authority to file suits against officials and private citizens who hindered registration. But its remedies were judicial, time-consuming, and expensive. By contrast, the Voting Rights Act became effective almost immediately.

Under the 1965 Voting Rights Act, the attorney general's certification became the unchallengeable basis for bringing states and political subdivisions under the act's provisions and for the appointment of federal registrars and observers to monitor elections. In addition, covered states and covered local governmental units could not change any voting procedure or standard unless the attorney general or the US district court for the District of Columbia precleared the change as not having the purpose or effect of racial discrimination.

The Voting Rights Act has been successfully amended several times to prohibit "tests or devices" that had been used to disenfranchise racial minorities—literacy tests, education requirements, character tests, racial gerrymandering, and English-only elections in some districts; require that a covered jurisdiction seek and gain federal permission for any changes in election law or procedures to assure such changes do not abridge the right to vote based on race, color, or language minority status; and make clear that if the *effect* of a practice is discrimination, regardless of the *intent*, it is unlawful.

MORE BLACKS REGISTERED in Selma the week after the Voting Rights Act became law than in all the years of the twentieth century. A year later, Black registration doubled in South Carolina, Georgia, Louisiana, Mississippi, and Alabama. By 1970, as many Blacks had registered in Alabama, Mississippi, Georgia, Louisiana, and North and South Carolina as had registered in the previous hundred years. If the civil rights movement from Montgomery in 1955 to Selma in 1965 made Southern Blacks visible, the Voting Rights Act turned visibility into influence. One result was the election of first-time Black officeholders—to Congress from Georgia and Texas in 1972, as Atlanta's mayor in 1973, and as Virginia's governor in 1989; and the renaissance in the early 1970s of white progressives—Arkansas's Dale Bumpers, Florida's Reuben Askew, Georgia's Jimmy Carter, and Virginia's Linwood Holton—represented a new, nonracist populism. Alabama's George Wallace crowned a Black homecoming queen—and kissed her; Bull Connor tried to win Black votes by singing "We Shall Overcome"—he lost.

The increase in Black officeholders did not come from changing attitudes or voluntary reforms; it was the product of federal obligations forced on recalcitrant jurisdictions. Without the race-conscious requirements of the Voting Rights Act, Black and Hispanic office holding in the South would be nearly nonexistent. In the voting booth, racially polarized voting by whites remains pervasive. In early July 2006, the US House of Representatives voted 390 to 33 and the Senate 98 to 0 to renew portions of the act. President George W. Bush signed it into law.

Then, in 2013, the US Supreme Court, in a catastrophic 5–4 decision in *Shelby County Alabama v. Holder*, struck down the portion of the Voting Rights Act specifying which municipalities and states would be subject to preclearance, saying that formula was "based on 40-year-old facts having no logical relation to the present day" and thus unconstitutional. As these crucial protections were dismantled, voter suppression efforts surged.

TWENTY-TWO

VIETNAM, BLACK POWER, AND THE ASSASSINATION OF MARTIN LUTHER KING

B Y 1965, THE white South had been forced to change against its will by a federal government many had long viewed as hostile and remote. The 1965 Voting Rights Act and court-ordered reapportionment had changed the movement's focus from desegregation to seeking political power. Blacks were elected where none had served since the end of Reconstruction.

My campaign for the Georgia House of Representatives in 1965 was an attempt to take the techniques SNCC had learned in the rural South into an urban setting, and to carry forward SNCC's belief that grassroots politics could provide answers to problems faced by America's urban Blacks. In keeping with SNCC's style, a platform was developed in consultation with the voters. The campaign supported a $2.00 hourly minimum wage, repeal of the anti-union, right-to-work law, and abolition of the death penalty. Resentment of the changes the movement had wrought found a focus in my election to the Georgia House of Representatives. I was elected to a one-year term in the Georgia House in 1965 in a court-ordered special election and set to take office on January 10, 1966.

But that didn't happen.

On January 3, 1966, a Black SNCC worker named Samuel Younge was shot in the back and killed in his hometown of Tuskegee, Alabama. Sammy was a veteran who had lost one of his kidneys in navy service and, as a consequence, had to go to the bathroom more often than most. When he tried to use the segregated bathroom at a white-owned gas station, the station owner shot and killed him. The irony of a man being killed because he lost a kidney in service to his country was too great.[1] Younge had taken forty Blacks to register and been threatened by the Tuskegee registrar with a knife just before he was killed. For SNCC, the death of this navy veteran for trying to use a bathroom "symbolized . . . the racism and hypocrisy that infected the nation."[2]

In 1965, the McComb MFDP branch became the first Black political organization to express opposition to the war in Vietnam. State MFDP officials not only refused to repudiate the McComb statement, they reprinted it in the state MFDP newsletter, giving it wider circulation and laying the groundwork for future Black opponents of the war.

Three days after Younge's death, SNCC released a statement condemning the Vietnam War as "murder" and charging "the United States government has been deceptive in its claims of concern for freedom of the Vietnamese people, just as the government has been deceptive in claiming concern for the freedom of colored people in such other countries as the Dominican Republic, the Congo, South Africa, Rhodesia, and in the United States itself."[3] When SNCC began to speak out against the war, our donor contributions fell off, and we began to suffer financially.

I think initially it wasn't a pacifist notion that turned most of us against the war—though it was for some people—but the assault on Black men and the idea that we were spending all these resources in a war that was not our business. There was no chance of my going to Vietnam; I had been classified 1-Y (mentally, physically, or morally unfit for service) because I had been arrested in a sit-in demonstration. It wasn't common to exempt civil rights activists from the draft. In fact, it seemed like Southern draft boards were targeting people in the movement. The head of my draft board was later quoted in *Newsweek* as saying, "That nigger Julian Bond, we let him slip through our fingers."

I thought the big fight was here at home. Sammy getting killed heightened our awareness of the essential wrongness of asking these young men to defend the country overseas. I hadn't written SNCC's statement, but I was SNCC's communications director, and I supported it. A week later, I presented myself to be sworn in at the Georgia House of Representatives. Several of my white colleagues-to-be had filed petitions challenging my right to take the seat because of my statements in opposition to the Vietnam War. When I appeared to take the oath of office, hostility from white legislators was nearly absolute.

After a brief hearing, the House voted 184 to 12 to deny me my seat, declaring the seat vacant and ordering a new election. I ran in that election and won, and a special House committee again denied me my seat. That fall there was another election; I ran and won again, elected three times to a seat I had yet to occupy.

Nine months after I had been expelled, in November 1966, my case was argued before the Supreme Court. My case was called *Bond v. Floyd*, and I was defended before the Supreme Court by my brother-in-law, Howard Moore (who later went on to defend Angela Davis), and attorney Leonard Boudin. I never met Chief Justice Earl Warren but watched him preside as the court heard arguments about whether or not I could take my place in the Georgia House of Representatives.

At the Supreme Court, I sat just behind the bar, where the lawyers sit to watch the argument, with attorney Boudin's law partner, Victor Rabinowitz, and I still remember when Justice Byron White interrupted the attorney general of Georgia, Arthur Bolton. Bolton was trying to argue that Georgia had a right to expel me. "Is that all you have?" Justice White asked. "You've come all the way up here and that's all you have?" I turned to Rabinowitz and asked, "We're winning, aren't we?" and he responded, "Yes, we are."

On December 5, the court unanimously ordered the legislature to seat me. Chief Justice Earl Warren's opinion in *Bond v. Floyd* was more than a victory for the First Amendment; it was a reaffirmation of my constituents' right to free choice in casting their votes. In January 1967, a year after I had been turned away, I took my seat in the Georgia House of Representatives.

The House years were not happy years. I was in the House that I had been expelled from. My nemesis, James H. "Sloppy" Floyd, was still there. Every two years when we'd get sworn in, he'd always walk out of the chamber. He wouldn't be sworn in with me.

MARTIN LUTHER KING, too, was revolted at the hypocrisy of America's claims for freedom overseas when Blacks enjoyed few freedoms here. War abroad, he said, stole from Americans at home. "The pursuit of widened war," he said, "has narrowed domestic welfare programs, making the poor, white and Negro, bear the heaviest burdens at the front and at home."[4] A couple months after my Supreme Court case was settled, at a speech at New York's Riverside Church in 1967, King called the United States "the greatest purveyor of violence in the world" and set off a firestorm of criticism. *Life* magazine called the speech "demagogic slander that sounded like a script for Radio Hanoi." The *Washington Post* declared that King had "diminished his usefulness to his cause, his country, his people."[5]

In the meantime, the divisions between SNCC and the white New Left were increasing. SNCC's freewheeling, anti-bureaucratic style served as inspiration for the predominately white college students who launched the antiwar and students' rights movements of the middle 1960s. But SNCC was changing. Although the groups were linked through their antiwar activities and critiques of American society, SNCC was separately developing an analysis that challenged the cultural assumptions and power differentials that underlay white racist attitudes and assumptions of leadership and Black feelings of inferiority and powerlessness. Staff members argued for grassroots leadership—Black leadership—of local organizing efforts.

Questions about white participation in the movement had surfaced first in debates about Freedom Summer, 1964. The most prominent exemplar of racial separatism was SNCC's Atlanta Project, begun initially in early 1966 to rally my constituents when the legislature expelled me. The project attracted a new generation of SNCC workers, half of them Northerners, none veterans of SNCC's integrationist beginnings. Several had been involved with nationalist organizations like the Nation of Islam. They promoted "black control of the black community," a long-held if seldom articulated SNCC goal. But they additionally argued against white participation in the civil rights movement. White participation, they said, bolstered Black feelings of inferiority. A single white participant in a meeting changed the course of the meeting—instead of talking about race and prejudice, the meeting would turn to discussions of brotherhood and love.

SNCC rejected the Atlanta Project's demands to expel whites, but the project had given voice to unspoken sentiments in many Black and some white SNCC workers. A May 1966 SNCC meeting heard arguments for local campaigns similar to my successful race for the legislature, for adopting a nationalist posture to aid in organizing Black people; and for having SNCC's white members organize in white communities where racism originated.

Stokely Carmichael replaced John Lewis as chairman of SNCC. Lewis had faced internal criticism for his involvement in the 1966 White House Conference on Civil Rights. Carmichael had won many supporters because of his successful organizing of the Lowndes County Freedom Organization in Alabama, popularly known as the Black Panther Party in 1965. The LCFO was "an independent political party which would prove to be a factor in Alabama politics for years to come. . . . The political consciousness of some of Alabama's Blacks had been raised to another level."[6] The party was formed in reaction to the racism of local and state Democratic parties. Like the MFDP, the new party was open to whites, but no whites in Lowndes County would participate in a Black-dominated political effort.

Carmichael's election was both hailed as a triumph of Black Nationalism and condemned as a takeover by antiwhite elements. But SNCC argued that being pro-Black did not mean being antiwhite. Whites could play an important role, Carmichael said, by going "into the white communities and . . . developing those moderate bases that people talk about that do not now exist." A Black man, he said, wants "to build something of his own, something that he builds with his own hands. And that is *not* antiwhite. When you build your own house, it doesn't mean you tear down the house across the street."[7] Later he said: "Black people . . . don't want to 'get whitey'; they just want to get him off their backs."[8] Among the few whites who publicly agreed was Anne Braden. Asking whites to organize in white communities where Blacks could not go "may be providing this generation with the last chance white people may ever have to overcome the racism and white supremacy by which western man has come close to destroying this planet."[9]

Then, on June 5, 1966, James Meredith, who had bravely integrated Ole Miss in 1962, was wounded by three shotgun blasts as he embarked on a one-man "March Against Fear" through Mississippi. Carmichael, King, and CORE's Floyd McKissick agreed to continue the march. Nightly rallies staged along the march route became contests in which the three leaders paraded their differences and competed for their Black audience's loyalty. Carmichael and McKissick promoted greater militancy and condemned the federal government's inaction; King, on the defensive, promoted nonviolence. Carmichael had unsuccessfully argued against allowing whites to march, but successfully argued for the inclusion of the Deacons for Defense and Justice, a self-defense organization formed in 1964 to guard and defend nonviolent civil rights marchers in Jonesboro, Louisiana, but most prominent in a series of confrontations between the Ku Klux Klan and CORE demonstrators in Bogalusa, Louisiana. The antiwhite rhetoric and the inclusion of the Deacons caused the NAACP and the Urban League to withdraw from the march.[10]

On June 16 in Greenwood, Mississippi, police arrested and held Stokely Carmichael temporarily. That night, taking a cue from SNCC organizer Willie Ricks, Carmichael electrified the crowd when he said: "This is the twenty-seventh time I've been arrested—and I ain't going to jail no more." He said Blacks had been asking for freedom for six years and had received little. "What we gonna start saying now is 'Black Power'!" and the audience responded enthusiastically.[11]

King saw Black Power as a positive way for "black people to amass the political and economic strength to achieve their legitimate goals."[12] But he remained troubled that Black Power supporters focused too much attention on what he felt were harmful—Black separatism, retaliatory violence, and isolationism—and that they had a defeatist attitude. At the same time, he also highlighted how unending white resistance and disregard lead to uprisings. A riot, he said, "is the language of the unheard. And what is it that America has failed to hear? It has failed to hear that the plight of the Negro poor has worsened over the past twelve to fifteen years. It has failed to hear that the promises of freedom and justice have not been met."[13]

Conversely, Carmichael and members of SNCC and CORE defined Black Power as "a call for black people in this country to unite, to recognize their heritage, to build a sense of community."[14] Writing with Charles V. Hamilton, Carmichael stated, *"Before a group can enter the open society, it must first close ranks. By this we mean that group solidarity is necessary before a group can operate effectively from a bargaining position of strength in a pluralistic society."*[15] From the Greenwood rally forward, definitions of the precise meaning of Black Power varied greatly. Nevertheless, its introduction marked a break from the Kingian rhetorical and organizing style, and the term in due course came to be adopted by Black Nationalist and revolutionary organizations of the late 1960s and early 1970s.

For King, the phrase was "an unfortunate choice of words," and pundits across the country condemned it.[16] Only later did Carmichael begin to construct and expound an ideological rationale for "Black Power." It did not preclude Black-white alliances, he said. Only when Blacks controlled their own communities would they be able to negotiate with whites. This was only possible if whites exercised their ability to organize other whites. Whites preferred to organize Blacks, he said. "They admonish blacks to be nonviolent," he wrote. "Let them preach nonviolence to the white community."[17] Whatever Carmichael's intentions, the antiwhite connotations of his rhetoric had undeniable appeal for many of his Black listeners, but it was that element of his message that also attracted his Black critics. The NAACP's Roy Wilkins denounced SNCC, but, no matter how it was interpreted, the Black masses were clearly attracted to Black Power.

Writing about Black Power as it developed in Philadelphia, but in ways that fit its development nationwide, historian Matthew J. Countryman said, "Black Power activists . . . sought to build organizations that were accountable solely to the black community and in which leadership was based not on professional degrees or middle-class status but on one's proximity to and ability to identify with poor and working-class blacks."[18] Civil rights strategy, he states:

> had been based on the liberal presumption that racism was an unfortunate distortion of American values and institutions and that it could be remedied through specific legal and political reforms. In contrast, the black nationalist tradition viewed racism as constitutive to the American social structure. And therefore, only movement strategies based on intraracial solidarity within the black community, not the goodwill of whites, and committed to the collective advancement of the black community as a whole, not just the liberal vision of equal opportunity and individual advancement, could solve the race problem in America.[19]

The presence of the Deacons during the Meredith march punctured the old racial double standard of self-defense—it was a given for whites, but provocative and self-defeating for Blacks. The Deacons also highlighted a double standard of police protection—safety and peace guaranteed for whites but ignored for Blacks.

Their presence and the nightly rhetorical battles along the march route between King, McKissick, and Carmichael revived and heightened old movement debates about nonviolence that had frequently arisen in the modern movement. These included the rhetorical exchanges between King and Malcolm X in 1963 over using children in Birmingham and the 1960 written debate between King and Robert Williams first published in *Liberation* magazine and then in the pages of the *Southern Patriot*.[20]

Clearly, there was great misunderstanding on both sides—for example, those who advocated self-defense misunderstood what King meant by "nonviolence." King's critics interpreted it as "passivity" and "submissiveness." Those who criticized "self-defense" misunderstood what its proponents meant. The critics characterized it as "violence." It revived simplistic views of the civil rights movement—Booker T. Washington versus W. E. B. Du Bois, integration versus separation, Martin Luther King versus Malcolm X, nonviolence versus violence. The frightening implication that "Black Power" meant Black violence and suggested it was imminent created an immediate backlash among whites.

For King, nonviolence was an alternative to wanton violence. Nonviolence was courageous, not cowardly. It was active resistance to evil, leading toward the creation of what he called "the beloved community." It attacked an evil system, not the evildoers themselves. It eradicated not only physical violence but "the violence of the spirit." It used love as a lever, tilting the majority toward justice and equality.

From the beginning of the sit-ins, many believed nonviolence might succeed on the picket line, but few were willing to adopt it in their private lives. King's argument that nonviolence could wear down and defeat *any* enemy ran counter to the common sense of most Blacks, and the continued equation of nonviolence with *passive* resistance reinforced, for many, that the practice was cowardly and unmanly. For some, like Robert Williams and Malcolm X, it was debasing. It might have limited tactical utility but not personal application.

King himself understood distinctions in the nonviolence/violence construct—he believed there were three categories of behavior: pure nonviolence, self-defense, and "the advocacy of violence as a tool of advancement, as in warfare, deliberately and consciously." And like Gandhi, he sanctioned self-defense for those unable to adopt and accept pure nonviolence. "When the Negro uses force in self-defense," he said, "he does not forfeit support—he may even win it, by the courage and self-respect which it reflects."[21]

But King and Robert Williams and Malcolm X were talking past each other, King mistaking Williams's call to "meet violence with violence" as an invitation to kill whites with impunity, and Williams failing to understand the militancy of King's direct action and—as others did—equating nonviolence with pacifism, acquiescence, gradualism. Journalists, and eventually historians, and even many movement activists, would continue to use "violence" as an opposite to "nonviolence"—each the opposite of the other, but each having different meanings for many.

For many in the movement, "violence" as a word used by whites describing Blacks meant murder or unprovoked violence against whites, despite there being almost no examples in twentieth-century history of any civil rights–connected gratuitous, wanton violence by Blacks against whites. Self-defense for Blacks was a means of combating disrespect; for Malcolm X and Robert Williams, Blacks could not relinquish self-defense in the battle for human rights—indeed, self-defense was central to the mission.

As what had seemed to be complete victory was realized as only partial and incomplete, and as more and more understood that there was much more struggle ahead, a critical and sober reassessment set in. First a few, and then more and more, began to question the worthiness and value of nonviolence. The tactic that had seemed perfectly suited to attacks on the petty apartheid of segregated lunch counters and bus seats seemed woefully inadequate to a nationwide struggle against deeply rooted, systemic white supremacy and economic marginalization.

A series of defeats further heightened disillusionment and the search for alternatives. There had always been divisions among movement organizations, but the larger interracial coalition seemed firm. The refusal of the Democratic Party to accept the Mississippi Freedom Democratic Party in 1964 opened fissures in the movement's publicly seamless political coalition. H. Rap Brown would later write that the MFDP's failure showed that "even when you're right, you lose. . . . When the people cannot find a redress of their grievances within a system, they have no choice but to destroy the system which is responsible in the first place for their grievances."[22] On the surface, the movement showed interorganizational and interracial unity. But there were always undeniable cracks in movement unity—in Albany in 1961 and in Selma in 1965.

The Lowndes County Freedom Party—the original Black Panther Party—emerged in rural Alabama in 1965, the same year as the armed Black self-defense unit, the Deacons for Defense and Justice, in Louisiana.[23] What would become the more famous Black Panther Party surfaced in California in 1966, and by the close of the year both SNCC and CORE— always on the movement's most radical wing, had begun to publicly question nonviolence.[24] Disappointment at the hollowness of the movement's goals was coupled with a renaissance of Black militancy and assertive pride, the former kindled by the movement that produced the latter. This new assertiveness raised expectations as disappointment reduced the domination of integrationist over nationalist thought that had characterized the movement's public face for most of the twentieth century.

SNCC's view of the struggle was also expanding. At a retreat in May 1966, Ivanhoe Donaldson argued in favor of SNCC's replicating its successful Southern political organizing efforts in the North, and the staff agreed. Donaldson and Robert Moses suggested that techniques learned in Southern campaigns could be employed to ease SNCC's passage into Northern cities.[25] Organizing for political power and community control could mobilize Northern urban dwellers, they contended. Michael Thelwell proposed in 1966 that the organization move "to the ghetto and organize those communities to control themselves. The organization must be attempted in Northern and Southern areas as well as in the rural Black belt of the South."[26]

Projects were established in Washington, DC, to fight for home rule. In Columbus, Ohio, a community foundation was organized. In New York City's Harlem, SNCC workers organized early efforts at community control of public schools. There, SNCC worker William Hall helped a Harlem group working for community control of Intermediate School 201 in fall 1966. His efforts laid the groundwork for later successful protests for community control of schools throughout the city. In Los Angeles, SNCC helped monitor local police and joined an effort at creating a "Freedom City" in Black neighborhoods, and SNCC workers in Chicago began to build an independent political party and demonstrated against segregated schools. In each of these cities, the Southern experiences of SNCC organizers informed their work.

As SNCC chair, Marion Barry had written members of Congress in 1960 to "urge immediate action to provide self-government to the vote-less residents of our nation's capital, the District of Columbia." In February 1966, Barry, then director of SNCC's Washington office, announced the formation of the "Free DC Movement" (FDCM). He wrote, "The premise . . . is that we want to organize Black people for Black power." Barry and the FDCM conducted a successful boycott of Washington merchants who did not support home rule.[27] As the focus of the Southern movement had changed, so would the aim of the Northern organizer. Desegregation had proven both elusive and insufficient to meet the problems of American Blacks, North or South. Their ability to control the Black community itself, and to direct the community's elected officials, had become paramount in rural Mississippi and in urban New York.

Just as its concern for social change had never been limited to the Southern states alone, SNCC's concern for human rights had long extended beyond the borders of the United States. It had linked the fight of American Blacks with the struggle for African independence from its first public statements. At its founding conference, SNCC first announced its identification with the African liberation struggle. "We identify ourselves with the African struggle as a concern for all mankind," they said. At SNCC's fall 1960 conference in Atlanta, a featured speaker was Alphonse Okuku, an Antioch College student and brother of Kenya labor leader Tom Mboya. The mass meeting program said, "[Okuku] brings to our attention the great significance of the African struggle and its relationship to our fight."[28] SNCC chairman John Lewis told the March on Washington in 1963, "One man, one vote is the African cry. It must be ours!"

In December 1963, as documented by my former student, Dr. Timothy Lovelace, SNCC "forged new political strategies and alliances within the global freedom struggle."[29] SNCC workers in Atlanta conferred with Kenyan leader Oginga Odinga. James Forman, SNCC executive director, recalled: "A group of us went to the Peachtree Manor [Atlanta's only integrated hotel] where he was staying, brought him gifts, sang freedom songs and chanted 'Uhuru'—'freedom'—with him. Inspired by the visit, we went on to a Toddle House restaurant for coffee."[30] When the Toddle House, as expected, refused to serve them, twenty-one SNCC protesters were arrested, prompting Odinga to declare, "[The United States] practices segregation—which is what we are fighting in Africa."[31]

The next month, January 1964, the entire fourteen-nation UN Sub-Commission on the Prevention of Discrimination and Protection of Minorities chose to visit Atlanta. It was this visit that would extend SNCC's influence well beyond the United States. In the process, SNCC accomplished what many sub-commission members—and Eleanor Roosevelt, as chair of the UN Committee on Human Rights—had been unable or unwilling to do.

The sub-commission was invited to Atlanta by Georgia native and former Atlanta attorney Morris Abram. As Lovelace writes, Abram believed "promoting civil rights at home would strengthen the United States's image abroad. . . . For Abram and many other Cold War liberals, Atlanta was an ideal city for a State Department–sponsored visit to the United States because Atlanta, renowned for its spirit of biracial communication among business-oriented, racial moderates, seemed to embody American exceptionalism and exemplify much-needed progress in Southern race relations."[32]

Atlanta's motto, after all, was "the city too busy to hate." But Atlanta was also the home of SNCC, which a month before the sub-commission's visit had given Oginga Odinga a different view of Atlanta from what the State Department had in mind. SNCC would do the same for the sub-commission members. Admonished by Mayor Ivan Allen not to hold protests during the sub-commission's visit that would "embarrass the city," I responded, as SNCC's communications director, that "it would embarrass us *not* to have the demonstrations."[33]

I don't remember how, but we got the unpublished itinerary of the sub-commission, enabling us to confront them at every stop. We greeted their arrivals at the airport and their hotel with signs that read "Atlanta's Image Is a Fraud" and "Welcome to Atlanta, a Segregated City."[34]

We delivered a letter to each member's hotel room, stressing our interest in their getting "a realistic view of this city and the South." We explained that our efforts sought to secure "the rights America guarantees to all her citizens [including] the right to vote, the right to earn a decent living, to buy a home where he chooses, or to send his children to a decent school." The letter concluded: "Attempts at voluntary integration or voluntary compliance with the law of the land have failed. We are convinced that such pressures must continue until all men are equal here and across the South."[35]

SNCC DISTRIBUTED LITERATURE throughout the community, showing that Atlanta had "failed to live up to its image as a progressive city 'too busy to hate,'" and proclaimed: "We have no shame in showing the world the truth, for we are acting out of the strongest belief in American democracy and the knowledge that Justice and Freedom are real and can be for all people." At one point, as the sub-commission members left a private luncheon, they were greeted by about three hundred student protesters singing freedom songs and carrying placards that read "Atlanta Needs UN Help."[36]

Lovelace argues that these demonstrations made an indelible impression on the sub-commission, so much so that SNCC "helped to reframe the human rights debate under [the global treaty]" that the sub-commission drafted. Originally when the sub-commission was drafting the treaty against discrimination, it was fearless about condemning apartheid in South Africa but made no mention about "Negroes in the segregated United States."

SNCC's protests changed that. The day after the sub-commission members left Atlanta and returned to UN headquarters, they amended the treaty to include the prohibition of "racial segregation" along with "eradication of apartheid."

In September 1964, an eleven-member SNCC delegation, which I took part in, went to Guinea as guests of that country's president, Sekou Toure, an advocate of African socialism and nonalignment who had made his small country politically independent of the West. It was an eye-opener for most of us.[37] Mississippi sharecropper and SNCC worker Fannie Lou Hamer said: "I saw black men flying airplanes, driving buses, sitting behind big desks in the banks and just doing everything I was used to see white people do."[38]

After the rest of us returned to the United States, John Lewis and Don Harris continued on a month-long tour of Liberia, Ghana, Zambia, Kenya, Ethiopia, and Egypt. An unexpected encounter was a meeting with Malcolm X in Nairobi. He had just broken with Elijah Muhammad and the narrow focus of the Nation of Islam.

The trip did much to strengthen the emotional bonds many young activists felt toward Africa. As John Lewis explained, "The social, economic, and political destiny of the black people of America is inseparable from that of our black brothers in Africa. It matters not whether it is in Angola, Mozambique, South-west Africa, or Mississippi, Alabama, Georgia, Harlem, United States of America. The struggle is one of the same. . . . It is a struggle against a vicious and evil system that is controlled and kept in order for many by a few white men throughout the world."[39]

In October 1965, two SNCC workers represented SNCC at the annual meeting of the Organization of African Unity (OAU) in Ghana.[40] SNCC's January 1966 antiwar statement charged the United States with being "deceptive in claiming concern for the freedom of colored people in such other countries as the Dominican Republic, the Congo, South Africa, Rhodesia and in the United States itself."[41]

Singer Harry Belafonte organized a supportive reception at the United Nations with fifteen African diplomats and me in early 1966. On March 22, 1966, seven SNCC workers were arrested at the South African consulate in New York, preceding by twenty years the "Free South Africa Movement" that later saw hundreds arrested, including me, at the South African embassy in Washington.[42]

At a June 1967 staff meeting, SNCC declared itself a human rights organization, dedicated to the "liberation not only of Black people in the United States but of all oppressed peoples, especially those in Africa, Asia, and Latin America." At that meeting, Forman became director of SNCC's International Affairs Commission; in this capacity, he visited Tanzania and Zambia.[43] SNCC chair Stokely Carmichael visited Algeria, Syria, Egypt, Guinea, and Tanzania in mid-1967. In November 1967, Forman testified for SNCC before the UN's Fourth Committee against American Investments in South Africa.[44]

THERE ARE MANY reasons for the demise of this important organization. The three years from the March on Washington in 1963 to the Meredith march in Mississippi in 1966, from where the slogan "Black Power" exploded, were years of progress and frustration for the movement. The 1964 Civil Rights Act and the 1965 Voting Rights Act had satisfied two of the movement's major demands. Even as this progress was being celebrated, even as Blacks rushed to registration booths and polling places, and even as Blacks began to win elections, it became clear that access to voting booths, lunch counters, and public office alone would not produce the necessary material improvements in Black people's lives. Blacks outside the South had long enjoyed the right to vote and to enjoy integrated cups of coffee without seeing the gap between Black and white income, education, and other life chances disappear; they still lived at the margins of American economic life.

The current of nationalism, ever-present in Black America, widened at the end of the 1960s to become a rushing torrent that swept away the hopeful notion of Black and white together that the decade's beginning had promised. In December 1966, SNCC officially voted to expel its white staff members. Nineteen voted for expulsion; eighteen voted against, and twenty-four—including the nine white staff members present—abstained. SNCC's white staff members were asked to leave the organization and devote their energies to organizing in white communities; some agreed, but most believed this action repudiated the movement's hopeful call to "Americans all, side by equal side." The shift of one Black vote from yes to no or the participation of one white staffer would have made the difference.[45]

For many on the staff, both white and Black, nearly a decade's worth of hard work at irregular, subsistence-level pay, under an atmosphere of constant tension, interrupted by jailings, beatings, and official and private terror, proved too much. In May 1967, H. Rap Brown succeeded Stokely Carmichael as SNCC's national director. Among his first statements as SNCC's new head, in the face of continued violence against the movement, were "Violence is as American as cherry pie" and "If America don't come around, we're gonna' burn it down"—thereby equating SNCC with violence and reinforcing fears of Black Power.[46]

1968

On March 17, 1968, Memphis pastor James Lawson, an early tutor in non-violence for King as well as the Nashville students, called King at his Los Angeles hotel to ask if he couldn't arrange a stop in Memphis to add his support to a month-old strike by Black sanitation workers. The workers were angered by "an incident that had sent twenty-two black sewer workers home without pay because of bad weather, while white employees had been kept on and paid" and outraged at the death of two workers, crushed to death in a malfunctioning garbage truck.[47]

King was then in the middle of a cross-country tour trying to gather support for and participants in a planned Poor People's March on Washington, an idea initially proposed to him by Marian Wright, then a lawyer for the NAACP Legal Defense and Education Fund, and the first Black woman to pass the Mississippi bar.[48] He eagerly accepted the idea.

King arrived in a city where the sanitation workers' strike had already begun to have some effect. A boycott of downtown stores had cut sales 35 percent, but the city remained adamantly opposed to negotiations. After speaking to an enthusiastic crowd, King agreed to return on Friday, March 22. An unexpected snowstorm forced the cancelation and rescheduled that march.

King was facing some hostility from his own staff to his insistence that the Poor People's Campaign be multicultural, involving poor whites, Hispanics, and Asians. Fund-raising for the campaign was anemic. But he also faced hostility from a familiar enemy, the FBI, aided by informants inside and outside the civil rights community. One historian noted: "In some cities, such as Chicago, Detroit, and Washington, undercover FBI operatives were interfering with the campaign's progress by staging dirty tricks or fanning internal dissension. FBI executives were expanding surveillance and penetration programs aimed at the black community."[49]

Before his return to Memphis, he traveled to speak in Batesville, Marks, Clarksdale, Greenwood, Grenada, Laurel, Jackson, and Hattiesburg, Mississippi; and Waycross, Albany, Macon, and Augusta, Georgia. King also flew to New York, where he spoke in Harlem, flew upstate to the annual conference of the Rabbinical Assembly, had lunch with a welfare recipient in Harlem, spoke to a group of community activists, spoke to groups of clergymen in Queens and Newark, met with twenty-five businessmen at New Jersey Bell Telephone, visited with playwright and author LeRoi Jones (later Amiri Baraka), and addressed rallies in Paterson, Newark, and Jersey City before flying back to Atlanta late at night. Early the next morning, he was back at the Atlanta airport to fly to Memphis. King's frantic pace tells us the urgency he felt and may lead credence to the notion that he knew his days were numbered.

The rescheduled march began peacefully, but suddenly the sound of broken glass was heard and some marchers and bystanders began to loot stores. King's closest aide, Bernard Lee, flagged down a car and drove King to the Rivermont Hotel, while back at the disrupted march police teargassed what had become a rock-throwing crowd and shot and killed a teenager they believed was a looter. Visitors to King's hotel room found him fully dressed—under the bedcovers—discouraged and depressed.

Jim Harrison, an FBI informant who worked in the SCLC office as the comptroller, telephoned his FBI contact, Al Sentinella, to tell him the news of the march's dissolution. At bureau headquarters, "top-ranking FBI executives ordered that special efforts be made to develop full information on King's involvement in the riot-torn march. Such information might be leaked to cooperative reporters as part of the FBI program to disrupt the Poor People's Campaign."[50] "I had never seen him more depressed," King's closest friend Ralph Abernathy said later.

King flew to Washington to preach at the National Cathedral. That evening his sprit was buoyed by the surprise announcement that President Lyndon Johnson would not run for re-election. Earlier, King had announced that SCLC would for the first time drop its nonpartisan stance and endorse a presidential candidate. King had verbally encouraged both Senators Robert Kennedy and Eugene McCarthy to run against Johnson and privately favored Kennedy.

On April 3, King and Abernathy flew to Memphis, where King and his staff met with the Invaders, the group of youths who had been blamed for the outbreak of violence in the first march. The youths asked for funds for their community organizing programs as a price for participating in a second march. King agreed.

Abernathy went to the Mason Temple to speak at that night's mass meeting. King had not planned to go for fear a small audience would add to suspicion that he was losing his ability to lead. But when Abernathy sensed that the crowd of about two thousand was disappointed in not seeing King, he called him at the Lorraine Motel and asked him to come over, and he did. King closed what would be his last speech with these words:

> It really doesn't matter what happens now. I left Atlanta this morning, and as we got started on the plane, there were six of us. The pilot said over the public address system, "We are sorry for the delay, but we have Dr. Martin Luther King on the plane. And to be sure that all of the bags were checked, and to be sure that nothing would be wrong with the plane, we had to check out everything carefully. And we've had the plane protected and guarded all night."
>
> And then I got into Memphis. And some began to say that threats, or talk about the threats that were out. What would happen to me from some of our sick white brothers?
>
> Well, I don't know what will happen now. We've got some difficult days ahead. But it doesn't matter with me now. Because I've been to the

mountaintop. And I don't mind. Like anybody, I would like to live a long life. Longevity has its place. But I'm not concerned about that now. I just want to do God's will. And He's allowed me to go up to the mountain. And I've looked over. And I've seen the promised land. I may not get there with you. But I want you to know tonight, that we, as a people will get to the promised land. And so I'm happy, tonight. I'm not worried about anything. I'm not fearing any man. Mine eyes have seen the glory of the coming of the Lord![51]

Some of the people in the pulpit with him thought he was so overcome by emotion he was crying. Ralph Abernathy and Andrew Young—who had heard him speak these worlds countless times—thought he had "gone beyond the maudlin to the morbid."[52]

He slept until noon April 4.

Memphis police had stationed Black police officer Ed Redditt and a partner at Fire Station Number 2, across the street from the Lorraine Motel, where King was staying in Room 306. Taping a newspaper over a window and cutting two eyeholes in the paper, Redditt and his partners watched federal marshals serve an injunction on King forbidding another march—and then watched while the marshals requested—and were granted—a "grip and grin" photograph with King.

At four o'clock, Redditt was removed from his surveillance duties at the firehouse. An informant had reported a plot to kill a Black police officer, and even though the plot centered on Knoxville, not Memphis, it was thought best to place Redditt and his family in safety, under police guard, under an assumed name, at another hotel. Redditt's partner, officer Willie Richmond, took over surveillance alone.

Historian Taylor Branch wrote:

At four o'clock an escaped convict bought a pair of Bushnell binoculars just up Main Street at York Arms Company, one of the businesses whose windows were smashed on March 28. . . . The convict had driven from Atlanta, where the newspapers said King was leaving for a march in Memphis, arriving late the previous night. This day, reading front-page news that King was staying at the Lorraine, and perhaps hearing radio reports that specified Room 306, he had located and studied the motel until an hour ago, when he rented a room for $8.50 per week in

Bessie Brewer's flophouse next door to Fire Station Number 2. With the seven-power Bushnells, he could read room numbers on the motel doors seventy yards distant, and the same strength on his Redfield scope would make human figures seem only thirty feet away. The scope was mounted on a .30–06 Remington Gamemaster, which was engineered so that its 150-grain slug would lose less than .01 inch in altitude and reach the motel balcony with 2,370 pounds of knockdown power— enough to drop a rhinoceros.[53]

On April 4, 1968, that convict, James Earl Ray, shot and killed Martin Luther King as he stood on the second-floor balcony of the Lorraine Motel. In the aftermath of King's murder, wild conspiracy theories flourished, as they frequently do when a nonentity suddenly strikes down a major figure. King's aide James Bevel argued, "There is no way a ten-cent white boy could develop a plan to kill a million dollar black man."[54]

In 1997, Dexter King proclaimed James Earl Ray innocent of his father's murder. But Ray possessed all the ingredients necessary to carry off the crime—he had means, motive, and opportunity, all the successful elements of any crime. He bought the gun that fired the shot that killed King. His fingerprints were on the gun and on the windowsill from which the shot was fired. He fled the scene, displaying guilty knowledge. And he confessed. He told his brother on the morning of April 4—"I'm going to get the big nigger."

Six days after King was murdered, and while riot flames and smoke still filled the air over many cities and gun emplacements guarded the Capitol Building in Washington, fair housing legislation, which had passed the United States Senate a month earlier, passed the House. Like previous civil rights bills, it was weak and ineffectual. Its most stringent provisions were aimed not at discriminatory owners and landlords but at rioters. It combined weak prohibitions against discrimination and strong punishments for anyone who broke the law in rebellious protest against weak solutions to the ancient problem of race.

After a bitter fight over the MFDP's challenge in 1964, the Democratic Party promised that all future delegations would be racially integrated and fairly chosen. Four years later, in 1968, there was no presidential primary in Georgia. All delegates, almost all white, were handpicked by the party chairman. Its membership included people pledged to vote for Alabama governor George Wallace, a third-party candidate, not for any of the Democratic candidates.

To highlight this problem, the alternative delegation I headed was chosen democratically, in an open convention in Macon. Our delegation fairly represented the Democratic candidates—Hubert Humphrey and Eugene McCarthy. I went to Chicago a week before the convention with Taylor Branch, who received the Pulitzer Prize years later for his wonderful three-volume history of the civil rights movement, collectively called *America in the King Years.* Our job was to secure housing and transportation for our sixty-member delegation—hotel rooms for them to stay in and buses to transport them to the convention center.

There was not a room to be had or a bus to be secured. Furthermore, unlike other delegations supported by their state political parties, we were challenging the legitimacy of our state's party and their leadership; we were nearly penniless. We were sadly walking Chicago's streets when a well-dressed Black man recognized me and approached us to ask if he could help. We explained our problem. He took us to a hotel we had already unsuccessfully approached, and after a quick conversation with the manager he secured sixty rooms.

We were astounded but still had no money to bring our delegation from scattered locations around Georgia to Chicago. This man suggested I ask his employer, the Honorable Elijah Muhammad, the head of the Nation of Islam. We were incredulous. Members of the Nation of Islam were forbidden to vote or participate in politics. They believed in racial separation, not integration. Why would the head of an organization that regularly characterized all whites as "blue-eyed devils" want to contribute to bringing an integrated group to a meeting where voting and political participation was the main idea?

Nonetheless, our new friend arranged for me to have dinner with Mr. Muhammad at his mansion in Chicago's Hyde Park. After the meal, I explained our problem, and Mr. Muhammad asked me to return the next day. He gave me three thousand dollars in hundred-dollar bills—more than $22,000 today. I wired the money to Georgia, our delegation arrived, and after days of lobbying and arguing, the convention voted to split Georgia's seats—half for us, half for the regular party. Most of the regulars walked out in anger, and the Georgia Loyal National Delegation got to occupy most of Georgia's seats and cast most of Georgia's votes.

I have often wondered why Mr. Muhammad did it—why a man who had built a movement on racial separatism and a withdrawal from the country's political institutions gave money to bring a group of Black and white Georgians to a political convention. Perhaps he remembered his early years in Georgia with some fondness or was even then looking forward to the day when the Nation of Islam would shed its opposition to politics and would enter the political mainstream.

At the convention, I was nominated to be the vice president of the United States. Obviously, I didn't win. At twenty-eight years old, I was too young to hold the office. Maine senator Edmund Muskie became the Democrats' 1968 vice presidential nominee—and the convention ended in a police riot.

SNCC: WHAT WE DID

The movement had important effects that were difficult to quantify immediately in the North and South. Since Montgomery in 1955, Southern Blacks had gained a sense of agency and efficacy. Northern Blacks, who could already sit on the front seats of buses, took inspiration from the Southern campaigns that played out on their television screens and newspaper front pages. The majority of Blacks, most not actual participants in the movement, felt empowered by the early movement's success.

We are a different country today than when I was first beckoned into the civil rights movement. That is only because thousands upon thousands of Americans put their bodies on the line for freedom and justice.

Throughout its brief history, SNCC insisted on group-centered leadership and community-based politics. It made clear the connection between economic power and racial oppression. It refused to define racism as solely Southern, to describe racial inequality as caused by irrational prejudice alone, or to limit its struggle solely to guaranteeing legal equality. It challenged American imperialism while mainstream civil rights organizations were silent or curried favor with President Lyndon Johnson, condemning SNCC's linkage of domestic poverty and racism with overseas adventurism. SNCC refused to apply political tests to its membership or supporters, opposing the red-baiting that other organizations and leaders endorsed or condoned. It created an atmosphere of expectation and anticipation among the people with whom it worked, trusting them to make decisions about their own lives.

SNCC widened the definition of politics beyond campaigns and elections. For SNCC, politics encompassed not only electoral races but also organizing political parties, labor unions, producer cooperatives, and alternative schools. It initially sought to liberalize Southern politics by organizing and enfranchising Blacks. One proof of its success was the increase in Black elected officials in the Southern states from 72 in 1965 to 388 in 1968.[55] But SNCC also sought to liberalize the ends of political participation, by enlarging the issues of political debate to include the economic and foreign policy concerns of American Blacks.

SNCC's articulation and advocacy of Black Power redefined the relationship between Black Americans and white power. No longer would political equity be considered a privilege; it had become a right.

One legacy from the movement is the destruction of the psychological shackles that had kept Black Southerners in physical and mental peonage. The Student Nonviolent Coordinating Committee helped to break those chains forever. What began more than a half century ago is not history. It was a part of a mighty movement that started many years ago and that continues to this day—ordinary women and men proving they can perform extraordinary tasks in the pursuit of freedom. They did then and can do so again.

WE ARE IN NEED OF SHAKING

by Vann R. Newkirk II

I WAS NOT lucky enough to take an entire class taught by Julian Bond or to experience the full range of his lectures. My only encounter with Julian Bond the professor came during a few weeks at Morehouse College in 2009. Professor Clayborne Carson, himself an esteemed historian and an official biographer of Dr. Martin Luther King Jr., invited Professor Bond to a few sessions of his class on King's legacy.

It was the kind of recursive setup that could veer almost into the parodical: Morehouse graduate Julian Bond guest-lecturing a class on Morehouse graduate Martin Luther King Jr., taught by a King historian a couple hundred yards away from the King statue on Morehouse campus. But it turns out that there might not have been a group of students who needed the intervention more. What even Black students were taught about the movement mostly amounted to a set of constraints—the idolization of a sepia-toned aesthetic—that didn't grapple much with our own needs in the present. At the college, we were all young Black men who had lived in the shadow of a figure we believed to be King. We were steeped in the politics of respectability. We were taught to dress like King. We were taught to speak like him. We were taught to aspire to be leaders like him. But even then, we knew the task of becoming the mythological, stone-statue version of King was impossible. So why bother?

The living history that Julian Bond presented to us, however, along with the clarity of his urgency—even then, in 2009—were antidotes to the anesthetized, inert version of progress that we had all ingested in bits and bites, here and there. Those lessons were antidotes to the paralysis inflicted on my classes by our curricula. Bond inspired us to learn from history, to critique historical figures, and to understand just how the conditions of today were built and maintained. Professor Bond shook us up. We were in need of shaking.

The tremors still radiate in this volume. Though Bond is now among the ranks of the departed, years after his death his lectures and commentary retain their relevance and urgency. These works from Bond function as a chronology, dramatis personae, and geographical primer of the civil rights movement. As a work of history—with the authority of a man at the center of events—they are a remarkable resource. One with absolutely no knowledge of the story of race and racism in this country could do worse than using this book as a starting point.

Yet we should all know by the end of this book that Bond did not intend his work to live on purely as a dusty tome of history. He spoke to the moment. He spoke to how we got here and endeavored in his drawing of lines to ensure that they were never as straight as they seemed in pop history. Bond struggled against the "master narrative" and worked to provide a counter narrative, one that not only relied on his authority but also on his ability to step outside of himself and outside of time. What he managed to deliver was titanic yet intimate, definitive yet unfinished. But in this case, we should beware of the finished story. Bond endeavored to keep learning, to refine and reassess his lectures as more information came, and to consider his own limitations as a guide. The result was a set of lectures that acknowledges that history is not done, and that to treat it as such robs young people of the ability to change their own circumstances.

It became clear in that classroom at Morehouse that we had all been infected by the seductiveness of the master narrative. Even there on the campus that made King—perhaps, *especially* there—we were subject to a version of the story of struggle that made progress seem inevitable, and made the study of the civil rights movement the study of a few good men. Good Negroes and bad racists played the starring roles in the history I consumed. Economic history was often ignored. Women in the movement were cherished but mostly for a perceived role in helping the great men at the top. The force of the intellect and rhetoric of King, embodied in singular moments like the "Dream" speech, was emphasized. His journey as a human, and the role of mentors, friends, and the pressures of the moment in shaping him—the exact pieces of information that might be useful for young men trying to figure out exactly *how* to become leaders and how to respond to struggles outside of our own—were largely marginalized.

The history was steeped in the tropes Bond fought hard to dismantle. "Booker T. Washington versus W. E. B. Du Bois, integration versus separation, Martin Luther King versus Malcolm X, nonviolence versus violence," as he put it.

What Professor Bond offered, instead, was a more complex view. He admonished us for a myopic view of the contributions of women, lecturing on Rosa Parks, Septima Clark, and Ella Baker and their origin stories, showing them to be operatives who carried a movement. Years before the 2016 presidential election, he spoke of the constant presence of white backlash and of the push and pull between activism and resistance that shaped the conditions of the Jim Crow South. He provided a more nuanced view of the interplay between nonviolence, self-defense, and racist violence. He talked about the diverse and often fractious nature of civil rights activism, and he ridiculed the respectability politics that we'd grown to believe in, as a matter of course. Above all, he stressed that the work was not fully done, and that it could be undone.

In helping rescue us from a version of history in which we were passive actors, he also empowered us. The reality of the movement was messier, subtler, and indeed scarier than we'd known. Yet the complexity made it clear that we all still had roles to play, that we hadn't reached the end of history, and that the courses of our own lives would be dynamic and sometimes contentious. He helped give us the ability to see that our own circumstances had been created and that we could re-create them should we choose. He helped us see that the giants of the civil rights movement were just regular people who had made remarkable decisions. Maybe it was impossible to become the mythologized figures conventional history gave us, but Professor Bond offered us pathways to act, just as his contemporaries had done. Those takeaways—distilled and even more powerful—should also be animating forces after reading this book.

These lessons come at a critical time. Bond noted how residential segregation had already shaped American cities fifty years after the Emancipation Proclamation. It has now been over a century since the moment he identifies, and gentrification, redlining, and the racialization of concentrated poverty are the universal constants of living in America. Bond pointed to the New Deal as the dawn of the racial wealth gap. Decades later, the gap only yawns more widely. School districts across the country are returning to a state of segregation as deep and formalized as they were on the eve of 1954. And problems that were not always recognized as central concerns of the movement have become ever more urgent. Since the Great Recession, Black landownership has contracted again. Research pinpoints racial disparities in pollution as a major factor in the gulf between white and Black life spans. And climate change advances, threatening Black families and Black towns in our most vulnerable areas.

Synthesize all these concerns into the larger story of justice in America at the moment—from LGBTQ rights to the twin scourges of xenophobia and anti-Semitism—and it's clear that Julian Bond still has something to say. In a particularly prescient lecture, he noted that "the consequences of slavery were neither incidental nor secondary aspects of American history but constitute its central theme." Perhaps as new journalistic and historical works recast the story of American democracy as the story of racial struggle, the rest of the country is finally catching up to the wisdom of that insight. Perhaps not.

What Bond offers in his most incisive moments is that idea that human history is human. It is messy. It is contradictory. Progress is not linear, and regress is guaranteed. We repeat ourselves in endlessly dull motifs yet are capable of beautiful improvisation. The machinery of the powers that be is mighty, but ordinary women and men, young and old, can dismantle it. They did before, and they will again. The present is full of potential Julian Bonds, Ella Bakers, and Rosa Parkses—not because there is a modern glut of talent or intelligence but because every person is capable of transformation. Taken altogether, these offerings should inspire us to look at the fractious present—the political defeats, the strength of white backlash, the social-media hellscape, and the relentlessly petty and venal actions of people in power—and see not the seeds of doom but the fertile ground for a paradigm shift. Taken one step further, Bond's lectures should indict the hubris of throwing up our hands and declaring the world hopeless. Such is the end goal of the master narrative, and we should resist it.

I was honored to write this afterword for *Julian Bond's Time to Teach*. Jeanne Theoharis and Pam Horowitz asked me to consider what this book might offer for the future. I think, reflecting on my brief time learning from Professor Bond, that the offering is in the title. It is always time to teach, because it is always time to do. The master narrative is constantly created. It must be constantly combatted. The master narrative teaches that history is divorced from the present and invites inertia by way of either complacency or despair. And Julian Bond knew that inertia is the enemy of progress. We are in need of shaking.

ACKNOWLEDGMENTS

O UR FIRST THANKS goes to Erik Wallenberg whose research assistance, citation work, vision, patience, and diligence made this book possible. We are grateful to Gayatri Patnaik, our editor, who loved this book idea from the first moment we brought it to her and to all the staff at Beacon Press for their care, commitment, and attention in bringing this book into the world; to Vann Newkirk for the gorgeous afterword to this book; and to Danny Lyon, whose photos make the book sparkle.

—JT and PH

FIRST, TO JULIAN—for writing out his lectures so beautifully that getting them ready for publication was pure pleasure. And to Jeanne—who had hoped to write a different book with Julian and graciously turned to me to do this one with her. And to Danny Lyon, whose love for Julian and incredible generosity allowed us to use his wonderful photos.

—PH

I AM DEEPLY GRATEFUL to Julian for teaching me how to tell this history and to Pam for sharing this book and this journey with me.

—JT

ANNOTATED BIBLIOGRAPHY
BY JULIAN BOND*

C HOOSING READING MATERIALS is a daunting challenge. The civil rights bibliography is lengthy and constantly expanding. Books on the following list are followed by descriptions. If you are a fast reader, consume the Taylor Branch trilogy—they are the very best books on the American civil rights movement and tell its familiar story with fascinating new detail and analysis—*Parting the Waters*, *Pillar of Fire*, and *At Canaan's Edge*.

Aldon Morris's *Origins of the Civil Rights Movement* provides excellent background to the movement. Glenn Eskew's *But for Birmingham* describes that city's movement. Vincent Harding's *Hope and History* places the civil rights movement in a modern context.

An exciting book that is certainly worthwhile, *Hands on the Freedom Plow: Personal Accounts by Women in SNCC*, includes fifty-two women—Northern and Southern, young and old, urban and rural, Black, white, and Latina—who share their courageous personal stories of working for the Student Nonviolent Coordinating Committee on the front lines of the civil rights movement. Another recommended book—written by my former TA when I taught at Harvard, Jeanne Theoharis—is *The Rebellious Life of Mrs. Rosa Parks*.

J. Mills Thornton's *Dividing Lines* places municipal politics in Montgomery, Selma, and Birmingham at the center of the freedom movement.

---

*Professor Bond created this annotated bibliography for the civil rights tours he led through the South under the auspices of the University of Virginia from 2007 to 2015.

Howell Raines's *My Soul Is Rested* tells the movement story in the movement makers' own words.

All the books on this list are worthy.

Bayard Rustin: Troubles I've Seen: A Biography, by Jervis Anderson (University of California Press, 1998).

Freedom Riders: 1961 and the Struggle for Racial Justice, by Raymond Arsenault (Oxford University Press, 2006). Detailed and powerful history of participants in the Freedom Rides.

Parting the Waters: America in the King Years, 1954–1963, by Taylor Branch (Simon & Schuster, 1988). This is the Pulitzer Prize–winning first book of Branch's three-volume history of the movement, which together cover the movement's early years, the March on Washington, the Montgomery bus boycott, the sit-ins and Freedom Rides, the Albany (Georgia), Birmingham, and St. Augustine movements, and much more.

Pillar of Fire: America in the King Years, 1963–1965, by Taylor Branch (Simon & Schuster, 1998). Volume 2 of Taylor's trilogy includes the movement in the North, Freedom Summer, and the Mississippi Freedom Democratic Party challenge.

At Canaan's Edge: America in the King Years, 1965–68, by Taylor Branch (Simon & Schuster, 2006). Volume 3 of Branch's history includes the Selma voting rights campaign, the march to Montgomery, Black Power, the Meredith march, the Chicago Campaign, and anti–Vietnam War protests.

Ready for Revolution: The Life and Struggles of Stokely Carmichael (Kwame Ture), by Stokely Carmichael with Ekwueme Michael Thelwell (Scribner, 2003). Autobiography of the freedom fighter who headed SNCC for a time.

In Struggle: SNCC and the Black Awakening of the 1960s, by Clayborne Carson (Harvard University Press, 1981). History of SNCC from the sit-ins and Freedom Rides through community organizing, Freedom Summer, Black Power, and dispersal.

Deep in Our Hearts: Nine White Women in the Freedom Movement, edited by Constance Curry et al. (University of Georgia Press, 2000). Nine first-person memoirs of the Southern freedom movement.

Silver Rights: The Story of the Carter Family's Brave Decision to Send Their Children to an All-White School and Claim Their Civil Rights, by Constance Curry (Harcourt, 1998). The powerful story of an African American sharecropper family on a plantation in Sunflower County, Mississippi, who sent seven of their thirteen children to desegregate the all-white school system in 1965.

The Good Doctors: The Medical Committee for Human Rights and the Struggle for Social Justice in Health Care, by John Dittmer (Bloomsbury Press, 2009). Story of the courageous MCHR doctors, nurses, and health professionals who cared for the injured and struggled for justice and health-care equality during Freedom Summer and the antiwar movement, in Selma, Chicago, Alcatraz, Wounded Knee, and elsewhere.

Local People: The Struggle for Civil Rights in Mississippi, by John Dittmer (University of Illinois Press, 1995). The movement in Mississippi from the point of view of the local people who lived it.

Cold War Civil Rights: Race and the Image of American Democracy, by Mary L. Dudziak (Princeton University Press, 2002). Analyzing impact of Cold War foreign affairs on US civil rights reform and how international relations affected domestic issues, this book interprets the civil rights movement as a Cold War feature and argues that the Cold War helped facilitate social reforms, including desegregation.

But for Birmingham: The Local and National Movements in the Civil Rights Struggle, by Glenn T. Eskew (University of North Carolina Press, 1996). Detailed historical examination of the Birmingham struggle in 1950s and 1960s.

Race and Democracy: The Civil Rights Struggle in Louisiana, 1915–1972, by Adam Fairclough (University of Georgia Press, 1999). British scholar Fairclough examines the history of the civil rights movement in Louisiana from 1915, when the New Orleans branch of the NAACP was founded, through the start of the first administration of Governor Edwin Edwards in 1972. He has written the most comprehensive account yet of the movement in Louisiana. Especially valuable is the discussion of the movement during the decades before the Supreme Court's Brown decision, a period that many scholars have neglected.

Lay Bare the Heart: An Autobiography of the Civil Rights Movement, by James Farmer (Texas Christian University Press, 1998). Personal story of the CORE leader and one of the major figures of the movement.

Soon We Will Not Cry: The Liberation of Ruby Doris Smith Robinson, by Cynthia Griggs Fleming (Rowman & Littlefield, 1998). Biography of a major leader and activist in SNCC and the struggle for women's rights.

The Making of Black Revolutionaries, by James Forman (University of Washington Press, 1997). Autobiography and movement history by SNCC executive director Jim Forman, originally published in 1972.

Subversive Southerner: Anne Braden and the Struggle for Racial Justice in the Cold War South, by Catherine Fosl (Palgrave Macmillan, 2002). Biography of famed civil rights activist Anne Braden.

A White Preacher's Message on Race and Reconciliation: Based on His Experiences Beginning with the Montgomery Bus Boycott, by Robert S. Graetz (New South Books, 2006). In addition to Graetz's Montgomery bus boycott memoirs, this book includes provocative chapters on white privilege, Black forgiveness, and the present-day challenges for human and civil rights.

Ella Baker: Freedom Bound, by Joanne Grant (John Wiley & Sons, 1998). Profile of Ella Baker and her central role in the movement.

Hope and History: Why We Must Share the Story of the Movement, by Vincent Harding (Orbis Books, 1990). Essays by movement veteran Vincent Harding on how the civil rights movement affected all aspects of American life.

Open Wide the Freedom Gates: A Memoir, by Dorothy Height (Public Affairs, 2003). Personal memoir of a major figure in the civil rights movement. A contemporary of Dr. King, W. E. B. Du Bois, Marcus Garvey, Eleanor Roosevelt, Mary McLeod Bethune, Adam Clayton Powell Sr., and Langston Hughes, Height was often the only woman involved in the movement at the highest leadership level.

Hands on the Freedom Plow: Personal Accounts by Women in SNCC, edited by Faith Holsaert et al. (University of Illinois Press, 2012). An unprecedented women's history of the civil rights movement, from sit-ins to Black Power, told by the largely little-known women who made it happen.

Going Down Jericho Road: The Memphis Strike, Martin Luther King's Last Campaign, by Michael Honey (W. W. Norton, 2007). Labor activist and historian Honey describes the strike and King's effort to build a new mass movement to push beyond civil rights to economic justice for the poor and working class.

Bloody Lowndes: Civil Rights and Black Power in Alabama's Black Belt, by Hasan Kwame Jeffries (New York University Press, 2009). Story of SNCC organizing in Lowndes County, the Lowndes County Freedom Organization, and the emergence of Black Power.

Simple Justice: The History of Brown v. Board of Education *and Black America's Struggle for Equality,* by Richard Kluger (Vintage, 2004). Major overview of not only the Brown case but also the movement as a whole, first published in 1975. This edition, updated to coincide with the fiftieth anniversary of Brown, includes analysis of the Republican "Southern strategy."

Judgment Days: Lyndon Baines Johnson, Martin Luther King, Jr., and the Laws That Changed America, by Nick Kotz (Houghton Mifflin, 2005). Covers the interactions and relationship between King and LBJ around the passage of the Civil Rights Act of 1964 and Voting Rights Act of 1965.

Memories of the Southern Civil Rights Movement, by Danny Lyon (University of North Carolina Press, 1992), with foreword by Julian Bond. Republished by Twin Palms in 2010, including a new afterword. This book by the SNCC photographer who covered major freedom movement campaigns and projects contains some of the most moving and powerful images to come out of the movement.

Freedom Summer, by Doug McAdam (Oxford University Press, 1968). Analysis of the 1964 Freedom Summer in Mississippi.

A Voting Rights Odyssey: Black Enfranchisement in Georgia, by Laughlin McDonald (Cambridge University Press, 2003). McDonald tells the story of the efforts of the white leadership in Georgia to maintain white supremacy by denying Blacks the right to vote and hold elected office. Narrated chronologically, most of the story is told by those who participated, from Alexander H. Stephens, vice president of the Confederate States, to Carl Sanders, governor of Georgia in the 1960s, to Emma Gresham, Black mayor of Keysville, in rural Burke County.

CORE: A Study in the Civil Rights Movement 1942–1968, by August Meier
and Elliott Rudwick (Oxford University Press, 1973).

*Struggle for a Better South: The Southern Student Organizing Commit-
tee, 1964–1969*, by Gregg L. Michel (Palgrave Macmillan, 2004). The
Southern Student Organizing Committee was an organization of
Southern white students who struggled in local white communities
against racism, to end the war in Vietnam, and to build an interracial
movement for justice and equality.

This Little Light of Mine: The Life of Fannie Lou Hamer, by Kay Mills
(Dutton, 1994). Moving biography of a central figure in the civil
rights movement.

*The Origins of the Civil Rights Movement: Black Communities Organizing
for Change*, by Aldon D. Morris (Free Press, 1986). Comprehensive
study of the movement's origin and strategies, with emphasis on the
roles played by women.

Reaping the Whirlwind: The Civil Rights Movement in Tuskegee, by Robert J. Norrell (University of North Carolina Press, 1998). In this classic and compelling account, Norrell traces the course of the civil
rights movement in Tuskegee, Alabama, capturing both the unique
aspects of this key Southern town's experience and the elements that
it shared with other communities during this period.

*I've Got the Light of Freedom: The Organizing Tradition and the Missis-
sippi Freedom Struggle*, by Charles Payne (University of California
Press, 1995). Uses one Mississippi community to explain how the
movement organized.

*Killing the Dream: James Earl Ray and the Assassination of Martin Luther
King*, by Gerald L. Posner (Random House, 1998). Argues that Ray
was the lone assassin and that there was no broader conspiracy.

My Soul Is Rested: Movement Days in the Deep South Remembered, by
Howell Raines (Putnam, 1977). Personal statements and recollections
of movement activists and leaders from the Montgomery bus boycott
through King's assassination.

*The Race Beat: The Press, the Civil Rights Struggle, and the Awakening of a
Nation*, by Gene Roberts and Hank Klibanoff (Knopf, 2006).

*Everybody Says Freedom: A History of the Civil Rights Movement in Songs
and Pictures*, by Pete Seeger and Bob Reiser (Norton, 1989). History
of the civil rights movement in songs, pictures, and interviews.

Lift Every Voice: The NAACP and the Making of the Civil Rights Move-ment, by Patricia Sullivan (New Press, 2009). A history of the oldest, largest civil rights organization.

The Rebellious Life of Mrs. Rosa Parks, by Jeanne Theoharis (Beacon Press, 2013). Presenting a corrective to the popular notion of Rosa Parks as the quiet seamstress who, with a single act, birthed the modern civil rights movement, Theoharis provides a revealing win-dow into Parks's politics and years of activism. She shows readers how this civil rights movement radical sought—for more than a half a century—to expose and eradicate the American racial-caste system in jobs, schools, public services, and criminal justice.

Dividing Lines: Municipal Politics and the Struggle for Civil Rights in Montgomery, Birmingham, and Selma, by J. Mills Thornton (Univer-sity of Alabama Press, 2006). Detailed, comprehensive history of the Montgomery bus boycott and movements in Selma and Birming-ham, with heavy emphasis on municipal politics.

Radio Free Dixie: Robert F. Williams and the Roots of Black Power, by Timothy B. Tyson (University of North Carolina Press, 1999). Biogra-phy of Robert F. Williams and his advocacy of "armed self-reliance" by Blacks.

Freedom Summer: The Savage Season That Made Mississippi Burn and Made America a Democracy, by Bruce Watson (Viking, 2010). De-scribes the overall freedom movement in Mississippi and the his-tory of the Mississippi Summer Project, including personal stories of more than fifty participants.

RECOMMENDED READINGS

CHAPTER ONE: WHITE SUPREMACY AND THE FOUNDING OF THE NAACP

W. E. B. Du Bois, *The Souls of Black Folk*

John Hope Franklin, *From Slavery to Freedom: A History of African Americans*

Grace Elizabeth Hale, *Making Whiteness: The Culture of Segregation in the South, 1890–1940*

David Levering Lewis, *W. E. B. Du Bois: A Biography, 1868–1963*

Nancy MacLean, *Behind the Mask of Chivalry: The Making of the Second Ku Klux Klan*

Mary White Ovington, *Black and White Together: The Reminiscences of an NAACP Founder*

CHAPTER TWO: ORIGINS OF THE CIVIL RIGHTS MOVEMENT

Evelyn Brooks Higginbotham, *Righteous Discontent: The Women's Movement in the Black Baptist Church*

Gilbert King, *Devil in the Grove: Thurgood Marshall, the Groveland Boys, and the Dawn of a New America*

Leon Litwack, *Trouble in Mind: Black Southerners in the Age of Jim Crow*

Harvard Sitkoff, *A New Deal for Blacks: The Emergence of Civil Rights as a National Issue: The Depression Decade*

Patricia Sullivan, *Lift Every Voice: The NAACP and the Making of the Civil Rights Movement*

CHAPTER THREE: WORLD WAR II

Jervis Anderson, *A. Philip Randolph: A Biographical Portrait*

Gunnar Myrdal, *An American Dilemma: The Negro Problem and Modern Democracy*

Isabel Wilkerson, *The Warmth of Other Suns: The Epic Story of America's Great Migration*

CHAPTER FOUR: PRESIDENT TRUMAN AND THE ROAD
TO BROWN V. BOARD OF EDUCATION

Anne Braden, *The Wall Between*

Martin Duberman, *Paul Robeson: A Biography*

Catherine Fosl, *Subversive Southerner: Ann Braden and the Struggle for Racial Justice in the Cold War South*

Myles Horton and Paulo Freire, *We Make the Road by Walking: Conversations on Education and Social Change*

CHAPTER FIVE: BROWN V. BOARD OF EDUCATION

Devery Anderson, *Emmett Till: The Murder That Shocked the World and Propelled the Civil Rights Movement*

Richard Kluger, *Simple Justice: The History of* Brown v. Board of Education *and Black America's Struggle for Equality*

Neil R. McMillen, *The Citizens' Council: A History of Organized Southern White Resistance to the Second Reconstruction*

Aldon Morris, *The Origins of the Civil Rights Movement: Black Communities Organizing for Change*

Howell Raines, *My Soul Is Rested: Movement Days in the Deep South Remembered*

CHAPTER SIX: THE MONTGOMERY BUS BOYCOTT

Virginia Foster Durr, *Outside the Magic Circle: The Autobiography of Virginia Foster Durr*

Robert Graetz, *A White Preacher's Message on Race and Reconciliation*

Fred Gray, *Bus Ride to Justice*

Martin Luther King Jr., *The Autobiography of Martin Luther King, Jr.*

Martin Luther King Jr., *Stride Toward Freedom: The Montgomery Story*

Rosa Parks, *Rosa Parks: My Story*

Jo Ann Gibson Robinson, *The Montgomery Bus Boycott and the Women Who Started It*

Jeanne Theoharis, *The Rebellious Life of Mrs. Rosa Parks*

CHAPTER SEVEN: THE 1956 PRESIDENTIAL ELECTION
AND THE 1957 CIVIL RIGHTS ACT

Jack Bass, *Taming the Storm: The Life and Times of Judge Frank M. John-son and the South's Fight over Civil Rights*

Jack Bloom, *Class, Race, and the Civil Rights Movement: The Changing Political Economy of Southern Racism*

Robert Dallek, *Lone Star Rising: Lyndon Johnson and His Times, 1908–1960*

Adam Fairclough, *To Redeem the Soul of America: The Southern Christian Leadership Conference and Martin Luther King, Jr.*

CHAPTER EIGHT: LITTLE ROCK, 1957

Carol Anderson, *White Rage: The Unspoken Truth of Our Racial Divide*

Daisy Bates, *The Long Shadow of Little Rock: A Memoir*

Melba Patillo Beals, *Warriors Don't Cry: A Searing Memoir of the Battle to Integrate Little Rock's Central High*

CHAPTER NINE: THE SOUTHERN CHRISTIAN LEADERSHIP CONFERENCE

Ralph Abernathy, *And the Walls Came Tumbling Down: An Autobiography*

Constance Curry, et al., eds. *Deep in Our Hearts: Nine White Women of the Civil Rights Movement*

Adam Fairclough, *To Redeem the Soul of America: The Southern Christian Leadership Conference and Martin Luther King, Jr.*

Joanne Grant, *Ella Baker: Freedom Bound*

Barbara Ransby, *Ella Baker and the Black Freedom Movement: A Radical Democratic Vision*

CHAPTER TEN: THE SIT-INS AND THE FOUNDING OF SNCC

William Chafe, *Civilities and Civil Rights: Greensboro, North Carolina, and the Black Struggle for Freedom*

Wesley Hogan, *Many Minds, One Heart: SNCC's Dream for a New America*

Faith Holsaert, et al., eds. *Hands on the Freedom Plow: Personal Accounts by Women in SNCC*

CHAPTER ELEVEN: THE STUDENT NONVIOLENT COORDINATING COMMITTEE

Clayborne Carson, *In Struggle: SNCC and the Black Awakening of the 1960s*

John Lewis with Michael D'Orso, *Walking with the Wind: A Memoir of the Movement*

Howard Zinn, *SNCC: The New Abolitionists*

CHAPTER TWELVE: THE FREEDOM RIDES

Raymond Arsenault, *Freedom Riders: 1961 and the Struggle for Racial Justice*

James Farmer, *Lay Bare the Heart: An Autobiography of the Civil Rights Movement*

Timothy Tyson, *Radio Free Dixie: Robert F. Williams and the Roots of Black Power*

CHAPTER THIRTEEN: KENNEDY AND CIVIL RIGHTS, 1961

Vicki L. Crawford, Jacqueline Anne Rouse, and Barbara Woods, eds., *Women in the Civil Rights Movement: Trailblazers and Torchbearers, 1941–1965*

Roy Wilkins and Tom Matthews, *Standing Fast: The Autobiography of Roy Wilkins*

Harris Wofford, *Of Kennedys and Kings: Making Sense of the Sixties*

CHAPTER FOURTEEN: ALBANY, GEORGIA, 1961

Clayborne Carson, ed., *The "Student Voice," 1960–1965: Periodical of the Student Nonviolent Coordinating Committee*

Cynthia Griggs Fleming, *Soon We Will Not Cry: The Liberation of Ruby Doris Smith Robinson*

Lynne Olson, *Freedom's Daughters: The Unsung Heroines of the Civil Rights Movement from 1830 to 1970*

Fred Powledge, *Free at Last? The Civil Rights Movement and the People Who Made It*

CHAPTER FIFTEEN: MISSISSIPPI VOTER REGISTRATION

John Dittmer, *Local People: The Struggle for Civil Rights in Mississippi*

Chana Kai Lee, *For Freedom's Sake: The Life of Fannie Lou Hamer*

Kay Mills, *This Little Light of Mine: The Life of Fannie Lou Hamer*

Charles Payne, *I've Got the Light of Freedom: The Organizing Tradition and the Mississippi Freedom Struggle*

CHAPTER SIXTEEN: BIRMINGHAM

Taylor Branch, *Pillar of Fire: America in the King Years, 1963–65*

Thomas Jackson, *From Civil Rights to Human Rights: Martin Luther King, Jr. and the Struggle for Economic Justice*

Diane McWhorter, *Carry Me Home: Birmingham, Alabama: The Climactic Battle of the Civil Rights Revolution*

CHAPTER SEVENTEEN: MISSISSIPPI, MEDGAR EVERS, AND THE CIVIL RIGHTS BILL

Charlie Cobb, *This Nonviolent Stuff'll Get You Killed: How Guns Made the Civil Rights Movement Possible*

James Forman, *The Making of Black Revolutionaries*

Robert D. Loevy, *To End All Segregation: The Politics of the Passage of the Civil Rights Act of 1964*

CHAPTER EIGHTEEN: THE MARCH ON WASHINGTON

John D'Emilio, *Lost Prophet: The Life and Times of Bayard Rustin*

Kenneth O'Reilly, *"Racial Matters": The FBI's Secret File on Black America, 1960–1972*

Athan Theoharis and John Stuart Cox, *The Boss: J. Edgar Hoover and the Great American Inquisition*

Gary Younge, *The Speech: The Story Behind Dr. Martin Luther King Jr.'s Dream*

CHAPTER NINETEEN: THE CIVIL RIGHTS ACT

Robert Caro, *Master of the Senate: The Years of Lyndon B Johnson*

Lyndon Baines Johnson, *The Vantage Point: Perspectives of the Presidency, 1963–69*

Barbara Jordan and Elspeth D. Rostow, eds., *The Great Society: A Twenty-Year Critique*

Charles Whalen and Barbara Whalen, *The Longest Debate: A Legislative History of the 1964 Civil Rights Act*

CHAPTER TWENTY: MISSISSIPPI FREEDOM SUMMER, 1964

Eric Burner, *And Gently He Shall Lead Them: Robert Parris Moses and Civil Rights in Mississippi*

Elizabeth Sutherland Martínez, *Letters from Mississippi: Reports from Civil Rights Volunteers and Freedom School Poetry of the 1964 Freedom Summer*

Nicolaus Mills, *Like a Holy Crusade: Mississippi 1964, the Turning Point of the Civil Rights Movement in America*

Howard Zinn, *The Zinn Reader: Writings on Disobedience and Democracy*

CHAPTER TWENTY-ONE: SELMA, ALABAMA,
AND THE 1965 VOTING RIGHTS ACT

John Dittmer, *The Good Doctors: The Medical Committee for Human Rights and the Struggle for Social Justice in Health Care*

Gary May, *The Informant: The FBI, the Ku Klux Klan, and the Murder of Viola Liuzzo*

Sheyann Webb, *Selma, Lord, Selma: Girlhood Memories of the Civil Rights Days*

Howard Zinn, *The Southern Mystique*

CHAPTER TWENTY-TWO: VIETNAM, BLACK POWER,
AND THE ASSASSINATION OF MARTIN LUTHER KING

H. Rap Brown, *Die Nigger Die!*

Stokely Carmichael (Kwame Ture) and Ekwueme Michael Thelwell, *Ready for Revolution: The Life and Struggles of Stokely Carmichael (Kwame Ture)*

Matthew Countryman, *Up South: Civil Rights and Black Power in Philadelphia*

Michael Honey, *Going Down Jericho Road: The Memphis Strike, Martin Luther King's Last Campaign*

Hasan Kwame Jeffries, *Bloody Lowndes: Civil Rights and Black Power in Alabama's Black Belt*

Peniel Joseph, *The Sword and the Shield: The Revolutionary Lives of Martin Luther King, Jr. and Malcolm X*

Martin Luther King Jr., *Where Do We Go from Here: Chaos or Community?*

Hampton Sides, *Hellhound on His Trail: The Electrifying Account of the Largest Manhunt in American History*

GENERAL

Julian Bond and Andrew Lewis, *Gonna Sit at the Welcome Table*

Clayborne Carson, *The Eyes on the Prize Civil Rights Reader: Documents, Speeches, and Firsthand Accounts from the Black Freedom Struggle, 1954–1990*

Henry Hampton, *Voices of Freedom: An Oral History of the Civil Rights Movement from the 1950s Through the 1980s*

NOTES

FOREWORD

1. Cynthia Bond, "The UVA Class the White Supremacists Didn't Take," *Village Voice*, August 22, 2017.

2. Email from David Koppelman (May 6, 2019).

3. Email from Angela Dorn (May 29, 2019).

4. Email from Daniel Gutman (May 10, 2019).

5. Phyllis Leffler, *Black Leaders on Leadership: Conversations with Julian Bond* (New York: Palgrave Macmillan, 2014), 184.

6. John F. Kennedy Presidential Library and Museum, Papers of JFK, Presidential Recordings, audiotape 112.6 (September 23, 1963).

7. Julian Bond, "SNCC: What We Did," *Monthly Review*, October 1, 2000.

8. Bond v. Floyd, 385 U.S. 116 (1966).

9. Danny Lyon, *Memories of the Southern Civil Rights Movement*, foreword by Julian Bond (Chapel Hill: University of North Carolina Press, 1992), 5.

10. Leffler, *Black Leaders on Leadership*, 184.

INTRODUCTION: WHAT JULIAN BOND TAUGHT ME

1. Jenny Jarvie, "An Uneasy Standoff Between Police and Protesters as Black Lives Matter Returns to the Streets," *Los Angeles Times*, July 9, 2016.

2. Barbara Reynolds, "I Was a Civil Rights Activist in the 1960s. But It's Hard for Me to Get Behind Black Lives Matter," *Washington Post*, August 24, 2015.

3. Charlie Cobb, *This Nonviolent Stuff'll Get You Killed: How Guns Made the Civil Rights Movement* (New York: Basic Books, 2014), 247.

4. As quoted in Charles Payne, "Introduction to the 2007 Edition," *I've Got the Light of Freedom: The Organizing Tradition and the Mississippi Freedom Struggle* (Berkeley: University of California Press, 2007), viii-ix.

5. Julian Bond, *Race Man: Selected Works, 1960–2015*, ed. Michael Long (San Francisco: City Lights Books, 2020), 3.

6. Data from the Roper Center for Public Research, quoted in Elahe Izadi, "Black Lives Matter and America's Long History of Resisting Civil Rights Protest," *Washington Post*, April 19, 2016.

7. Izadi, "Black Lives Matter and America's Long History of Resisting Civil Rights Protest."

8. Sheldon Appleton, "Martin Luther King in Life . . . and Memory," *Public Perspective* (February–March 1995): 12.

9. Fred Powledge, "Polls Show Whites in City Resent Civil Rights Protest," *New York Times*, September 21, 1964.

10. "Dr. King's Error," editorial, *New York Times*, April 7, 1967.

11. Jeanne Theoharis, *The Rebellious Life of Mrs. Rosa Parks* (Boston: Beacon Press, 2013).

12. Julian Bond, author phone interview (November 15, 2010).

CHAPTER ONE: WHITE SUPREMACY AND THE FOUNDING OF THE NAACP

1. Martin Luther King Jr., quoted in R. C. Smith, *Racism in the Post–Civil Rights Era: Now You See It, Now You Don't* (Albany: State University of New York Press, 1995).

2. W. E. B. Du Bois, "The Niagara Movement," *Voice of the Negro*, September 1905, 619–22.

3. John W. Cell, "Race Relations," in *Encyclopedia of Southern Culture*, ed. Charles Reagan Wilson and William Ferris (Chapel Hill: University of North Carolina Press, 1989), 189.

4. Charles Carroll, *The Negro a Beast, or, In the Image of God?* (St. Louis: American Book and Bible House, 1900); Robert Wilson Shufeldt, *The Negro: A Menace to American Civilization* (Boston: R. G. Badger, 1907).

5. Eric Foner lays out the Dunning School argument and the profound changes in the ways Reconstruction is now understood in "Reconstruction Revisited," *Reviews in American History* 10, no. 4 (1982).

6. *Report of the United States Commission on Civil Rights, 1959*, https://www2.law .umaryland.edu/marshall/usccr/documents/cr11959.pdf.

7. C. Vann Woodward, *The Strange Career of Jim Crow* (New York: Oxford University Press, 1955); Leon Litwack, *North of Slavery: The Negro in the Free States, 1790–1860* (Chicago: University of Chicago Press, 1961); Richard Wade, *Slavery in the Cities: The South, 1820–1860* (New York: Oxford University Press, 1964); Joel Williamson, *After Slavery: The Negro in South Carolina During Reconstruction, 1861–1877* (Chapel Hill: University of North Carolina Press, 1965).

8. John Hope Franklin, *From Slavery to Freedom: A History of African Americans* (New York: Alfred A. Knopf, 1969).

9. W. E. B. DuBois, *The Souls of Black Folk: Essays and Sketches* (Chicago: A. C. McClurg, 1903).

10. Peter Lau, *Democracy Rising: South Carolina and the Fight for Black Equality Since 1865* (Lexington: University of Kentucky Press, 2006), 3.

11. Franklin, *From Slavery to Freedom*, 311.

12. Ida B. Wells's *Red Record* documented this sordid history of lynching.

13. Quoted in Gunnar Myrdal, *An American Dilemma: The Negro Problem and Modern Democracy*, vol. 2 (New Brunswick, NJ: Transaction Publishers, 1996), 819.

14. Du Bois, *The Souls of Black Folk*, 50.

15. See David Levering Lewis, *W. E. B. Du Bois: A Biography, 1868–1963* (New York: Holt, 2009).

CHAPTER TWO: ORIGINS OF THE CIVIL RIGHTS MOVEMENT

1. Harvard Sitkoff, *A New Deal for Blacks: The Emergence of Civil Rights as a National Issue: The Depression Decade* (Oxford, UK: Oxford University Press, 1978), 6.

2. Philip Dray, *Capitol Men: The Epic Story of Reconstruction Through the Lives of the First Black Congressmen* (New York: Houghton Mifflin, 2008); Philip Dray, "NAACP's Hundred Year Fight Against Hate," *New York Post*, February 15, 2009.

3. "Imperial Wizard," *Time*, June 23, 1924.

4. See Patricia Sullivan, *Lift Every Voice: The NAACP and the Making of the Civil Rights Movement* (New York: New Press, 2009).

5. Amy Jacques-Garvey, ed., *The Philosophy and Opinions of Marcus Garvey, or Africa for the Africans* (New York: Universal Publishing House, 1925), 38–39.

6. W. E. B. Du Bois, "A Lunatic or a Traitor," *Crisis*, May 1924, 8.

7. Quoted in John Hope Franklin and August Meier, eds., *Black Leaders of the Twentieth Century* (Chicago: University of Illinois Press, 1982), 134.

8. Quoted in Tony Martin, *Race First: The Ideological and Organizational Struggles of Marcus Garvey and the Universal Negro Improvement Association* (Dover, MA: Majority Press, 1976), 23.

9. Franklin, *From Slavery to Freedom*, 360.

10. Sitkoff, *A New Deal for Blacks*; Ta-Nehisi Coates, "The Case for Reparations," *Atlantic*, June 2014.

11. Sitkoff, *A New Deal for Blacks*, 332.

CHAPTER THREE: WORLD WAR II

1. Manning Marable, *Race, Reform, and Rebellion: The Second Reconstruction and Beyond in Black America, 1945–2006*, 3rd ed. (Jackson: University Press of Mississippi, 2007), 20.

2. Quoted in Franklin and Meier, *Black Leaders of the Twentieth Century*, 155.

3. Franklin and Meier, *Black Leaders of the Twentieth Century*, 155.

4. Franklin D. Roosevelt, Executive Order 8802, June 25, 1941, US Equal Employment Opportunity Commission, https://www.eeoc.gov/eeoc/history/35th/thelaw/eo-8802.html.

5. William J. Collins, "African-American Economic Mobility in the 1940s: A Portrait from the Palmer Survey," *Journal of Economic History* 60, no. 3 (2000): 756–81, Mary S. Bedell, "Employment and Income of Negro Workers—1940–1952," *Monthly Labor Review* (June 1953).

6. Quoted in Martha Biondi, *To Stand and Fight: The Struggle for Civil Rights in Postwar New York City* (Cambridge, MA: Harvard University Press, 2003), 16.

7. Quoted in Myrdal, *An American Dilemma*, 1016, 1017.

8. Myrdal, *An American Dilemma*, 1016.

9. Ronald Takaki, *Double Victory: A Multicultural History of America in World War II* (New York: Little, Brown, 2000).

CHAPTER FOUR: PRESIDENT TRUMAN AND THE ROAD TO BROWN

1. Harry S. Truman, "Special Message to the Congress on Greece and Turkey: The Truman Doctrine," March 12, 1947, Harry S. Truman Library and Museum, https://www.trumanlibrary.gov/library/public-papers/56/special-message-congress-greece-and-turkey-truman-doctrine.

2. Interviewed in 2014 about Woodard, Julian Bond broke into tears, saying, "I still weep for this blinded soldier." Richard Gergel, *Unexampled Courage: The Blinding of Sgt. Isaac Woodard and the Awakening of President Harry S. Truman and Judge J. Waties Waring* (New York: Farrar, Straus and Giroux, 2019), 5–6.

3. Kevin M. Schultz, "The FEPC and the Legacy of the Labor-Based Civil Rights Movement of the 1940s," *Labor History* 49, no. 1 (2008): 71–92; Sullivan, *Lift Every Voice.*

4. Quoted in Philip A. Klinkner with Roger M. Smith, *The Unsteady March: The Rise and Decline of Racial Equality in America* (Chicago: University of Chicago Press, 1999), 209.

5. Harry S. Truman, *To Secure These Rights: The Report of the President's Committee on Civil Rights*, 1946, https://www.trumanlibrary.gov/library/to-secure-these-rights.

6. Quoted in Donald R. McCoy and Richard T. Ruetten, *Quest and Response: Minority Rights and the Truman Administration* (Lawrence: University Press of Kansas, 1973), 99.

7. Quoted in Nadine Cohodas, *Strom Thurmond & the Politics of Southern Change* (Macon, GA: Mercer University Press, 1993), 166; Hubert Horatio Humphrey, *Beyond Civil Rights: A New Day of Equality* (New York: Random House, 1968), 37.

8. Harry S. Truman, "Executive Order 9980," July 26, 1948, Harry S. Truman Library and Museum, https://www.trumanlibrary.gov/library/executive-orders/9980/executive-order-9980.

9. Quoted in Terry H. Anderson, *The Pursuit of Fairness: A History of Affirmative Action* (New York: Oxford University Press, 2004), 43.

10. Quoted in Richard Kirkendall, "The Presidential Election of 1948," in Robert D. Marcus and David Burner, eds., *The American Scene: Varieties of American History*, vol. 2 (New York: Appleton-Century-Crofts, 1971), 420.

11. Harry S. Truman, *Public Papers of the Presidents of the United States: Harry S. Truman: Containing the Public Messages, Speeches, and Statements of the President, January 1 to December 31, 1948* (Washington, DC: National Archives and Record Services, 1961–1966), 850–52.

12. Truman, *Public Papers of the Presidents of the United States*, 925.

CHAPTER FIVE: *BROWN V. BOARD OF EDUCATION*
1. Derrick Bell, *Silent Covenants:* Brown v. Board of Education *and the Unfulfilled Hopes for Racial Reform* (New York: Oxford University Press, 2004).

2. For more on *Brown*, see Julian Bond, "With All Deliberate Speed: *Brown v. Board of Education*," *Indiana Law Journal* 90, no. 4 (2015).

3. Slaughter House Cases, 16 Wall. 36, 67–72 (1873); Strauder v. West Virginia, 100 U.S. 303, 307–8 (1880).

4. Plessy v. Ferguson, 163 U.S. 537 (1896).

5. Brown v. Board of Education, 347 U.S. at 489.

6. Alfred H. Kelley, "An Inside View of *Brown v. Board of Education*," reprinted in *Congressional Record* 108 (September 11, 1962), 19025–28.

7. Quoted in Jack M. Bloom, *Class, Race, and the Civil Rights Movement: The Changing Political Economy of Southern Racism* (Bloomington: Indiana University Press, 1987), 126.

8. Thomas P. Brady, *Black Monday* (Association of Citizens Councils, 1955), 89.

9. Earl Warren and Supreme Court of the United States, *U.S. Reports: Brown v. Board of Education*, 347 U.S. 483. Emphasis added.

10. Carol Anderson, *White Rage: The Unspoken Truth of Our Racial Divide* (New York: Bloomsbury, 2016).

11. David S. Cecelski, *Along Freedom Road: Hyde County, North Carolina, and the Fate of Black Schools in the South* (Chapel Hill: University of North Carolina Press, 1994).

12. Green v. New Kent County School Board, 391 U.S. 430, 439 (1967). Emphasis in original.

13. Freeman v. Pitts, 503 U.S. 467 (1992); Board of Education v. Dowell, 498 U.S. 237 (1991).

14. Richard Kluger, *Simple Justice: The History of* Brown v. Board of Education *and Black America's Struggle for Equality* (New York: Alfred A. Knopf, 1975), 748–49.

15. Philip Dray, *At the Hands of Persons Unknown: The Lynching of Black America* (New York: Modern Library, 2003), 426, 430.

16. Sara Bullard, *Free at Last: A History of the Civil Rights Movement and Those Who Died in the Struggle* (New York: Oxford University Press, 1995), 44. See also Mamie Till-Mobley and Christopher Benson, *The Death of Innocence: The Story of the Hate Crime That Changed America* (New York: One World, 2003); and Devery Anderson, *Emmett Till: The Murder That Shocked the World and Propelled the Civil Rights Movement* (Jackson: University of Mississippi Press, 2015).

17. Roy Wilkins and Tom Matthews, *Standing Fast: The Autobiography of Roy Wilkins* (New York: Viking, 1982); Yvonne Ryan, *Roy Wilkins: The Quiet Revolutionary and the NAACP* (Lexington: University Press of Kentucky, 2014).

CHAPTER SIX: THE MONTGOMERY BUS BOYCOTT

1. Aldon D. Morris, *The Origins of the Civil Rights Movement: Black Communities Organizing for Change* (New York: Free Press, 1984), 1.

2. Morris, *The Origins of the Civil Rights Movement*, 1.

3. Morris, *The Origins of the Civil Rights Movement*, 140.

4. Martin Luther King Jr., *The Papers of Martin Luther King, Jr.*, vol. 1: *Called to Serve, January 1929–June 1951*, ed. Clayborne Carson (Berkeley: University of California Press, 1992), 45.

5. King, *The Papers of Martin Luther King, Jr.*, vol. 1, 53.

6. Michael Eric Dyson, *I May Not Get There with You: The True Martin Luther King, Jr.* (New York: Free Press, 2000), 212.

7. Isabel Wilkerson, *The Warmth of Other Suns: The Epic Story of America's Great Migration* (New York: Random House, 2010), 45.

8. Lee Augustus McGriggs, *The Odyssey of Martin Luther King, Jr.* (Lanham, MD: University Press of America, 1978), 24; Jo Ann Gibson Robinson, *The Montgomery Bus Boycott and the Women Who Started it: The Memoir of Jo Ann Gibson Robinson* (Knoxville: University of Tennessee Press, 1987).

9. Robinson, *The Montgomery Bus Boycott and the Women Who Started It*, 36.

10. Frederick Douglass, *Life and Times of Frederick Douglass: His Early Life as a Slave, His Escape from Bondage, and His Complete History to the Present Time, Including His Connection with the Anti-slavery Movement* (London: Park Publishing, 1892), 277.

11. Stetson Kennedy, *Jim Crow Guide to the U.S.A.: The Laws, Customs and Etiquette Governing the Conduct of Nonwhites and Other Minorities as Second-Class Citizens* (1959; repr., Tuscaloosa: University of Alabama Press, 2011); Woodward, *The Strange Career of Jim Crow*, 23.

12. Martin Luther King Jr., *The Autobiography of Martin Luther King, Jr.*, ed. Clayborne Carson (New York: Grand Central Publishing, 2001).

13. Shannon Frystak, *Our Minds on Freedom: Women and the Struggle for Black Equality in Louisiana, 1924–1968* (Baton Rouge: Louisiana State University Press, 2009).

14. Mary Fair Burks, "Trailblazers: Women in the Montgomery Bus Boycott," in *Women in the Civil Rights Movement: Torchbearers & Trailblazers, 1941-1965*, ed. Vicki L. Crawford, Jacqueline Anne Rouse, Barbara Woods, and Broadus Butler (Bloomington: Indiana University Press, 1993).

15. Danielle L. McGuire, *At the Dark End of the Street: Black Women, Rape, and Resistance—a New History of the Civil Rights Movement from Rosa Parks to the Rise of Black Power* (New York: Vintage, 2010).

16. Robinson, *The Montgomery Bus Boycott and the Women Who Started It*, 16.

17. Lewis V. Baldwin and Aprille V. Woodson, *Freedom Is Never Free: A Biographical Portrait of Edgar Daniel Nixon* (Nashville: Office of Minority Affairs, Tennessee General Assembly, 1992), 9.

18. Quoted in Baldwin and Woodson, *Freedom Is Never Free*, 13.

19. Jeanne Theoharis, *The Rebellious Life of Mrs. Rosa Parks* (Boston: Beacon Press, 2013), 56–60.

20. Theoharis, *The Rebellious Life of Mrs. Rosa Parks*, 13. See, also, Rosa Parks with Jim Haskins, *Rosa Parks: My Story* (New York: Dial, 1992).

21. Theoharis, *The Rebellious Life of Mrs. Rosa Parks*, 61.

22. Theoharis, *The Rebellious Life of Mrs. Rosa Parks*, 28.

23. Theoharis, *The Rebellious Life of Mrs. Rosa Parks*, 59.

24. Theoharis, *The Rebellious Life of Mrs. Rosa Parks*, 60–71.

25. Robinson, *The Montgomery Bus Boycott and the Women Who Started It*, 45–46.

26. Robinson, *The Montgomery Bus Boycott and the Women Who Started It*, 50.

27. Robinson, *The Montgomery Bus Boycott and the Women Who Started It*, 46–47.

28. Jon Meacham, ed., *Voices in Our Blood: America's Best on the Civil Rights Movement* (New York: Random House, 2001), 7.

29. Robert Graetz, *A White Preacher's Memoir: The Montgomery Bus Boycott* (Montgomery: Black Belt Press, 1998).

30. Theoharis, *The Rebellious Life of Mrs. Rosa Parks*, 88–89.

31. Donnie Williams with Wayne Greenhaw, *The Thunder of Angels: The Montgomery Bus Boycott and the People Who Broke the Back of Jim Crow* (Chicago: Lawrence Hill, 2006), 60; Baldwin and Watson, *Freedom Is Never Free*, 48.

32. Taylor Branch, *Parting the Waters: America in the King Years, 1954–63* (New York: Simon & Schuster, 2007), 136–37.

33. Branch, *Parting the Waters*, 138.

34. Martin Luther King Jr., "MIA Mass Meeting at Holt Street Baptist Church" (speech), 1955, Martin Luther King, Jr. Research and Education Institute, https://kinginstitute.stanford.edu/king-papers/documents/mia-mass-meeting-holt-street-baptist-church.

35. Theoharis, *The Rebellious Life of Mrs. Rosa Parks*, 102.

36. Ralph Abernathy, *And the Walls Came Tumbling Down: An Autobiography* (New York: Harper & Row, 1989), 154.

37. Stewart Burns, ed., *Daybreak of Freedom: The Montgomery Bus Boycott* (Chapel Hill: University of North Carolina Press, 2012), 98.

38. Martin Luther King Jr., *Stride Toward Freedom: The Montgomery Story* (orig. 1958; New York: Harper & Row, 1986), 112.

39. See Theoharis, *The Rebellious Life of Mrs. Rosa Parks*, ch. 4, for more on the boycott.

40. Burns, *Daybreak of Freedom*, 110.

41. David J. Garrow, *Bearing the Cross: Martin Luther King Jr. and the Southern Christian Leadership Conference* (New York: HarperCollins, 1986), 31.

42. Burns, *Daybreak of Freedom*, 109.

43. For more on the FBI surveillance of the civil rights movement, see Kenneth O'Reilly, *"Racial Matters": The FBI's Secret File on Black America, 1960–1972* (New York: Free Press, 1991).

44. Mills Thornton, *Dividing Lines: Municipal Politics and the Struggle for Civil Rights in Montgomery, Birmingham, and Selma* (Montgomery: University of Alabama, 2002), 598.

45. Branch, *Parting the Waters*, 150; Jack Bass, *Taming the Storm: The Life and Times of Judge Frank M. Johnson, Jr., and the South's Fight over Civil Rights* (Athens: University of Georgia Press, 2002).

46. Peter J. Albert and Ronald Hoffman, eds., *We Shall Overcome: Martin Luther King Jr, and the Black Freedom Struggle* (New York: Da Capo Press, 1993), 17.

47. Martin Luther King Jr., *The Papers of Martin Luther King, Jr.*, vol. 3, *Birth of a New Age, December 1955–December 1956*, ed. Clayborne Carson (Berkeley: University of California Press, 1992), 8.

48. Quoted in Garrow, *Bearing the Cross*, 57–58.

49. Quoted in Branch, *Parting the Waters*, 166.

50. Garrow, *Bearing the Cross*, 61.

51. Frye Gaillard, *Cradle of Freedom: Alabama and the Movement That Changed America* (Tuscaloosa: University of Alabama Press, 2004), 42.

52. Patricia Sullivan, ed., *Freedom Writer: Virginia Foster Durr, Letters from the Civil Rights Years* (Athens: University of Georgia Press, 2006), 109.

53. John D'Emilio, *Lost Prophet: The Life and Times of Bayard Rustin* (New York: Free Press, 2003).

54. Gary Younge, *The Speech: The Story Behind Dr. Martin Luther King Jr.'s Dream* (Chicago: Haymarket, 2013), 28–29.

55. See Charlie Cobb, *This Nonviolent Stuff'll Get You Killed: How Guns Made the Civil Rights Movement Possible* (New York: Basic Books, 2014).

56. Martin Luther King Jr., *The Papers of Martin Luther King, Jr.*, vol. 5, *Threshold of a New Decade, January 1959–December 1960*, ed. Clayborne Carson (Berkeley: University of California Press, 1992), 302.

57. Martin Luther King Jr., "The Social Organization of Nonviolence," *Liberation*, October 1959.

58. Phillip Hoose, *Claudette Colvin: Twice Toward Justice* (New York: Farrar, Straus and Giroux, 2009), 87.

59. Branch, *Parting the Waters*, 195.

60. King, *Papers of Martin Luther King, Jr.*, vol. 3, 482.

61. Theoharis, *The Rebellious Life of Mrs. Rosa Parks*, 134.

62. John Ansbro, *Martin Luther King, Jr.: Nonviolent Strategies and Tactics for Social Change* (New York: Madison Books, 2000), 162.

63. "Rev. Martin Luther King," *Time*, February 18, 1957.

CHAPTER SEVEN: THE 1956 PRESIDENTIAL ELECTION
AND THE 1957 CIVIL RIGHTS ACT

1. Kluger, *Simple Justice*, 749.

2. Brief for the United States as amicus curiae at 6, Brown, 347 U.S. 483.

3. Michael J. Hogan, *A Cross of Iron: Harry S. Truman and the Origins of the National Security State, 1945–1954* (New York: Cambridge University Press, 2000), 255.

4. Women's Armed Services Integration Act of 1947: Hearings Before the Committee on Armed Services, US Senate, 80th Cong., 1st Session, July 2, 9, 15, 1947.

5. Steven F. Lawson, *Black Ballots: Voting Rights in the South, 1944–1969* (New York: Lexington Books, 1999), 149.

6. Lawson, *Black Ballots*, 153.

7. Robert Dallek, *Lone Star Rising: Lyndon Johnson and His Times, 1908–1960* (New York: Oxford University Press, 1991), 352.

8. Dallek, *Lone Star Rising*, 78.

9. Mark Solomon, *The Cry Was Unity: Communists and African Americans, 1917–1936* (Jackson: University Press of Mississippi, 1998), 234.

10. Sitkoff, *A New Deal for Blacks*.

11. Quoting Harold Ickes on Roosevelt, Dallek, *Lone Star Rising*, 161.

12. Dallek, *Lone Star Rising*, 347. Ellipses in original.

13. Dallek, *Lone Star Rising*, 368.

14. Dallek, *Lone Star Rising*.

15. Lawson, *Black Ballots*, 195.

CHAPTER EIGHT: LITTLE ROCK, 1957

1. Daisy Bates, *The Long Shadow of Little Rock: A Memoir* (Fayetteville: University of Arkansas Press, 2007), 6.

2. Bates, *The Long Shadow of Little Rock*.

3. John Jackson, *American Bandstand: Dick Clark and the Making of a Rock 'n' Roll Empire* (New York: Oxford University Press, 1997).

4. Richard Aquila, *That Old-Time Rock and Roll: A Chronicle of an Era, 1954–1963* (Urbana: University of Illinois Press, 2000), 10.

5. Bates, *The Long Shadow of Little Rock*.

6. Jack Greenberg, *"Brown v. Board of Education": Witness to a Landmark Decision* (Northport, NY: Twelve Tables Press, 2004).

7. William R. McIntyre, *School Integration: Fifth Year*, Editorial Research Reports (Washington, DC: CQ Press, 1958), http://library.cqpress.com/cqresearcher/document.php?id=cqresrre1958082700.

CHAPTER NINE: THE SOUTHERN CHRISTIAN LEADERSHIP CONFERENCE

1. Bloom, *Class, Race, and the Civil Rights Movement*.

2. D'Emilio, *Lost Prophet*, 246–48; memo from Bayard Rustin, December 23, 1956, at https://kinginstitute.stanford.edu/king-papers/documents/bayard-rustin-0.

3. Cornel West, *Prophetic Fragments: Illuminations of the Crisis in American Religion and Culture* (Trenton, NJ: Africa World Press, 1993), 4.

4. Barbara Ransby, *Ella Baker and the Black Freedom Movement: A Radical Democratic Vision* (Chapel Hill: University of North Carolina Press, 2003).

5. Much of the Baker biographical material comes from Susan Bernice Youngblood, "Testing the Current: The Formative Years of Ella Jo Baker's Development as an Organizational Leader in the Modern Civil Rights Movement," master's thesis, University of Virginia, August 1989. See also Ransby, *Ella Baker and the Black Freedom Movement*.

6. Dyson, *I May Not Get There with You*, 245.

7. Bass, *Taming the Storm*, 165.

CHAPTER TEN: THE SIT-INS AND THE FOUNDING OF SNCC

1. Quoted in William H. Chafe, *The Unfinished Journey: America Since World War II* (New York: Oxford University Press, 1991), 166.

2. William H. Chafe, *Civilities and Civil Rights: Greensboro, North Carolina, and the Black Struggle for Freedom* (New York: Oxford University Press, 1980), 83.

3. Quoted in Pat Watters, *Down to Now: Reflections on the Southern Civil Rights Movement* (1971; repr., Athens: University of Georgia Press, 1993), 74.

4. Chafe, *Civilities and Civil Rights*, 84.

5. Chafe, *Civilities and Civil Rights*, 80–86.

6. Unpublished article written by Charlie Cobb with letter to David Llorens, assistant editor, *Negro Digest*, June 16, 1966, quoting Stokely Carmichael.

7. Harvard Sitkoff, *The Struggle for Black Equality, 1954–1980* (New York: Hill and Wang, 1988), 89.

CHAPTER ELEVEN: THE STUDENT NONVIOLENT COORDINATING COMMITTEE

1. Clayborne Carson, *In Struggle: SNCC and the Black Awakening of the 1960s* (Cambridge, MA: Harvard University Press, 1981), 24.

2. Carson, *In Struggle*, 21.

3. Wesley Hogan, *Many Minds, One Heart: SNCC's Dream for a New America* (Chapel Hill: University of North Carolina Press, 2013), 19; Carson, *In Struggle*, 21.

4. John Lewis with Michael D'Orso, *Walking with the Wind: A Memoir of the Movement* (New York: Simon and Schuster, 1998), 61.

5. Carson, *In Struggle*, 23.

6. Clayborne Carson, "Toward Freedom and Community: The Evolution of Ideas in the Student Nonviolent Coordinating Committee, 1960–1966," PhD diss., University of California, Los Angeles, 1975, 62.

7. Sitkoff, *The Struggle for Black Equality*, 83.

8. Sitkoff, *The Struggle for Black Equality*.

9. Quoted in introduction to Elizabeth Sutherland Martinez, ed., *Letters from Mississippi: Reports from Civil Rights Volunteers and Freedom School Poetry of the 1964 Freedom Summer* (Brookline, MA: Zephyr Press, 2002), xi, vi. Brackets in original.

10. Quoted in Carson, *In Struggle*, 24.

11. Charles Payne, *I've Got The Light of Freedom: The Organizing Tradition and the Mississippi Freedom Struggle* (Berkeley: University of California Press, 1995), 104–7; John Dittmer, *Local People: The Struggle for Civil Rights in Mississippi* (Urbana: University of Illinois Press, 1995), 101–3.

12. Carson, *Toward Freedom and Community*, 85.

13. Statement submitted by SNCC to Platform Committee of National Democratic Convention, Los Angeles, California, July 7, 1960.

14. Quoted in Carson, *In Struggle*, 27.

15. Carson, *In Struggle*, 27, 28.

16. Quoted in Carson, *In Struggle*.

17. David Garrow, ed., *Martin Luther King, Jr. and the Civil Rights Movement*, vol. 9, *Atlanta, Georgia, 1960–1961: Sit-Ins and Student Activism* (Brooklyn, NY: Carlson Publishers, 1989), 130.

18. "An Appeal for Human Rights," *Atlanta Daily World*, *Atlanta Constitution*, and *Atlanta Journal*, March 9, 1960.

19. Herman Mason, *Politics, Civil Rights, and Law in Black Atlanta, 1870–1970* (Charleston, SC: Arcadia, 2000), 6.

20. Bloom, *Class, Race, and the Civil Rights Movement*, 223.

21. Branch, *Parting the Waters*, 350.

22. Branch, *Parting the Waters*, 351.

23. Branch, *Parting the Waters*, 353–56.

24. Branch, *Parting the Waters*, 359–60.

25. Quoted in Branch, *Parting the Waters*, 361.

26. Branch, *Parting the Waters*, 362.

27. Branch, *Parting the Waters*, 365.

28. Branch, *Parting the Waters*, 366.

29. Branch, *Parting the Waters*, 367.

30. Branch, *Parting the Waters*, 368–70.

31. *Congressional Record: Proceedings and Debates of the 89th Cong., 2nd Sess.* (Washington, DC: US Government Printing Office, October 10, 1966), 25956.

32. Winston A. Grady-Willis, *Challenging U.S. Apartheid: Atlanta and Black Struggles for Human Rights, 1960–1977* (Durham, NC: Duke University Press, 2006), 7.

33. Grady-Willis, *Challenging U.S. Apartheid*, 26.

34. Gayraud S. Wilmore, *Black Religion and Black Radicalism: An Interpretation of the Religious History of African Americans* (Maryknoll, NY: Orbis Books, 1998).

35. Howard Zinn, *SNCC: The New Abolitionists* (Boston: Beacon Press, 1964), 17–18.

36. Carson, *In Struggle*, 33.

CHAPTER TWELVE: THE FREEDOM RIDES

1. Raymond Arsenault, *Freedom Riders: 1961 and the Struggle for Racial Justice* (New York: Oxford University Press, 2007), 13.

2. Arsenault, *Freedom Riders*, 11–12.

3. James Farmer, *Lay Bare the Heart: An Autobiography of the Civil Rights Movement* (Fort Worth: Texas Christian University Press, 1998), 195.

4. Lewis and D'Orso, *Walking with the Wind*, 137–38.

5. Farmer, *Lay Bare the Heart.*

6. Arsenault, *Freedom Riders*, 101.

7. Branch, *Parting the Waters*, 419.

8. King, *The Autobiography of Martin Luther King, Jr.*

9. Quoted in Branch, *Parting the Waters*, 425.

10. Branch, *Parting the Waters*, 429.

11. Quoted in Branch, *Parting the Waters*, 430.

12. Arsenault, *Freedom Riders*, 145.

13. Branch, *Parting the Waters*, 447.

14. Branch, *Parting the Waters*, 450.

15. In 1962, Kennedy appointed White to the Supreme Court.

16. Hogan, *Many Minds, One Heart*, 49.

17. Farmer, *Lay Bare the Heart.*

18. Farmer, *Lay Bare the Heart*, 3.

19. Quoted in Philip A. Goduti, *Robert F. Kennedy and the Shaping of Civil Rights, 1960–1964* (Jefferson, NC: McFarland, 2012), 93.

20. Quoted in Derek Catsam, *Freedom's Main Line: The Journey of Reconciliation and the Freedom Rides* (Lexington: University Press of Kentucky, 2009), 266.

21. Eric Foner, "Bound for Glory," review of Arsenault's *Freedom Riders*, *New York Times*, March 19, 2006.

22. Quoted in L. D. Ervin, *Step by Step: The Reverend Fred L. Shuttlesworth* (Paducah, KY: Turner Publishing, 1999), 81–82.

23. Quoted in Cynthia Griggs Fleming, *Soon We Will Not Cry: The Liberation of Ruby Doris Smith Robinson* (New York: Rowman & Littlefield, 2000), 87. First brackets in original.

24. Leslie W. Dunbar, "The Southern Regional Council," *Annals of the American Academy of Political and Social Science* 357, no. 1 (January 1965): 108–12.

25. When Rowe's picture appeared in the *Birmingham Post Herald*, his FBI handlers instructed him to deny the photo showed him. Four years later, on March 25, 1965, he was one of four Klansmen who followed and then shot Viola Liuzzo—although Rowe testified later he did not fire a shot.

CHAPTER THIRTEEN: KENNEDY AND CIVIL RIGHTS, 1961

1. *Platforms of the Democratic Party and the Republican Party* (Washington, DC: US Government Printing Office, 1960), 45.

2. Hal Bochin, *Richard Nixon: Rhetorical Strategist* (New York: Greenwood Press, 1990), 51.

3. Virginia Foster Durr, *Outside the Magic Circle: The Autobiography of Virginia Foster Durr* (Tuscaloosa: University of Alabama Press, 1985), 177–79.

4. Carson, *In Struggle*, 38–39.

5. Carson, *In Struggle*, 40.

6. Carson, *In Struggle*, 41.

7. Carson, *In Struggle*, 41.

8. Sitkoff, *The Struggle for Black Equality*, 106.

9. Quoted in Grace Jordan McFadden, "Septima P. Clark and the Struggle for Human Rights," in Crawford, Rouse, and Woods, *Women in the Civil Rights Movement*,

85–86. See, also, Katherine Mellen Charron, *Freedom's Teacher: The Life of Septima Clark* (Chapel Hill: University of North Carolina Press, 2009).

10. Quoted in McFadden, "Septima P. Clark and the Struggle for Human Rights," 87.

11. McFadden, "Septima P. Clark and the Struggle for Human Rights."

12. Payne, *I've Got the Light of Freedom*, 72–73.

13. Sandra B. Oldendorf, "The South Carolina Sea Island Citizenship Schools, 1957–1961," in Crawford, Rouse, and Woods, *Women in the Civil Rights Movement*, 172.

14. Oldendorf, "The South Carolina Sea Island Citizenship Schools," 174.

15. Branch, *Parting the Waters*, 575.

16. "Dave Dennis," SNCC Digital Legacy Project, https://snccdigital.org/people /dave-dennis.

17. Payne, *I've Got the Light of Freedom*, 116–17.

18. Payne, *I've Got the Light of Freedom*, 120.

19. Michael Newton, *The Ku Klux Klan in Mississippi: A History* (Jefferson, NC: McFarland, 2009), 134.

20. Dittmer, *Local People*, 219.

21. Quoted in Zinn, *SNCC*, 76.

22. Carson, *In Struggle*, 52.

CHAPTER FOURTEEN: ALBANY, GEORGIA, 1961

1. Quoted in Gene Roberts and Hank Klibanoff, *The Race Beat: The Press, the Civil Rights Struggle, and the Awakening of a Nation* (New York: Knopf Doubleday, 2008), 198.

2. Fred Powledge, *Free at Last? The Civil Rights Movement and the People Who Made It* (New York: Little Brown, 1991), 411–13.

3. Branch, *Parting the Waters*, 536.

4. Lynne Olson, *Freedom's Daughters: The Unsung Heroines of the Civil Rights Movement from 1830 to 1970* (New York: Scribner, 2001), 212.

5. Belinda Robnett, *How Long? How Long? African-American Women in the Struggle for Civil Rights* (New York: Oxford University Press, 1997), 107.

6. Branch, *Parting the Waters*, 604.

7. William Moses Kunstler, *Deep in My Heart* (New York: Morrow, 1966), 103.

8. Morris, *The Origins of the Civil Rights Movement*, 248.

9. Pam McAllister, *Reweaving the Web of Life: Feminism and Nonviolence* (Philadelphia: New Society Publishers, 1982), 121.

10. Olson, *Freedom's Daughters*, 240.

11. Howard Zinn, *The Southern Mystique* (Cambridge, MA: South End Press, 2002), 188.

12. David L. Chappell, *Inside Agitators: White Southerners in the Civil Rights Movement* (Baltimore: Johns Hopkins University Press, 1996), 136.

13. Branch, *Parting the Waters*, 624.

14. James Forman, *The Making of Black Revolutionaries* (orig. 1972; repr. Washington: Open Hand, 1985), 247.

15. Julian Bond did a whole lecture on music; this is just a few paragraphs from it. He thought it was essential to understand the centrality of music to the struggle and wanted students, in the midst of the difficult subjects the class was covering, to experience the uplifting power of movement song. He played "Dog, Dog," "Oh Pritchett, Oh Kelley,"

"This Little Light of Mine," "If You Miss Me from the Back of the Bus," "I'm Gonna Sit at the Welcome Table," "We Shall Overcome," "Governor Wallace," and a movement reinterpretation of "Go Tell It on the Mountain," providing commentary on all the songs.

16. "Rights Song Has Own History of Integration," *New York Times*, July 23, 1963.

CHAPTER FIFTEEN: MISSISSIPPI VOTER REGISTRATION
1. Carson, *In Struggle*, 77.
2. Quoted in Carson, *In Struggle*. Brackets and ellipses in original.
3. James Hilty, *Robert Kennedy: Brother Protector* (Philadelphia: Temple University Press, 1997), 331.
4. Quoted in Leonard Harris, ed., *Key Concepts in Critical Theory: Racism* (Amherst, NY: Humanity Books, 1999), 438.
5. Quoted in Kay Mills, *This Little Light of Mine: The Life of Fannie Lou Hamer* (Lexington: University Press of Kentucky, 2007), 31.
6. Mills, *This Little Light of Mine*, 32. See, also, Chana Kai Lee, *For Freedom's Sake: The Life of Fannie Lou Hamer* (Urbana: University of Illinois Press, 1999).
7. Mills, *This Little Light of Mine*, 23–24.
8. Mills, *This Little Light of Mine*, 8.
9. Mills, *This Little Light of Mine*, 11.
10. Mills, *This Little Light of Mine*, 11–12.
11. Mills, *This Little Light of Mine*, 14–15. Brackets and emphasis in original.
12. Mills, *This Little Light of Mine*, 15.
13. Mills, *This Little Light of Mine*, 22.
14. Mills, *This Little Light of Mine*, 24.
15. Mills, *This Little Light of Mine*, 24.
16. Mills, *This Little Light of Mine*, 36.
17. Mills, *This Little Light of Mine*, 36–37. Ellipses in original.
18. Mills, *This Little Light of Mine*, 37.
19. Mills, *This Little Light of Mine*, 38.
20. Mills, *This Little Light of Mine*, 42.
21. "Hartman Turnbow," SNCC Digital Gateway, https://snccdigital.org/people/hartman-turnbow.
22. Branch, *Parting the Waters*, 638–39.
23. Quoted in Eric Burner, *And Gently He Shall Lead Them: Robert Parris Moses and Civil Rights in Mississippi* (New York: New York University Press, 1995), 84.

CHAPTER SIXTEEN: BIRMINGHAM
1. Quoted in Adam Fairclough, *To Redeem the Soul of America: The Southern Christian Leadership Conference and Martin Luther King, Jr.* (Athens: University of Georgia Press, 2001), 112.
2. Diane McWhorter, *Carry Me Home: Birmingham, Alabama: The Climactic Battle of the Civil Rights Revolution* (New York: Simon and Schuster, 2001), 150.
3. Andrew Manis, *A Fire You Can't Put Out: The Civil Rights Life of Birmingham's Reverend Fred Shuttlesworth* (Tuscaloosa: University of Alabama Press, 2001), 332.
4. Glenn Eskew, *But for Birmingham: The Local and National Movements in the Civil Rights Struggle* (Chapel Hill: University of North Carolina Press, 2000).

5. King's "Letter from Birmingham Jail" was published partially in the *New York Post Magazine*, May 19, 1963, and in full in *New Leader*, June 24, 1963.

6. Branch, *Parting the Waters*, 714.

7. Branch, *Parting the Waters*, 718.

8. Branch, *Parting the Waters*, 720.

9. Peter Guralnick, *Dream Boogie: The Triumph of Sam Cooke* (New York: Little, Brown, 2014); "Dick Gregory," SNCC Digital Gateway, https://snccdigital.org/people/dick-gregory.

10. Branch, *Parting the Waters*, 528.

11. Branch, *Parting the Waters*, 868.

12. Branch, *Parting the Waters*, 758.

13. David J. Garrow, *Protest at Selma: Martin Luther King, Jr., and the Voting Rights Act of 1965* (New Haven, CT: Yale University Press, 1978).

14. Juan Williams, *Eyes on the Prize: America's Civil Rights Years, 1954–1965* (New York: Penguin Books, 1988), 190.

15. Branch, *Parting the Waters*, 762.

16. Branch, *Parting the Waters*, 763.

17. Branch, *Parting the Waters*, 788–89; McWhorter, *Carry Me Home*, 419–20.

18. Tom Hayden, *The Long Sixties: From 1960 to Barack Obama* (New York: Routledge, 2016), 28.

19. Garrow, *Bearing the Cross*, 267.

20. Branch, *Parting the Waters*, 807.

21. John F. Kennedy, "Radio and Television Report to the American People on Civil Rights, June 11, 1963," full address available at https://www.jfklibrary.org/archives/other-resources/john-f-kennedy-speeches/civil-rights-radio-and-television-report-19630611.

CHAPTER SEVENTEEN: MISSISSIPPI, MEDGAR EVERS,
AND THE CIVIL RIGHTS BILL

1. Branch, *Parting the Waters*, 818.

2. Mills, *This Little Light of Mine*, 60.

3. Bettye Collier-Thomas and V. P. Franklin, eds., *Sisters in the Struggle: African American Women in the Civil Rights–Black Power Movement* (New York: New York University Press, 2001), 151.

4. She would become Eleanor Holmes Norton, a DC delegate to the US House of Representatives.

5. Quoted in Richard Lentz, *Symbols, the News Magazines and Martin Luther King* (Baton Rouge: Louisiana State University Press, 1999), 101.

6. Robert D. Loevy, *To End All Segregation: The Politics of the Passage of the Civil Rights Act of 1964* (Lanham, MD: University Press of America, 1990), 16.

7. Adam Fairclough, *Better Day Coming: Blacks and Equality, 1890–2000* (New York: Viking Press, 2001).

8. Quoted in Sitkoff, *The Struggle for Black Equality*, 156.

9. Mildred A. Schwartz, *Trends in White Attitudes Toward Negroes* (Chicago: National Opinion Research Center, University of Chicago,1967), https://www.norc.org/PDFs/publications/NORCRpt_119.pdf.

10. Jeanne Theoharis, *A More Beautiful and Terrible History: The Uses and Misuses of Civil Rights History* (Boston: Beacon Press, 2018), 46–47.

11. Federal Fair Employment Practices Act (Washington, DC: US Government Printing Office, 1949). Emphasis added.

12. This and other information about the congressional debate and presidential strategy on the Civil Rights Bill of 1963 is drawn largely from Hugh Davis Graham, *The Civil Rights Era: Origins and Development of National Policy, 1960–1972* (New York: Oxford University Press, 1990).

CHAPTER EIGHTEEN: THE MARCH ON WASHINGTON

1. D'Emilio, *Lost Prophet*, 328.

2. Garrow, *Bearing the Cross*, 271.

3. Quoted in Jervis Anderson, *Bayard Rustin: Troubles I've Seen* (New York: Harper Collins, 1997), 15.

4. Quoted in Garrow, *Bearing the Cross*, 272.

5. Much of the following information comes from Kenneth O'Reilly, *"Racial Matters": The FBI's Secret File on Black America, 1960–1972* (New York: Free Press, 1989); Athan Theoharis and John Stuart Cox, *The Boss: J. Edgar Hoover and the Great American Inquisition* (New York: Bantam Books, 1990); and David Garrow, *The FBI and Martin Luther King, Jr.: From "Solo" to Memphis* (New York: Penguin Books, 1983).

6. Garrow, *The FBI and Martin Luther King, Jr.*

7. Quoted in Branch, *Parting the Waters*, 845.

8. Branch, *Parting the Waters*, 845. Emphasis in original.

9. Athan Theoharis, ed., *The FBI: A Comprehensive Reference Guide* (Phoenix: Oryx Press, 1999), 135–36, 335.

10. O'Reilly, *"Racial Matters,"* 13.

11. O'Reilly, *"Racial Matters,"* 19.

12. O'Reilly, *"Racial Matters,"* 20.

13. O'Reilly, *"Racial Matters,"* 20.

14. Garrow, *The FBI and Martin Luther King, Jr.*

15. Garrow, *The FBI and Martin Luther King, Jr.*

16. FBI jargon referred to wiretaps as "a confidential source who has furnished reliable information in the past"; internal FBI documents called wiretaps "technical surveillance." Break-ins were called "black bag jobs."

17. O'Reilly, *"Racial Matters,"* 130.

18. Garrow, *Bearing the Cross*, 280.

19. Lewis and D'Orso, *Walking with the Wind*, 219–21.

20. Theoharis, *A More Beautiful and Terrible History*, 166–67.

21. Theoharis, *A More Beautiful and Terrible History*, 168.

22. Malcolm X, "Message to the Grassroots," speech, Detroit, December 10, 1963, *BlackPast*, https://www.blackpast.org/african-american-history/speeches-african-american-history/1963-malcolm-x-message-grassroots.

23. Younge, *The Speech*, 74–75.

24. Nick Bryant, *The Bystander: John F. Kennedy and the Struggle for Black Equality* (New York: Basic Books, 2006).

25. Garrow, *Bearing the Cross*, 287.

26. James Baldwin, *No Name in the Street* (orig., 1972; New York: Knopf, 2013), 140.

27. Sara Evans, *Personal Politics: The Roots of Women's Liberation in the Civil Rights Movement and the New Left* (New York: Vintage, 1979), 41.

28. Lance Hill, *The Deacons for Defense: Armed Resistance and the Civil Rights Movement* (Chapel Hill: University of North Carolina Press, 2006).

29. Danny Lyon captured that moment in the photo that graces this book's cover.

30. Garrow, *Bearing the Cross*, 307.

CHAPTER NINETEEN: THE CIVIL RIGHTS ACT

1. Lyndon Baines Johnson, *The Vantage Point: Perspectives of the Presidency, 1963–69* (New York: Holt, Rinehart, and Winston, 1971), 156.

2. Johnson, *The Vantage Point*, 29.

3. Johnson, *The Vantage Point*, 34.

4. Johnson, *The Vantage Point*, 37.

5. Johnson, *The Vantage Point*, 37.

6. Johnson, *The Vantage Point*, 38.

7. Barbara Jordan and Elspeth D. Rostow, eds., *The Great Society: A Twenty-Year Critique* (Austin: University of Texas Press, 1986), 78.

8. Jordan and Rostow, *The Great Society*, 158.

9. Jordan and Rostow, *The Great Society*, 158.

10. Jordan and Rostow, *The Great Society*, 158.

11. Jordan and Rostow, *The Great Society*, 159–60.

12. Jordan and Rostow, *The Great Society*, 79.

13. Charles Whalen and Barbara Whalen, *The Longest Debate: A Legislative History of the 1964 Civil Rights Act* (Cabin John, MD: Seven Locks Press, 1985), 116.

14. Whalen and Whalen, *The Longest Debate*, 117.

CHAPTER TWENTY: MISSISSIPPI FREEDOM SUMMER, 1964

1. Carson, *In Struggle*, 99–100; Hogan, *Many Minds, One Heart*, 149–54.

2. Burner, *And Gently He Shall Lead Them*, 152.

3. Michael Ezra, *Civil Rights Movement: People and Perspectives* (Santa Barbara, CA: ABC-CLIO, 2009), 28.

4. Frank would later be elected to Congress from Massachusetts in 1980.

5. Peter Levy, *The Civil Rights Movement in America: From Black Nationalism to the Women's Political Council* (Santa Barbara, CA: ABC-CLIO, 2015), 317.

6. Julian Bond laid out these figures in his June 28, 2014, address at the fiftieth anniversary of Freedom Summer in Jackson, Mississippi. For the full speech, go to https://www.crmvet.org/comm/bond14.htm.

7. See Crmvet.org, https://www.crmvet.org/comm/bond14.htm.

8. Burner, *And Gently He Shall Lead Them*, 158.

9. Burner, *And Gently He Shall Lead Them*, 157.

10. Doug McAdam, *Freedom Summer* (New York: Oxford University Press, 1990), 83.

11. Susie Erenrich, ed., *Freedom Is a Constant Struggle: An Anthology of the Mississippi Civil Rights Movement* (Montgomery, AL: Black Belt Press, 1999), 82.

CHAPTER TWENTY-ONE: SELMA, ALABAMA, AND THE 1965 VOTING RIGHTS ACT

1. J. L. Chestnut Jr. and Julia Cass, *Black in Selma: The Uncommon Life of J. L. Chestnut, Jr.* (New York: Farrar, Straus and Giroux, 1990), 148.

2. Bloom, *Class, Race, and the Civil Rights Movement*.

3. Forman, *The Making of Black Revolutionaries*, 348–49.

4. David Garrow, *Protest at Selma: Martin Luther King, Jr., and the Voting Rights Act of 1965* (New Haven, CT: Yale University Press, 2015).

5. Dittmer, *Local People*, 292–96.

6. Dittmer, *Local People*, 289.

7. Mills, *This Little Light of Mine*, 5.

8. Mills, *This Little Light of Mine*, 300.

9. Mills, *This Little Light of Mine*, 299.

10. Steven Lawson, *In Pursuit of Power: Southern Blacks and Electoral Politics, 1965–1982* (New York: Columbia University Press, 1985), 94.

11. Frank Parker, *Black Votes Count: Political Empowerment in Mississippi After 1965* (Chapel Hill: University of North Carolina Press, 1990), 71–72.

12. John Dittmer, *The Good Doctors: The Medical Committee for Human Rights and the Struggle for Social Justice in Health Care* (New York: Bloomsbury Press, 2009), x–xi.

13. Hugh Davis Graham, *The Civil Rights Era: Origins and Development of National Policy, 1960–1972* (New York: Oxford University Press, 1990), 162.

14. Garth E. Pauley, *LBJ's American Promise: The 1965 Voting Rights Address* (College Station: Texas A&M University Press, 2007), 76.

15. Jack Blum, *Years of Discord: American Politics and Society, 1961–1974* (New York: W. W. Norton, 1992), 164.

16. Garrow, *Bearing the Cross*, 375–76.

17. Payne, *I've Got the Light of Freedom*, 76–77, 92–93; Dyson, *I May Not Get There with You*, 212–13.

18. Quoted in Garrow, *Bearing the Cross*, 376. Ellipses in original.

19. Garrow, *Bearing the Cross*, 373.

20. Garrow, *Bearing the Cross*, 374.

21. Garrow, *Bearing the Cross*, 371–72.

22. Garrow, *Bearing the Cross*, 379.

23. Garrow, *Bearing the Cross*, 381.

24. Garrow, *Bearing the Cross*, 381.

25. Garrow, *Bearing the Cross*, 382.

26. Garrow, *Bearing the Cross*, 386.

27. Garrow, *Bearing the Cross*, 385.

28. Dyson, *I May Not Get There with You*, 30.

29. Garrow, *Bearing the Cross*, 386–87.

30. Garrow, *Bearing the Cross*, 390–91.

31. George Breitman, ed., *Malcolm X: By Any Means Necessary* (New York: Pathfinder, 1970), 92.

32. James H. Cone, *Martin and Malcolm and America: A Dream or a Nightmare* (Maryknoll, NY: Orbis Books, 1991).

33. Gubernatorial press secretary Bill Jones quoted in Garrow, *Bearing the Cross*, 395.

34. Carson, *In Struggle*, 158.

35. "Civil Rights Movement History 1965: Selma and the March to Montgomery," Crmvet.org, https://www.crmvet.org/tim/timhis65.htm.

36. Garrow, *Bearing the Cross*, 398–99.

37. Babbitt later became President Clinton's secretary of the interior.

38. Nick Kotz, *Judgment Days: Lyndon Baines Johnson, Martin Luther King, Jr., and the Laws That Changed America* (New York: Houghton Mifflin, 2006), 305–6.

39. Garrow, *Bearing the Cross*, 407.

40. Garrow, *Bearing the Cross*, 408–9.

41. Garrow, *Bearing the Cross*, 410.

42. King, *The Autobiography of Martin Luther King, Jr.*

CHAPTER TWENTY-TWO: VIETNAM, BLACK POWER,
AND THE ASSASSINATION OF MARTIN LUTHER KING

1. *National Guardian* 18 (1965): 3.

2. Carson, *In Struggle*, 188.

3. Forman, *The Making of Black Revolutionaries*, 445.

4. Jo Ann Robinson, *Abraham Went Out: A Biography of A. J. Muste* (Philadelphia: Temple University Press, 1981), 133.

5. Jeff Cohen and Norman Solomon, "The Martin Luther King You Don't See on TV," *Common Dreams*, April 4, 2007.

6. Hardy Thomas Frye, "The Rise of a Black Political Party: Institutional Consequences of Emerging Political Consciousness," PhD diss., University of California, Berkeley, 1975, 68. See, also, Hasan Kwame Jeffries, *Bloody Lowndes: Civil Rights and Black Power in Alabama's Black Belt* (New York: New York University Press, 2010).

7. Quoted in Carson, *In Struggle*, 205. Ellipses and emphasis in original.

8. Stokely Carmichael, "What We Want," *New York Review of Books* 7 (September 22, 1966).

9. Anne Braden, "The SNCC Trends: Challenge to White America," *Southern Patriot*, May 1966.

10. Hill, *The Deacons for Defense*.

11. Stokely Carmichael (Kwame Ture) and Ekwueme Michael Thelwell, *Ready for Revolution: The Life and Struggles of Stokely Carmichael (Kwame Ture)* (New York: Scribner, 2003), 507.

12. Martin Luther King Jr., *Where Do We Go From Here: Chaos or Community?* (Boston: Beacon Press, 1967), 36.

13. Martin Luther King Jr., "The Other America," speech, Grosse Pointe High School, Grosse Pointe, Michigan, March 14, 1968, Grosse Pointe Historical Society, https://www.gphistorical.org/mlk/mlkspeech.

14. Peniel E. Joseph, *Dark Days, Bright Nights: From Black Power to Barack Obama* (New York: Basic Books, 2010), 26.

15. Kwame Ture [Stokely Carmichael] and Charles V. Hamilton, *Black Power: The Politics of Liberation in America*, new ed. (New York: Vintage, 1992), 44.

16. Marable, *Race, Reform, and Rebellion*, 92–95.

17. Carmichael, "What We Want."

18. Matthew Countryman, *Up South: Civil Rights and Black Power in Philadelphia* (Philadelphia: University of Pennsylvania Press, 2006), 8.

19. Countryman, *Up South*, 7–8.

20. Timothy B. Tyson, *Radio Free Dixie: Robert F. Williams and the Roots of Black Power* (Chapel Hill: University of North Carolina Press, 1999), 214–16.

21. King, "The Social Organization of Nonviolence."

22. H. Rap Brown (Jamil Abdullah Al-Amin), *Die Nigger Die! A Political Autobiography of H. Rap Brown (Jamil Abdullah Al-Amin)* (New York: Dial Press, 1969), 54.

23. Jeffries, *Bloody Lowndes*; Hill, *The Deacons for Defense.*

24. See Bobby Seale, *A Lonely Rage: The Autobiography of Bobby Seale* (New York: Times Books, 1978); Donna Jean Murch, *Living for the City: Migration, Education, and the Rise of the Black Panther Party in Oakland, California* (Chapel Hill: University of North Carolina Press, 2010); Charles Jones and Judson Jeffries, *The Black Panther Party [Reconsidered]* (Baltimore: Black Classic Press, 1998).

25. Bond, introduction to Martínez, ed., *Letters from Mississippi*, ix.

26. Michael Thelwell quoted in Julian Bond, "What We Did," *Monthly Review*, October 1, 2000, https://monthlyreview.org/2000/10/01/sncc-what-we-did.

27. Quoted in Bond, "What We Did."

28. Bond, "What We Did."

29. H. Timothy Lovelace Jr., "Making the World in Atlanta's Image: The Student Nonviolent Coordinating Committee, Morris Abram, and the Legislative History of the United Nations Race Convention," *Law and History Review* 32, no. 2 (May 2014): 396.

30. Lovelace, "Making the World in Atlanta's Image," 396.

31. Lovelace, "Making the World in Atlanta's Image," 397.

32. Lovelace, "Making the World in Atlanta's Image," 400,

33. Lovelace, "Making the World in Atlanta's Image," 409–10.

34. Lovelace, "Making the World in Atlanta's Image," 410.

35. Lovelace, "Making the World in Atlanta's Image."

36. Lovelace, "Making the World in Atlanta's Image," 410–11, 413.

37. Forman, *The Making of Black Revolutionaries*, 408–11.

38. Harry G. Lefever, *Undaunted by the Fight: Spelman College and the Civil Rights Movement, 1957–1967* (Macon, GA: Mercer University Press, 2005), 207.

39. *Congressional Record: Proceedings and Debates of the 89th Congress of United States, First Session* (Washington, DC: US Government Printing Office, 1965), 5303.

40. Letter from Donna Richards and Robert Moses to Dr. Horace Mann Bond, October 6, 1965.

41. Forman, *The Making of Black Revolutionaries*, 445.

42. *Atlanta Journal*, March 22, 1966. The seven were John Lewis, James Bond, James Forman, Cleveland Sellers, Willie Ricks, Judy Richardson, and William Hall.

43. Forman, *The Making of Black Revolutionaries*, 480–92.

44. Martínez, *Letters from Mississippi*, xii; Forman, *The Making of Black Revolutionaries*, 499.

45. Carson, *In Struggle*, 239–41.

46. Brown, *Die Nigger Die!*, 112.

47. Garrow, *Bearing the Cross*, 604.

48. In 1973, Marian Wright Edelman founded the Children's Defense Fund.

49. Garrow, *Bearing the Cross*, 607.

50. Garrow, *Bearing the Cross*, 611.

51. Martin Luther King Jr., *"All Labor Has Dignity"* (Boston: Beacon Press, 2011).

52. Garrow, *Bearing the Cross*, 621.

53. Taylor Branch, *At Canaan's Edge: America in the King Years, 1965–68* (New York: Simon & Schuster, 2006), 763–64.

54. Branch, *At Canaan's Edge*, 770.

55. John B. Morris, ed., *Black Elected Officials in the Southern States* (Atlanta: Voter Education Project of the Southern Regional Council, 1969).

INDEX

Page references to images are in italics, as insert.

ABOUT THE CONTRIBUTORS

PAMELA HOROWITZ was one of the first lawyers hired at the Southern Poverty Law Center. During her tenure there, she successfully argued a historic gender discrimination case before the US Supreme Court. She now sits on the SPLC board. Her thirty-year legal career also included being a legislative counsel with the national ACLU and a partner in a Washington, DC, law firm. She also worked in partnership with her late husband, Julian Bond, in multiple public, private, and academic projects and is involved in several activities honoring his legacy.

JEANNE THEOHARIS is Distinguished Professor of Political Science at Brooklyn College of the City University of New York and the author or coauthor of nine books and numerous articles on the civil rights and Black Power movements, the politics of race and education, and social welfare and civil rights in post-9/11 America. Her widely acclaimed biography *The Rebellious Life of Mrs. Rosa Parks* won a 2014 NAACP Image Award and the Letitia Woods Brown Award from the Association of Black Women Historians; her book *A More Beautiful and Terrible History: The Uses and Misuses of Civil Rights History* won the 2018 Brooklyn Public Library Prize for Nonfiction. Her work has appeared in the *New York Times*, the *Washington Post*, MSNBC, *The Nation, Slate, Salon, The Intercept*, and the *Chronicle of Higher Education*.

DANNY LYON is a photographer, filmmaker, and writer. His pictures of SNCC, bikers, and Texas prisons from the 1960s are now considered part of the New Journalism. In 1962, Lyon began working as a photographer with the

Student Nonviolent Coordinating Committee and was present at many of the major events of the Southern civil rights movement. His many books include *The Bikeriders*, *The Destruction of Lower Manhattan*, *Conversations with the Dead*, *Knave of Hearts*, *Like a Thief's Dream*, and *Deep Sea Diver*. His nonfiction essays have been published by Karma, as *American Blood*. Widely exhibited and collected, Lyon has been awarded Guggenheim Fellowships twice, a Rockefeller Fellowship, the Missouri Honor Medal in Journalism, and National Endowment for the Arts grants multiple times. Lyon is an active blogger at bleakbeauty.com. His Instagram is dannylyonphotos.

VANN R. NEWKIRK II is a senior editor at *The Atlantic*. He has covered the battles for voting rights since the 2013 *Shelby County* Supreme Court decision, the fate of communities on the front lines of climate change and disasters, and the Black vote in the 2018 and 2020 elections. He is the host of *The Atlantic's* podcast *Floodlines*, a narrative series about Hurricane Katrina. Newkirk was a 2020 11th Hour Fellow at New America and a 2018 recipient of the American Society of Magazine Editors' ASME Next Award.

ABOUT THE AUTHOR

FROM HIS CIVIL RIGHTS AND ANTIWAR ACTIVISM in the 1960s to his support for gay rights in the new millennium, Julian Bond was on the cutting edge of social change,

As a college student in 1960, he was a leader of the Atlanta sit-in movement and a founder of the Student Nonviolent Coordinating Committee (SNCC). For the next five years, as SNCC's communications director, he covered or participated in every major event of the Southern civil rights movement.

When Bond won election to the Georgia House, in 1965, his fellow legislators refused to seat him because of his opposition to the war in Vietnam. It took two more electoral victories and a unanimous US Supreme Court decision for him to be seated. That fight captured the country's attention and made Bond a household name, leading to his becoming, in 1968, the first African American to be nominated to the vice presidency of the United States. At aged twenty-eight, he was too young to serve.

After twenty years in the Georgia House and Senate, he began a twenty-five-year career as a college professor, teaching first at Drexel University, then at the University of Pennsylvania, Williams College, and Harvard University, and then permanently at the University of Virginia and American University.

His lifetime of activism took him from serving as the first president of the Southern Poverty Law Center during the 1970s to the chairmanship of the NAACP, the nation's oldest and largest civil rights organization, from

1998 to 2010. He was the first national Black leader to support the fight for marriage equality.

Bond was also a television commentator, a writer, a host of *Saturday Night Live*, an actor (*Ray*, *5 to 7*), and the narrator of several prize-winning documentaries, including *A Time for Justice* and *Eyes on the Prize*.